Gendered Nations

Gendered Nations

Nationalisms and Gender Order in the Long Nineteenth Century

Edited by
Ida Blom, Karen Hagemann, Catherine Hall

Oxford • New York

First published in 2000 by
Berg
Editorial offices:
150 Cowley Road, Oxford, OX4 1JJ, UK
838 Broadway, Third Floor, New York, NY 10003-4812, USA

Berg is an imprint of Oxford International Publishers Ltd.

Library of Congress Cataloging-in-Publication Data
A catalogue record for this book is available from the Library of Congress.

British Library Cataloguing-in-Publication Data
A catalogue record for this book is available from the British Library.

ISBN 1 85973 259 3 (Cloth)
       1 85973 264 X (Paper)

Typeset by JS Typesetting, Wellingborough, Northants.
Printed in the United Kingdom by WBC Book Manufacturers, Mid Glamorgan.

For Karin Hausen

Contents

Contents

List of Illustrations

List of Contributors

Beth Baron is associate professor of history at the City College and the Graduate School of the City University of New York, USA, where she teaches courses on the history of the Middle East. At City College, City University of New York, she has just started a Middle East Studies Program. Beth Baron is author of the *The Women's Awakening in Egypt: Culture, Society, and the Press* (1994) and co-editor with Nikki Keddie of *Women in Middle Eastern European History* (1991). She is currently completing a manuscript on *Gender and Nationalisms in Egypt.*

Ida Blom is professor of European history and gender history in the Department of History at the University of Bergen, Norway. Her publications include books on women and reproductive health and on the gendered fight against tuberculosis. She is editor and co-author of a Norwegian three-volume women's world history and a one-volume Norwegian history with a gender perspective. Both will be published in 1999. At the moment she is working on gendered welfare history as well as on gendered approaches to global history.

Helen Bradford is professor of South African history at the Department of History of the University of Cape Town, South Africa. Most of her early work focused on the African resistance, epitomized in her book *A Taste of Freedom: The ICU in the South African Countryside* (1987). Together with Bill Nasson she edited *Southern African Research Papers* (1988). Currently she is trying to gender key events in South African history.

Geoff Eley is professor of German and European history at the Department of History of the University of Michigan, Ann Arbor, US. He has published widely in German history, including *Reshaping the German Right: Radical Nationalisms and Political Change after Bismarck* (1980), *The Peculiarities of German History: Bourgeois Society and Politics in Nineteenth-Century Germany* (1984), and *Wilhelminismus, Nationalismus, Faschismus: Zur historischen Kontinuität in Deutschland* (1991). He also co-edited *Becoming National: A Reader* (1996) with Ronald Grigor Suny, and *Culture/Power/History: A Reader in Contemporary Social Theory* (1994) with Nicholas Dirks and Sherry Ortner. He has just finished a general history of the European left between the mid-nineteenth century and the present.

Karen Hagemann was assistant professor at the Department of History and later at the Centre for Interdisciplinary Studies on Women and Gender at the Technical University of Berlin and is now research fellow in history of the German Research Foundation at this centre. She has published widely in the field of gendered German history of the nineteenth and twentieth century. Her publications include *Frauenalltag und Männerpolitik. Alltagsleben und gesellschaftliches Handeln von Arbeiterfrauen in der Weimarer Republik* (1991) and *Landsknechte, Soldatenfrauen und Nationalkrieger. Militär, Krieg und Geschlechterordnung im historischen Wandel* (1998), which she co-edited with Ralf Pröve. She is now writing a book on the nation, war and the gender order in Prussia in the period of the anti-Napoleonic wars.

Catherine Hall is professor of modern British social and cultural history at University College, London. She has published widely on British history and women's and gender history. Her publications include the books *Family Fortunes. Men and Women of the English Middle Class, 1780-1850* (together with Leonore Davidoff, 1987) and *White, Male and Middle Class. Explorations in Feminism and History* (1992). Her current work focuses on the relation between Britain and its empire in the nineteenth century. Her most recent book, written with Keith McClelland and Jane Rendall, is *Defining the Victorian Nation: Class, Race, Gender and the Reform Act of 1867* (2000).

Marilyn Lake holds a personal chair in history at the La Trobe University, Australia, where she was also foundation director of women's studies. She teaches courses on feminist theory, feminism and post-coloniality and the history of Australian gender relations. She has published widely on gender, nation, race and citizenship, in Australia and internationally, is co-author of the feminist history of Australia, *Creating a Nation* (1994), co-editor of *Gender and War: Australians at War in the Twentieth Century* (1995) and has just completed a history of feminism called *Pursuit of Equality: Hundred Years of Feminism in Australia,* which will be published in 1999.

List of Contributors

Jitka Malečková is assistant professor in history at the Institute of Near Eastern and African Studies of the philosophical faculty at Charles University in Prague, Czech Republic. She published on the nineteenth-century cultural and social history of the Ottoman empire and on women and nationalism in Central and Eastern Europe and is co-author of *The Struggle for a Modern State in the Muslim World* (1989, in Czech). Her current research focuses on gendered images and nationalism in nineteenth-century East Central Europe and the Ottoman Empire.

Irina Novikova is docent of the Department of English at the University of Latvia, Riga, and director of the Center for Gender Studies at the same university. Her publications include articles on women's autobiographical writing, gender and representation, and gender and genre. She is the editor of the recently published Conference Proceedings *Women's Studies and Gender Research in the Baltic and Nordic Countries: Mapping the Situation* (1999), of the first collection of essays on feminist theories and methodologies in the Latvian language, and of the forthcoming newspaper *Women in the Baltics* in the Russian language. Her most recent article is on 'Fashioning Our Minds: Mass Media Representations of Minority Women in Latvia' (1999).

Ruth Roach Pierson is professor at the Ontario Institute for Studies in Education at the University of Toronto, Canada and teaches women's history and feminist studies. She is author of *'They're Still Women After All': The Second World War and Canadian Womenhood* (1986), co-author of *Canadian Women's Issues: Twenty-Five Years of Women's Activism in English Canada* (2 vols, 1993 and 1995), editor of *Women and Peace: Theoretical, Historical and Practical Perspectives* (1987), co-editor of *Writing Women's History: International Perspectives* (1991), and co-editor of *Nation, Empire, Colony: Historicizing Gender and Race* (1998).

Angelika Schaser was assistant professor at the Department of History of the Free University of Berlin, Germany, and is now research fellow in history of the German Research Foundation at this Department. Her study on Transylvanian social and economic history from the sixteenth to the eighteenth century was published in 1989 as *Josephinische Reformen und sozialer Wandel in Siebenbürgen. Die Bedeutung des Konzivilitätsreskriptes für Hermannstadt.* Her recent publications include studies on minorities, on the women's movement in Germany during the nineteenth and twentieth century and on gender and nation in the German history of the Wilhelmian Empire.

List of Contributors

Viktoria Schmidt-Linsenhoff is professor of art history at the Department of Art History of the University of Trier, Germany, and teaches mainly in the field of women and gender studies. From 1981 till 1990 she worked at the Historical Museum of Frankfurt and organized several exhibitions on the art and cultural history of the sixteenth to the twentieth century. She has published extensively on the field of gendered art history and is co-editor of *Projektionen. Rassismus und Sexismus in der visuellen Kultur* (1997).

Carroll Smith-Rosenberg is professor of women's studies, history and American culture at the Department of History of the University of Michigan, Ann Arbor, US. She has published widely in the fields of American history and women's and gender history. Her work includes the book *Disorderly Conduct. Visions of Gender in Victorian America* (1986) as well as important articles such as 'Discovering the subject of the "great constitutional discussion"', in *Journal of American History* (December, 1991) and 'Subject female: authorizing American identity', in *American Literary History* (Fall, 1993). She is now writing a book entitled *America Embodied: Constituting the American Subject 1770–1860*.

Margaret Ward is research fellow in history at the Bath Spa University college, United Kingdom, and vice chair of the British Association for Irish Studies. She has been writing on the subject of women, nationalisms and feminisms in Ireland since the 1970s. Her recent work includes *In Their Own Voice: Women and Irish Nationalism* (1995) as well as her biography of Irish suffragist and republican Hanna Sheehy, *Hanna Sheehy-Skeffington: Suffragist and Sinn Feiner*, which was published in 1997.

Silke Wenk is Professor for Art History and Cultural Studies at the Department of Art History of the Carl von Ossietzky University Oldenburg, Germany. She has published widely on sculpture in public space, on representation of gender in the nation state, on art in fascism and on methodological problems of a feminist art history. Her most recent book is *Versteinerte Weiblichkeit. Allegorien in der Skulptur der Moderne* (1996).

Preface

This book started life as Karen Hagemann's idea. In March 1998 she organized a symposium that took place in Berlin on 'Gendered Nations: Nationalisms and Gender Order in the long nineteenth century: International Comparisons'. Planned in cooperation with Ida Blom this symposium brought together 39 scholars from 16 different countries to discuss intensively, over three days, issues concerning the gendering of nations and nationalisms. The symposium was hosted by the Centre for Interdisciplinary Studies on Women and Gender at the Technical University of Berlin and the Einstein Forum Potsdam. The aim of this meeting was to gather together scholars who have been working on questions of gender and nation. We presented research to each other, discussed key questions that are emerging from the work that has been done and assessed important areas of investigation for the future. The focus was on discussion: written papers were circulated in advance so that we could spend our time talking, exchanging ideas, reflecting on comparative material and on the similarities and differences between both national formations and nationalisms.

The past two decades have seen an explosion of writing on questions of nation: a reflection of the political conjuncture in which we live. Yet questions of gender have been seriously neglected in much of this work. The writing that has focused on gender and nation has come mainly from literary scholars and to date relatively little has been published by feminist historians in this field. This book contributes to that growing body of research and aims to place questions of national belonging, citizenship, nation formation, and national iconography, to name some of our concerns, firmly in a historical frame. Although cultural critics have enabled us to make sense of the representations of the nation as female, and sociological analysts have theorized the different ways in which men and women belong to the nation, there are particular historical questions that need to be addressed. What difference does it make to our understanding of national belonging when gender is taken into account? How central are questions of sexual difference to categories of citizenship? What is the relation between hierarchies of class and those of gender in any given nation? What are the critical moments in nation formation and how does gender inflect those moments? As nations always include and exclude at the very same moment, what hierarchies of difference are in play? How do race, ethnicity, religion and generation intersect in national histories? What is the complex of relations between nationalisms and feminisms? And finally, as historians have played a critical part in the construction of imagined nations, what part are we playing now in our rewritings of histories?

These are some of the questions that were at the heart of the symposium and remain central to this book, which focuses on the constitutive phase of modern nationalisms. This period is extraordinarily relevant to the problem of gender and nation but has received relatively little attention until now. The developmental phase of modern nationalisms seems to have been more important for the social and cultural construction of both nation and gender, as it was during this period that the 'basic patterns' were created which were to exert a long-term influence upon the political culture of gendered nations/ nationalisms. The aim of this book is to produce an assessment of the state of research in different European countries and beyond while inspiring future research with new questions and encouraging scholars to engage in more international comparison. For that reason, the book begins with an introduction section on 'nation/ nationalisms and gender' with four theoretical and methodological essays, which discuss the contributions to the volume from various perspectives and place them within the more general development of research. The first essay, by Ida Blom, deals with questions of 'nation and gender in international comparison'. From the viewpoint of cultural-historical research on nationalism, Geoff Eley reflects upon the relationships among 'culture, nation and gender'. Ruth Roach Pierson addresses the key problem of race, empire and nations from the standpoint of gender history. Finally, Silke Wenk comments upon 'images and representations of the gendered nation' from an art historical perspective. The nine essays in the main part of the book, all of them case studies from recently completed research projects or work in progress, deal with four central problems within research on nation and gender. In the first section on 'nation states, ethnicity and gender order', the articles by Viktoria Schmidt-Linsenhoff, Catherine Hall, Beth Baron and Marilyn Lake on revolutionary France, Britain, Egypt, and Australia respectively, examine the formation of nation states and citizenship in the light of ethnicity and gender. An important aspect of their papers is the connections among the nation state, colonialism, imperialism, and the gender order, connections which construct hierarchical relationships within and among nations that already exist or

Preface

are struggling to come into being. The contributions in the second section on 'national wars, military systems and gender relations' by Karen Hagemann and Helen Bradford, on Prussia and South Africa, centre on the links among nation, military, and gender order. They discuss the significance of gender images for the mobilization of national 'defence capabilities' and readiness for war and ask about the consequences of changes in the military system and means of waging war for the construction of nation and gender images as well as gender relations. In the third section on 'nations in social and cultural practice – gender-specific participation in national movements' the articles by Margret Ward and Angelika Schaser on Ireland and Wilhelmine Germany focus on the specific participation of women and men in national movements, and on the specific, gendered forms and scopes of action in the cultural and social practices of nations. The fourth and final section on 'national symbols, rituals and myths – gender images and cultural representations of nations', with papers by Carroll Smith-Rosenberg, Jitka Malecková, and Irina Novikova on the American Republic, the Czech National Movement and Latvia considers the significance of gender images for the cultural construction of the national myths, symbols, and rituals that represent the political order. The book was edited collectively by Ida Blom, Karen Hagemann and Catherine Hall.

Many debts have accumulated in the process of transforming an idea into a symposium, a three-day workshop into a book. The generous sponsorship of the German Research Foundation, the British Council, the German Marshall Fund, the Hans Boeckler Foundation, the Heinrich Boell Foundation, and the Technical University of Berlin made possible the symposium. The discussions that took place there made it possible for authors to revise their contributions in ways that reflect the significance of the collective debates which took place: the finished essays have benefited from the intellectual generosity of all the participants. The organizational skills of Annette Langguth and the intelligent and meticulous minute taking of Patricia R. Stokes helped make the conference a success and smoothed the way for publication of the contributions. The Technical University of Berlin has provided further help, which has enabled us to put together this book, and to include some coloured as well as black-and-white illustrations. Stefan Grob has patiently dealt with the vagaries of the mail and the pleasures and pains of electronic communication, and taken many tedious tasks from the hands of the editors. Maike Bohn has been a constructive and sympathetic editor.

We would like to dedicate this book to Karin Hausen, one of the most well known German historians internationally. She belonged to the first generation of women academics who began to research, write and teach women's history in the 1970s and 1980s. Her stimulating and unconventional work inspired many feminist scholars, and without her efforts, women's and gender history in Germany would never have reached its present level. Today Karin Hausen is director of the Centre for Interdisciplinary Studies on Women and Gender at the Technical University of Berlin, which was founded in 1995. This book is our belated gift for her sixtieth birthday, which she celebrated in March 1998, just a few days before the symposium that gave rise to this book.

Bergen, Berlin and London, April 1999
Ida Blom, Karen Hagemann and Catherine Hall

Part 1
Nations/Nationalisms and Gender

Gender and Nation in International Comparison
Ida Blom

From Gendered Cultural Histories to Gendered Nations – a Historiographical Approach

The construction of nations and nation states has mostly been studied as a phenomenon originating in Western societies and gradually spreading to other parts of the world. However, as has been pointed out, the concept of the unitary nation state was affecting people in different parts of the world during roughly the same period of time – the late nineteenth and early twentieth centuries.[1] Consequently, it seems reasonable to expect that international comparative studies may broaden our understanding of the process of creating national identities and nation states.

In my attempt to sketch approaches to such comparisons, let me start with some historiographical ponderings.

I would posit that not only has gender been a neglected category of analysis in the flowering field of historical research on nation building, the nation state and nationalisms, but it may also be said that, historiographically, the understanding of history as primarily *the history of nations*, of governments, of kings and statesmen, in short, of the public sphere, has been an obstacle to historical research on gender, on the private sphere and civil society. There seems to have been, from the beginning, a built-in antithesis between the two fields of history, histories of nations and histories of gender. Since the early nineteenth century, the focus of historical research on national histories has drowned any interest that may have existed in analysing gender relations and gender orders. Furthermore, during the late nineteenth century, new research disciplines, such as anthropology, sociology and ethnology to a certain degree appropriated the field of researching civil society and the private sphere, including gender relations, although these disciplines have also, until the 1960s and 1970s, more-or-less neglected the existence of gender orders.[2]

However, as the concept of *gendered nations* is now slowly taking root in the historical sciences, we are, in fact, in certain ways returning to a research tradition prevailing during the last decades of the eighteenth century. Enlightenment philosophers as well as enlightenment historians, in France, Germany and Britain, were looking for explanations of why some peoples developed into 'civilized' cultures, while others remained 'barbarians'. They created theories of development by stages, suggesting that historical change could be understood as a teleological process from the childhood of a culture, through youth to cultural adulthood, or as following cultural stages, where people would change from wild, to barbaric, to half-cultivated, ending up fully cultivated people. Eurocentrism was open and conspicuous in these histories. The fully cultivated peoples were the Europeans.[3]

An interesting feature in these comparative global histories was that they incorporated everyday life. They described living conditions and lifestyles, food traditions, fashions, mentalities and feelings. In these cultural histories, women and children formed part of a cultural totality. Moreover, some historians even wrote separate women's histories. John Millar's *Observations Concerning the Distinction of Ranks in Society*, published in London in 1773, opened with an analysis of women's position in different cultures, stressing the importance of the conditions of production, of religion and of politics to explain differences among gender orders in different cultures. A Danish historian published a history of women in Scandinavia before the advent of Christianity, and the German historian, Christoph Meiners, in a four-volume *Geschichte des weiblichen Geschlechts*, published between 1788 and 1800, discussed differences between southern and northern European women.[4] Meiners explicitly reasoned about the problems involved for a male historian when writing women's history, and about the differences that might exist between the lived history as perceived in bygone days and the reconstruction of history by historians.

There is, however, a very important difference between modern historians incorporating a gender analysis into the history of nations and nation states and our enlightenment predecessors. For the eighteenth-century historian, the term 'nation' signified 'people', 'tribe' or 'culture', not the nation state or the group of people imagining themselves as part of a national community.[5]

As the formation of nation states started out in early nineteenth-century Europe, the understanding of the term 'nation' gradually changed. At the same time, and parallel with the development of history into a professional science, the focus of research narrowed from the history of different cultures to the history of Western nation states. In that process, the gender perspective was lost, as was the grand design of comparative cultural history.

Much research on nationalisms and on the gendered nation still concentrates on one nation state.[6] This approach generates a lot of valuable knowledge, needed also if we want to widen the perspective to comparative analysis of similar processes in different nations. Studies limited to one individual nation are – and will remain – the cornerstones on which to build international comparisons . However, international comparative research may yield even more insight into the interaction of gender orders, nationalisms and nation building, also in individual nations. I do not, then, propose either single nation analysis or international comparison, but both. This is a research strategy that will, I think, enrich both approaches.

So, let me enlarge on the gains and problems of international comparisons of nation and gender.

Transcultural Comparative Approaches

Comparisons are inherent in historical research. They range from microcosmic to macrocosmic comparisons, and they may be made at different levels, from the individual to the global. Where a number of nation states within a number of cultures are compared, the German historian Jürgen Osterhammel suggests that we speak of *transkulturel vergleichende Geschichtswissenschaft – transcultural comparative history*.[7] Transcultural comparative history discusses the history of global phenomena such as urbanization and industrialization, and among them of nationalisms and nation states. It also analyses institutions such as village communities, urban societies, family and kinship systems – global phenomena shaped by changing historical, geographical and cultural contexts – and is now beginning to include studies of the interaction between nation and gender.

The Sri Lankan sociologist Kumari Jayawardena published her study of the interaction of *Feminism and Nationalism in the Third World* in 1986. This featured twelve nations in Asia and the Middle East during the late nineteenth and early twentieth century.[8] Her comparisons highlight culturally determined variations as well as cross-cultural common aspects. Among common aspects of nationalism are, according to Jayawardena, the wish to modernize society through reforms, with an aim to strengthen the fight against colonial powers, attempts to abolish pre-capitalist structures such as dynastic absolutism and religious orthodoxies, and finally efforts to create national identities that would mobilize for the fight for national independence.

Jayawardena situates the fight for women's emancipation in this setting as a central feature of endeavours to construct modern independent nations. Institutionalized education of girls and women is seen as one of the important means to strengthen the nation. In particular, educating middle-class women to become better wives, better mothers and cleverer housewives is, in Jayawardena's view, a cross-cultural phenomenon in struggles to create a positive and dynamic national identity. As a result, the nations under study saw the growth of a long number of women's organizations and women's groups, supporting different political parties and taking part in central reform movements, all with the common goal of constructing a strong nation.

Even as Jayawardena shows striking parallels among twelve nations within cultures as different as those of Islam, Hinduism, and Confucianism, she also points to differences rooted in cultural and ideological traditions. She underlines internal as well as external factors that have influenced developments. As she focuses on nations that have been subdued by imperialism, Europe plays a secondary role in her story. She does not draw parallels with the gendering of European nations, but Europe is given a place as representing colonial powers and as inspiring liberal and national ideologies. To a Scandinavian historian it seems especially interesting to see the importance she gives to Henrik Ibsen's play, *A Doll's House.* She underscores the discussions in many Asian countries of the meaning of Nora leaving the safe haven of marriage, children and home. Nora was seen as a symbol of rupture with traditional and widely accepted social norms and with orthodox morality. She was understood as an expression of the possibility of reaching a clear consciousness of self, a message directed to subjected women as well as to subjected nations. This understanding of nationalism as a gendered phenomenon indicates gender-specific involvements in nation building and in the construction of national identities, even as it demonstrates how 'woman' symbolized 'nation' – in this case nations struggling to find themselves and become independent.

Jayawardena's study encourages research – which is well under way today – to analyse parallels and differences within Asian, African and Western cultures in the interaction of gender and nationalism.[9] As such studies multiply, we can begin the daunting task of picturing a global comparison of the interaction of gender and nation around the turn of the century.

But – and there are some very important reservations to be made here

– transcultural comparative history mostly remains at a high level of abstraction, supporting findings and observations as much by philosophical and social science theories as by historical evidence. It hardly comes as a surprise that sociologists and political scientists with an interest in historical processes have been the pioneers of this research.[10] In fact, interdisciplinarity is a salient characteristic of what is also termed 'global history'. Such research tends to build generalizations and may run counter to fundamental features of historical method: the nearness to historical evidence and the critical evaluation of evidence. Transcultural comparative history may endanger the process of grading and arguing for and against probabilities, the principle of individualizing and the holistic wish to understand individual phenomena in relation to a connected whole, diachronically or synchronically.[11] In sum, the resulting observations should be taken with a grain of salt.

Does that mean that historians should refrain from 'global' comparisons, or transcultural comparative research? I think not. As Heinz Gerhardt Haupt and Jürgen Kocka have maintained, large-scale comparisons may serve as points of references for more detailed investigations. They may help evaluate concepts and theories and contribute to throw light on and urge reflections on 'Westocentric' approaches.[12] Moreover, a large-scale comparative approach may highlight considerations of the advantages and disadvantages of analysis 'from outside' the culture under study. For the historian to be rooted in a different culture from the one he or she is studying may be a barrier to proper understanding, but it does not necessarily represent an insoluble problem. Openly acknowledged distance may lead to other perspectives and other understandings than those stemming from unreflected nearness and implicitness. The point is to avoid normative characteristics, especially those burried in seemingly value-neutral statements.[13]

Despite all this, we may turn to more limited comparisons, nearer the methodology of historical sciences.

Limited Comparisons

Comparisons limited to a few entities are more manageable and do not so easily run contrary to normal historical methodology. Researchers will be able to study two, three or four nations thoroughly. They will usually have thorough knowledge of one of these national histories, and may highlight meaningful problems to be researched in the context of other nations. Results of these more limited comparisons may later be related to more general observations and processes, to evaluate similarities and differences. Comparing with a view to finding contrasts in the interaction of nation and gender within a smaller number of nations will enhance understanding of each individual case, while attempts to find similarities will point to more general patterns.[14] Even limited comparisons may therefore contribute to innovation and fine tuning theories by building on more verifiable evidence.

Allow me to illustrate this with one of my own fledgling attempts at international comparison of gendered nations.

National Symbolism and National Citizenship

Inspired by Jayawardena, and co-operating with Indian and Japanese colleagues, I have studied similarities and differences in the process of constructing nation states within Asian cultures as diverse as Japan and India, comparing them with northern European culture as represented by Sweden and Norway – all around the end of the nineteenth century. I have connected two classical aspects of the nation, what Friedrich Meinicke termed the 'state-nation' (Staats-Nation) and the 'culture-nation' (Kultur-Nation).[15] From my knowledge of Norwegian history, I have argued that national symbols rooted in traditions of loyalty to family and in traditional understandings of gender paved the way for a gendered approach to citizenship in the democratic nation state.

Not surprisingly, in all four nations (Japan, India, Sweden and Norway) the family was central to national symbolism. Concepts such as 'father-land' and 'mother tongue' indicate the gendered family as a symbol of the nation. At least since the French revolution, it was common for Western European nations to conceive of themselves as families. Identifying the nation with the family – a timeless and global unity of loyalty, evoking sentiments as well as hierarchies of gender and age – facilitated the construction of national identities and national loyalties. This symbolism also served as a guarantee for the continuation of traditional bonds between individuals as the process of nation building widened the understanding of loyalty to include the national community.[16] Women as national mothers are visible not only in Western national rhetoric, but also in Asian nations, for instance in the widely used concept of 'mother India'.[17] In the Nordic countries, as well as in India, the mother figure represented the nation. In Bengal, anti-British feelings around the turn of the century were imbued with a Hindu nationalism, invoking the mother-goddess Kali, also the goddess of strength, to liberate Mother India. When the British pointed to the subjugated position of Indian women as a sign of what they perceived as the uncivilized character of

Indian culture, Indian nationalists would cite old Hindu traditions – the *shakti* – where powerful goddesses invested women with strength and steadfastness. However, mothers were mostly seen as generating cultural strength, educating children to respect national norms of gendered behaviour and teaching them the national language.

Differences in national symbols were also obvious. In authoritarian Japanese society the father figure, not the mother, dominated national symbols. Education and ideology stressed the Emperor as the father of the nation, demanding full obedience from sons as well as from all women. The mother image became that of the subservient figure. She would perceive her sons as the sons of the Emperor, and would happily sacrifice their lives – and the life of her husband – to the needs of the Japanese nation. Although such thoughts were not completely absent in the other three nations, they were very explicitly expressed by the state-supported women's organization, Aikoku Fujinkai, established in 1901. The aim of this organization, soon to become the biggest women's organisation in Japan, was to console women who had lost sons and/or husbands in war, at the same time exhorting them to fulfil the ideal of the Japanese mother. The Dainippon Rengo Fujinkai had a similar mission in the 1930s.

Gendered national symbols of family loyalty mirrored the ways individuals were included or excluded from rights in the nation state. The interaction of the private with the public was evident in the construction of all four nations. Full inclusion as measured by access to suffrage rights was very clearly gendered. From the beginning, in all four nations, only men were regarded as entitled to suffrage rights. But gradually, gender changed meaning. Women were, at least in some quarters, accepted as worthy of being incorporated in the nation as individual citizens through suffrage rights. The argument was either that femininity was seen as representing values other than masculinity – values needed in the nation to complement the masculine character of nationhood – or (but less frequently) that women were perceived as individuals with the same potential as men and who consequently deserved the same rights in the nation. However, gender relations understood as a process where the meaning of gender changed over time, evidenced different time aspects. The authoritarian Japan long maintained regulations that prohibited women from taking part in party politics – a parallel to the situation in Prussia from the early 1850s until 1908 – and full membership in the nation through political citizenship was not conveyed on Japanese women until 1945. In India, national suffrage was gradually extended to women throughout the 1920s, with full acceptance in 1948. In Sweden and Norway gender lost importance in the question of access to national suffrage much earlier, in 1920 and 1913 respectively.

Parallel developments in the interaction between gender and nation were tinged by cultural differences. In some respects these differences revealed gaps in the understanding of gender in the four nations involved. All four nations understood masculinity as a key to public rights and obligations in the nation, but the understanding of femininity varied. In the two northern European countries, femininity had wide connotations. Discussions concerned problems such as women's rights to university education and admission to jobs within the national civil service, married women as legal subjects, and their admission to paid work. In India and Japan womanhood was limited within narrow confines. Conflicts concerned the total subjugation of married women under husbands and mothers in law, questions such as concubinage, child marriages, and the harsh conditions to which widows were subjected. Discussions of how to explain such cultural differences may lead to fruitful reflections on effects of modernization, of the weight of religious fundamentalism on nation-building and nationalism, and of collectivity versus individualism as value systems.[18]

The Indian sociologist Suma Chitnis, working to explain the lack of support for Western feminism among today's Indian women, analyses, among other factors, the impact of accepted value systems and of traditional understandings of femininity.[19] She explains the embeddedness of Indian women in a web of very strict hierarchies, hierarchies of caste and class, of generations and of gender. All these hierarchies are imbued with a strong sense of deference to superiors, but also – and this is important – with a sense of mutuality, expressed in behavioural codes that bend superiors to fulfil their obligations to inferiors. Add to this a philosophy of self-denial and the contrast with Western value systems stands out clearly. Concepts of equality and of individuality, central not only to Western feminism but to Western philosophy as such, seem foreign to the value systems respected by Indian women.

Such observations may help the historian understand the very different strands in Indian and British nationalism, and the different problems that women in the two nations had to cope with in attempts to be accepted as national citizens on par with men.

Chitnis also makes us aware that there are different ways of interpreting national symbolism rooted in cultural traditions. Very potent Hindu legends, conditioning women to serve their husbands as devotees serve their gods, be it the legend of Satyavan and Savitri or of Rama and Sita, have generally emphasized women's willing self-immolation. Interpreters of these legends have overlooked that the very same women exhibited sharp wits, intelligence, resourcefulness, tenacity and affection. All these positive elements, according to Chitnis, have never been held up for emulation. But they are there, and Chitnis suggests that they may be used to transform the impact of traditions on women's lives as well as on power hierarchies. A historian may ask if these positive elements in traditional Hindu legends were not part of Gandhi's successful appeal to women, mobilizing them for the national struggle? That Gandhi's understanding of gender also resulted in important differences in the ways women and men were supposed to serve the nation should, of course, not be forgotten. Gandhi saw the goddess Sita, the self-sacrificing and loyal wife of the god Rama, as a model for Indian womanhood and found women especially suited for non-violent resistance.[20]

Gender and Class in Historical Traditions

Comparisons of historical traditions within culturally closely related nations may point to other important aspects of national symbolism.

In the search for national identities, romantic nationalism in the middle of the nineteenth century in a number of western European countries singled out the peasant population as bearers of age-old traditions, sometimes of long-lost democratic institutions. The revival of national history meant upgrading folklore in the form of popular 'folktales' and 'folkdances'. It included reviving popular food recipes and not least popular ways of dressing. Wearing clothes patterned on peasants' Sunday dress, or clothes used for church-going, marriages and funerals, in a number of nascent nations signalled awareness of national singularity. Analyses of this process in two northern European nations, Iceland and Norway, demonstrates the changing meanings of gender and class for national symbolism.[21]

Similarities in this process in both countries might indicate more general patterns. The national costume was a created costume, and not identical to any of the costumes that had been or still was in use among the peasant population. It was also worn by urban people, and signalled attachment to the national movement. In Norway wearing a national costume at the same time indicated a critical attitude to the new urban culture, and resistance to international fashion trends and modern international ready-made products. Priority was given to clothes produced in the nation, preferably by hand. At the outset, Norwegian national costumes were worn by women and men alike; in Iceland national costumes were worn by women exclusively. Gradually, however, this tradition also became much less popular with men in Norway.

Already at the World Exhibitions in 1856 and again in 1862, the Norwegian national dress was said to attract enormous attention as expressing something typical Norwegian The national dress gained momentum in the 1880s as the opposition to the political union with Sweden grew stronger, and gradually it became a symbol of the nation itself. As tourism started to flourish in the Norwegian fjords, the first tourist hotels had their waitresses dress up in national costumes. Small dolls in national costumes became popular souvenirs and specially made costumes would be used as presents to important foreign guests, such as a French prince and the German Kaiser Wilhelm II. The British Princess

Figure 1.1 *Norwegian Woman from Ulvik,* Hardanger, around 1900 – an example of Norwegian national costume, highlighting women's importance to the nation as mothers and housewives. Photo by K. Knudsen (Bergen University Library, Norway)

Maud, visiting the Norwegian fjords in the 1890s, was photographed in a Norwegian national dress. Twelve years later she was to return to Norway as the first queen of the fully independent nation. The photograph became a popular postcard with the text 'the Queen of Norway' – a uniting symbol of the free, independent nation.

Gradually, however, wearing the national costume became in the main reserved for women. Although women continued to symbolize tradition, the understanding of national masculinity was changing. At the turn of the century, the peasant as a symbol of the democratic Norwegian nation was met by a new urban elitist nationalism. The hero of this competing nationalism was the intellectual progressive urban man and the lonely masculine skier, fighting the wild nature of the arctic world – as personified in Fridtjof Nansen who, in the 1880s, crossed Greenland on skies.[22]

In Iceland national costumes played a similar role. But the gendering was much clearer. Only women wore national costumes. Attempts to create such costumes for men, never succeeded. And what is more, the female national costume was created by a man – the artist Sigmundur Gudmundson, founder of the National Museum of Iceland – and propagated by men, not by women. Gudmundson explained that the national costume was meant as a symbol of the nation as a mother. The Icelandic national costume had a tight corset, lifting and exposing women's breasts, symbolizing the mountainous nature of Iceland. The full skirt that could easily be enlarged during pregnancies indicated the fertile plains and the maternal womb. According to Inga Dora Björnsdottir, the apron that went with the dress, pointed to women's duties in the domestic sphere.

This exposure of the motherly nature of the female body may also be found in some versions of the Norwegian national dress. But one of the most popular versions resembled the then rather popular 'reform dress', freeing women from the grip of the corset. This costume was designed by Hulda Garborg, who moved in a circle of friends active within the women's suffrage movement. It seems no coincidence that after a while Hulda Garborg stopped using the apron that originally accompanied this dress. The Norwegian national costume could be understood both as a symbol of women as mothers of the nation, and as an indication of a new freedom for women within the nation.

The symbolism of the national costume in the two Nordic countries lends itself to a double interpretation. The creation of a national costume, in Iceland exclusively for women, in Norway mostly for women, seemed to further polarize understandings of femininity and masculinity in both nations. At the same time, however, it made women visible as members of the nation and served to support the argument that women, as national mothers or even as free individuals, should be entitled to full suffrage rights.

It would be tempting to analyse further the meaning attached to the use of national dresses in other nations. It springs to the eye, that women in Africa and Asia generally have also tended to dress in traditional clothes for a much longer time than men. Will parallel analyses of the meaning of using traditional clothes show similar understandings in African and Asian nations as those revealed for Iceland and Norway? Let me at least add that it does not come as a surprise to learn that Gandhi urged women not only to wear, but also to produce, home-spun cotton saris. To this very day, Indian and Bangladeshi women wear saris and men wear Western business suits. In Egypt, in around 1900, for women to discard the veil was seen as a symbol of a modern nation, well capable of freeing itself from British authority. In present day Egypt, as in a number of Islamic countries, wearing the veil and even the chador, symbolizes opposition to Western decadent cultural and political influences.[23] This demonstrates the political importance attached to gendered attires.

In her analysis of the gendered meaning of the Icelandic national costume, Inga Dora Bjørnsdottir points to the fact that – in contrast with the highly decorative clothes worn by a frivolous male aristocracy – the Western male suit was a symbol of bourgeois austerity and the Protestant work ethic. The male suit thus had a function of symbolizing the rising middle classes and their values. In contrast with Icelandic women's national costume, which pointed to mainly one identity for women – that of mother and housewife – the male suit covered multiple professions and personalities. This gender difference could substantiate Anne McClintock's observation that men represented national modernity, while women stood for retrograde cultural nationalism.[24]

Comparative research on gender and nations, crossing cultural boundaries, confirms the international character of nationalism as well as of the fight for women's emancipation. Highlighting cross-cultural parallels alongside decisive culturally determined differences, such research tears down the walls often constructed between the public and the private, between culture and state, between symbols and realities, and points to gendered ambiguities in the construction of nations.

Duties in the Nation: Defence and Reproduction

Such ambiguities also apply to mechanisms of rights and duties in the nation state. The creation of nation states made suffrage an important right and a means of including or excluding individuals from the national community. However, citizen's rights in the nation state were seen as resting on the performance of certain duties to the state. Defending the national territory has been seen as a fundamental duty.

The importance of gender for the military seems straightforward. The military was conceived as a masculine arena. Men were understood to be strong and courageous, women as weak and fearful, in need of protection. This comes out very clearly in all military rhetoric.

If for a moment we revert to the transcultural comparative histories of the Enlightenment, Michael Harbsmeier has pointed out that courage was seen as a characteristic found in white men, whereas cowardice was associated with the feminine and with people of colour. 'Westocentric' approaches highlighted European culture as the apotheosis of cultural developments, and described non-Europeans, not only as 'hideous' and 'dark-complexioned' but also as harbouring unsympathetic qualities such as a 'more-than-feminine cowardice'.[25] Karen Hagemann has found similar 'feminization of the other', this time of men of the enemy nation, in Prussian war rhetoric during the anti-Napoleonic wars 1812–14. The French were characterized as 'vain and feminine weaklings', while the typical German man was seen as 'valorous, strong' and capable of defending his fatherland.[26]

Military *practices*, at first glance, seemed to confirm the perception of military defence of the nation as a masculine undertaking. A complicated process, starting in the second half of the seventeenth century, led to standing armies and in some nation states to the conscription of male citizens. This process seemed to change the military from a joint masculine-feminine undertaking, as had been the case as long as women followed the armies to cook, clean and take care of the wounded, to a men-only project.[27] The gendered meaning of this shift in military practices was strengthened by the parallel growth in Darwinistic biologism. Increasingly, gender was seen as a biological given, stressing the uniformity of all members of the female sex as opposed to all members of the male sex. This underpinned the presupposition that *all women* were weak and needed protection, whereas to be strong and bellicose was a characteristic shared by *all men*. A person with a masculine biology who demonstrated feminine characteristics – and vice versa – was seen as an anomaly.

However, as has been shown by a number of researchers, wars between nations were not an exclusively masculine phenomenon.[28] Although national conscription did not include women, this should not blind the historian to women's co-responsibility for national wars. Recent Scandinavian and German research has revealed the eagerness of groups of middle class and aristocratic women to support national defence, collecting money to strengthen the national army or navy, to construct fortifications and assisting the military by preparing sanitary material and furnishing sanitary assistance in war situations.[29] The important services rendered by women in the belligerent nations during the First World War – as nurses, doctors, ambulance drivers, ammunition workers, agricultural labourers, etc., are well-known examples of women as supporters and even as indispensable to, national wars. If all these women seemed less bellicose than their male counterparts, their acceptance of military violence as a means of solving national problems and their assistance with such violence was not to be doubted.[30]

Finally, if women have only to a minor degree lost their lives in direct battles to protect the nation or believing that they defended the honour of the nation, women had in different ways suffered for the same purposes. Suffice it to mention the broad acceptance of rape as a war measure, humiliating the men of the enemy nation who were not capable of protecting their women, and in some historical context causing the rape victims to be expelled from the family and neighbourhood networks on which their lives depended.[31]

We may ask whether there was not a systematically gendered difference between all these female war activities and sufferings and the experiences of the male soldier. Was not the soldier, as a man, in a much more direct way willing to sacrifice his life for the nation?

A good deal of evidence points in a different direction. First, not all men were part of the military. Not all nations used national conscription, and even where this existed, there were means of avoiding being called up. To take Norway as an example: when, in 1814, the Norwegian state was established as separate from the Danish crown, national conscription was accepted as a principle but it was not enacted as part of the legal system until 1854, and rich people could, until 1876, still pay someone else to do military service.[32] To this day, clergymen and missionaries are excepted from military service.[33] In some nations, like the US, race and ethnicity might decide a man's function within the military, and consequently how exposed he would be to losing his life.[34]

Second, if women did not sacrifice their lives for the nation through military service, they did it in a different way. Women's maternal capacities created life for the nation, created the new generations. Around the turn of the century, and still for many decades, despite the important consequences of the discovery of antiseptics and aseptics, death in childbirth was a common phenomenon.[35]

But the nation needed citizens, and giving birth and raising children were often referred to as 'women's maternal duties'. The American President, Theodore Roosevelt, compared the 'cowardly' and 'selfish' woman who shirked her duty to become a mother with the man who 'fears to do his duty in battle when the country calls him'. Both, in different ways, let down the nation. In 1886, August Bebel declared that 'a woman who brings children into the world does the community at least as great a service as a man who defends his country'. He found the number of casualties among child bearers to be probably greater than among soldiers on the battlefield, and saw in this fact an important reason to entitle women to complete equality with men. Not many men would have agreed with Bebel's statement at that time.

But the above reasoning demonstrates that the private (bearing children) was as necessary to maintain the nation as the public (the defence of the nation). However, the two services to the nation were evaluated in the light of the prevalent understanding of femininity and masculinity. To create life resulted in a need for protection and consequently in dependence, whereas to be prepared to take life resulted in independence and rights in the nation.[36]

Much more comparative research is needed to reach a better understanding of the gendered meaning of duties to the nation. Comparisons of gender and the military over time within one nation, and comparisons of this relationship between different nations will yield interesting insights into a number of problems pertaining to gendered nations and gendered nationalisms as well as into the construction of gender identities. The investigation of correspondence and lack of correspondence between understandings of gender and actual gendered behaviour in the relation to war and the military must be a fascinating task.

National Identities and Other Identities

However, studies of the importance of gender as a marker of belonging to and of exclusion from the national community do not stop at analysing the shifting relations between women and men and the common nation. Failure to comply with dominant gender models – with prevailing understandings of femininity and masculinity – could be used as arguments for grading nations as more or less capable of stability and independence. Certain understandings of masculinity could be seen as indicating national superiority.

Mrinilina Sinha has studied the process through which national masculine identities are made by constructing men of a different nationality – the other male – as effeminate.[37] She has looked at relations between British administrators and Hindu middle-class men in Bengal around the year 1900. She has also analysed debates concerning the Act of Consent, enacted in 1891. This law allowed the continuation of the tradition of marrying off girls under twelve years of age, but at the same time, it forbade consummation of a marriage before the bride's twelfth birthday. Sinha discusses many implications of this law, such as the reluctance of British officials to intervene in the private sphere of Hindu traditions. In the context of this chapter, the interesting feature is her observation that the British officials, all men, acted in accordance with their Victorian understanding of masculinity. To British officials, the masculine ideal was a person in full control of himself, not least in sexual matters, and with a tall, strong and healthy bodily appearance. Contrasting with this ideal, the British pointed to the small, delicate bodies of Hindu middle-class men and interpreted their tradition of child marriages as a sign of lack of self-control. In fact, the British picture of Hindu men approached the contemporary picture of homosexual men, so harshly stigmatized in British society. Such men, in the opinion of the British, could not govern themselves, let alone a whole society. They would have to be educated by 'proper men' – namely the British – but it was deemed doubtful that education would ever bring Hindu men to comply with British ideas of proper masculinity. This way of understanding masculinities not only underpinned the British imperial project, but also allowed British men to cushion their own masculinity in contempt of 'the other'.

No doubt, this British understanding of masculinity was also tinged by expectations as to skin colour. The interaction of racism and gender in the formation of nation states is a field that historians have only just begun to explore. The persistent doubts about the possibility of 'educating' Indian men to become proper men may have been embedded in ideas of biological determination, alongside the belief in the possibility of cultural change. If this holds true, Bengali–British relations may bear witness to the same process as the one Catherine Hall has analysed for the 1830s and 1840s. Hall finds that a liberal cultural racism, perceiving blacks as small brothers and sisters, was transformed into an aggressive biological racism, understanding blacks as a different species, born to be mastered.[38] Comparative analyses of how nationalism tended to marginalize specific groups, of the working of racism, and of the importance of gendered racism to the process of creating modern nations, are still few. Such studies may be located in nations dominated by whites, to compare possible different processes of marginalization of different groups of coloured people, or – for the latter half of the twentieth century, in nations dominated by coloured people to compare different processes of relations between one-time-white-masters and present-day coloured masters.

This raises the question of how different identities interact in periods of nation building. How do race, ethnicity, gender and class identities confirm or undermine national identity? To what extent have dominating social groups, such as white middle-class men and women attempted to make other ethnic groups or working class individuals conform to a white middle-class perception of national identity? Which codes of behaviour would signal the 'correct' national identity ?

I would suggest that in situations of little or no tension between two nations, gender identities could produce friendly cooperation among women, as was the case with Norwegian and Swedish middle-class women during the 1880s and 1890s.[39] But when national conflicts sharpened awareness of national identities, gender solidarity could wane. In 1905, the year of the abrogation of the political union between Norway and Sweden, the most prominent of Norwegian feminists launched a vitriolic attack on Sweden, characterizing the Swedish nation as a 'sly robber'. Immediately, Swedish feminists shied away from cooperation with their Norwegian counterparts. In both countries, for a while, national identity took priority over gender identity. In this context, however, class – and political conviction – made a difference. All through the national conflict, men and women socialists maintained a friendly and smooth cooperation across the Norwegian–Swedish border. The fact that class still, to some extent, meant exclusion from civil rights, for men as well as for women, undermined attachment to nation and tinged the construction of national identity. The international character of socialism also bound working-class individuals together, and gave class identity the first place. Socialists – most clearly in Sweden – found their special national identity, different from the middle class national identity, seeing the working class as *the* national class that would liberate the nation from the pressures of international capitalism. In both countries socialists maintained that general suffrage, in Norway explicitly including women's suffrage, was a better way of protecting the nation than national military services. Rather than maintaining that class identity dominated over national identity, it may be said that Norwegian and Swedish socialists developed a socialist national identity. In Norway, this identity even had a gendered character, as socialist women saw themselves as the best promoters and guarantors of a peaceful future for the nation.

It may also be pertinent that where gender and/or class marginalized individuals from the nation, marginalized groups would look across national boundaries for identification. Thus middle-class women were eagerly involving themselves in international women's organizations, such as the International Council of Women (ICW), seeking support from women of other nationalities in a common feeling of exclusion from their respective nations. However, even in such fora, national identities might cause conflicts, as was the case during the process that lead to the abrogation of the Norwegian-Swedish union in 1905. This conflict lead to a change of statutes within the ICW, stating that matters of nationality and religion should not be discussed within this organization.

An interesting subject to pursue would thus be the importance of national identity to the workings of international organizations, with a special view to women's organizations.

Together with race, class and gender, religious identity might also challenge national loyalties. This was evident in the formation of the German nation, where the Catholic south for long was opposed to the Protestant north. In India, Muslim and Hindu women organized separately, and in many countries Jewish women build their special organizations paralleling Christian women's organizations within the same nation.[40] To what extent religion helped splinter or strengthen national identity, and in which ways gender coloured this process is, as far as I know, a still-unexplored area of nation building.

Conclusion

Nationalism and nations are, even today, contested themes and cross-cultural understanding is a difficult project within gender history. Mechanisms to avoid cultural imperialism and teleological – even 'Westocentric' – approaches must be sought out carefully to facilitate cross-cultural understanding in the research process as well as in discussions among researchers of different nationalities and with different cultural identities. What historians should strive to achieve is a working atmosphere of what Nira Yuval-Davis has called 'tranversalism'.[41] She recommends researchers to be fully and openly aware of their own 'rooting' in their specific nation, culture, class, race, *and* at the same time be prepared to 'shift' – to attempt to understand the rootedness of 'the other'. Dialogues – be they the dialogue between the researcher and the evidence of a historical past, or the dialogue among researchers, must, according to Yuval-Davis, be carried out with respect for two points. One is that neither of the participants should lose awareness of their own rooting; the other is that groups taking part in the dialogue should never be understood as homogeneous and dichotomous. Yuval-Davis warns that, desirable as this method may be, it is only applicable as long as none of the participants insists on continuing or creating hierarchies of power or on adhering to an essentialistic understanding of identity that results in exclusions of others.

My conclusion is that international comparisons of the gendering of nationalisms and nation states is well under way. I am sure that the future will see much more of cross-cultural comparative history as well as of more limited comparisons in this field, and that future research will bring fascinating new understandings of the interrelations of gender and nation at a global level. It is to be hoped that historians working in this area of the past will consider the importance of transversalism and attempt to avoid power hierarchies so easily constructed within cross-cultural research.

Notes

1. For an excellent introduction, see Eley, G. and Suny, R. G. (1990), 'Introduction: From the Moment of Social History to the Work of Cultural Representation,' in Eley, G. and Suny, R. G., *Becoming National. A Reader*, Oxford and New York: Oxford University Press, 3–37. For the global impact of nationalism, see also Arjun Appandurai (1990), 'Disjuncture and Difference in the Global Cultural Economy;' in Featherstone, M. (ed.), *Globalization and Modernity*, London: Sage, 295–310.
2. Blom, I. (1997), 'World History as Gender History: The Case of the Nation State' in Tønnesson, St., Koponen, J., Steensgaard, N. and Svensson, Th. (eds.), *Between National Histories and Global History*, (Helsingfors: FHS, 71–91. Blom, I. (1994), *Det er forskjell på folk – nå som før. Om kjønn og andre former for sosial differensiering*, Oslo: Universitets forlaget, 11–12.
3. Harbsmeier, M. (1989), 'World Histories Before Domestication. The Writing of Universal Histories, Histories of Mankind and World Histories in Late Eighteenth Century Germany,' *Culture and History*. (Copenhagen: Akademisk forlag, 93–131.
4. Blom, I., *Det er forskjell*, 18. Barbara Stollberg-Rilinger (1996), 'Vaeter der Frauengeschichte? Das Geschlecht als historische Kategorie im 18. und 19. Jahrhunderts,' *Historische Zeitschrift*, Vol. 262: 39–71.

5. Hobsbawm, E. (1990), *Nations and Nationalism Since 1780: Programme, Myth, Reality*, Cambridge: Cambridge University Press.
6. See for Instance Sewell Jr., W. H. (1988), 'Le Citoyen/la citoyenne: Activity, Passivity and the Revolutionary Concept of Citizenship,' in Lukas, C. (ed.), *The Political Culture of the French Revolution* vol. 2 of *The French Revolution and the Creation of Modern Political Culture*, Oxford: Pergamon, 105–123. Offen, K. (1992), 'Depopulation, Nationalism, and Feminism in Fin-de-Siecle France,' *The American Historical Review*, vol. 97, no.2: 349–378. Lake, M. (1992), 'Mission Impossible: How Men Gave Birth to the Australian Nation. Nationalism, Gender and Other Siminal Acts,' in *Gender and History*, vol. 4, no. 3: 305–322. Curthoys, A. (1993), 'Identity Crisis: Colonialism, Nation and Gender in Australian History,' *Gender and History*, vol. 5, no. 2: 165–176.
7. Osterhammel, J. (1996), 'Transkulturell vergleichende Geschichtswissenschaft,' in Haupt, H.-G. and Kocka, J. (eds), *Geschichte und Vergleich. Ansätze und Ergebnisse international vergleichender Geschichstschreibung*, Frankfurt and New York: Campus, 271–314.
8. Jayawardena, K. (1986), *Feminism and Nationalism in the Third World*. (London and New Delhi:
9. See for instance Pierson, R. R. and Chaudhuri, N. (1998), *Nation, Empire, Colony: Historicizing Gender and Race*, Bloomington: Indiana University Press. Sinha, M., Guy, D. J. and Woollacott, A. (1998), *Feminism and Internationalism*, Special issue of *Gender and History*, vol. 10, no. 3.
10. Osterhammel, J. (1996), 'Transkulturell vergleichende Geschichtswissenschaft,' in Haupt, H.-G. and Kocka, J. (eds), *Geschichte und Vergleich. Ansätze und Ergebnisse international vergleichender Geschichstschreibung*, Frankfurt and New York: Campus, 283–291.
11. Haupt, H.-G. and Kocka, J. (1996), 'Historischer Vergleich: Methoden, Aufgaben, Probleme. Eine Einleitung,' in Haupt, H.-G. and Kocka, J. (eds), *Geschichte und Vergleich. Ansätze und Ergebnisse international vergleichender Geschichstschreibung*, Frankfurt and New York: Campus, 9–45.
12. *Ibid.*
13. Blom, I. (1991), A Global Women's History: Organising Principles and Cross-Cultural Understandings,' in Offen, K., Pierson, R. R. and Rendall, J. (eds), *Writing Women's History: International Perspectives*, Bloomington and London: Indiana University Press, 135–149.
14. Osterhammel, J. (1996), 'Transkulturell vergleichende Geschichtswissenschaft,' Macmillan and Haupt, H.-G. and Kocka, J., Historischer

Vergleich: Methoden, Aufgaben, Probleme. Eine Einleitung,' in Haupt, H.-G. and Kocka, J. (eds), *Geschichte und Vergleich. Ansätze und Ergebnisse international vergleichender Geschichstschreibung,* Frankfurt and New York.

15. Meinicke, Fr. (1908), *Weltbürgertum und Nationalstaat,* Berlin: R. Oldenburg. For India, see Basu, A. (1995), 'Feminism and Nationalism in India, 1917–1947,' in *Journal of Women's History,* vol. 7, no. 4: 95–107. For Japan, see Hayakawa, N. (1995), 'Feminism and Nationalism in Japan, 1868–1945, in *Journal of Women's History,* vol. 7, no. 4: 108–119. Blom, I. (1995), 'Feminism and Nationalism in the Early Twentieth Century: A Cross-Cultural Perspective', in *Journal of Women's History,* vol. 7, no. 4: 82–94. See also Blom, I. (1996), 'Das Zusammenwirken von Nationalismus und Feminismus um die Jahrhunderswende: Ein Versuch zur vergleichenden Geschlechtergeschichte,' in Haupt, H.-G. and Kocka, J. (eds), *Geschichte und Vergleich. Ansätze und Ergebnisse international vergleichender Geschichstschreibung.* Frankfurt and New York: Campus, 315–338. Blom, I. (1996), 'Nation–Class–Gender: Scandinavia at the Turn of the Century,' in *Scandinavian Journal of History,* vol. 21: 1–16. Blom, I., 'World History as Gender History: The Case of the Nation State' in Tønnesson, St., Koponen, J., Steensgaard, N. and Svensson, Th. (eds), *Between National Histories and Global History,* (Helsingfors: FHS.

16. See Hagemann, K., chapter 9.

17. Ramusak, B. (1988), 'Women in South and South East Asia,' in Berger, I. et al., (eds), *Restoring Women to History: Teaching Packets for Integrating Women's History into Courses on Africa, Asia, Latin America, The Caribbean and the Middle East.* Bloomington: Organization of American Historians, 1–63. Sievers, S. L. (1988), 'Women in China, Japan and Korea',' in Berger, I. et al.,)eds), *Restoring Women to History: Teaching Packets for Integrating Women's History into Courses on Africa, Asia, Latin America, The Caribbean and the Middle East.* Bloomington: Organization of American Historians, 63–118. Blom, I. (1995), 'Feminism and Nationalism in the Early Twentieth Century: A Cross-Cultural Perspective', in *Journal of Women's History,* vol. 7, no. 4: 82–94.

18. Blom, I., 'Das Zusammenwirken von Nationalismus und Feminismus um die Jahrhundertwende: Ein Versuch zur vergleichenden Geschlechtergeschichte,' in Haupt, H.-G. and Krocka, J. (eds), *Geschichte und Vergleich. Ansätze und Ergebnisse international vergleichender Geschichstschreibung,* Frankfurt and New York: Campus, 315–338.

Blom, I., (1995), 'Feminism and Nationalism in the Early Twentieth Century: A Cross-Cultural Perspective', in *Journal of Women's History*, vol. 7, no. 4: 82–94.

19. Chitnis, S., (1998), 'Feminism: Indian Ethos and Indian Convictions,' in Ghadially, R. (ed.), *Women in Indian Society. A Reader*, New Delhi and London: Sage Publications, 81–95.

20. Ramusak, B. (1988), 'Women in South and South East Asia,' in Berger, I. et al., (eds), *Restoring Women to History: Teaching Packets for Integrating Women's History into Courses on Africa, Asia, Latin America, The Caribbean and the Middle East*. Bloomington: Organization of American Historians, 1–63. Blom, I. (ed.) (1992), *Cappelens kvinnehistorie*, vol. 2, Oslo: Cappelen forlag.

21. For Norway, see Oxaal, A. (1994), 'Folkedrakt som uniform,' in Sørensen, Ø. (ed.), *Nasjonal identitet – et kunstprodukt?*, Oslo: NFR, 91–112. For Iceland, see Björnsdottir, I. D. (1997), 'Nationalism, Gender and the Body in Icelandic Nationalist Discourse,' in *NORA, Nordic Journal of Women's Studies*, vol. 5, no. 1: 3–13.

22. Stenseth, B. (1994), 'Borgerlig nasjonlisme og bygdenasjonalisme,' in Sørensen, Ø. (ed.), *Nasjonal identitet – et kunstprodukt?*, Oslo: NFR, 159–169. Goksøyr, M. (1994), 'Nasjonale idrætter – et 1800-tals produkt?,' in Sørensen, Ø. (ed.), *Nasjonal identitet – et kunstprodukt?*, Oslo: NFR, 53–67.

23. Ray, B. 'Freedom Movement and Women's Awakening in Bengal, 1911–1929,' *The Indian Historical Review*, vol. 12, nos. 1–2: 130–163. Blom, I. and Vogt, K. (1992), 'Kampen om sløret,' in Blom, I. (ed.), *Cappelens kvinnehistorie*, vol. 2, Oslo: Cappelen forlag, 216–223.

24. McClintock, A. (1996), 'No Longer in a Future Heaven: Nationalism, Gender and Race,' in Eley, G. (ed.) *Becoming National*, Oxford: Oxford University Press, 260–284.

25. Harbsmeier, M. (1989), 'World Histories Before Domestication. The Writing of Universal Histories, Histories of Mankind and World Histories in Late Eighteenth Century Germany,' *Culture and History*. (Copenhagen: Akademisk forlag, 92–131.

26. See chapter 9.

27. Hagemann, K. (1997), 'Militär, Krieg und Geschlechterverhältnisse. Untersuchungen, Überlegungen und Fragen zur Militärgeschichte der Frühen Neuzeit,' in Pröve, R. (ed.), *Klio in Uniform? Probleme und Perspektiven einer modernen Militärgeschichte der Frühen Neuzeit*, Köln, Weimer and Wien: 35–88. Hagemann, K. and Pröve, R. (eds) (1998), *Landsknechte, Soldatenfrauen und Nationalkrieger. Militär,*

Krieg und Geschlechterordnung im historischen Wandel, Frankfurt a.M. and New York: Campus Verlag.

28. Yuval-Davis, N. (1997), *Gender and Nation*, London: Sage 93–115.
29. For Norway and Sweden, see Blom, I. (1996), 'Nation–Class–Gender: Scandinavia at the Turn of the Century,' in *Scandinavian Journal of History*, vol. 21: 1–16. For Denmark see Vammen, T. (1992), 'Kanonkvinnorna fostrade sönerna till soldater,' *Kvinnovetenskaplig Tidskrift*, vol. 13, no. 4: 150–154. For Germany, see note 20.
30. Braybon, G. and Summerfield, P. (1987), *Out of the Cage. Women's Experience in Two World Wars*, London and New York: Pandora. See also Helen Bradford's analysis of gender and warfare in chapter 10 of this volume.
31. Hagemann, K. (1997), 'Militär, Krieg und Geschlechterverhältnisse. Untersuchungen, Überlegungen und Fragen zur Militärgeschichte der Frühen Neuzeit,' in Pröve, R. (ed.), *Klio in Uniform? Probleme und Perspektiven einer modernen Militärgeschichte der Frühen Neuzeit*, Köln, Weimar and Wien: 35–88. Blom, I. (in press), 'Global kjønnshistorie – en utfordring til framtidens historikere,' in Quarsell, R. and Sundin, J. (eds), *Historieforskningen inför framtiden*.
32. Pryser, T. (1985), *Norsk historie 1800–1870. Frå standssamfunn mot kiassesamfurm*, Oslo: Det norske sam laget, 20–22.
33. Pax leksikon.
34. Yuval-Davis, N. (1997), *Gender and Nation*, London: Sage, 96. Native Americans and Japanese Americans had the highest rates of combat fighting in American forces during World War II, while American blacks were almost absent from the front.
35. Blom, I. (1980), *Den haarde Dyst: Fødsler og fødsleshjelp gjennom 150 år*, Oslo: Cappelen forlag, 216.
36. Pateman, C. (1992), 'Equality, difference, subordination: the politics of motherhood and women's citizenship' in Bock, G. and James, S. (eds), *Beyond Equality and Difference: citizenship – feminist politics – female subjectivity*, London and New York: Routledge, 17–31.
37. Sinha, M. (1987), 'Gender and Imperialism: Colonial Policy and the Ideology of Moral Imperialism in Late Nineteenth Century Bengal,' in Kimmel, M. (ed.), *Changing Men: New Directions in Research on Men and Masculinity*, London and New Delhi: Sage, 217–231.
38. Hall, C. (1988), 'Missionary Stories: gender and ethnicity in England in the 1830s and 1840s,' in Hall, C., *White, Male and Middle Class*, Cambridge: Polity Press, 207–254.
39. Blom, I. (1996), 'Nation – Class – Gender: Scandinavia at the Turn of the Century,' in *Scandinavian Journal of History*, vol. 21: 1–16.

40. Frevert, U. (1989), *Women in German History: From Bourgeois Emancipation to Sexual Liberation*, New York, Oxford and Munich: Berg Publishers, 111–113.
41. Yuval-Davis (1999) *Gender and Nations*, London: Sage, 116–134.

2

Culture, Nation and Gender
Geoff Eley[1]

There are many ways of organizing a discussion of nations and nationalism. In this particular volume, the 'long nineteenth century' provides the temporal boundaries, and so here 'the national' refers more to the processes of nation *forming* than to differences and complexities of the nation form in already constituted national states. Either nations were still being imagined, founded, and fought for in state-territorial ways (the essays on Egypt, Afrikanerdom, Ireland, Czechoslovakia, Latvia), or else populations were being reshaped within old territorial states in a new and distinctively 'national' manner (England/Britain, France, Prussia/ Germany). In a third category, the state-nation was being violently refounded through wars and an expanding frontier (United States, Australia).

Of course, this categorization immediately throws up problems. Thus Prussia was certainly an 'old' state, and 'Germany' enjoyed complex state-institutional existence between the sixteenth and nineteenth centuries, but unified Germany was an entirely *new* state in 1871, and had to be freshly proposed and imagined as such. Likewise, the US was already independent by the end of the eighteenth century, but experienced huge upheaval and redefinition during the civil war, and arguably had to be imagined 'after the fact'. Afrikanerdom was a newly imagined nation in terms of the aspiration to statehood, but as a frontier nation conjoined in a larger South African project of state-territorial consolidation.

The imperial dimension and the complex dialectics of colonialism further confuse these distinctions. One axis of difference was intra-European, between the old-established territorial states, where sovereignty preceded the nationalist era (England/Britain, France, ambiguously Prussia/Germany), and the smaller nations claiming their own sovereign existence against imperial rule (Ireland, Czechoslovakia, Latvia). *National* demands were overdetermined by dilemmas of *social* development. Where societal conflicts of bourgeoisie and aristocracy could be resolved in existing sovereign states (classically in England/Britain, Netherlands, France), a sense of nationality materialized in the institutions and cultures of dominant classes. But among the smaller subject peoples of the European periphery, the conditions of progress (bourgeois society, capitalist economy) required casting off the domination of foreign, metropolitan, or 'de-nationalized' bourgeois-aristocratic rulers, and for this purpose populist forms of nationalist mobilization became excellently fitted. For the dominant nationalities, this field of differences became normalized into languages of superiority, in the nineteenth-century condescension of 'historic' nations to 'history-less peoples', which the twentieth-century discourse of national self-determination has still only partially overcome. Given nineteenth-century Europe's political geography, smaller nationalities (Irish, Czechs, Latvians) could only define themselves via long conflicts with normally intransigent imperial powers (England/Britain, Russia, Austria-Hungary, imperial Germany).

On metropolitan Europe's nationality frontiers – between the English and Irish, Germans and Poles, Germans and Czechs, Hungarians and Slovaks, Russians and the subject peoples, and so on – struggles were violent and impassioned, assuming all the forms of the colonial relationship. Moreover, within the old-established national states, the drive for standardization and cultural uniformity, particularly via conscription and schooling, entailed similar systematic attacks on subaltern linguistic cultures and regional or local identities, which were invariably peasant, peripheralized, and pre-literate. That is, even nominally 'national' cultures had to be created as such, and supposedly homogenous 'French' or 'German' populations had first to be codified, counted, and ordered into shape.[2] Outside Europe, the colonizing process was the more dramatic. This volume contains two instances of extra-European anti-colonial nationalism, each of them in a highly complex relationship both with competing state projects (local, imperial, European), and with the ethno-religious demographics of the region – Beth Baron's discussion of 'the making of the Egyptian nation', and Helen Bradford's dissection of the Anglo-Boer War's role in 'regendering Afrikanerdom'. The volume also addresses the nationalisms of the *colonizing* as well as the *colonized* societies: notably, in Catherine Hall's reading of race and empire against class and gender in the English nation-defining moment of 1832; and Marilyn Lake's reflection on the constitutive interaction of race and gender in the discourse of Australian nationhood between the 1880s and 1930s.

What I am really stressing here is the inchoateness and non-fixity of national meanings and identifications in the nineteenth century. This was a period where the boundaries of the national category were anything but fixed. Increasingly over the last decade, we've come to see the indeterminacy, constructedness, and contingency of national identity as central to the subject in general, and certainly not confined to the period before the First World War. But, at the same time, there were vital ways in which national affiliations became hardened into continuities after 1918, in juridical, institutional, ideological, and other terms. In the period covered by this book, on the other hand, the fully articulated ideal of the nation-people-citizenry, as the basis for state-political organization, whether or not political independence was already attained, was still being proposed.

Let me spell out more extensively what I mean. The transition to statehood marks a key watershed in the development of any nationalist movement. Possessing the nation state, with its juridical machinery of constitutions, legal codes, courts and police, its centralized administrative systems, its society-wide institutions in governmental, party-political and associational terms, its organized cultural life, and so on, has made an enormous difference to the strength of national identifications, as well as to the range of modalities through which the latter can be built. The ideal of 'the nation', as opposed to some other principle of state-political organization, became a source of extraordinary legitimizing power in the centralizing drives of government during the nineteenth century, enabling demands on the population's loyalties going far beyond the expectations of earlier forms of government – even allowing for the momentary surges of millennial and other popular mobilizations in earlier times. As Benedict Anderson famously put it, the willingness to *die* for the nation, to sacrifice one's body, memorialized in poetry and monuments, became the extreme heroic form for this suturing of the individual and the nation together.[3]

It made a huge difference to this discourse of sacrificial inscription – which was inescapably gendered in its allegories and public symbolics – whether the nationalism concerned was a campaigning or insurgent movement demanding its rights, or a state already wielding its independence. Different temporalities of state formation were in play. On the one hand, infrastructures of national identification in the old states of Western Europe (the cumulative histories of legal and institutional sedimentation) allowed practical consciousness of national belonging to coalesce. On the other hand, purposeful movements of political creation generated explicit demands for national independence. The coordinates of nationalism in England and France were profoundly different from those in Germany and Italy, still more from the moving nationalist frontier of Eastern Europe. Outside the 'core' states of the West, nationality lacked the faculty of established statehood. For the German nationalists of the anti-Napoleonic wars, the *Vormärz*, and the 1860s, or the pioneers of Czech and Latvian nationality in the later nineteenth century, the real work of proposing and elaborating the national category – inventing the nation as a political programme – was conducted without benefit of existing state institutions. The architecture of national identification, and the process of imagining the nation as an organized, proselytizing act, in a politics of continuous nationalist pedagogy, depended on private rather than official bodies, individuals and voluntary associations rather than governments. Moreover, this process of proposing the (German, Czech, Latvian) national category was to a great extent identical, or at least coterminous, with the emergence of a public sphere in Habermas's sense, so that 'the nation' became conceived simultaneously as a political community of citizens.[4] Indeed, the very virtue of 'publicness' in its civic sense, and the associated coalescence of civil society, were entailments of the demand for the nation.

The complex interpenetration of these two ideas – *nation* and *citizenry* – in the political languages of the nineteenth century was extraordinarily important. There was a key tension in processes of national unification between the coalescing of national consciousness in institutional ways (as an *effect* of longer-term histories) and the campaigning of the nationalist movement *per se*. For example, a political identity of Germanness may have cohered institutionally over a long period, in response to state policies, constitutional frameworks, juridical definitions, and political opportunity structures, but German *nationalism* required new languages of political subjectivity that called on the inhabitants of this central European region to think of themselves in *national* as opposed to other ways.

It is worth thinking about this tension for a moment, by naming both the *inventedness* of national identity and the *constraints* in which the inventiveness had to move. Thus on the one hand, the element of political innovation has become key to how we think of nations and nationalism nowadays: nationality was *not* a natural consequence or outgrowth of common culture of great antiquity; nations were not so much discovered or awakened, as they were invented by the labours of intellectuals. That is, nationalisms rested on specific political histories and ideals of citizenship far more than they arose spontaneously out of pre-established cultural communities. Moreover, achieving continuity in national culture required hard, repeated, creative ideological and political efforts by intellectuals and nationalist leaderships. It did not occur by itself. Yet, on the other hand, nationalists could only work with the cultural materials at hand – not with cultures of their own choosing, but with cultures directly encountered, given, and transmitted from the past. For all the power of the 'constructionist' insight (the inventedness and contingency of nations), it was this complicated dialectic of political innovation and actually existing cultures that provided the key to the particular histories that nation building involved.

Furthermore, these days we have become acutely sensitized to the indeterminacies and contingencies, not only of the nation, nationhood, and national identity, but also of other key political terms, from *citizenship* to the *state*. So far from being stable or transparent in meaning, or juridically fixed, these terms are also culturally constructed. If we examine the particular contexts of constitution making in the long nineteenth century, or the practical dynamics and consciousness of political movements, citizenship rested on explicit, subtle, and disguised languages and mechanisms of inclusion and exclusion; it was subject to disagreement, conflict, counterinterpretations, and contestations; and it might also be transformed. As well as the formal political contests between dominant and oppositional social forces, and their party-political arenas, wider differences of meaning circulated less visibly through the political cultures. Complicated processes of delegitimization and entitlement were involved, privileging some social groups and categories of people over others. Such differences among the national citizenry – or among those accorded the full faculties of citizenship and those who were not – were ordered by gender, class, race, religion, sexual orientation, and other logics of centredness and marginalization.

The unifying strength of the essays in this volume is to have brought this fissiparous and fractured quality of nineteenth-century political cultures into focus. Eventually, nations attained a presence independently of the political practices that originally proposed them – they acquired an instituted and renewable everydayness, which built them into the underlying framework of collective identification in a society, part of the assumed architecture of political order and its common-sense intelligibility. With the attainment of sovereignty or political self-determination at the latest, the nation became a discursive formation – ideologically, institutionally, culturally, practically in myriad small ways – of immense power, which already prescribed the possible forms of political action and belief, what was thinkable and what not. In Tom Nairn's words, in these circumstances nationalism turned into 'a name for the general condition of the modern body politic, more like the [overall] climate of political and social thought than just another [free-standing] doctrine'.[5] In the nineteenth century, however, this hard wiring could not be presupposed. Accordingly, these essays explore the contexts in which this came to be the case. In fascinating diverse but convergent ways, they each choose a moment of *making* – a process of the nation's configuring through a very specific set of histories, focusing especially on the boundaries of exclusion and inclusion, for which gender analysis has become an essential tool.

It has become a commonplace of feminism that the default languages of modern political thought were shot through with gendered partialities of understanding, not least in the doubled context of Enlightenment and French Revolution from which so many of the key terms of democratic discourse descend. This founding conjuncture of modern political meaning, which also invented the language of nationality, was pervaded by binary orders of assumptions about woman and man, which became inscribed in the constitutions, codes of law, and political mobilizations, as well as the formal philosophical discourse around the universals of reason, law and nature, embedding such talk in an ideologically constructed system of differences in gender.[6] Caroll Smith-Rosenberg dissects the language of one such foundational moment, the late eighteenth-century discourse of representation, but the 'en-gendering' of political language is presupposed by the volume's contributors in general. Across the emergent national contexts of the nineteenth century, this translated into the exclusion of women from citizenship, most obviously through denial of the franchise, but more elaborately through a complex repertoire of silencings and disabilities, barring them from property, education, profession, and politics, or all the roles that qualified men for the public sphere. It was not until the second quarter of the twentieth century and later, in most parts of the world, that women were allowed formal entry into the political process.

Thus membership in the nation has been a powerfully gendered faculty. Nations have invariably been imagined through the metaphors of family, thereby replicating the patriarchy and hetero-normative axioms of conventional familial forms. National identity's referents of 'common descent', 'shared lineage', and 'the relatedness of the community' (see Baron in Chapter 7 of this volume), had a natural affinity for the languages of family and household. In one recurring chain of associations, women were addressed as mothers of the nation, reproducing its biological future, nurturing the next generations, teaching the 'mother tongue' – reproducers rather than producers, prized and revered objects of protection, rather than agents in their own right. Anxieties about the national health, the nation's demographic future and productive efficiencies, its global competitiveness, or the stabilities of the social fabric, invariably authorized a politics directed to and against women, whether through systems of mother-and-child welfare, rhetoric of family values, or policy offensives around reproductive health, regulation of sexuality, or direct control over women's bodies. Maternalism has been a recurring and mobile discursive formation in this sense, focusing forms of welfare-state intervention, condensing large-scale programmes of reform, resonating with popular hopes and fears, and working with or against competing conceptions of citizenship. In twentieth-century contexts, especially, it is impossible to discuss nationalism without encountering this systematic and explicit gendered dimension.[7]

In the nineteenth-century contexts of this collection, the relational field of 'family' and 'nation' figured differently. In varying ways, the pioneers of nation making found familial metaphors excellently suited for a modernizing vocabulary of reform that simultaneously upheld the gender regimes of men. Advocacy of political reform imagined new boundaries of the public and private. Baron's essay on Egypt shows one set of linkages, in the pre-parliamentary ordering of political capacities around dominant-class household economies, whose 'unravelling' through the end of slavery placed the 'woman question' at the centre of debate. As nationalists argued over the best strategies for reforming the polity, they made household into the 'building block of the nation'. In this case, gender relations (in the reordering of sexuality, reproduction, family, household) became a primary medium of politics, providing 'the fault line along which men and women negotiated ethnic boundaries, cultural identity, and social transformations'.

In Chapter 10 of this volume, on the Anglo-Boer War of 1899–1902, Helen Bradford shows another version of the household/nation duality, here in the exceptional circumstances of guerrilla warfare and brutal counter-insurgency, through which Afrikaner women appropriated patriotic agency ('the strongest element in our nation') and briefly occupied centre ground. They displaced men from the vanguard of nationalist intransigence, and 'gatecrashed into a homosocial *volk*', in Bradford's striking phrase, 'proving themselves more irreconcilable, and more manly, than many men'. Here the comparative possibilities of the volume are particularly rich – with 'the homo-social nation' of other frontier or settler societies (Australia, or the nineteenth-century US), with rural or peasant-based nationalisms in conflict with imperial powers (Ireland, the Baltic), with societies mobilized for war (Ireland, Prussia), and so on. In Bradford's analysis, republican Boer women broke the subaltern spell of family in a particularly interesting way. Like some of the volume's other essays – Beth Baron's, Margaret Ward's on women's role in the Irish Land War, and the two essays on Germany (Karen Hagemann's treatment of the anti-Napoleonic Wars, and Angelika Schaser's discussion of women's activism in Imperial Germany) – she also grounds the argument in a richly understood social history, showing how the best 'constructionist' analytic relies simultaneously on a social account.

In this way, the volume significantly destabilizes the main scholarly consensus on nationalism emerging from the 1980s, in which *modernist* approaches of one kind or another had comprehensively defeated *primordialist* ones.[8] The main alternative to primordialist views took shape in the 1960s and 1970s in the works primarily of sociologists and social historians, beginning with heterodox and sometimes idiosyncratic individuals like Elie Kedourie and Ernest Gellner, who considered nationalism as a set of responses to modernization, or a series of effects of the modernizing process, understood mainly as a process of capitalist industrialization.[9] This line of work stressed the inventiveness of states and intelligentsias. It charted the spread of nationalism and the dynamics of nation forming in relation to the experience of social groups, especially the peasantry and the middle classes. The latter were seen as the objects of policy, the constituencies for mobilization, and the source of the wide variations, complexities, and subtleties in the content and meanings of nationalist ideas and nationalist beliefs. These approaches explicitly acknowledged conflict and contestation in the processes of national identification.

Even in its best versions – Eric Hobsbawm's writings on nationalism between the 1960s and 1990s would be one example, or Miroslav Hroch's pioneering social histories of nation forming among the smaller peoples of Europe[10] – this stress on the contingent modernity of nations still contains a kind of immanent 'unifying' logic, privileging the developmental trajectory of sameness over the differences and conflicts that disrupt the nation's longer-term power. Now, Hobsbawm in particular has always stressed the competing projects lodged in any nationalism, and their relationship to the interests and organized agency of rival social forces. Moreover, more recently globalization and larger processes of regional integration like the EU have unsettled both the sufficiencies of the nation state and our assumptions about its future viability. So this tendency to see the unifying consequences of nationalism, within the steadily expanding hegemony of the nation form, is certainly not simplistic or unqualified by other recognitions. But nonetheless, it tends to play down some of the complex relations of superiority and subordination through which particular national identities are formed and in which they remain held. 'Modernist' approaches have remained blunt in relation to two key dimensions – those of the colonial 'outsides', and the gendered 'insides' of the nations concerned.

An enormous push for the recognition and exploration of these dimensions has come during the last two decades from cultural studies, and in this respect the influences in the English-speaking world (especially in the US) have been mainly literary. I am thinking, here, of the impact on writings about nationalism of Edward Said, Homi Bhabha, and Gaytri Spivak, although in their various ways Benedict Anderson, Stuart Hall, and Paul Gilroy have developed their critiques and proposals from a much broader range of disciplinary and intellectual bases.[11] Without going into the history of these approaches in any detail, I want to stress that the essays in this volume begin to show how the problematizing of gender, race, and cultural difference in cultural studies can be put to work for historical analysis. During the past decade in particular, there have been endless articles, books, and anthologies exploring race and gender in the constructions of nation and nationness in the nineteenth and twentieth centuries in particular literary texts, whether canonical or popular. Such analyses have migrated to powerful effect across other contexts of the arts and culture too, particularly in popular reading genres and the rich domain of visual representations (in art, photography, film, television, museums, exhibitions, fashion, style, and so on). The great virtue of this current volume is to show how these approaches can also be deployed by social and cultural historians.

The essays seldom draw directly on the formal repertoire of approaches now summarized for convenience as cultural studies. But several essays move onto the ground of the latter, and develop arguments that come practically very close, in a cognate cultural history that would be further enriched by an explicit conversation. Viktoria Schmidt-Linsenhoff's essay on racialized constructions of masculinity in the visual culture of the French Revolution draws mainly on the techniques of the history of art (old and new), reading visual representations against the surrounding contexts of social, cultural, and political change. She shows how the reading strategies developed in another discipline can enormously enrich our ability to go inside the instabilities and coherences of public discourse in a moment of dramatic and accelerated change like the French Revolution. Likewise, Jitka Maleckova and Irina Novikova both demonstrate the value of returning to similar terrains of cultural history – mythology, iconography, painting, folk song, opera, poetry, chronicles, novels, and the general festival culture of the Czech and Latvian nationalist movements. This is actually the classic terrain of the historiography of nationalist movements in Eastern and Central Europe, and both authors demonstrate the gains to be made by building on *both* the social history corpus accumulated since the 1960s, *and* the very different interdisciplinarity more recently registered by the new cultural history. The complexities of popular agency in the Czech and Latvian nationalist movements, given the gendered constructions presented in these two essays, can be compellingly opened up if we went further and began explicit and sustained dialogues with cultural studies.

In fact, it is impossible to imagine the discussions by Catherine Hall, Karen Hagemann, and Caroll Smith-Rosenberg in particular unless such dialogues had already been taking place. In making this case I have no intention of being prescriptive in a narrow or sectarian methodological or theoretical way. There is certainly no uniformity of approach to the essays in this collection. Their strength is precisely their varying combinations of social, cultural, intellectual, and political analysis, each dimension enriching the others. The mutually constitutive importance of these different 'regions' of history escapes the older hierarchies of explanation, whether those of 'base and superstructure' and other versions of a materialist social history, or other systems for assigning causal priority to this or that 'level' of social structure, practice, and experience. There is no question that cultural studies have incited these historians to think differently. Catherine Hall (Chapter 6) is writing immediately about the new approaches to 'nation and empire', but her remark that 'Feminist, post-colonial and post-structuralist approaches to history writing have opened up new ways of thinking' extends more generally to the project of this volume, the conference discussions preceding it, and the continuing international effort to illuminate the history and politics of 'gendered nations'.

Hall's own essay is a model of what can be achieved. It shows how the meanings of national identity (in this case Englishness-Britishness) have to be specified via extremely careful analyses of particular conjunctures, in which not only the dynamics of class and gender, but also the 'wider frame of empire' need to be addressed, in what Partha Chatterjee calls 'the rule of colonial difference'[12] Even as persuasive an approach as that of Linda Colley tends to dissolve once we subject it to the complexities of the forces acting on the political process from what are conventionally regarded as the margins or the periphery – whether that periphery is *social* (as in the classic critiques of Edward Thompson and his many successors), *geographical* (as in the relationship of events in Westminster to events in Ireland or Jamaica), or conceived via the categories of *race* and *gender* in the manner of Hall's approach.[13]

Finally, in aggregate these essays make a powerful case for the defining importance of particular moments or conjunctures in the shaping of a nation's gendered construction (and the same applies, as Hall points out, to 'classed' and 'raced' dimensions of the latter's presence as well). Whether in the more classic foundational moments of the great French revolution and the wider transatlantic contexts of democratic republicanism (see Chapters 5 and 13), in the cognate moment of the anti-Napoleonic 'War of Liberation' in Prussia (Hagemann), or in the case-specific 'nation-defining moments' chosen by the other contributors, a resilient and hegemonic frame – simultaneously empowering and constraining – was established for the future. The 1832 Reform Act (Chapter 6), the South African War of 1899–1902 (Chapter 10), and the Irish Land War (Chapter 11) are the most dramatic and concentrated examples of such 'moments'. But the founding phases of Czech and Latvian nationalism (Chapters 14 and 15), and the end of harem slavery in Egypt (Chapter 7) function analogously, as do more diffusely the Wilhelmine conjuncture of German nationalism (Chapter 12) and Australian nationalist discourse at the turn of the twentieth century (Chapter 8).

In each case, these were moments of crisis, where normativities gave way to fragility and instability – both in the languages of political agency and identification and in the instituted practices and relations of the established political system. The gender order was also brought into question. Such moments allow us to ask: what was the space for women's political agency in nationalist movements, and where were the cracks in the political dominance of men? This cannot be answered as a straightforward question of membership and formal participation because, as we learn from these essays, such participation could usually be predicated on various kinds of containment and subordination, as well as effective exclusion from the fronts of the struggle. That is, the question of women's political agency is also a matter of the specific political opportunities allowed discursively for women's presence, in terms of visibility, efficacy, and recognition. In these terms, how far did the primary languages of familialism and gendered solidarity leave space for egalitarian models of women's participation? We need to search for the contradictions, to allow us to see the spaces where a different kind of politics might have cohered. Dramatic moments of political rupture, whether the French Revolution or the 1832 Reform Act, or the others mentioned above, deliver some of the best answers to this question.

Notes

1. These comments are based on discussions at the conference on 'gendered nations', in Berlin, 25–28 March 1998, as well as on the

particular contributions included in this volume. They also build on arguments in Eley, G. and Suny, R.G. (1996) 'From the Moment of Social History to the Work of Cultural Representation', in Eley, G. and Suny, R.G. (eds), *Becoming National: A Reader,* New York: Oxford University Press 3–37.

2. Weber, E. (1976) *Peasants into Frenchmen: The Modernization of Rural France, 1870–1914,* Stanford: Stanford University Press, is one classic study of this process.

3. Anderson, B. (1991) *Imagined Communities: Reflections on the Origin and Spread of Nationalism,* rev.ed, London: Verso, 7, 9ff.

4. See Habermas, J. (1993) *The Structural Transformation of the Public Sphere: An Inquiry into a Category of Bourgeois Society,* Cambridge: MIT Press; and Eley, G. (1992) 'Nations, Publics, and Political Cultures: Placing Habermas in the Nineteenth Century', in Calhoun, C. (ed.), *Habermas and the Public Sphere,* Cambridge: MIT Press, 289–339.

5. Nairn, T. (1996) 'Scotland and Europe', in Eley, G. and Suny, R.G. (eds), *Becoming National,* 80.

6. Carole Pateman has been a key influence here. See (1988, 1989) *The Sexual Contract* and *The Disorder of Women,* Cambridge: Cambridge University Press. For pointed and eloquent discussion, see Benton, S. (1991) 'Gender, Sexuality, and Citizenship', in Andrews, G. (ed.) (1991), *Citizenship,* London: Lawrence & Wishart, 151–63, and Phillips, A. 'Citizenship and Feminist Politics', in Andrews, G. (ed.) (1991), *Citizenship,* London: Lawrence & Wishart, 76–88.

7. The literature here is huge, but relatively few examples deal directly with the issues of national citizenship. See for France, Offen, K. (1984), 'Depopulation, Nationalism, and Feminism in Fin de Siècle France', *American Historical Review,* 89, 648–76; and Jensen, J. (1986), 'Gender and Reproduction or Babies and the State', *Studies in Political Economy,* 20: 9–46. For Britain, see Davin, A. (1978), 'Imperialism and Motherhood', *History Workshop Journal,* 5: 9–65; and Pedersen, S. (1990) 'Gender, Welfare, and Citizenship in Britain during the Second World War', *American Historical Review,* 95: 983–1006. For Germany, see Eley, G. and Grossmann, A. (1997) 'Maternalism and Citizenship: The Gendered Politics of Welfare', *Central European History,* 30, 1: 67–75.

8. 'Primordialists' saw nations as cultural formations of long antiquity rooted in communities of culture that precede the growth of political consciousness, the emergence of nationalist movements, and the creation of nation-states. Alternatively, the 'primordial' refers to a

pre-political level of cultural identity based on kinship, social relations of family, household and community, and conditions of everyday life.

9. See Kedourie, E. (1960), *Nationalism,* London: Hutchinson; Gellner, E. (1983), *Nations and Nationalism,* Oxford: Blackwell.

10. For the former, see Hobsbawm, E.J. (1990), *Nations and Nationalism since 1780: Programme, Myth, Reality,* Cambridge: Cambridge University Press; Hobsbawm, E.J. (1972), 'Some Reflections on Nationalism', in Nossiter, T.J. Hanson, A.H., and Rokkan, S. (eds), *Imagination and Precision in the Social Sciences: Essays in Memory of Peter Nettl,* London: Faber & Faber, 385–406; Hobsbawm, E.J. and Ranger, T. (eds) (1983), *The Invention of Tradition,* Cambridge: Cambridge University Press. For the latter, see Hroch, M. (1985), *Social Preconditions of National Revival in Europe: A Comparative Analysis of the Social Composition of Patriotic Groups among the Smaller European Nations,* Cambridge: Cambridge University Press; and Hroch, M. 'From National Movement to the Fully-Formed Nation: The Nation-Building Process in Europe', in Eley, G. and Suny, R.G. (eds), *Becoming National,* 60–77.

11. Said, E. (1978), *Orientalism,* New York: Pantheon; Said, E. (1994), *Culture and Imperialism,* London: Chatto & Windus; Bhabha, H. (ed.), (1990), *Nation and Narration,* London: Routledge; Spivak, G.C. (1988), 'Can the Subaltern Speak?', in Grossberg, L. and Nelson, C. (eds) *Marxism and the Interpretation of Culture,* Urbana: University of Illinois Press, 271–317; Anderson, B. (1991), *Imagined Communities: Reflections on the Origin and Spread of Nationalism,* rev.ed, London; Stuart Hall, 'Ethnicity: Identity and Difference', in Eley, G. and Suny, R.G. (eds), *Becoming National,* 337–49; Gilroy, P. 'One Nation under a Groove: The Cultural Politics of "Race" and Racism in Britain', in Eley, G. and Suny, R.G. (eds), *Becoming National,* 350–69.

12. Chatterjee, P. (1993), *The Nation and its Fragments: Colonial and Postcolonial Histories,* Princeton: Princeton University Press, 10. The literature on the complex interrelations among race, class, and gender in the colonial setting is growing rapidly. For an indication, see the following collections: Melman, B. (ed.) (1998), *Borderlines: Genders and Identities in War and Peace 1870–1930,* New York: Routledge; Cooper, F. and Stoler, A.L. (eds), (1997), *Tensions of Empire: Colonial Cultures in a Bourgeois World,* Berkeley and Los Angeles: University of California Press; Chambers, I. and Curti, L. (eds) (1996), *The Post-Colonial Question: Common Skies, Divided Horizons,* London:

Routledge; Pierson, R.R. and Chaudhuri, N. (eds) (1998), *Nation, Empire, Colony: Historicizing Gender and Race,* Bloomington: Indiana University Press.

13. Colley, L. (1992), *Britons: Forging the Nation, 1707–1837,* New Haven and London: Yale University Press.

3

Nations: Gendered, Racialized, Crossed With Empire

Ruth Roach Pierson

As a number of the following chapters testify, it is difficult today to reflect on nationalism without reference to Benedict Anderson's work.[1] Something like canonical status has been deservedly achieved for his definition of nation as 'an imagined political community' as well as for his analysis of print capitalism as the material foundation for the emergence and dissemination of a sense of shared nationality. Yet when I assign Anderson's book to my students in Canada, although they accept as useful the notion of the constructedness of nations, a number always find his work too bloodless and abstract to provide a satisfactory answer to the question he himself poses in his introduction, the question as to why over the past two centuries so many millions of people have been willing, not so much to kill for their nation as to die for it.[2] Perhaps the fault lies in four shortcomings to which the March 1998 Berlin conference 'Gendered Nations: Nationalisms and Gender Order in the Long Nineteenth Century' and this ensuing book offer correctives.

The first shortcoming is evident in the following statement from Anderson's introduction: 'in the modern world everyone can, should, will "have" a nationality, as he or she "has" a gender'.[3] This sharp separation of nationality and gender is an indication of Anderson's failure to consider nation as gendered and consequently one's nationality, one's sense of national identity, as inextricably and ineluctably intertwined with one's gender. The phrase 'gendered nations' in the title of both the Berlin conference and this present book indicates the commitment of all involved to continue the important initiatives undertaken by scholars of women's history and gender history to foreground the 'technologies of gender' in studies of the construction of nations, nationalities, nationalisms.[4]

A second and related shortcoming is the inability of Anderson's analysis, perhaps given its tremendous breadth and attention to instrumentalities, to delve far enough into the deep structures of subjectivity and identity formation. As Karen Hagemann reminded the conference, people's connection to nation is emotional, not rational. These emotional attachments are shaped, tapped into and evoked through the mobilization of symbols and images that have been imprinted deep into our psyches. A number of this volume's papers investigate the processes, the ritualizations and mythologizations, involved in the imaging of the imagined community. Other papers explore the charging of these images with sexual and erotic investments. At work is the very constitution of subjectivities through national narratives.

The third shortcoming lies in Anderson's conviction that nationalism and racism have separate origins and goals and hence travel along separate trajectories.[5] I find more convincing George Mosse's argument that racism is a 'scavenger ideology' that has proven itself capable of 'annexing' nationalism.[6] The long century saw not only the creation and consolidation of nations but the further expansion of European imperialism and colonialism. The heyday of this expansion coincided with the extension of the Enlightenment quest for encyclopaedic knowledge of the world, its mania for classification and categorization. Order was also to be brought into the immense diversity of humankind through attempts to sort humans into racial categories. These were defined by moral and intellectual as well as physical attributes and, in keeping with discourses of civilization, progress and degeneration, arranged in hierarchical order. The age of 'scientific' racism was born. Nations came to be perceived as not only gendered but also 'raced'.[7] Only some of the contributions to this volume make 'race' an integral and central component of their analysis. It is undeniably difficult to attend simultaneously to all the social categories recognized as constituting the crucial axes of power and identity formation in the modern world. But as Catherine Hall exhorted the conference:

> if our symposium on gendered nations fails to reflect on the range of historical forces which have articulated nations, we will be guilty of reproducing the gender blindness of previous historians of nations and nationalism in another key.

A possible fourth shortcoming lies in Anderson's insufficient emphasis on the violence inherent in the national project, and this despite his allusion to people's willingness to kill and be killed for the nation. Anderson's focus is more on the centripetal forces at work in nation building; he would seem to hold an optimistic view of the eventual and easy inclusion of those initially excluded from the national community. Historians persuaded by a more Foucauldian outlook, however, emphasize the centrifugal as well as the centripetal in the national project. Within the discursive fields of nation and nationalism, national identities are generated in relation to bipolar opposites and through the embracing of the positive and the rejection of the negative: pure versus impure, normal versus abnormal, healthy versus degenerate, beautiful versus ugly. Resting on such bipolarities, national identity is unstable, shot through with contradictions, as the excluded 'other', the repressed, threatens reappearance. The result is a national subject beset with tensions and ambiguities, exclusions and inclusions.

In my following commentary on *Gendered Nations/Nationalisms and Gender Order in the Long Nineteenth Century – Europe and Beyond,* I shall focus on the themes of gender, identity formation, race, and violence as they are taken up (or not taken up) in the contributions to this book. Important also to my consideration of these themes will be the distinction between nation and state and the imperialist/colonialist context for much European nation building.

The exclusion of women from the body politic and the ambivalent and soon-to-be revoked emancipation of slaves in the French colonies provide the historical frame for the two paintings from the time of the French Revolution examined by Viktoria Schmidt-Linsenhoff. Her close and nuanced reading reveals a subtle play of difference and desire in Girodet's *Endymion by Moonlight* and his portrait of the Black legislator Belley. She finds the French nation depicted in the former as an homoerotic, passive hero and in the latter as an emancipated, but because of his too-vigorous sexuality, not fully assimilated Black. According to Schmidt-Linsenhoff, Girodet posed therewith the subversive possibility that the masculine subject position over against the nation might not have to be that of bodily service/servility/surrender, but given his failure to contest either women's exclusion from the body politic or the racist stereotype of Africans as oversexualized, I would contest Schmidt-Linsenhoff's conclusion that Girodet called the biological nature of race/ethnicity and gender into question.

What relationship exists between the figuration of woman in the iconography of the nation and women's exercise of direct, active agency in the political sphere of the nation state or of the nation state in formation – the nationalist movement? A number of feminist historians looking at the French Revolution have pointed to the frequency with which the empty space created by the king's dethronement was filled by deindividualized female figures, whether living (and appearing as allegorical figures in national *fêtes*) or carved in stone. As allegorical representations they were used to personify the nation at its most sublime and to stand for the highest principles of the Revolution – truth, reason, virtue. Woman, *das Ewig-weibliche*,[8] in conformity with racialized aesthetic ideals,[9] became the symbol of that which was immortal and unchanging in the nation. But most noteworthy, according to these feminist scholars, is the inverse relationship between the prominence of female figures in the allegoriz-ations of nation and the degree of access granted women to the political apparatus of the state. (Note the distinction between nation and state.) It is precisely women's exclusion from political life that rendered their images fit to represent the high cause of the nation for which men were willing to kill and be killed.[10]

The strategies of 'normalizing power' that Foucault identified in *Discipline and Punish: the Birth of the Prison*[11] – comparison, differ-entiation, hierarchization, homogenization, exclusion – can be seen at work in the formation and maintenance of nations. The violence inherent in these processes is unmistakable – for instance, in the near genocide of aboriginal peoples in Australia and North America, or the so-called acts of 'ethnic cleansing' committed in the name of nation building down to the present day. Pointing to 'one of his more famous theoretical moves', Patrìcia Molloy reminds us that Foucault inverted Clausewitz's famous dictum to argue that politics, in the era of the modern nation-state, is 'the continuation of war by other means'.[12] But Anderson underplays even the traditional field of violence for nations: war. Perhaps he felt the traditional accounts by historians and political scientists had already devoted sufficient attention to the importance of war for the achievement of nationhood. The connection is crucial, however, as the conference discussion indicated and a number of this volume's articles highlight: wars have indisputably served as defining moments in the emergence of nations, in the consolidation of national identities, and in the inflaming of nationalist sentiments.

Students of modern European history have traditionally seen the French Revolution as sowing the seeds of nationalism in Europe: first by transformations within France – of the body politic from dynastic state into nation state, of the state's male subjects into citizens, and of a professional army into a *levée en masse* charged with defending revol-utionary France against all the reactionary powers of Europe. And second, by Napoleon's wars of conquest, which sent ripples from the French storm throughout the continent as his invading soldiers, the ideals of the French Revolution in their knapsacks, scattered the seeds of not only *liberté*, *egalité*, and *fraternité* but also *nationalité* in the fertile soil of reaction to, and resentment against, French imperialism and the Napoleonic redrawing of the map of Europe. A century of wars of national liberation and national unification followed.[13]

Missing from the traditional accounts has been a gender analysis of the constitution of nation and nationality in that defining moment of war. Karen Hagemann traces the play of gender in the construction of the myth of German nationhood and of a German people (*Volk*) at the time of the anti-Napoleonic wars, 1806–15. France's 1806–7 crushing military defeat of Prussia, destined in the eyes of patriots to head the emerging German nation, was interpreted both as a divine judgement and as a devastating failure of manliness. This is similar to the way Abouali Farmanfarmaian has read the Gulf War of 1990–1 as the cure to the castration anxiety and fear of an emasculated American manhood following the debacle of the Vietnam War.[14] Hagemann discerns in the enlistment propaganda for the Wars of Liberation appeals to young men both to prove their manliness and to restore manliness and valour to the image of Prussia and Germanness. This militarization of Prussian/German masculinity and masculinization of the nation/state went hand in hand, Hagemann reminds us, with the bourgeoisification (embourgeoisement) of the military and society as well as with the changing European discourse of gender differences. Their anchoring in anatomy increased their polarization, and this polarity was increasingly construed as both 'natural' and hierarchical.[15]

The alliance that nationalism would form with bourgeois respectability and the latter's spread in the course of the nineteenth century up and down through the ranks of European society rested firmly on the notion of the propriety of a strict division of labour and traits between male and female in civilized nations.[16] This became a racialized gender order, as race 'theory' read a low degree of distinction between the sexes as a manifestation of low racial status and lack of civilization.[17]

In keeping with this gender order, the introduction of universal conscription in Prussia during the Wars of Liberation was limited to men, just as the National Convention during the French Revolution had prohibited women's bearing of arms in defence of the Republic.[18] The linking of eligibility for full citizenship to capacity to render military service coupled with women's exclusion from military obligation tended to gender citizenship male. But if, as Geoff Eley commented at the conference, 'nation makes its appearance in connection with the creation of the political category of citizenship', did the military service-citizenship nexus mean that women were excluded from the nation? Floya Anthias and Nira Yuval-Davis draw a helpful distinction between the concepts of 'nation' and 'state,'[19] a distinction already noted in the context of women and the French Revolution. The distinction has not only an analytical dimension but also an ontological dimension. Those imagining themselves a national community have sought to acquire the machinery of state power for their nation. Attainment of this goal has brought the coupling of nation and state, the apparent fusion of the two in 'the nation state', and finally the total elision of 'state' in formulations such as the League of Nations or, today, the United Nations. But in order to track the place of women as well as 'racialized' others in the nation, it is helpful to retrieve the 'state' from its disappearance into 'nation' and to keep in mind that the two concepts can operate to designate separate levels of being.

In Hagemann's Prussia, as military service was the key to the possibility of full state citizenship and to the promise of more civil rights, women were excluded from the political arena of the state. But they were not excluded from the national embrace. The emerging nation may have been militarized and masculinized, but it was also 'familialized', construed as a 'patriarchally and hierarchically organized folk family'. Within that family, women, embodying the canon of female virtues, found their properly subordinate and dichotomous place as defined by the new bourgeois gender order.

Since 'Jewish emancipation' occurred in the German states over the same century as Germany's national unification, one is left wondering how these two processes interconnected. To what degree were 'assimilated' German Jews integrated into or marginalized from the construction of the German *Volksfamilie*? Was the admission of Jews (gender-specifically) to civil rights and degrees of citizenship equated with or differentiated from acceptance into the body of the nation?[20] As members of the nation, men and women both have been called to its service in gender-specific ways. How has the service of citizen subjects not regarded as members of the national community been categorized?

Insofar as women have been accepted into military service in wars of national defence or liberation, historians and political scientists have uncovered a relatively common pattern at work. In moments of crisis, women's active involvement has been tolerated, sometimes even solicited and celebrated. Afterwards, however, regardless of whether the struggle has ended in victory or defeat, women's former prowess has often been resented and suppressed or reinterpreted and repressed.[21] Helen Bradford's account of the role of Boer women in the Anglo-Boer War of 1899–1902 bears traces of this pattern. To account for women's exclusion from the military, some have theorized a fear of women's potentially terrifying bellicosity and anxieties 'over women's sexual and reproductive powers'.[22] To be eligible for inclusion in the national narrative, the exceptional few (twenty-three) women who fought in the Prussian/ German Wars of Liberation, Hagemann informs us, had to have been virgins and preferably to have died in battle. Is it that during periods of crisis the fears of women's dangerous potential recede in the face of the greater threat, only to reassert themselves once the crisis is past?

Margaret Ward has given us the example of Anna Parnell and the Ladies' Land League in Ireland during the so-called 'Irish Land War' of 1879–82. As political/nationalist visionaries the women proved themselves more radical and intransigent than the men. But rather than their display of bravery and skill winning them praise and immortalization, their efforts were either erased from the chronicles of Irish nationalism or vilified and denounced. And their one-time male comrades succeeded in excluding women from all Irish nationalist organization for an entire generation. A succeeding generation of women played a significant role in the Irish war of independence of 1919–22, but its aftermath saw the reassertion of gender conservatism and women's relegation to the private sphere. The primacy of women's domestic responsibilities was to define the relationship between women and the Irish nation for much of the rest of the twentieth century.[23] As Louise Ryan has argued, women's exclusion from the public world of nation-building was based at least in part on 'demonised images of the deviant non-domestic woman,'[24] – violators of the bourgeois gender order.

In his classic 'What is a Nation?' of 1882, Ernest Renan passed in review five possible foundations of nationhood – dynastic principle, race, language, religion, and geography. His conclusion, an early articulation of the modernist, constructionist position, dismissed the notion of 'pure race' as a chimera and rejected the rest of the purportedly 'natural' bases for nation as historically unfounded. He opted instead for the 'spiritual principle' of civic consent.[25] But those 'naturally given' criteria of nation dismissed by Renan were fervently invoked by nationalists during his lifetime and after. For that reason they continue to provide the categories in contemporary typologies of nation and nationalism.[26] Evidence suggests that when language, culture and ethnic descent are seen as the binding elements of nation, the figure of the mother as bearer and educator of the young and preserver of culture acquires national stature.[27] In the ethnolinguistic nationalism of Latvia, an 'agroliterate' society, the image of women as national mothers and the role of motherhood (and sisterhood), according to Irina Novikova, came to occupy places of importance. Mothers were heralded as teachers of the national language to the next generation (a relationship enshrined in English with 'mother tongue' and in German with *Muttersprache*)[28] and as guardians of the nation's cultural heritage. With reference to the latter, mothers were recognized for their role as collectors of *dainas*, the folk songs regarded as the receptacles of the national past. Beginning in 1873, folk song festivals assumed a central role in the process of nationalization. In those rituals of inclusion and exclusion, women performed alongside men, and sisters alongside brothers as the sons and daughters of the national family in formation.

It is one of Anderson's insightful claims that, to compensate for the relatively short history of the nation, nationalists turn myth into history to give the nation a long and distinguished past.[29] Nations are constructions, fictions; but the politicians and intelligentsia who articulate nations into being – the missionaries of nationalism – start with already existing materials. The extent, however, to which these 'primordial' materials (such as language, culture, and notions of common lineage) are manipulated can never be underestimated. For example, according to Ida Blom, the properly gendered 'national costume' fashioned for male and female dolls in Norway and elsewhere in the nineteenth century had no historically pre-existent referent. Instead it had to be patched together out of a mixture of local styles of dress.

In the invention of a national past for the Czech nation, Jitka Malecková informs us, female figures from ancient myths were exalted as national heroines: in this case not in the role of national mother, but as icons of women's elevated status in Czech society. The mythical Libuše, princess, prophetess and founder of Prague, and Vlasta, the woman warrior who led a women's revolt, were written, to varying degrees, into the history of the Czech nation as real historical figures.[30] There they served as proof to Czech nationalists of the antiquity of the Czech nation, to Czech feminists of the equality of Czech women in the pagan past, and to both as a model for contemporary womanhood. Above all, as emblems of the high position of Czech women, they served as proof of Czech cultural and societal superiority over their German oppressors whose national principle was masculine. Perhaps because both the discourse of Czech nationalism and that of women's emancipation depicted Libuše and Vlasta as such powerful female figures, these mythical/historical images helped create the myth of a tradition of 'gender harmony' in Czech history. This myth, according to Malecková, 'forms a part of the [contemporary] Czechs' self-perception', a clear example of the inscription of nationalist symbolization on subjectivity.

Whether one reads nationalism as filling the vacuum left by the march of secularization, or as capable of joining forces with religion,[31] nationalism can elevate the nation to the level of divine purpose. Such elevation has encouraged the scripting of narrations of sacrifice, especially in time of war. These, too, have been highly gendered. In Europe the vision of the young male soldier's sacrificial and heroic death borrowed from models of Christian martyrdom and ancient pagan heroism. Female figures were used to represent what these young men died for, as in the winged, majestically angelic victory holding out the crown of glory.[32] But women were offered and created their own scripts of sacrifice, in keeping with the roles assigned women within the bourgeois gender order. As agents of ostentatious consumption they offered up their jewellery; as creatures of beauty they offered up its crowing glory, their hair; as wives and mothers they offered up their husbands and sons.[33] Hagemann refers briefly to Prussian/German women's introduction to patriotic sacrifice at the start of the long nineteenth century. At its end Käthe Kollwitz provides an example of how deeply these gendered narratives of sacrifice had been incorporated into women's subjectivities. With the outbreak of the First World War, Kollwitz, as Regina Schulte has shown, 'entered an alliance of sacrifice with her son.'[34] She encouraged her son's decision to volunteer, against her husband's, the father's, resistance, fully anticipating her son's sacrificial death. When it came, but a few months later, she embraced it as 'fiery' and purifying. Infused with new energy and purpose, she dedicated herself henceforth to the role of sacrificing mother and her art to the commemoration and immortalization of the son who had met a warrior hero's death.

German Jews also responded with fervour to the call to sacrifice. But the racialized and racist discourses of nation enabled non-Jewish Germans of the officer corps and imperial war regime to cast doubt on the sacrificial will of German Jews. The anti-Semitic suspicion of German Jews as malingerers led the Prussian War Ministry in the fall of 1916 to order a census of the Jews (*Judenzählung*) to determine whether their participation in the German war effort, particularly as soldiers at the front, was commensurate with their proportion of the total German population. This singling out was experienced by many German Jews as a wounding affront to their sense of membership in the German nation, and by German Jewish veterans as a denial of their German masculinity. The *Reichsbund jüdischer Frontsoldaten*, the Veterans Association of German Jews, laboured throughout the Weimar Republic to contest and disprove this exile from the national body.[35]

In the course of the nineteenth century, in other words, nationalist narratives played themselves out in a world increasingly organized according to the discourses of 'race' animating Europe and her settler colonies. Various theories of race would, by the end of the century, join with evolutionary theory and social Darwinism to give shape to a discourse of civilization that ranked nations and hierarchized and excluded social groups within nations. In Helen Bradford's study of the Anglo-Boer war, gender constructions are inseparably and complicatedly intertwined with imperialist/colonialist race and ethnic relations. It was a war declared by two Boer 'male-only, white-only' republics, the Transvaal and the Orange Free State, against the British Empire and its two South African colonies, the Cape and Natal. Although the war was to be waged only by men mobilized as 'broeder Afrikaners', Bradford found that during it Afrikaner women proved to be 'the fiercest advocates of war to the bitter end.' Ann Stoler has theorized the regulation of white women's sexuality as central to the policing of racial borders and the preservation of white supremacy in Southeast Asian colonialism in the late nineteenth and early twentieth centuries.[36] During the Boer war it was Afrikaner women who raised the fear of race degeneration through hybridity and the crossing of racial borders. To shame their men into greater militancy, the women sounded the alarm that conquest would bring 'equality between black and white, and miscegenation'. For Afrikaner women, their nationalist hostility to British imperialism was part and parcel of their racist, colonialist sense of superiority over black Africans. Once defeated, Afrikaner men were willing to sink their differences with the former British foe in order to make 'white' common cause against black Africans, to engage, in the words of Bradford, 'in the fraternal politics of race, creating an Anglo-Afrikaner alliance to subordinate black men'. For Afrikaner men, the politics of race now took precedence over the politics of nationalism. In exchange they reaped the reward of restored patriarchal authority, over both their own women, now portrayed as helpless white innocents threatened by the black rapist, and over black African men. Afrikaner women retreated into the home to be idealized as mothers of the *volk*. There they became the developers and cultivators of an Afrikaner nationalism composed of the 'mother tongue' (Afrikaans), religion (Dutch Reformed Church), and race hatred.

Marilyn Lake positions non-Aboriginal white women in Australia more ambiguously over against the founding racism of their colonial settler society. Once again the nation/state distinction has relevance. Although non-Aboriginal white women were admitted to citizenship in the new Commonwealth of Australia,[37] 'national independence from Britain was conceptualized as a coming to 'manhood' for non-Aboriginal white men, and the national community was imagined as the fraternal mateship of rough, tough bushmen, a male- and white-exclusive fraternity. There was a difference, then, between place in political representation within the state apparatus (which women shared with men so long as they were white Europeans) and place in the cultural representation of the nation (monopolized by white European males). Feminists resented women's exclusion from the cultural representation of the nation. To correct it, they sought 'to retrieve' the 'pioneer women "lost to fame" and inscribe them in the historical record as nation-builders.' To do so, however, was to ignore women's complicity in the racist foundation of Australia, the dispossession of the Aborigines.[38] Or one could 'innocent'[39] oneself by invoking the 'comforting conceit' of imperialist/colonialist discourse about conquered indigenous peoples, the notion of 'a dying race' inevitably slated to disappear 'by the impersonal force of evolution'.[40] Lake finds a later generation of Australian feminists (in the 1920s and 1930s) divided between those still committed to securing a place for white women within the triumphalist account of Australia's nation building and those 'determined to call' the nation state 'to account for its treatment of Aboriginal people,' particularly Aboriginal women. But in their focus on 'the victimization of Aboriginal women' and in their campaigns to relieve the worst of the abuses, these maternalist feminist reformers were doing more than exercising their political subjecthood. Were they not also securing the position of benefactress ascribed to them by the bourgeois gender order and accomplished in their relationship to the victimized 'other'? If, as Lake writes, 'nation building was haunted by the original sin of dispossession', so apparently are attempts at reform of the nation-state in such settler colonial societies as Australia and, for that matter, Canada.

Catherine Hall makes clear that, in the typology of nationalisms, imperialist nationalism belongs high on the list. In the case of those European nation-states with imperial possessions, empire imbricates nation. Antoinette Burton has argued that British colonialism/imperialism 'provided the opportunity for Britons of all classes to conceive of the nation and to experience themselves as members of a "national culture"'.[41] For Hall, empire was a determining factor 'in defining the boundaries of the [British] nation.' Her study heeds both aims of the 'post-colonial studies' project: (a) to attend to the 'subaltern', to the perspective of those on the 'margins', and (b) to treat the imperial metropole as not separate from and untouched by empire and colony. According to the arguments of Edward Said,[42] Inderpal Grewal,[43] and others, the metropolis needs to be seen as riddled with the effects of empire. While Said attends largely to the cultural effects, these are inseparable from the economic fruits and power relations resulting from imperialist ventures, and these latter are what principally concern Hall. If we applaud with Ann Stoler the growth of a post-colonial scholarship which attempts to bring together 'metropole and colony in a single analytic field',[44] we also concede with her the difficulty of this project for the Eurocentrically trained historian. Hall's paper comes as close to accomplishing this goal as any I've read. She takes up Partha Chatterjee's concept of 'the rule of colonial difference', expands it into the 'rule of difference' and uses it to conceptualize the shifting hierarchies of gender, class, race, ethnicity, religion, colonizer/ colonized, and slave/free at a pivotal moment of British nation formation: the period leading up to and immediately following the passage of the English Parliamentary Reform Act of 1832. It is a time of great political turmoil and destabilization of the hierarchies on which the 'rule of difference' is predicated, at home in the 'mother country' as well as in the colonies. The sites Hall focuses on are far flung: anti-colonialist Irish Catholic nationalism in Ireland, a major slave rebellion in Jamaica, agitation among both middle and working classes for parliamentary reform in England. Hall does not treat each as a separate narrative unit. Rather showing how they crosscut and intersect with one another, she simulates 'homogeneous time', the peculiar kind of simultaneity that Anderson saw as characteristic of national consciousness.[45] The restabilization in 1832 rested on a reworking of all the hierarchies of difference, not into a fixed pattern but into the prelude to further shifts to come later in the century. Not the least of these would be the contestation of the male gendering of citizenship.

The hierarchical binaries around which colonial and imperial ruling is organized, according to post-colonial theorists, are as unstable as the inclusions and exclusions through which nations are constructed. According to Beth Baron's account, the Egyptian nation in formation offers a field day for such complexification. The decline of the Ottoman Empire early in the century was the precondition of an emerging Egyptian nation, but colonization by the British later in the century was its limitation. Caught between two empires, Egypt tried to assert its own imperialism over the Sudan. Many of the strategies of 'normalizing power' are detectable in the creation of a new Egyptian national identity: out of the suppression of harem slavery yet fight to retain the domestic slavery of Sudanese; the exclusion of Circassian and Syrian ethnicities but inclusion of the Copt religious minority; the Egyptianizing through homogenization of the old Ottoman-Egyptian elite; the invidious comparison of the light-skinned, modest 'Egyptian' woman with, and differentiation from, her dark-skinned, highly sexualized Sudanese sister. Two competing nationalist movements emerge, one secular, led by landholding Copts, and preferred by the British, the other pan-Islamic and fiercely anti-British. Running through all this like a red thread: debates over marriage, divorce, and women's work, education, veiling, seclusion. The 'Woman Question' was, according to Baron, 'the fault line' of Egyptian national identity formation. And women as well as men were active in these debates.

According to Prasenjit Duara, 'nationalism is a relational identity'.[46] For Anderson, the relationship on which nations have been founded was a horizontal one between and among scattered strangers bound together by a sense of simultaneity, homogeneity, community. To that notion Duara opposes one of 'fluid relationships' between 'a constantly changing Self and Other'.[47] In the foregoing papers we have observed men standing in different relationship to nation from women of the same social group, social groups' differences defined in part through differing relationships to nation, and all of these relationships in flux. Nation itself is defined in relation to other nations, a shifting relationship, as we have seen, often expressed in gendered or racialized terms.

We feminist women's historians in the West have harboured shifting, ambivalent feelings toward women's relationship to the national project. In the heady early years of the revival of feminism, it often seemed to white, middle-class, university-educated feminists in north America and Europe that theories of patriarchy and male domination provided an explanation for militarism, nationalism, and the wars they bred.[48] The tendency was to unearth the histories of women as victims of nationalist/sexist violence or as contributors to movements of world peace.[49] With alacrity white feminists, especially if inclined toward pacifism, embraced Virginia Woolf's famous dictum: 'as a woman, I have no country. As a woman I want no country. As a woman my country is the whole world'.[50] This 'dream of a global sisterhood of women', as Caren Kaplan has called it,[51] posited women as a homogenous universal and ignored the radically different positions women occupy within nations and within the unequal distribution of power internationally. Who but a woman with a secure place within a nation can speak high-mindedly about not wanting a country. It is precisely that lack that sentences millions of women with their children to languish, stateless, in refugee camps.[52]

Justified critiques by Third World women and women of colour together with the advent of post-modern theories of multiple and shifting identities have ruptured the universalist and totalizing dream and exposed the violences inherent in its repressions.[53] More recent scholarship, like that contained in this volume, has made us aware of the complexity of women's relation to nation and nationalism and to the colonialist and imperialist ventures of nations.[54] Across the world, and over time, 'woman' has functioned as signifier for nation in a great variety of ways.[55] The struggle for women's emancipation has often been waged in alliance with, as well as in opposition to, nationalist, imperialist movements.[56] And while implicated in ways differentiated by gender, women have by no means been universally innocent of the violence, the racism, the imperialism and colonialism carried out in the name of nation.

Notes

1. Anderson, B. (1983, rev. ed 1991), *Imagined Communities: Reflections on the Origin and Spread of Nationalism,* London: Verso.
2. Anderson, B. (1983, rev. ed 1991), *Imagined Communities: Reflections on the Origin and Spread of Nationalism,* London: Verso, 7, 141–4.
3. Anderson, B. (1983, rev. ed 1991), *Imagined Communities: Reflections on the Origin and Spread of Nationalism,* London: Verso, 5.
4. See, for example, McClintock, A. (1995), 'No Longer In A Future Heaven: Nationalism, Gender and Race,' in *Imperial Leather: Race, Gender and Sexuality in the Colonial Context,* New York and London: Routledge, 352–68.
5. Anderson, B. (1983, rev. ed 1991), *Imagined Communities: Reflections on the Origin and Spread of Nationalism,* London: Verso, 141–53.
6. Mosse, G.L. (1978), *Toward the Final Solution: A History of European Racism,* New York: Harper Colophon Books, Harper & Row, 234.
7. Pierson, R.R. (1998), 'Introduction,' in Pierson, R.R. and Chauduri, N. (eds) with the assistance of Beth McAuley *Nation, Empire, Colony: Historicizing Gender and Race,* Bloomington and Indianapolis: Indiana University Press, 1–20.
8. 'The eternal feminine.'
9. See Mosse, G.L. (1978), *Toward the Final Solution: A History of European Racism,* New York: Harper Colophon Books, Harper & Row, 21–32.
10. Hoffmann-Curtius, K. (1991), 'Opfermodelle am Altar des Vaterlandes seit der Französischen Revolution,' in Gudrun Kohn-Waechter (ed.), *Schrift der Flammen: Opfermythen und Weiblichkeitsentwürfe im 20. Jahrhundert,* Berlin: Orlanda Frauenverlag, 61–3. See also Landes, J.B. (1988), *Women in the Public Sphere in the Age of the*

French Revolution, Ithica/London: Cornell University Press; Outram, D. *The Body and the French Revolution: Sex, Class and Political Culture,* New Haven/London; Wenk, S. (1996), *Versteinerte Weiblichkeit: Allegorien in der Skulptur der Moderne,* Köln/Weimar/Wien: Böhlau Verlag, 103–27.

11. Foucault, M. (1979), trans. by Alan Sheridan, *Discipline and Punish: The Birth of the Prison,* Toronto: Random House of Canada, originally published in France as Foucault, M. (1975), *Surveiller et Punir: Naissance de la prison,* Paris: Éditions Gallimard.

12. Patricia Molloy, (1999), 'From the Strategic Self to the Ethical Relation: Pedagogies of War and Peace,' University of Toronto Ph.D. thesis.

13. See, for example, Minogue, K.R. (1967), *Nationalism,* London: Methuen..

14. Farmanfarmaian, A. (1992), 'Did You Measure Up? The Role of Race and Sexuality in the Gulf War,' in C. Peters, ed., *Collateral Damage: The New World Order at Home and Abroad,* Boston: South End Press, 111–38.

15. See Laqueur, T. (1990), *Making Sex: Body and Gender from the Greeks to Freud,* Cambridge, MA: Harvard University Press. A gender ideology based in a notion of biological bipolarity became fully elaborated during the Victorian era. See, for example, Poovey, M. (1988), *Uneven Developments: The Ideological Work of Gender in Mid-Victorian England,* Chicago: The University of Chicago Press.

16. Mosse, G.L. (1985), *Nationalism and Sexuality: Respectability and Abnormal Sexuality in Modern Europe,* New York: Howard Fertig.

17. Schiebinger, L. (1993), *Nature's Body: Gender in the Making of Modern Science,* Boston: Beacon Press.

18. Abray, J. (1975), 'Feminism in the French Revolution,' *The American Historical Review* 80 (1): 43–62.

19. Anthias, F. and Yuval-Davis, N. (1989), 'Introduction,' *Woman – Nation – State,* London: Macmillan, 6–7.

20. For a discussion of the relation of anti-Jewish enmity to the emerging sense of German nationality in the Wars of Liberation, see Chapter Four of Hagemann, K. (forthcoming) *Männlicher Mut und Teutsche Ehre. Entwürfe von Nation, Krieg und Männlichkeit in Preußen zur Zeit der antinapoleonischen Kriege, 1806–1815 [Manly Valor and German Honor: Nation, War and Gender in Prussia during the Antinapoleonic Wars, 1806–1815].*

21. See, for example, Goldman, N.L. (ed.) (1982), *Female Soldiers– Combatants or Noncombatants? Historical and Contemporary*

Perspectives, Westport, Connecticut: Greenwood Press; Pierson, R.R. (1986), *'They're Still Women After All': The Second World War and Canadian Womanhood,* Toronto: McClelland & Stewart; Higonnet, M.R., Jensen, J., Michel, S., and Weitz, M.C. (eds) (1987), *Behind the Lines: Gender and the Two World Wars* (New Haven and London: Yale University Press; Ruth Roach Pierson, 'Beautiful Soul or Just Warrior: Gender and War,' *Gender & History* 1 (1) (Spring 1989), 77–86.

22. Bourke, J. (1998), 'Military Training and the Construction of Masculinity Prior to the First World War,' paper delivered at the March 1998 Berlin conference 'Gendered Nations: Nationalisms and Gender Order in the Long Nineteenth Century,' 18.

23. That the women of the Irish Ladies' Land League had violated the gender order with their radical nationalism is also evident in the reaction of the British authorities: when thirteen women of the Ladies' Land League were arrested, they were not incarcerated as political prisoners like the men but rather 'imprisoned under statutes designed to keep prostitutes off the streets.'

24. Ryan, L. (1998), 'Negotiating Modernity and Tradition: newspaper debates on the modern girl' in the Irish Free State,' *Journal of Gender Studies* 7,(2): 181–97.

25. Renan, E. (1990), 'What is a nation?' trans. by Martin Thom, in Bhabha, H.K. (ed.), *Nation and Narration,* London and New York: Routledge, 8–22.

26. See, for example, Dominique Schnapper, 'Beyond Opposition: Civic Nation versus Ethnic Nation,' in Couture, J., Nielsen, K., and Seymour, M. (eds) (1996), *Rethinking Nationalism, Canadian Journal of Philosophy* Supplementary, vol. 22, Calgary, Alberta: University of Calgary Press, 219–34. Although the project of Anthias and Yuval-Davis is not to classify different types of nationalisms, the outlines of a typology emerge nonetheless: ethnic nationalism, civic nationalism, cultural nationalism, religious nationalism, imperialist nationalism. One of their points, however, is that any and all of these principles of inclusion in/exclusion from nation may be racialized to serve racist ends. Anthias, F. and Yuval-Davis, N. (1992), *Racialized Boundaries: Race, Nation, Gender, Colour and Class and the Anti-Racist Struggle,* New York and London: Routledge.

27. Mosse has argued that as the triumph of the male-headed nuclear family 'coincided with the rise of nationalism and respectability' and the middle-class stereotype and national stereotype merged, woman acquired a national symbolizing role as the guardian of the nation's

morality, of its traditional values, of what was transcendental and immutable in the nation. Mosse, G.L. (1985), *Nationalism and Sexuality: Respectability and Abnormal Sexuality in Modern Europe,* New York: Howard Fertig, 16–18.

28. To Marlene Norbese Philip, speaking for peoples in former English colonies who were robbed of their 'mother tongues' by slavery and colonization, English 'is both mother *and* father tongue,' the latter because it 'comes tainted with a certain history of colonialism and imperialism.' Philip, M.N. (1997), 'Father Tongue,' in *A Genealogy of Resistance and Other Essays,* Toronto: The Mercury Press, 129.

29. Anderson, B, (1983, rev. ed 1991), *Imagined Communities: Reflections on the Origin and Spread of Nationalism,* London: Verso, 187–206.

30. For examples of female historical figures mythologized and written into Canadian History as national symbols, see Morgan, C. (1996), '"Of Slender Frame and Delicate Appearance": The Placing of Laura Secord in the Narratives of Canadian Loyalist History,' and Coates, C.M. (1996), 'Commemorating the Woman Warrior of New France: Madeleine de Verchères, 1696–1930,' in Parr, J. and Rosenfeld, M. (eds) (1996), *Gender and History in Canada,* Toronto: Copp Clark Ltd, 103–36.

31. Anthias and Yuval-Davis contest the modernist view that nationalism replaces religion and point to the compatibility between nationalism and religion in a world in which religion is on the increase. Anthias, F. and Yuval-Davis, N. *Racialized Boundaries: Race, Nation, Gender, Colour and Class and the Anti-Racist Struggle,* New York and London: Routledge, 34–6.

32. For example, the Viktoria on top of the Siegesäule in Berlin. See Wenk, S. (1996), *Versteinerte Weiblichkeit: Allegorien in der Skulptur der Moderne,* Köln/Weimar/Wien: Böhlau Verlag, 87–102.

33. Hoffmann-Curtius, K. (1991), 'Opfermodelle am Altar des Vaterlandes seit der Französischen Revolution,' in Kohn-Waechter, G. (Hg.), *Schrift der Flammen: Opfermythen und Weiblichkeitsentwürfe im 20. Jahrhundert,* Berlin: Orlanda Frauenverlag,, 77–9.

34. Schulte, R. (1996), 'Käthe Kollwitz's Sacrifice,' trans. by Pamela Selwyn, *History Workshop Journal,* 41: 194. This essay originally appeared as 'Käthe Kollwitz' Opfer,' in Jansen, C., Niethammer L., und Weisbrod, B. (Hg.) (1995), *Von der Aufgabe der Freiheit: Politische Verantwortung und bürgerliche Gesellschaft im 19. und 20. Jahrhundert. Festschrift für Hans Mommsen zum 5. November 1995,* Berlin: Weisbrod.

35. Pierson, R. (1974), 'Embattled Veterans: The *Reichbund jüdischer Frontsoldaten,*' *Leo Baeck Institute Year Book XIX,* London: Secker & Warburg, 142.
36. Stoler, A.L. (1991), 'Carnal Knowledge and Imperial Power,' in di Leonardo, M. (ed.) *Gender at the Crossroads: Feminist Anthropology in the Post-Modern Era,* Berkeley: University of California Press, 51–101; Ann Laura Stoler, 'Sexual Affronts and Racial Frontiers: European Identities and the Cultural Politics of Exclusion in Colonial Southeast Asia,' in Cooper, F. and Stoler, A.L. (eds) (1997) *Tensions of Empire: Colonial Cultures in a Bourgeois World,* Berkeley: University of California Press, 198–237.
37. The Commonwealth of Australia was created in 1901 and one year later, in 1902, non-Aboriginal white women were given the franchise and the right to be elected into the national parliament.
38. For analysis of a Canadian feminist's efforts to write white British women into the building of Canada as a white nation while fully accepting the naturalness of slave holding and the exclusion of Natives as 'savages,' see Boutilier, B. (1997), 'Women's Rights and Duties: Sarah Anne Curzon and the Politics of Canadian History,' in Boutilier, B. and Prentice, A. (eds) *Creating Historical Memory: English-Canadian Women and the Work of History,* Vancouver: UBC Press, 51–74.
39. Lake's terminology resonates with the analysis given by the anti-racist, feminist legal scholar Sherene Razack to the moves those implicated in structures of domination make in order to 'secure innocence,' i.e., the illusion (fiction) of non-involvement as the dominant party in relations of domination and subordination. See Razack, S.H (1998) *Looking White People in the Eye: Gender, Race, and Culture in Courtrooms and Classrooms,* Toronto: University of Toronto Press. For narratives of 'innocent' white women victimized by 'savage' aboriginal men, see Carter, S. (1997), *Capturing Women: The Manipulation of Cultural Imagery in Canada's Prairie West,* Montreal and Kingston: McGill Queen's University Press.
40. See, for example, Rosaldo, R. (1989), 'Imperialist Nostalgia,' *Representations* 26, 107–22.
41. Burton, A. (1997), 'Who Needs the Nation? Interrogating 'British' History,' *Journal of Historical Sociology* 10, (3): 228.
42. Said, E.W. (1993) *Culture and Imperialism,* New York: Alfred A. Knopf.
43. Grewal argues: '[t]o focus merely on what happens to the colony is...to leave out a major factor in the discourse of colonization.'

Grewal, I. (1996), *Home and Harem: Nation, Gender, Empire and the Cultures of Travel,* Durham and London: Duke University Press, 9.

44. 'dismantling the careful bracketing that contained metropolitan and colonial history . . . has not only become unwieldy as an individual effort, but difficult for either fledgling graduate student or seasoned scholar to sustain.' Stoler, A.L. (1995), *Race and the Education of Desire: Foucault's History of Sexuality and the Colonial Order of Things,* Durham and London: Duke University Press, xii.

45. Anderson, B. (1983, rev. ed. 1991), *Imagined Communities: Reflections on the Origin and Spread of Nationalism,* London: Verso, 24.

46. Duara, P. (1995), *Rescuing History from the Nation: Questioning Narratives of Modern China,* Chicago: University of Chicago Press, 15, cited in Wong, Y.R. (1999), 'In-between Nationalism and Colonialism: The Making of the Hong Kong-Chinese Identity in the Development of China,' Ph.D. thesis, University of Toronto.

47. Duara, P. (1993), 'Deconstructing the Chinese Nation,' *The Australian Journal of Chinese Affairs,* 30, (3): 2, cited in cited in Wong, Y.R. (1999), 'In-between Nationalism and Colonialism: The Making of the Hong Kong-Chinese Identity in the Development of China,' Ph.D. thesis, University of Toronto.

48. For example, see Reardon, B.A. (1985), *Sexism and the War System,* New York and London: Teachers College, Columbia University.

49. See, for example, Swerdlow, A. (1982), 'Ladies' Day at the Capitol: Women Strike for Peace Versus HUAC,' *Feminist Studies* 8, (3): 493–520; Jill Liddington, 'The Women's Peace Crusade: The History of a Forgotten Campaign,' in Thompson, D. (ed.) *Over Our Dead Bodies: Women Against the Bomb,* London: Virago, 180–98; Florence M.S., Marshall, C., Ogden, C.K. (1987), in Kamester, M. and Vellacot, J. (eds) *Militarism Versus Feminism: Writings on Women and War*, London: Virago; Liddington, J. (1989), *The Long Road to Greenham: Feminism and Anti-Militarism in Britain since 1820,* London: Virago; Oldfield, S. (1989), *Women Against the Iron First: Alternatives to Militarism 1900–1989,* Oxford: Basil Blackwell.

    I myself, although rejecting the easy association of women with peace, still hoped to find an inherent connection between feminism and pacifism. See Pierson, R.R. (1987), 'Introduction,' in Pierson, R.R. (ed.) *Women and Peace: Theoretical, Historical and Practical Perspectives,* London: Croom Helm.

50. Woolf, V. (1938) *Three Guineas* (London: Hogarth Press), 197. In 1984 the Cambridge Women's Peace Collective used a part of this

quotation for the title of their collection of writings by women on issues of peace and war. Cambridge Women's Peace Collective (1984), *My Country is the Whole World: An Anthology of Women's Work on Peace and War,* London: Pandora Press.

51. Kaplan, C. (1994), 'The Politics of Location as Transnational Feminist Critical Practice,' in Grewal, I. and Kaplan, C. (eds), *Scattered Hegemonies,* Minneapolis/London: University of Minnesota Press, 137.

52. According to figures of the United Nations High Commission for Refugees (UNHCR), a disproportionate 80 per cent of the world's uprooted people are women and children. See Brazeau, A. (Senior Co-ordinator for Refugee Women at UNHCR) (1991), 'Introduction' in Martin, S.F. *Refugee Women* London: Zed Books, ix.

53. Mohanty, C.T. (1991), '"Under Western Eyes": Feminist Scholarship and Colonial Discourses", in Mohanty, C.T., Russo, A., Torres, L. (eds) *Third World Women and the Politics of Feminism,* Bloomington and Indianapolis: Indiana University Press, 51–80.

54. See, for example, Grimshaw, P., Lake, M., McGrath, A., and Quartly, M. (1994), *Creating a Nation,* Ringwood, Victoria, Australia: McPhee Gribble; Gravenhorst, L., Tatschmurat, C. (ed.) (1900), *Töchter Fragen NS-Frauen Geschichte,* Freiburg: Kore Verlag; Heinsohn, K., Vogel, B., Weckel, U. (ed.) (1997,) *Zwischen Karriere und Verfolgung: Handlungsräume von Frauen im nationalsozialistischen Deutschland,* Frankfurt am Main: Campus Verlag; Wildenthal, L. (1998), '"When Men Are Weak": The Imperial Feminism of Frieda von Bülow,' *Gender and History* 10, 53–77.

55. See, for instance, Chatterjee, P. (1989), 'The Nationalist Resolution of the Women's Question,' in Sangari, K. and Vaid, S. (eds) *Recasting Women: Essays in Colonial History,* New Delhi: Kali for Women, 233–53; Natarajan, N. (1994), 'Woman, Nation, and Narration in *Midnight's Children,*' in Grewal, I. and Kaplan, C. (eds) *Scattered Hegemonies,* Minneapolis/London: University of Minnesota Press, 76–89.

56. See, for example, Burton, A. (1994), *Burdens of History: British Feminists, Indian Women, and Imperial Culture, 1865–1915,* Chapel Hill and London: University of North Carolina Press; Liu, L. (1994), 'The Female Body and Nationalist Discourse: *The Field of Life and Death* Revisited,' in Grewal, I. and Kaplan, C. (eds) (1994), *Scattered Hegemonies,* Minneapolis/London: University of Minnesota Press, 41–4; Cano, G. (1997), 'The *Porfirato* and the Mexican Revolution: Constructions of Feminism and Nationalism,' in *Nation, Empire,*

Colony, 106–20; Gray, B. and Ryan, L. (1997), 'The Politics of Irish Identity and the Interconnections between Feminism, Nationhood, and Colonialism,' in *Nation, Empire, Colony*, 121–38; West L., (ed.), *Feminist Nationalism,* New York & London: Routledge.

–4–

Gendered Representations of the Nation's Past and Future

Silke Wenk

Translated by Tom Lampert

The present volume provides manifold evidence that the 'invention' of the nation was supported by the modern construction of the two sexes. Not only were national movements frequently structured from their very beginnings according to modern conceptions of gender polarity – men fight battles, women concern themselves with reproduction – but the descriptions and articulations of nations clearly cannot do without images or metaphors of gender as well. This is true not only of Western Europe and North America, but also of eastern European countries and anti-colonial movements, for example in Egypt or Australia, to mention only two examples presented in this book.

Given the extensive dissemination of images and metaphors of the feminine used to describe one's own 'nation' – both its past and its future – the silence which historians and political scientists have maintained in regard to the 'gendering' of the nation in modernity can itself be read as symptomatic. This silence indicates, on the one hand, how something that was historically produced becomes, as it were, nature: the modern order of the two sexes, which, according to recent historical investigations, was only established as the decisive order in the course of the eighteenth century, was declared to be 'natural,' or even 'necessary for nature'.[1] At the same time, it also makes clear the way in which constructions of gender have left their mark on ideas about the bonds of a community as a nation.

That which holds the nation, the 'imagined community', together can be understood as a system of cultural representations and practices that produce and reproduce the meanings of the nation.[2] The nation is constituted as a 'natural' unity through linguistic and visual represent-ations, through verbal and non-verbal practices and rituals, which connect the perceptions, emotions and memories of individuals with those of the collective, and thus signify belonging. This, however, is by no means simply a matter of explicit designations of the nation, for example, the national flag, the national anthem or national narratives. Explicit designations are ultimately connected to words and images that are understood within the community and that build upon this understanding. 'National memory,' writes Alon Cofino, can offer insights not only into 'what people remember of the past, but also how they internalize an impersonal world by putting it in familiar and intelligible categories.'[3] According to Maurice Halbwuchs, 'collective memory' forms the frame in which particular memories are localized and brought into an order that makes 'sense.'[4] Collective memory functions, at the same time, as a reservoir for images that explain and support each other, which are related to one another as well as to the thoughts and actions of the members of that respective collective – silently, without requiring any kind of linguistic, literary or theoretical explanation. This is particularly true of gender specific representations.

Benedict Anderson writes at the end of his book *Imagined Communities*[5] that the language that the patriot learns as a little boy 'at mother's knee' and that he parts with 'only at the grave' is the language in which he conjures up the past and in which he dreams of the future. As is well known, Anderson was not interested in examining the significance of gender. Ruth Roach Pierson points this out in her commentary in this volume. Anderson clearly holds gender differences to be inessential. Yet at the same time, he does come across them at two places in his own book, both of which are ultimately significant. Anderson characterizes the community, the invention and cohesion of which he wants to investigate, as a masculine community. With this, he has history on his side: as the contributions to the present volume indicate, the capacity to act politically was, above all, a male domain. Anderson himself speaks of 'a deep, horizontal comradeship' and of the 'fraternity' within the national community.[6] The other gender appears only in passing, but is, nevertheless, explicitly mentioned: Anderson writes of the mother when it is a matter of tradition, of the memory of belonging, and of that which, so to speak, frames the life of the responsible citizen – childhood and death. The context in which Anderson mentions the mother is language – the 'mother tongue' – and its significance for the ideal of communality, which Anderson judges to be very important. It is conspicuous, however, that the figure of the mother appears only briefly to illustrate the beginnings of 'political love' or *amor patriae*[7] – the critical explanation of which Anderson had promised – before disappearing immediately again into the background. Anderson names 'the mother' here: her presence appears to be as indispensable as it is self-evident in describing the origin of the patriot and his love for the nation. Yet at the same time, he reduces the figure of the mother to a sign.[8] The exclusion of women and the construction of masculinity are so self-evidently bound together for Anderson that they do not need to be thematized any further. In this, Anderson appears simply to have followed the historical development of the nation itself and its gender constructions. While the feminine is relegated here beyond history, beyond disputes and battles, it is, at the same time, reintroduced and, without expending too many words, fixed and preserved as an image or sign, which by no means merely stands for that from which the masculine must distinguish itself.

In national movements of the nineteenth century women were not accepted as political subjects and continued to be denied the right to vote far into the twentieth century. Civil rights were connected with the right and duty to bear arms – this was true in Prussia as much as in revolutionary France and America, as Karen Hagemann points out in her contribution on the anti-Napoleonic wars of liberation in this volume.[9] This connection marks the genesis of modern masculinity, and assigns women to a realm of action outside of political and state institutions. Women, however, do play an important role in the process of nation building or, as Angelika Schaser remarks, 'in historical moments in which the nation needed reassurance – in times of war, revolution or violent upheaval.' Women's responsibilities were articulated not merely in terms of familial reproduction and of caring for those wounded in battle, but also in terms of cultural responsibilities – in times of peace and, in particular, where a national movement had begun to form or a nation defined itself primarily as a cultural nation. Women were assigned the particular responsibility of preserving and imparting traditions, those of the 'national' language as well as of the 'national' culture (cf. Hagemann, Novikova, Schaser and others in this volume).

If, within the gender-specific division of labour, women were (and continue to be) excluded from state institutions, these gender-specific activities, at the same time, provided them with the possibility of public visibility. In her commentary, Ruth Roach Pierson correctly points to the decisive distinction here between nation and state. The public visibility of women, however, occurs outside of the space where politics is negotiated, and thus outside of the space where questions of political representation and the legitimacy of political representatives are discussed as well, as Caroll Smith-Rosenberg thematizes in this volume. It is, rather, in public festive performances that women present traditional culture as a part of national culture, or in songs and even in textiles as well, the function of which in forming collectivity is often underestimated,[10] as Irina Novikova shows in her contribution through the example of the Latvian national movement.[11] Women present tradition – that which should be anchored in the national memory – and thus become representatives of national culture, a culture that claims to have always already existed, and is transmitted outside of the official political realm. One could also say that women emerge as representatives of a 'timeless national memory.'[12] In this sense, they stand not only for that which 'the masculine' must constitute itself against, but, at the same time, for a past that is supposed to motivate the actions of those tied to the national community as well.

A national movement cannot exist and be effective without the reconstruction of a common history as well as a common language, a history that is capable of explaining the project of a future together and of providing it with a 'cause'. Gender images play an important role in such narratives. The description of the nation as a family, in which the gender roles are more-or-less clearly distributed, is widespread (cf. Hagemann and Novikova), as is the reconstruction of hereditary communities. The origins of such communities are sought in an archaic time, in a 'golden era', in which female founding figures play an important role. This is evident not only in the significance of Pharaonic women for the construction of an Egyptian nation, analysed by Beth Baron in this volume, but also in the rearticulation of Libuše in Czech narratives of origins, described here by Jitka Malecková. As Anne McClintock notes elsewhere, 'despite their myriad differences, nations are symbolically figured as domestic genealogies.'[13]

The particular and frequently dominant position of female figures in such national genealogies is remarkable. 'Mothers' clearly have a special position in narratives about the origins of nations, and not merely as the complement to masculine heroes or founding fathers. Thus, as Karen Hagemann notes, the royal family in Prussia was celebrated as the first family of the nation: king and queen were stylized into 'father of the country' and 'mother of the country'. In this construction, a specific mythification of the female figure, here Queen Luise of Prussia, developed which points beyond the familial metaphor. This can be seen in the cult around the Prussian queen, which had already been established in the early nineteenth century and that steadily consolidated after that. Not only was the image of the Prussian queen 'made bourgeois' from the very beginning; following her early death in 1811, she was immediately made in a figure whose biography served as metaphor for the 'destiny of the nation'.

The material for the idea of such female figures, who could be connected to national myths of foundation, arose from diverse traditions that were themselves reconstructed and altered. Existing myths were reworked, individual elements reweighed. In the construction of new myths, the variety and heterogeneity of traditional narratives were reduced. Ultimately, it was clearly a matter of constructing figures who could be identified with, and who allowed for the transcendence of social, and, if possible, ethnic differences. In this sense, one can speak of an allegorization of historical and mythical figures, in which concrete histories were pushed into the background and a general, ahistorical determination of the feminine became significant, a feminine that was supposed to refer to the nation and its origins – and perhaps to its future as well. In her contribution to this volume, Jitka Malecková demonstrates, for example, how the fullness of the concrete and, in part, contradictory narratives about the mythic figure of Libuše was gradually reduced. With this tendency, it was always a matter of constructing an original unity without differences. Violence is often evident in such reconstructions, particularly when the nation is supposed to be formed on a territory that cannot be asserted as having always already been 'its own': for example, Australian feminists, as Marilyn Lake reports in her contribution, sought to assert their superiority over Aborigine women on the basis of the Darwinist concept of a 'dying race'.

'All nationalisms are gendered, all are invented and all are dangerous', Anne McClintock writes in an article on 'nationalism, gender, and race:'

> the representation of male national power depends on the prior construction of gender difference . . . Excluded from direct action as national citizens, women are subsumed symbolically into the national body politic as its boundary and metaphoric limit . . . Women are symbolically constructed as the symbolic bearers of the nation, but are denied any direct relation to national agency.[14]

We find such a division of gender roles in many representations of national histories. While women stand for the nation and for its tradition – they 'appear in a metaphoric or symbolic role' – men usually come into the picture or are called upon as active agents, as those who do battle.[15] The role of men in the national scenario can be described as 'metonymic': 'men are contiguous with each other and with the national whole'.[16]

As is discussed in many contributions in the present volume, this male position does not simply exist: masculinity must itself be produced.[17] Carroll Smith-Rosenberg reminds us that masculinity, like femininity, must be produced and secured as 'the other side' of the modern two-sex

Figure 4.1 *Citizens – born free* (*Citoyens né libre*). Anonymous etching, 1793/94 (Musée Carnavalet, Paris)

model – both in relation to, and in opposition to, its counterpart, the feminine. In this process, however, the feminine by no means merely occupies that position from which the masculine must distinguish itself, as Smith-Rosenberg describes it. The feminine is also designed as a complement and a supplement to the masculine: through the defence of the feminine, masculinity produces and demonstrates itself. Masculinity is measured by its ability to defend the feminine, which can also mean 'the nation.' This model proves particularly effective in the competition among nations: national stereotypes, such as those of 'the Germans' as opposed to 'the French' (discussed by Karen Hagemann), operate according to this ideal of masculinity. The battle for national independence is equated with a 'manning' or coming to manhood, not only in a Prussia under Napoleon, but also in Australia under the British crown, as Marilyn Lake shows. Such 'mature masculinity' promises to be able to overlook class allegiance and social difference.

Anne McClintock connects the division of gender roles in the scenario of the nation with the doubled or contradictory temporal conception of the nation, as it has been analysed by theorists and historians (such as Tom Nairn and Homi K. Bhabha):[18] on the one hand, the nation presents itself as a project of the future, and, on the other hand, as a project grounded in a mythically original past as well.

> What is less often noticed is that the temporal anomaly within nationalism – veering between a nostalgia for the past and the impatient, progressive sloughing off of the past – is typically resolved by figuring the contradiction in the representation of time as a natural division of gender. Women are represented as the atavistic and authentic body of national tradition, . . . embodying nationalism's conservative principle of continuity.

Men would then stand ultimately for the opposite, for progress and also for discontinuity. 'Nationalism's anomalous relation to time is thus managed as a natural relation to gender.'[19] McClintock also points out that this model of the 'gendering of the nation' is by no means limited to Europe and North America. The current volume presents extensive material substantiating this thesis.

Up to this point, I have not thematized how the constellation described here came into being. In what follows, I would like to elucidate ways in which this occurred through an excursus on the French revolution. In the French revolution, gender differences attained a decisive and historically new function in political iconography, which had consequences for the representation of the nation as well as for the feminine. The process of constructing an image of femininity during the French revolution, an image that was supposed to 'embody' the new republic and its central values and orientation, is well known. Images of the feminine assumed the space that had become empty in the course of the dissolution or overcoming of absolutist power. Female personifications replaced the image of the king's body, assuming the meanings of the 'sacred centre' of power, [20] while modifying them.

This gradual process, which was by no means linear and free of contradiction, can be traced through a concrete example in 1792–93: the installation of a statuary image of the feminine was proceeded by the destruction of the image of the masculine ruler's body. In 1792, the equestrian statue, which had been erected on Louis XV Square in 1763, was taken down. Not far from its remains, the guillotine upon which Louis XVI would be beheaded, was erected. In the same year, a statue depicting *Liberté* – a seated enthroned female statue – was placed upon the empty pedestal in the middle of what had, in the meantime, been renamed the *Place de la Révolution*. The statue formed a central point in the procession of the festival of Republican Unity, which took place in August 1793. Part of the festival ritual was a fire in which the '*Liberté*' insignia of the old regime were sacrificed. These performances in 1793 depict, in a particularly heightened form, what had been taking place in illustrated journalism for a number of years. If we follow the two sketches by Monsiau from 1798 and 1800, the femininity of the Republic had already become self-understood by around 1800 (see Figures 4.2 and 4.3). Female personifications as a specific form of allegory now served the visualization or the visual 'embodiment' of the new order, which no longer had only the figure of the father as a single centre. This form of representing the nation established itself during the course of the nineteenth century in other Western European countries and in the US.[21] At times – I mention this only in passing – it seemed as if something comparable recently occurred in the former socialist countries following the collapse of the socialist order.

These forms of representing the nation are concerned with depicting something that is not representable: the nation as an 'imagined community', one that does not simply encompass a territory, but rather – following the descriptions of Anderson and others – encompasses the idea of a 'natural' – an ostensibly always already existing bond among a group of people. Allegories – in particular, personifications – provide a means of depicting this. Throughout history, personification has repeatedly served to represent that which cannot be mimetically illustrated. This alone, however, does not commit the personification to any particular gender: the fact that nations were, for the most part, personified by female figures cannot be explained by recourse to the tradition of iconography. In the history of allegorical personifications, gender attributions were never as unambiguous and as unchanging as they are depicted in the iconography of the modern, in which 'higher' values – precisely those values that are regarded as universally binding – are represented, above all, through images of femininity. In older traditions (such as those of

Figure 4.2 *Monument à la gloire de Louis XIV,* N.A. Monsiau. Engraving, 1789 (Musée de la Révolution Française, Vizilles)

Figure 4.3 *La liberté triomphante,* N.A. Monsiau. Engraving, 1800 (Musée de la Révolution Française, Vizilles)

the Middle Ages), vices as well as virtues could be personified as female.[22] Only since the early modern can one detect an alteration or regrouping of the gendered attributions used in personified representations. Art historians have pointed out that in the Renaissance, allegories – above all, female allegories – were increasingly used to visualize the new moral values. In addition to this, these female allegories were more clearly marked in their (sexualized) physicality.[23] It is, perhaps, not a coincidence that one of the earliest known personifications of democracy is female – in the expanded edition of the *Iconologia* by Cesare Ripa, a compendium published in 1630, primarily to support artists, in which the person-ifications of monarchy or aristocracy were assigned to the male sex.[24] Finally, during this historical era, a reorganization of gender relations also began – a gradual but far-reaching constitution of the two sexes, both in theoretical discussions and in the world of images.[25]

The new and increasing dissemination of female personifications in the political iconography of modern nations or nation states presupposed the self-evidence of an 'order of gender' based upon the 'naturalness' of the two sexes, an order that has been decisive in western Europe since the eighteenth century. In the political iconography of the modern nation, female allegories were not only disseminated in a new way, but also occupied a new position.[26] The substitution of the male ruler's body with the female personification of the values of the republic implied a profound change in status of female personifications – one that a merely icon-ographic account will fail to notice if a history of personifications is written as a history of motifs and omits the contexts and the medial forms of representation in which those personifications were historically present.[27] Finally, it is significant that the nation has been represented in the medium of sculpture. This medium promises the presence and permanence of that which is depicted, as well as a relative timelessness of expression in regard to the future on the basis of an origin without history.[28]

Referring to Kantorowicz's famous study on *The King's Two Bodies*,[29] one could say that the sculptural image of the female, in stepping onto the pedestal of the King's monument, assumes the meanings of King's 'eternal' body, and with this, the meanings of his immortality and legitimacy. At the same time, these meanings are modified through their connection with the implications of femininity itself. 'Femininity' and 'nature' appear as the justification for the legitimacy as well as for the continuity of the new order. The fact that images of femininity could be connected to these meanings presupposes the exclusion of women from the political public sphere. The legitimacy of this new order of the nation is understood as natural. The feminine, which refers to a place 'beyond history', thus appears suitable for establishing such an order. In place of traditional genealogy, which begins with the figure of the father, a new beginning emerges that can only be mythically thought. Through its connection to cyclical – invariable nature, femininity ultimately appears, at the same time, as a guarantee for a never-ending reproduction, and thus for the future as well.

The image of the feminine functions as an image of the nation, and thus as the image of something that exists only through performance and is produced through both representation and action.[30] Since the image of the feminine assumed the space previously occupied by the body of the king, there is a need for its visualization.[31] As there should and can be no empty space, this visualization is repeatedly produced, modified and reproduced. The silent reproduction of metaphors of the feminine for the imagined community ultimately occurs within a broad field of performative practices in which women have attempted to create public visibility for themselves. One could say that the paradox that Judith Butler problematizes in regard to the politics of the contemporary women's movement – that women represent on the political stage everything that they themselves have been excluded from in politics[32] – had its prehistory in early national movements. Future research on the history of gender must attempt to work out the connections between the construction of the two sexes and the invention of the nation, to make the implicit connections between them explicit. This requires that the analysis of political movements takes seriously the specific productivity of cultural representations, including those on the visual field.

Notes

1. Cf. for example Laqueur, T. (1990), *Making Sex. Body and Gender from the Greeks to Freud,* Cambridge; Schiebinger, L. (1993), 'Anatomie der Differenz, "Rasse" und Geschlecht in der Naturwissenschaft des 18. Jahrhundert,' *Feministische Studien* 1: 48–64 (original in Schiebinger, L. (1990) *Eighteenth Century* 23: 387–405); Honegger, C. (1990), *Die Ordnung der Geschlechter. Die Wissenschaften vom Menschen und das Weib* (Frankfurt a.M.).

2. Cf. Hall, S. (1992), 'The Question of Cultural Identity', in Hall, S., Held, D., and McGrew, T. (eds) *Modernity and its Futures*, Cambridge, 273–316.

3. Confino, A. (1993), 'The Nation as a Local Metaphor: Heimat, National Memory, and the German Empire, 1971–1918,' *History and Memory* 5: 42–86.

4. Cf. Halbwachs, M. (1985), *Das Gedächtnis und seine sozialen Bedingungen*, Frankfurt a.M.

5. Anderson, B. (1991), *Imagined Communities. Reflections on the Origin and Spread of Nationalism*, revised edition, London, 154.

6. Anderson, B. (1991), *Imagined Communities. Reflections on the Origin and Spread of Nationalism*, revised edition, London, 7.

7. Anderson, B. (1991), *Imagined Communities. Reflections on the Origin and Spread of Nationalism*, revised edition, London, 113f, 154.

8. This is particularly evident in the German translation, which renders the English original 'at mother's knee' as 'at mother's skirt strings' [*an Mutters Rockzipfel*] – see (1993), *Die Erfindung der Nation. Zur Karriere eines erfolgreichen Konzepts*, Frankfurt a.M./New York, 154. In the German translation, the mother becomes a sign in the order of clothing in modernity, an order that has the function, above all, of marking the distinction from the masculine, and that stands for everything from which the 'responsible' citizen must separate himself or should have separated himself from.

9. Cf. Kerber, L. (1997), 'The Republican Mother, Woman and the Enlightenment – an American Perspective,' in Linda Kerber, *Intellectual History of Women*, London, 41–62 and 63–99.

10. 'Like language, cloth in its communicative aspects can be used to coerce . . . We see this coercion in situations of complex, socially stratified, capitalist and colonial societies,' write Jane Schneider and Annette B. Weiner (1989) in their instructive book *Cloth and Human Experience*, Washington, 54. 'Valued as currency, shroud, ancestor, royalty, or fashion, cloth represents the key dilemmas of social and political life: how to bring the past actively into the present'. When women embroider the national flag, as Carola Lipp describes it, they thereby initiate an important community-building tradition within the sexual division of labour.

11. Cf. on this the study by Lipp, C., 'Frauen und Öffentlichkeit. Möglichkeiten und Grenzen politischer Partizipation in Vormärz und in der Revolution 1848/1849,' in Lipp, C. (1986), *Schimpfende Weiber und patriotische Jungfrauen. Frauen im Vormärz und in der*

Revolution 1848/1849, Moos/Baden-Baden, 270–307; and 'Liebe, Krieg und Revolution. Geschlechterbeziehung und Nationalismus in der Revolution 1848/1849,' also in Lipp, 353–84.

12. This is how Confino describes the concept *Heimat* or home. This notion of *Heimat*, as that which remains the same and is bound together with 'timeless national memory,' is of general significance in connection with femininity. Cf. Confino, A. (1993), 'The Nation as a Local Metaphor: Heimat, National Memory, and the German Empire, 1971–1918,' *History and Memory* 5: 42–86, 52f.

13. McClintock, A. (1996), '"No Longer in a Future Heaven": Nationalism, Gender, and Race' in Eley G. and Suny, R.G. (eds) *Becoming National. A Reader*, New York, 262.

14. McClintock, A. (1996), '"No Longer in a Future Heaven": Nationalism, Gender, and Race' in Eley G. and Suny, R.G. (eds) *Becoming National. A Reader*, New York, 260f.

15. A caricature of the 'plain honest German' (*der deutschen Michel*) as dopey and incapable of action only works in the context of this ideal of masculinity.

16. McClintock, A. (1996), '"No Longer in a Future Heaven": Nationalism, Gender, and Race' in Eley G. and Suny, R.G. (eds) *Becoming National. A Reader*, New York, 260f.

17. If one describes the discourse around masculinity at the turn of the eighteenth to the nineteenth century as a crisis of masculinity (as, for instance, Karen Hagemann does in her contribution to the present volume), one would then have to discuss how one avoids the danger of presuming the prior existence of fixed gender identities, and whether the intensification of the discourse around masculinity should not be understood as a way of producing modern masculinity. The contribution by Viktoria Schmidt-Linsenhoff in this volume provides some evidence for this thesis.

18. McClintock, A. (1996), '"No Longer in a Future Heaven": Nationalism, Gender, and Race' in Eley G. and Suny, R.G. (eds) *Becoming National. A Reader*, New York, 263. See also Bhabha, H.K. 'Dissemination, Time, Narrative and the Margins of the Modern Nation,' in Homi K. Bhabha, (1994), *The Location of Culture,* London/ New York, 139–46.

19. McClintock, A. (1996), '"No Longer in a Future Heaven": Nationalism, Gender, and Race' in Eley G. and Suny, R.G. (eds) *Becoming National. A Reader*, New York, 263.

20. Cf. Hunt, L. (1984), *Politics, Culture, and Class in the French Revolution,* Berkeley/ Los Angeles.

21. I have examined in detail analogous developments in France. See Wenk, S. (1996), *Versteinerte Weiblichkeit. Allegorien in der Skulptur der Moderne*, Köln/ Weimar/ Wien, 75–127. This development, however, is not limited to Western Europe, see Baron, B. (1997), 'Nationalist Iconography. Egypt as a Woman', in *Rethinking Nationalism in the Arab Middle East*, ed. James Jankowski and Israel Gershomi, New York, 105–24. On female personification in Finland, see Juntti, E. (1998), 'On Our Way to Europe. Finnish Women's Magazines and Discourse on Women, Nation, and Power', in *The European Journal of Women's Studies*, 5.

22. I note here that the gender specific depiction of personifications is not, as is often assumed, grounded in linguistic gender. The question of linguistic gender in allegorically depicted concepts is merely a displacement of the problem.

23. Cf. here Wittkower R. (1984), *Allegorie und Wandel der Symbole in Antike und Renaissance*, Köln; Schade, S., Wagner, M., Weigel, S. (1994), *Allegorien und Geschlechterdifferenz*, Köln/ Weimar/ Wien; and Wenk, S. (1996), *Versteinerte Weiblichkeit. Allegorien in der Skulptur der Moderne*, Köln/ Weimar/ Wien, 24. There is a reproduction of this image in Martin Warnke, 'Die Demokratie zwischen Vorbildern und Zerrbildern,' in Dario Gamboni (ed.) *Zeichen der Freiheit. Das Bild der Republik in der Kunst des 16. bis 20. Jahrhunderts*, Bern, 88f.

25. On this, see also Sigrid Schade and Silke Wenk, 'Inszenierungen des Sehens: Kunst, Geschichte und Geschlechterdifferenz', in Bußmann, H. and Hof, R. (eds) (1995), *Genus. Zur Geschlechterdifferenz in den Kulturwissenschaften*, Stuttgart, 340–407.

26. This did not begin abruptly with the French Revolution. Helga Möbius has shown a related change in the status of female personifications in the Dutch Republic of the 17th century, Helga Möbius, 'Frauenbilder für die Republik,' in Gamboni, D. (1991), *Zeichen der Freiheit. Das Bild der Republik in der Kunst des 16. bis 20. Jahrhunderts*, Bern, 53–74.

27. This is precisely the problem in the otherwise completely laudable study by Warner, M. (1985), *Monument and Maidens. The Allegory of the Female Form*, London. The claim to be an historically comprehensive compendium pushes an historical analysis of effects into the background.

28. Cf. on this Wenk, S. (1996), *Versteinerte Weiblichkeit. Allegorien in der Skulptur der Moderne*, Köln/ Weimar/ Wien, 81 f. – with reference to Michail Bachtin, 'Epos und Roman. Zur Methodologie der

Erforschung des Romans', in Hiersch, A. and Kowalski, E. (1969), *Konturen und Perspektiven*, Berlin/ DDR, 191–222.

29. Kantorowicz, E.H. (1957), *The King's Two Bodies: A Study in Medieval Political Theology,* Princeton.

30. I point out here that the German concept *Repräsentation* is ambiguous: *Repräsentation* can be translated not only as 'representation,' but also as 'performance' [*Vorstellung*] or depiction [*Darstellung*], and that this depiction can also mean 'production' [*Herstellung*]. Thus, one speaks in German, for example, of the *Darstellung* of a chemical substance, and means by this the production of a chemical substance. Cf. on this, Rheinberger, H.-J. (1997), 'Von der Zelle zum Gen: Repräsentationen der Molekularbiologie,' in Rheinberger, H.-J. (ed.) *Räume des Wissens: Repräsentationen, Codierung, Spur*, Berlin, 265f.

31. Cf. on this as well Wenk, S. (1999), 'Geschlechterdifferenz und visuelle Repräsentation des Politischen,' in *Frauen-Kunst-Wissenschaft*, Marburg, (27 May): 25–42.

32. Butler, J. (1990), *Gender Trouble,* London, 1990, Chapter 1.

Part 2
Nation States, Ethnicity and Gender Order

Male Alterity in the French Revolution – Two Paintings by Anne-Louis Girodet at the Salon of 1798

Viktoria Schmidt-Linsenhoff

Translated by Elizabeth Volk

In the wake of the growing importance of the media, feminist theory and art history have increasingly shown an interest in the meaning of visual culture and performance for the process of national and sexual identity formation. Unlike traditional political iconography attention is focused here on the interdisciplinary concept of representation, a 'nexus of aesthetics, semiotics, politics and psychoanalysis'.[1] In the sociopolitical realm representation means the representation of groups and interests by individual persons, and in the field of visual culture it means aesthetic representation through images and sculptures. Every nation is shaped not only by portrayals of people, places and events but also by illustrations of abstract ideas and emotive images. So far, art history has mainly concentrated on the gendered rhetoric of predominantly feminine alleg-ories of nation. The idealized femininity depicted in male political fantasies of a unified and united national body undermines women's right of political representation of their interests. It was often implied that the political and artistic subject of representation in a nation based on male association would be masculine and characterized by dominance and homogeneity. The following analysis of paintings, however, shows that the nationalization of masculinity necessitates its ethnic differentiation and creates a male otherness that is constructed in these paintings.

In 1798 the Paris Salon displayed two paintings by Anne-Louis Girodet (1767–1824), which do not have much in common concerning genre, pretension, and effect: the mythological portrayal *Endymion. Effet de lune* and the portrait of the Negro representative Jean Baptiste Belley (Figures 5.1 and 5.2). The seductive male nude of the *Sleeping Endymion* painted in 1791 in Rome, is the basis of the renown of this twenty-four-year-old student of David and is considered his most important work, stimulating renewed attempts at interpretation even up to the present. The portrait of Belley (1797) has received much less acclaim, although it had been bought by the French government in 1832 and has been on view to the public since then. Apparently only the dark skin colour of the person portrayed was of interest and the historical connection with the question of slavery in the French revolution. I would like to discuss both of these paintings at the same time, however, as they represent masculinity as alterity in a manner that is at once similar and unusual. With *Endymion* Girodet relied upon aesthetic patterns that had been developing in painting since the Renaissance to portray the female nude, and in the portrait of Belley he took recourse to that ideal figure representing critique of civilization, the 'noble savage'. The historical frame of reference for these two paintings is the politics of the French Revolution with regards to the sexes and the colonies that completely denied human and constitutional rights to women and only half-heartedly and temporarily granted them to male blacks in the colonies. The field of discourse where they spark debate even up to the present is the cultural construction of 'masculinity' as a criterion for membership in the collective *corp politique* of a democratically-constituted nation. My initial question regarding both paintings was: How do they stand up in the light of the imagination of a national body that, on the one hand, was conceived as white, male and heterosexual, and which was, on the other hand, endowed with the universal claim to human rights? Do the paintings, through a reinterpretation of qualities normally attributed to women and 'savages' plead for their political recognition? Or do they rather serve to promote the incorporation of these qualities into the European masculine ideal of universals? In the process of the examination other aspects came to the forefront: With his paintings, Girodet introduces to the revolutionary discourses on 'equality' and 'fraternity' difference and desire. The homosexual desires that he stages with the significants of 'femininity' and 'savagery' in connection with the picture of the male body raises the question of its subversive potential.

Endymion. Effet de Lune

Portrayed here is a mythological love affair of the gods: The Greek goddess of the moon Semele is united with her sleeping lover, the shepherd and hunter Endymion. The mortal Endymion had asked Zeus for eternal sleep in order to preserve his ephemeral beauty and youth for the pleasure of the goddess. Key to the understanding of the mysterious tale of the picture is the way the light is employed. The female main character is acting in the form of moonlight, which creates an unreal, submarine dream atmosphere that correctly reminded its interpreters of the contemporary interest in magnetism and mesmerism. The light sharply contours the oversized laurel and oak leaves (which in 1791 signify the glory of art and civic virtue) and the figure of Zephyr. On the other hand, the body lines of Endymion evaporate into a *sfumato á la Correggio* – a metaphor for the love act and proof of a *genie nocturne,* whose 'poetry' had enthused the critics of the Salon in 1793 just as much as the exceptional 'originality' of the painting's idea of making the female protagonist disappear.[2] Ever since Annibale Carraci's portrayal of the story in the frescoes of the Galleria Farnese in Rome around the year 1600, the material had provided an opportunity to represent female desire and the female view of the male nude. In the eighteenth century the interest in this topic grew along with the increasing pleasure taken in erotic role changing and role-playing, and which preceded its satirical trivialization in the years prior to 1790.[3] With the elimination of the female from the love story, the sleeping Endymion becomes an autonomous erotic nude. Girodet's concept takes recourse to the ephebe, which had already been linked in late antique reliefs with the iconography of Endymion: a body reclining in perfect passivity, there for the enjoyment of another. The gesture for defencelessness and unawareness is the arm, which has been placed above his head. Antique works of art famous in the eighteenth century, such as the *Barberini Faun* which had drawn admiration from the Marquis de Sade, connoted this gesture with homoerotic passivity. European Renaissance painting, however, attributed a feminine definition to it with the pictorial types of the 'sleeping Venus' and the 'nereid'. Since Giorgione's *Venus* (around 1507) the arm placed above the head of a sleeping woman designates – quoting here from the *Vatican Ariadne* – the subordination of the female body portrait to the male eye.[4] Girodet not only takes over this gesture, which can, in principle, designate the passivity of both sexes but he systematically transfers motives and composition schemes of the Venus iconography to the male hero – the naturalizing of the nude by embedding him in civilizationally-distant spaces of the landscape and the wilderness, of the dream and the unconscious; the availability to the viewer's eye of the body still in sleep or death; the mediating of the voyeuristic pleasure by a third party, internal to the painting, who acts in representation of the view and the desires of the viewer. Girodet fills this key role with the cupid, who as 'Zephyr' pulls aside the branches of the laurel tree in order to expose Endymion to the flood of moonlight. It is this third party within the painting that is at once witness and agent of the lust portrayed there, fitting our view into a homoerotic structure of desire. Endymion is no longer object of the female desires of the goddess, but of a male viewer. The painter changes the heterosexual love story, in which (for once) activity is on the part of the female lover and passivity is on the part of the male loved one, into an icon of male autonomy.

In recent years, Girodet's *Endymion* has become the object of controversy in research dealing with the art history of the French Revolution and with the aesthetic construction of sexual identities. In 1991 Thomas Crow refuted the stylistic attribution of the painting to post-revolutionary classicism, found in the older literature, and emphasized the political character of the composition before the backdrop of the relationships between David and his students. It was a reaction stemming from the weave of relationships and the competitive conditions in the David school, and in the last analysis, rooted in a rational concept of art and of politics in the sense of David.[5] Whitney Davis insisted, in 1994, upon an explicitly homoerotic component. He saw in Girodet's *Endymion* what we also perceive as an 'emancipatory' alternative to the rigid, Roman virtue of militarized masculinity, whose classical formulations are David's *Oath of the Horatii*, *The Death of Socrates* and *Brutus*: '. . . an opening toward a non-phallic and possibly homoerotic alternative'.[6] For Davis, *Endymion* signifies a renunciation on the part of the painter, who with this passive, sensual, dreaming ephebe casts off precisely that ideology of masculinity that had gained acceptance in the French Revolution and would still be the basis of Crow's concept of art, politics, and the public. Taking into consideration the overwhelming multitude of paintings showing male weakness and passivity, Abigail Solomon-Godeau had observed a significant feminization of masculinity around 1800, whose first and artistically most consequential manifestation was Girodet's *Endymion*.[7]

Of interest is a small controversy that the magazine *Texte zur Kunst* had sparked in an interview with Crow in 1994. Crow criticized Solomon-Godeau's terminology of 'feminized' and 'masculine' manliness on grounds that it was supposedly rooted in the customary stereotypes of binary sexual identities and closes with an emphatic profession to male universals:

> It is probably more to the point if one says that for a moment an exceptional trust was placed in the capability of the nude male body and in masculinity to encompass all desirable human qualities. If one wanted to show ideal beauty and sexuality, one didn't have to paint Venus, one could have drawn Adonis instead. And in 'Endymion' Girodet leaves the goddess out completely, so that only the male body remains . . .[8]

What is remarkable about this statement, which registers the omission of the goddess with undeniable satisfaction as a cultural victory, is the tenor of an unreflected, spontaneous anti-feminism. Solomon-Godeau's research concerning the concepts of masculinity in French painting of around 1800 depart from a feminist approach, which understands itself as a scientific criticism of male universals. The interpretations of both Crow and Davis are indebted to this approach, regardless of their controversy concerning the definition of 'masculinity' and 'politics', 'art' and 'the making of art history'. While Solomon-Godeau interprets the confusing and contradictory paintings of a bourgeois 'male trouble' in the French Revolution as a symptom of the structural adaptation of patriarchy to the egalitarian forms of democracy, the existence of women or of a second sex remains irrelevant for the interpretations of both Crow and Davis. Where Solomon-Godeau determines a dual movement of an 'expulsion' of the feminine and its 'incorporation' into the male self, Crow and Davis believe they can understand the discourse of masculinity in painting by excluding the feminine.[9] They overlook the fact that the imaginary male body of the people constitutes itself by way of what it excludes socially, but represents culturally. The absent femininity is – according to Judith Butler – its 'constituting external'.[10] I would like to refer the feminization of the autonomous male nude in the *Endymion* to the yet unstable fantasies of the French Revolution concerning the gender of the republican body of people, to the gendering of the collective subject of 'nation'.

At first glance the spectacular success enjoyed by the painting at the Salon of 1793 does not fit in at all with the political situation. Was the idealization of the pleasure taken in the male acceptable at just the moment when the revolution demanded its sacrifices? Girodet transfigured the sensual death out of love at a time when the nation was demanding death on the battleground; he legitimized the vice of infertile sodomy while the institutions of family and marriage were at the service of increasing the population; he tempted with the pleasures of privacy and passivity while the male sexual character was being defined as the public ability to act. An explanation of these (alleged) contradictions by assuming a division of the David school into the defenders of a rigid, Roman ideal of masculinity and on the other hand, propagators of a sensitive one which Davis suggests is as little plausible as a chronological development of the strict virtues of the Jacobins to the post-revolutionary hedonism of 'effeminate' masculinity purported by Solomon-Godeau. The situation is, in fact, much more complicated. Girodet's Jacobin inclinations during the years of his sojourn in Rome are clearly documented.[11]

Finally David himself politicized more than the pain-resistant body of the Roman soldier and stoic philosopher. With the paintings of the murdered representatives Marat and Pelletier in 1793 he pointed out the vulnerability of the male *corps politique* and, in 1794, transcended secularized death with the pedophile Eros of the dying child martyr Bara. But already in 1790/91 – during the months Girodet was working on the *Endymion* in Rome – in David's sketchbooks for the *Oath in the Ballroom,* it was not the equality of parallel, outstretched arms, raised to take an oath, but the tender emphasis in the embracings of the fraternization scene that was the departing point of his pictorial design.[12]

The sensitive and erotic aspects of 'fraternity' play a decisive role in the homosocial project of a nation that had been constituted through exclusion of women. In addition to the imagination of a male body of people, whose unanimity and 'unity' guaranteed the strength of the nation, there was a growing interest in paintings that focus on the themes of love and friendship under the auspices of difference. The most pronounced painting of the masculinity of the body of the people was the colossal figure of Hercules in 1793, which David had designed for the fourth station of the celebration of the first anniversary of the Republic (10 August 1793), having as a motto the 'unity and indivisibility of the republic'. Its gigantic proportions and militancy signalized the readiness to destroy with the brutal force of the popular movement of the *sans culottes* whatever threatened the 'unity' of this symbolic body – a symbolic threat that became reality with the passing of the *terreur* laws on 17 September 1793. This image of the body, which was spread through mass media during the Jacobin dictatorship, reacted defensively to the frequent dangers to the 'unity and indivisibility' of the republic: The escalation of the war with England, the Netherlands and Spain was perceived as a threat to the borders of the symbolic and territorial body of the state, which Hercules is defending in the painting as the 'people' and the 'devourer of the king' (Figure 5.3). With the patricide of the king on 21 January 1793, the splintering of the National Assembly and the gap between the elite and the citizen's movement worsened further. The bitter, mortal conflicts in Paris and the civil war in the Vendée caused 'equality' and the 'unity of the republic' to become empty phrases, which took on the character of an hysterically-mystic spell in official speech. Finally the aggressive interventions of the political clubs of women, the riots of the women *sans culottes* and the journalistic attacks against 'male tyranny', were regarded as an unbearable inner threat to the 'unity'. The Jacobin government met them by outlawing the women's clubs, by revoking the right of speech for women in public meetings,

Figure 5.1 A.L. Girodet, *Endymion*, 1791 (Paris, Louvre)

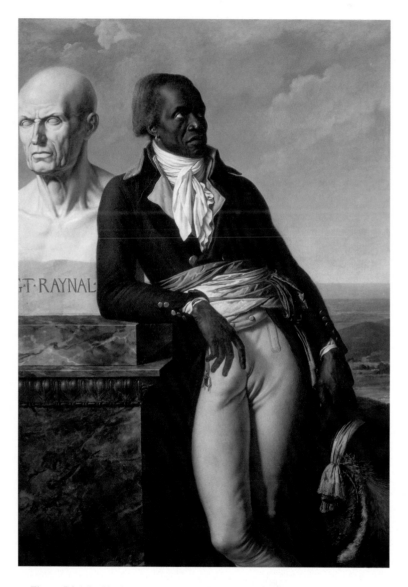

Figure 5.2 A.L. Girodet, *Jean Baptiste Belley*, 1797 (Musée du Château, Versailles)

Figure 5.3 *Le peuple mangeur du Rois,* anonymous etching, 1793 (In: *Les Révolutions de Paris,* December 1793, with the comment 'Statue colossale proposée par le journal des Révolutions de Paris, pour être placée sur les points les plus éminens des nos frontières')

and by the execution within six weeks of three of the most prominent women politicians of the revolution in the fall of 1793 – Marie Antoinette, Madame Roland and Olympe de Gouges. The Jacobin Hercules-iconography – which temporarily competed with the *Liberté* as state emblem – was not addressed to the female population in 1793, emphatically reminding them of the masculinity of a 'single and indivisible' body of people.[13] If Girodet himself, when working on the *Endymion* in Rome in 1791, had in mind rather a modification of the authority, with which David had placed art, politics and masculinity under the dictates of soldierly and philosophic asceticism, nevertheless the Salon public in Paris in 1793 saw above all the authority of the doctrine of 'unity and indivisibility' of the national body as modified. This in no way meant, however, that the authority of masculinity saw itself shaken. Quite the contrary, the *Endymion* confirmed the male claim to universal acceptance by its appropriation of the 'feminine'. Anti-feminist policies after the fall of 1793 and representational practices focused on the strength of the 'unity' and the universality of the male body of the state, the antagonism between Hercules and Endymion was dissolved. This twofold role of fantasies incorporating the masculinity of the body of the people and of the state remained relevant beyond the Thermidor – as relevant as the republican, Bonapartist and Bourbon anti-feminism.

Portrait du Citoyen Belley, ex-représentant des colonies

Nothing is known about the conditions of the contract or the relationship between Girodet, who had returned from Rome in 1796, and the emancipated slave, and only little is known about the person portrayed.[14] Belley was born on the Senegalese Island of Goré in 1747 and deported as a child by slave traders to the French colony of Santo Domingo. In 1791 he participated in the slave revolts led by Toussaint-Louverture and he joined the army of the French Revolution, in which he received the rank of captain of a battalion. After the Jacobin envoy Sonthonax confirmed the decree of the abolition of slavery in Santo Domingo in August 1793, Belley was elected as one of three representatives of the colonies. When the representatives entered the Paris National Assembly on 3 February 1794, the question of the colonies met with little attention due to the problems of the wars of the revolution and the war economy. Nevertheless the representative Camboulas gave a ceremonial speech, in which he condemned the 'aristocracy of skin colour' as intolerable for a republic and greeted the new representatives as 'free citizens of Santo Domingo', as reported by the Moniteur.[15] An embrace from the president of the assembly sealed the brotherhood of all men. One day later the convention unanimously abolished slavery in all French colonies. In a small pen-and-ink drawing Nicolas Monsiau lent this scene a pathos that shows the partiality of the artist rather than documenting the ambivalent and reserved attitude of the National Assembly towards the question of slavery (Figure 5.4). After the dissolution of the Convention by the government of the Directorate in 1795, he was taken into the 'Council of Five Hundred'. In the new elections in May 1797 he lost his seat and returned to Santo Domingo. All biographical traces of him were lost during the fighting of the Napoleonic punitive expedition, which aimed to reinstitute slavery in the colony in 1802.[16] Belley was not a prominent person of public life for the Salon public of 1798. There are no myths around his person, unlike the legendary *Negro General* Toussaint-Louverture. Two-thirds of the paintings exhibited at the Salon 1798 were portraits, among these remarkably many men who had earned honours for the fatherland while in the military. The critics singled out Girodet's Belley from the crowd as a politically explosive *portrait histoire,* which takes a general stand upon the controversial question of French slavery and colonial politics.[17]

Girodet shows the emancipated slave wearing the tricolours in the silk shawl and on the feathered hat. He leans in casual elegance against the base of an oversized bust of the encyclopedist Raynal, who had died in

Figure 5.4 *The Abolition of Slavery by the National Assembly on 4 February 1794*, Nicolas Monsieau. Wash drawing, undated (Musée Carnavalet, Paris)

1796. The low horizon of the *Cap Haitienne* and the expanse of a high, lightly clouded sky push the monument and the portrait into a close-plasticity at the front edge of the painting. The artistic touch of placing a dead or absent person in a relationship to a person portrayed by means of a bust was widespread in portrait painting of the eighteenth century. The symmetry of meaning, which Girodet installs between the monument and the physical presence is, however, unique. The painted bust is more than an attribute that gives information about an inclination of the person portrayed. Girodet has, rather, united two very different citizens of the French Nation in a Janus-faced double portrait. Guillaume-Thomas Raynal was the most radical critic of slavery and of French colonial policy in the *ancien regime*. His major work *Histoire philosophique et politique des etablissements et du commerce des Européens dans les deux Indes* (Amsterdam 1770) sharpened the abolitionist arguments in an anti-clerical manner. The *History of Both Indias* forced its author into exile, but its numerous printings caused it to become a standard work of abolitionism. The frontispiece to the fourth volume of the second printing of 1774

Figure 5.5 Frontispiece to Volume 4 of G.T. Raynal, *Histoire philosophique et politique des Européens dans les deux Indes, 1774,* Charles Eisen

contains a copper engraving by Charles Eisen (Figure 5.5). The personification of nature in the form of the (white-skinned) Isis nurses a light- and a dark-skinned boy equally lovingly at her breasts. With this concept of a double-portrait, Girodet identifies himself with this abolitionist iconography of the fraternity – in clear distinction from the central icon of the anti-slavery movement, whose emblem of the French Society of the *Amis des Noirs* was a kneeling black in chains, who in Christian humility prays for the granting of his freedom (Figure 5.6). This pictorial form appealed to the patriarchal consideration and Christian charity of the white man, who should bestow upon his 'black brother' the gift of freedom. Until the beginning of the twentieth century, it was to shape in many variations the relationships between 'whites' and 'blacks' in Christian-philanthropic circles. Monsiau integrates this emblematic figuration in an exposed position in the foreground of the aforementioned sketch for an historical portrayal of 2 April 1794 at the National Assembly in Paris. Girodet distances himself firmly from this concept of Christian fraternity in the spirit of paternalistic condescension. He is the first painter to grant an African a European subject status with a full-body portrait,

Figure 5.6 *Ne suis-je pas un homme? Un frère?* Medallion issued by the Association of Opponents of Slavery, 'Amis des Noirs'. Biscuit porcelain Sèvres, 1789 (Musée National Adrien-Dubouché, Limoges)

and connects this at the same time with a reflection upon European masculinity as well as the relationship between body, ethnicity, and nationality.[18] With *Mercure de France,* the Salon criticism praised the 'fortunate idea' the painter had to place Representative Belley supporting himself against Raynal, the 'eloquent advocate of the Blacks'. However, the author corrects the uneasy feeling of equality that is creeping over him with a well-meant suggestion to the contrary: 'If he were to embrace this sacred image, one could call the painting an homage to gratitude'.[19] No, Girodet is not showing us a 'Negro' in childish thankfulness, but rather a dead European and a self-assured African of stimulating liveliness. The painting is no homage to gratitude, but rather – if a homage at all – then to the physical elegance of the *homme de couleur.*

The portrait invites one to determine the differences between Raynal and Belley in a series of binary oppositions, which one can rattle off like verse: Black and white, antique and modern, past and future, death and life, thought and action, home country and colony, above and below, and so forth. The central dualism that refers back to all the others is, however, that of spirit and body, mind and body. Girodet brings the darkly-clothed upper torso of Belley into relationship to the bust of Raynal by placing the shoulders at the same height and Belley's arm bent at a right angle upon the bust. Belley's sash corresponds compositionally to the surface of the bust inscription; Belley's lower body, whose bulging hips are emphasized by the dark coat-tails, corresponds with the pedestal. The veins of the dark marble are a painterly equivalent to the veins in the representative's hands. Girodet plays the bust's representational form, which negates the bodies of important men as nature surmounted by the spirit, against the vibrantly exposed corporeality of the Black man. Though the masculine nakedness in the antique-like treatment of the bust points to the intellectuality of the person, which remains after his physical death, Girodet bestows upon the body of the representative a sensual energy, pulsating through the material of the European suit. The critic Chaussard crowned his praise of the 'simplicity' and 'magnitude' of the pose, which Girodet had given the representative, with the remark: *On sent les belles parties du nu sous l'habit même.*[20] This praise directed at the painter for his artistic ability in allowing us to 'sense' the beauty of the naked body in the painting of the clothed one, would have been just as impossible with any other portrait of a representative as it would have been unfitting for the model. While portrait painting, especially in the years of the French Revolution, establishes the authority of the masculinity of European politicians, military men, or intellectuals by negating the sensuality of the body, Girodet sexualizes the portrait of Belley by exhibiting his virility.

The index finger of his right hand points to his genitals, which shape the soft, yellow hose he is wearing and whose size brings to mind the European fantasy of the excessive sexuality of Africans. This sexualization of 'black masculinity' becomes clear in a comparison with a terse formulation of the new pictorial task of the portraits of the deputies. The portrait of Bertrand Barère de Vieuzac is today attributed to a student of David, J.J. Luneville, dated 1793 (Figure 5.7). It shows the Jacobin in his position as president of the National Assembly when on 4 January 1793 he reads out the indictment against Louis XVI. The emancipation of the men of the third estate from the 'slavery' of feudalism and superstition is legitimized as an act of self-liberation, relying upon treatise and law. The speaker's wooden bench, upon which the brief is lying, cuts across the lower body of the representative in the painting and diverts one's eye to that part whose delineation through the suit had captured the critics' notice in the portrait of Belley. Here, on the painted body of the parliamentary 'murderer of the king' Vieuzac, something else passes before the eyes of the viewer: The phallus is shifted from the body depicted to the script. This transformation of biological virility into phallogocentric law is opposed by the body of Belley in Girodet's portrayal. It is not so much the difference between the light and dark skins or the unpretentious and subtle colour contrasts in the suit, not the small, gold earring, which in contrast to Vieuzac and many other portraits of representatives, makes him a 'savage'. It is the difference in the construction of masculinity, which is in the one case presented as a corporeality in the painting and in the other case as its surmounting.

There is no doubt as to the immediate political message of the painting at the Salon of 1798. Girodet pleads for the 'freedom of the blacks' and their ability to assert civil rights, at a time when the growing influence of capital had again called this into question. His strongest argument is the ideal figure of the 'noble savage', which he superimposes over the portrait of Belley. The qualities he attributes to the African body in this pattern of interpretation, make his plea seem ambivalent, however. Granted, the African 'noble savage' had enjoyed a literary profile since Aphra Behn's novel *Oroonoko* in 1688, but it did not simply fit into the anthropological concepts of the enlightenment, for which what was 'noble' about the 'savage' was its alleged proximity to the original natural condition. Unlike the 'light-skinned' South Sea Islanders, whose erotic liberality was interpreted as their natural innocence, the blacks were considered as corrupted by European slavery and the ancient notion of their unbridled sexuality was rather associated with the threat of rebellion than childish innocence. Thus, the few portrayals of the 'noble black' in eighteenth-century paintings and graphic works divert the attention away from the body and toward the social role of the emancipated. Although 'blackamoor-servants' were racially-stereotyped as a symbol of wealth and pleasure in portrait and genre painting of the eighteenth century, blacks in portraiture were 'dark-skinned Europeans'. In 1768, for example, Thomas Gainsborough portrayed the former plantation slave

Figure 5.7 J.J. Luneville, *Bertrand Barère de Vieuzac demands a death sentence for Louis Capet,* 1793, (Kunsthalle Bremen)

Ignatius Sancho as a European intellectual. In 1770 in a portrait study of an anonymous black, Joshua Reynolds repressed the different physiognomic characteristics in favour of a mimic expression of English sentimentalism.[21] These portraits were supposed to prove that the 'physical difference of the Negro from the European', examined by S. Th. Sömmering,[22] was not at all a hindrance to acculturation. These blacks portrayed are not 'noble' because of their proximity to a fictitious natural condition, but rather because of their capability of being integrated into European culture. Girodet argues the opposite: Although Representative Belley has been socially integrated into the national *corp politique*, his body opposes this assimilation. By calling attention to the 'physical difference' rather than negating it, Girodet depicts Belley as the 'noble savage'. The underlying civilizational critique inherent to this perception clearly points out deficiencies in European masculinity: the loss of the physical. The idealization of black sexual masculinity will become part of the iconography of the romantic artists' revolt with works such as Johann Heinrich Füssli's *Avenged Negro* (1807), Theodor Gericault's *The Raft of the Medusa* (1809) and Eugène Delacroix's *The Death of Sardanapalus* (1827). The (insinuated) undisciplined vitality of the African body becomes a metaphor for protest against the discipline of the European.

The Marquis de Sade and Girodet

In de Sade's pornographic romance *La Philosophie dans le Boudoir* (1795), sodomy assumes a central role. It is the central model of debauchery as a radical transgression of norms that regulate the relationship of the individual to society. In this text, it stands for the liberation from despotism, for the revolutionizing of public customs and private morals, without which, according to de Sade, the democratic form of government only just attained could not be maintained. In the descriptive 'tableaux' of the sexual acts, sodomite practices dominate because they are considered to be the more passionate and stimulating. Dolmancé, 'sodomite par principe' teaches his student Eugénie about the privileged 'l'acte du libertinage': 'On la divise en deux classes, l'active et la passive: l'homme qui encule, soit un garçon, soit une femme, commet la sodomie active; il est sodomite passive quand il se fait fautre'.[23] In the chapter 'Français, encore un effort si vous voulez être republicains', the theoretical core of the novel, which plays upon the constitution of July 1795, de Sade defends 'le prétendu crime', because it is a natural inclination that the state should tolerate. The further argumentation, however, extends beyond the call for tolerance in two contradictory points. De Sade defends sodomy on grounds that it (a) creates the autonomy of the principle of lust in an act of excess and (b) because it is politically useful for the republic. He propagates the equality of all body parts and deems the differentiation of clean and unclean abstruse.[24] He makes fun of a population policy that proclaims the waste of semen a sin, although nature herself is highly indifferent to this.[25] De Sade grants privilege to the sodomite gesture in his catalogue of perversions because it most radically defends the natural urges of the individual against the institutions of family and state. In the outline of his culturally-relativistic history of homophile love and its universal occurrence, he raises it to a paradigm of republican manners and social thought. Sodomy is the pleasure of the great philosophers and heroes, and de Sade takes care to find the foremost authorities as proof of the usefulness of this vice in a republic – Plutarch, Strabo, Caesar, the Roman poets from Catullus to Vergil, Cook and Columbus, who found it in the egalitarian societies among the 'noble savages' in America and the South Seas. De Sade also finds no crime in feminine homosexuality and, referring to the Greeks as an example, emphasizes its uses for the male state interest. Pederasty had always been the vice of the republican brotherhoods and of warrior peoples, 'il donnait du courage et de la force, et qu'il servait à chasser les tyrans'.[26]

I would like to use *La Philosophie dans le Boudoir* for the inter-pretation of both paintings by Girodet, without suggesting in any way a type of illustrative connection. It is uncertain whether Girodet knew the text. It appeared anonymously in 1795 in Paris and disappeared 'without further ado into the collections of erotica of the nouveaux riches', to quote de Sade's biographer Pauvert.[27] The sense of a parallel reading cannot be to point out a social practice of homosexuality, which historians have reconstructed with other sources more suitable for this purpose. But de Sade sets the scene with such a clear discourse, placing homosexual desires in relationship to the nation and to republican customs, and this is the same thing Girodet also brings into painting with the aesthetic portrayal of difference and desire of the male body. With the simultaneous presentation of the paintings at the Salon of 1798, the allusions to the passive and active pederasty in *Endymion* and *Belley* were made clear, and so was the reference of these sexual practices to freedom and slavery as well as to the republic.

The subject was not at all limited to the off-limits area of pornography. Michel Foucault described the antique tradition that developed the philosophical discussion of pederasty from social and political aspects. The decisive section is the principle of isomorphism between sexual relationship and social relations.

[. . .] Departing from this, one can understand that in sexual behavior there is a role, which is esteemed honorable and completely positive: namely, the role of being active, of dominating, of penetrating and thus of establishing one's superiority. From out of this arise several consequences for the status of those who have to assume the passive role for this activity. Naturally, the slaves are at the disposal of their master: their position makes them sexual objects . . .'[28]

In Greek and Roman antiquity, it was in no way disgraceful for a free adult citizen to love a free youth or to use slaves for sexual purposes. But the sexual passivity of a free citizen who would allow himself to become a slave as an object of lust was considered to be very 'shameful'. 'In that world, classification was not according to gender – love of women, love of men – but according to activity and passivity', as Paul Veyne put it. 'To be active is to be male, no matter what gender the partner had who was regarded as passive'[29] The analogy between sexual practice and social order also applied to eighteenth-century France. Police reports about the Parisian homosexual scene between 1700 and 1750 differentiate – just like the antique philosophers – between active and passive sodomy. They record that the active role was normally assumed by the aristocracy, clerics and the wealthy, the passive by the plebeians, and that active sodomy was only regarded with slight moral disapproval while passive sodomy was regarded far more negatively.[30] The Enlightenment replaced the Biblical term 'sodomite' with 'pederast', which no longer refers to the Bible but to antiquity, and it came up with new linguistic constructions such as *le peché philosophique* or *le platonisme*. If sodomy was earlier the privilege of kings and the court, pederasty developed from about 1730 into an urban subculture, which was determined by aristocrats and bourgeois intellectuals.[31] Granted, the enlightenment chastized the 'aristocratic vice' as a feudal waste at the cost of population growth and shaped the masculinity of the father of the house against the negative image of the 'effeminate' aristocrat. By referring back to the Greek and Roman republics as an example for the present times, the problem gained new political dimensions, however – as the most revered *exempla virtutis* were given to the philosophic vice. Voltaire did use the aversion to the *peché infame* for his anti-clerical polemics, but he respected it in another place in a dictionary entry under the heading *amour nommé socratique* in connection with Alcibiades.[32] 'Just because Achilles loved Patroclus, Orestes loved Pylades, Aristogeiton loved Harmodius, Socrates loved Alcibiades etc. . . . were they of any less use to their country?' asks the republican Anarchasis Cloots.[33] De Sade praises the wisdom of Greek lawmakers, who outlawed *aucun genre de lubricité* to the citizens of

Sparta and Athens and he points out the philosophical hero of the revolution, Socrates: '. . . *le plus sage des philosophes de la terre, passant indifféremment des bras d'Aspasie dans ceux d'Alcibiade, n'en était pas moins la gloire de la Grèce.*'[34] When viewed before such a backdrop, the historical scene *Socrates tears Alcibiades from the arms of the hetaeras* (Paris, Louvre), shown by Jean Baptiste Regnault at the Salon in 1791, is not so much a plea for abstinence, as for pederasty, which serves the republic by contrast with the heterosexual debauchery.[35]

My attempt to interpret Girodet's portrayal of homoerotic desire in the *Endymion* and *Belley* using de Sade stems from the assumption that the author and the painter not only refer to the discourse of republican sodomy, but rather take subversive positions within the discourse. Both turn the social isometry of 'honourable' activity and 'shameful' passivity upside down. The libertine Dolmancé comments upon the question as to whether the active or the passive part gives more satisfaction in sodomite practices. Dolmancé assumes that both practices are equal, but thinks that the greater pleasure is to be had by the 'passive player', who offers himself to another man, who then treats him like a woman, a whore.[36] De Sade touches here upon the problem that, according to Foucault, bothered the antique authors the most. Even more shameful than having to endure the passive position is having to enjoy it. 'Their uneasiness referred to the object of desire, or more precisely, to this object, in as much as it was to become for its part, master in the desire which one was having with the others, as well as in the power which one exerts over oneself.' De Sade departs from this 'extreme of problematics': 'How is the object of desire to be turned into a subject which is master of his desires?'[37] In the *tableaux vivants* of debauchery that Dolmancé organizes systematically, men and women, aristocracy and plebeians, young and old, educated and uneducated assume every possible position of activity and passivity. The variations cancel out the social hierarchy of sexual activity and passivity. If each gender, each class, each age group can alternately carry out and enjoy each active and passive act, then the social order of a ruling 'subject of desire' and a ruled 'object of desire' no longer applies. Such an interchangeability of subject and object positions, of sexual activity and passivity is what Girodet is presenting in *Endymion*. Endymion is in no way a youthful ephebe, but rather a grown man who allows himself to become an object of desire and takes pleasure in it without loss of honour. The young Zephyr on the other hand, who would have a right to this passive position, is the active player. Before the background of this turning around of the logic of honour in republican male homosexual love, the question may again be asked: by whom can

Endymion be sodomized without being dishonoured? Whose object may he become without losing his standing as hero? Who takes the place of the moon goddess, who is the active subject, with whom the eye of the viewer identifies when gazing upon the male nude? I would suggest the following interpretation: The answer can only be the nation itself. The Jacobin Girodet in no way idealized the private pleasure of a *peché aristocratique* but rather the sacrifice for the revolution. He does not stage it – unlike David – as a self-denial in a stoic soldier's death, but rather as a homoerotic death out of love. The invisible collective subject, to whom Endymion conveys his body to be used passively and sensually, is the social 'upper strata', the state.

In the portrait of Belley Girodet accentuates phallic activity as a metaphor of social emancipation. Belley's affiliation with the French Nation means that he no longer – unlike the slaves, unlike women – needs to serve as passive object of desire. Being in possession of civil rights and his status as representative of the colony in the National Assembly make him a free man. With the set-up of relationships of republican male homosexual love – which interprets both the relationship of the citizens among themselves as well as each individual to the nation – Girodet at the same time marks the imperfection of Belley's freedom. He attributes a sexuality to his physical body, which denies any self-control. In the double-portrait of Belley and Raynal, the 'philosophical head', which corresponds to the 'philosophic vice', is European, the pleasure-taking body African. Granted, the portrait stylizes the emancipated slave into an 'active French citizen', but it denies him the necessary ability for this status to be 'master of his desires' (Foucault). Girodet's idealization of African physicality, which refuses assimilation, limits male autonomy. The uncontrollable self-will of the dark body legitimizes the European rule of reason.

Both *Endymion* and the portrait of the representative Belley cause a lot of confusion even today: A sensuous, passive hero and an unassimilated black represent the nation that still defines itself ideally as male, hetero-sexual and 'white'. It was from out of the criticism of these constructions of masculinity and nation that Girodet derived the 'originality' of his pictorial ideas. With them he presents the question as to whether a male, political subject position is not also possible without the servitude of one's own body. Within the framework of body and image policies in the French revolution, this question is always subversive. Girodet at the same time calls into question the biological nature of ethnicity and gender, which will regulate the membership of a nation in the nineteenth century and even beyond.

Notes

1 Bronfen, E. (1995), 'Weiblichkeit und Repräsentation – aus der Perspektive von Semiotik, Ästhetik und Psychoanalyse', in: Bußmann, H. and Hof, R. (eds) *Genus. Zur Geschlechterdifferenz in den Kulturwissenschaften*, Stuttgart, 408. Wenk, S. (1999), 'Geschlechterdifferenz und visuelle Repräsentation des Politischen', in: *Frauen, Kunst, Wissenschaft*, 27: 25.

2. Bordes, P. and Michel, R. (1988), *Aux Armes & Aux Arts! Les arts et la revolution 1789–1799*, Paris, 42. The authors report on Salon critiques.

3. Concerning the iconographic tradition, see Rubin, J.H. (1978), 'Endymion's dream as a myth of romantic inspiration', *Art Quarterly*, (Spring): 47.

4. Haskell, F., Penney, N. (1981), *Taste and the Antique: The Lure of Classical Sculpture 1500–1900,* London, 184, and 202, who document the history of the reception of the *Barberini Faun* and the *Vatican Ariadne*. Concerning the female nude in Renaissance painting, Hammer-Tugendhat, D. (1994), 'Körperbilder—Abbild der Natur? Zur Konstruktion von Geschlechterdifferenz in der Aktkunst der Frühen Neuzeit', in: *L'Homme. Zeitschrift für feministische Geschichtswissenschaft*, Year 5, 1: 45.

5. Crow, T. (1991), 'Revolutionary Activism and the Cult of Male Beauty in the Studio of David', in Fort, B. *Fictions of the French Revolution*, Evanston, 55.

6. Davis, W. (1994), 'The Renunciation of Reaction in Girodet's "Sleep of Endymion"', in Norman Bryson, N. (ed.) (1994), *Visual Culture. Images and Interpretations*, Hannover/London, 168.

7. Solomon-Godeau, A. (1993), 'Male Trouble: A Crisis in Representation', *Art History*, 16, (2): 286.

8. (1994), 'Ein Interview mit Tom Crow' *Texte zur Kunst*, 4: 69.

9. Solomon-Godeau, A. (1993), 'Male Trouble: A Crisis in Representation', *Art History*, 16, (2): 84, where the author points to an attempt, 'to escape sexual difference altogether' as a decisive step towards the 'masculinization of the visual culture of the elite'. Small, J. (1996), 'Making Trouble for Art History', *Art Journal*, 55, (4): 20, determines a connection between the sexualization of the male nude and the topics of exoticism. I am unable to follow his criticism that the feminist approach leads to a re-pathologization of male homosexuality. See also the differentiated thoughts concerning the aesthetics of body delineation for purposes of identity in Fend, M. (1997), 'Nebulöse

Identitäten. Girodet's Schlaf des Endymion', in: G. Härle (ed.), *Ikonen des Begehrens. Bildsprachen der männlichen und weiblichen Homosexualität in Literatur und Kunst*, Stuttgart.

10. Butler, J. (1995), *Körper von Gewicht*, Berlin 1995, 23. 'In this sense, therefore, the subject is constituted then by the power of exclusion and condemnation, by something which lends the subject a constituted exterior, a condemnable exterior, which basically lies "within" the subject as its internally-based rebuttal.' (Translation, e.v.)

11. Crow, T. (1991), 'Revolutionary Activism and the Cult of Male Beauty in the Studio of David', in Fort, B. *Fictions of the French Revolution*, Evanston, 74

12. Concerning the first sketches of male nude models in the so-called 'Carnet de Versailles', see Bordes, P. (1983), *Le Serment du Jeu de Paume de J. L. David*, Paris .

13. On the political dimensions of gender in the Hercules-iconography, see Schmidt-Linsenhoff, V. (ed.) (1989), *Sklavin oder Bürgerin?* Exhibition Catalogue of the Historisches Museum Frankfurt, 480f.

14. Exhibition catalogue (1972), *The Age of Neo-Classicism*, London, Cat. No. 106, 71; Honour, H. (1989), *The Image of the Black in Western Art, IV. From the American Revolution to World War I, 1. Slaves and Liberators,* Houston, 104. Weston, H.. (1994), 'Representing the right to represent. The Portrait of Citizen Belley, ex-representative of the colonies by A.L. Girodet', *Res. Anthropology and Aesthetics*, 26: 83.

15. Honour, H. (1989), *The Image of the Black in Western Art, IV. From the American Revolution to World War I, 1. Slaves and Liberators,* Houston, 322, note 267.

16. Benot, Y. (1989), *La Révolution francaise et la fin des colonies*, Paris, 254 states that Belley fought on the side of the Napoleonic army under General Leclerc, was sent back to France and deported then to the Belle Isle, where he died in 1805. A clearly arranged description of the slave-uprisings and of the war of independence of St. Domingue/Haiti within the context of the French Revolution is supplied by Bernecker, W.L. (1996), *Kleine Geschichte Haitis*, Frankfurt . Weston, H.. (1994), 'Representing the right to represent. The Portrait of Citizen Belley, ex-representative of the colonies by A.L. Girodet', *Res.Anthropology and Aesthetics*, 26: 83, describes the context in which Belley was politically active in Paris. Her historical reconstruction of Belley as politically active subject is convincing considering the literary sources used. What remains problematic, however, is the notion that Girodet's portrait is an

authentic portrait of the person because she overlooks the projected ideals on the part of the painter in his aesthetic staging.

17. Bordes, P. and Michel, R. (1988), *Aux Armes & Aux Arts! Les arts et al revolution 1789–1799*, Paris, 79.

18. A similar distancing from the emblem of the anti-slavery movement is taken by Johann Heinrich Füssli in his painting *The Avenged Negro*, 1807, Hamburger Kunsthalle. See Schmidt-Linsenhoff, V. (1997), 'Sklaverei und Männlichkeit um 1800', in Friedrich, A. (ed.),, *Projektionen. Rassismus und Sexismus in der Visuellen Kultur*, Marburg, 96.

19. Bordes, P. and Michel, R. (1988), *Aux Armes & Aux Arts! Les arts et al revolution 1789–1799*, Paris, 79

20. Bordes, P. and Michel, R. (1988), *Aux Armes & Aux Arts! Les arts et al revolution 1789–1799*, Paris, 79.

21. Concerning Thomas Gainsborough, *Ignatius Sancho*, 1768, Ottawa, National Gallery, see Honour, H. (1989), *The Image of the Black in Western Art, IV. From the American Revolution to World War I, 1. Slaves and Liberators,* Houston. On Joshua Reynolds, *Portrait-Study of a Black*, 1770, Exhibition catalogue, *Reynolds*. Royal Academy of Arts, London 1986, Cat. No. 77, 245 f.

22. Sömmering, S.T. (1785), *Über die körperliche Verschiedenheit des Negers vom Europäer*, Mainz/Frankfurt.

23. de Sade, D.A.F. (1968), *La Philosophie dans le Boudoir,* Oeuvres Complétes XXV, Paris, 113.

24. de Sade, D.A.F. (1968), *La Philosophie dans le Boudoir,* Oeuvres Complétes XXV, Paris, see note 22, 248–9.

25. de Sade, D.A.F. (1968), *La Philosophie dans le Boudoir,* Oeuvres Complétes XXV, Paris,, see note 22, 249 and 158.

26. de Sade, D.A.F. (1968), *La Philosophie dans le Boudoir,* Oeuvres Complétes XXV, Paris, see note 22, 252.

27. Pauvert, J.J. (1991), *Der göttliche Marquis, Leben und Werke*, Munich/Leipzig, 1099.

28. Foucault, M. (1984), *Sexualität und Wahrheit,* Vol. 2, Frankfurt, 273 (translation from the German, e.v.).

29. Veyne, P. (1982), 'Homosexualität im antiken Rom', in Ariès P., *Die Masken des Begehrens und die Metamorphosen der Sinnlichkeit*, Frankfurt, 43 (translation from the German, e.v.).

30. Rey, M. (1985), 'Parisian Homosexuals create a Lifestyle, 1700–1750. The Police Archives' in Maccubin, R. *Unauthorized sexual behaviour during Enlightenment, 18th Century Life*, special issue, 9: 179. See

also for what follows Coward, D.A. (1980), 'Attitudes to Homosexuality in 18th century France', *Journal of European Studies,* 10: 239.

31. Rey, M. (1985), 'Parisian Homosexuals create a Lifestyle, 1700–1750. The Police Archives' in Maccubin, R. *Unauthorized sexual behaviour during Enlightenment, 18th Century Life,* special issue, 9: 188. Coward, D.A. (1980), 'Attitudes to Homosexuality in 18th century France', *Journal of European Studies,* 10: 237.
32. Coward, D.A. (1980), 'Attitudes to Homosexuality in 18th century France', *Journal of European Studies,* 10: 241.
33. Cloots, A. (1979), *Ecrit Revolutionnaire, 1790–1794,* edited by Michel Duval, Paris, 124.
34. de Sade, D.A.F. (1968), *La Philosophie dans le Boudoir,* Oeuvres Complétes XXV, Paris, see note 22, 233
35. Sells, C. (1977), 'Socrate et Alcibiade de J.B. Regnault au Louvre', in *Revue du Louvre,* 354. See also Schmidt-Linsenhoff, V. (1991), 'Hercules als verfolgte Unschuld?' in: Daniela Hammer-Tugendhat and others *Die Verhältnisse der Geschlechter zum Tanzen bringen,* Marburg 1991.
36. de Sade, D.A.F. (1968), *La Philosophie dans le Boudoir,* Oeuvres Complétes XXV, Paris, see note 22, 113.
37. Foucault, M. (1984), *Sexualität und Wahrheit,* Vol. 2, Frankfurt, 286.

–6–

The Rule of Difference: Gender, Class and Empire in the Making of the 1832 Reform Act
Catherine Hall

This chapter is part of a wider project to develop an analysis of the relation between citizenship, nation and empire in nineteenth- and twentieth-century Britain.[1] It is presented as a schematic and provocative argument, setting an agenda for work that might be done rather than claiming to be a fully researched piece of historical writing.[2] The essay focuses on a key moment in the process of British nation formation – 1832, when the parliamentary franchise was significantly extended. The example that I am focusing on here is the national settlement represented by the English Parliamentary Reform Act of 1832. This was a politically decisive moment, when the basis of political citizenship changed. For two years the country was in turmoil, revolution was widely feared by the propertied classes and major changes took place in the organization of the franchise as a result. In 1832 217,000 voters were added to an electorate of 435,000, £10 householders in boroughs received the vote, pocket and rotten boroughs were significantly reduced in number, and the representation of the new industrial towns was increased. Approximately 1 in 5 adult men now had the vote in England and Wales in a population of 16 million.[3] At the same time it was specified for the first time that the franchise was granted to 'every Male Person of full Age, and not subject to any legal Incapacity'; the political citizen was formally named as masculine.[4]

A moment such as this can be seen as a defining instance in the life of a nation because although nations are always in process, always being made, there are particular defining moments, of key legislative change within the state, or military victory or defeat, for example, which can be utilised to examine the state of the nation. The particular sets of relations that preoccupy me here are those between subjects and citizens, nation, state and empire.

My argument is that a full understanding of nation making in the British context – the times when new conceptions of the nation were enshrined in institutions, legislation or political discourse and distinctive national identities engendered – depend on a grasp of a wider frame of empire. Nation, I suggest, as constituted in Britain in the nineteenth century, cannot be understood outside of empire. Anderson's thesis on the imagined community of the nation has been widely accepted but it has been much harder to persuade historians of nations and nationalisms that those communities and identities are gendered. Meanwhile, historians influenced by feminism and open to the significance of gender as a category of analysis have often been reluctant to take on other axes of differentiation such as race or ethnicity. However, nations and national identities are not only gendered – they are also raced, and racialized identities are central to the construction of imagined polities. The British Empire played a crucial part in defining the boundaries of the nation – what was the outside and what was the inside, who belonged where and in what ways, who were citizens and who were subjects. At one level such an argument is hardly new. C.L.R. James argued in *The Black Jacobins* in 1938 that French metropolitan politics were shaped by the colonial and vice versa. Frantz Fanon insisted that the making of the colonized was also about the making of Europe, of the colonizers.[5] For the most part, however, such insights have until recently only been used by the colonized. Feminist, post-colonial and post-structuralist approaches to history writing have opened up new ways of thinking about the relation between nation and empire and some historians have begun to try to put together the histories of colonizer and colonized.[6] At the same time the contemporary rediscovery of ethnicity, assumed by the great social theorists of the nineteenth century to be a form of social division that would gradually lose its salience in the constitution of modern ethnically mixed societies, has resulted in an explosion of work on ethnicity in the global world and a renewed interest amongst historians in ethnicity. British history, once constructed around a homogenized idea of the nation in which Welsh, Scots and Irish were rarely considered, has become much more contested as the claims of four nations to their separate but related histories have been absorbed.[7]

Empire, of course, means a number of different things. By the end of the Napoleonic Wars the British empire had made an astonishing recovery from the dark days following the loss of the north American colonies. By 1820, it is estimated, 26 per cent of the world population lived within British territories.[8] The constituent parts of that Empire figured very differently in nineteenth century metropolitan debates over appropriate forms of colonial rule. White settler colonies, Australia and Canada for example, lands constituted as 'empty' where indigenous populations were expected to die out, were constructed as colonies in the proper sense, offshoots of the mother country, were granted representative forms of government and were moving towards dominion status by the end of the century. Dependencies, territories with majority black populations, were seen very differently. In the 1830s enthusiastic abolitionists looked forward to freed slaves becoming political citizens but that vision declined in the wake of rebellions across the empire, particularly the 'Indian Mutiny' of 1857 and the Jamaican rebellion of 1865.[9] The time of political maturity for black people was seen to lie far ahead. Britain must shoulder its burden of responsibility and rule those who were unfit to rule themselves. Partha Chatterjee analyses this system of government as 'the rule of colonial difference', a rule predicated on the power of the metropolis over 'its' subject peoples. The premise of the colonial state, he argues, was 'the preservation of the alienness of the ruling group'.[10]

'The rule of colonial difference' helps us to think about the ways in which power is exercised by colonizers over some of the colonized. But white settler colonies, it must be remembered, have a somewhat differently inflected history with the ruling group being the white settlers. If different sites of Empire make it imperative to recognize different forms of colonial rule, it is also worth reflecting on the ways in which political power is exercised 'at home', by some men over others and by some men over women and what the connections are between one form of rule and another. 'The rule of difference' might be a way of conceptualizing the hierarchies that are created through gender and class hierarchies as well as ethnic and racial hierarchies and which cut across both nation and empire.[11] Grasping the complexity of 'the unequal relations among/ between peoples' requires something more than a simple focus on the binary oppositions of colonizer/colonized, male/female, aristocracy/ middle class.[12] Such binaries were continually threatened with dissolution as they crosscut and intersected with others: enslaved men were freed in 1834 and won their masculinity. Like their colonizers they acquired the right to have women and children as their dependants. Aristocratic women could vote neither before nor after 1832 but had the opportunities to exercise immense informal influence over other classed subjects both male and female. Irish Catholic men won the right to enter Parliament in 1829 but many had the franchise taken from them at the very same time because they were Irish and Catholic. These were the complexities of the 'rule of difference', differences encoded through gender, property, religion and race, differences that resulted in both formal and informal inequalities and which operated both at the level of the state (political citizenship) and the nation (the cultural identities associated with different kinds of belonging). It is the organization and interplay of these differences at a moment of national definition that this essay seeks to explore. To suggest that the moment of 1832 was about exclusion and differentiation is, of course, not new; but the classical accounts have focused on questions of class exclusion. My insistence on the salience of other kinds of difference may open up new understandings.

Linda Colley in *Britons* suggests that between 1707–1837 it was the experience of war that was crucial to the forging of a new nation, uniting English, Scots, Welsh and Irish in the late eighteenth and early nineteenth centuries, welding them into a new entity, Britain, characterized by its commitment to Protestantism and to its monarch, its powerful anti-Catholicism, and its long-term enmity with France.[13] This argument has its critics but it provides a powerful narrative of nation-building.[14] Colley sees the nation as redefined by the early 1830s. Re-defined by the inclusion of Catholics, through Catholic emancipation; by Parliamentary reform which resulted in very substantial changes and made the nation more uniformly British than it had previously been, and considerably more democratic than any other European country; and by the movement for anti-slavery that offered a new source of self-respect to the nation in the aftermath of the loss of the American colonies. 'Successful abolitionism became one of the vital underpinnings', she argues, 'of British supremacy in the Victorian era, offering as it seemed to do, irrefutable proof that British power was founded on religion, on freedom and on moral calibre, not just on a superior stock of armaments and capital'.[15]

I welcome Colley's attention to Catholicism and anti-slavery as well as the more familiar question of political reform but my reading is different. The idea of the nation, I suggest, enshrined as it was in these moments of political settlement, was always fragile. It depended on the construction of an imagined entity, a political and social body, held together on the basis of a series of inclusions and exclusions of different groups, locked momentarily in complex hierarchies presenting an illusion of homogeneity but always threatening dissolution. These hierarchies operated across the imagined empire as well as the nation, securing the rights of some Englishmen in relation to Irish Catholics, or slaves about to be freed in Jamaica, or women, or the English poor. My object of study is the hierarchies that were constructed and constantly reworked along the axes of race, ethnicity and gender as well as class, securing the boundaries of subject and citizen, 'mother country' and colony, nation and empire and securing it through 'the rule of difference'.

The year 1832 offers an opportunity to reflect on the nation as it was framed at that point: how were citizens defined, in the sense of those who had the right to vote and participate in government, who belonged and in what ways, who were the imagined insiders and who were the outsiders, what political and cultural identities were being constituted? The debates of 1829–32, which took place inside and outside of Parliament, were concerned with defining the different ways of belonging to the nation, 'drawing the lines'. But the relation between nation and empire was also at issue. Questions as to the rights of subjects were seriously debated, a quite different category from that of political citizen, defining forms of subjecthood as well as citizenship and what the hierarchies were within those categories. Class, race, ethnicity and gender were all crucially in play in these debates and provided the lines on which boundaries could be drawn up, and different social groups included or excluded from the imagined community of the nation/empire. That nation/empire had both a political definition - those who were citizens of the nation state, and the notion of a body politic which was monarchical and into which all subjects were born, but enjoyed particular and differentiated forms of cultural belonging.

The idea of the citizen drew on two major traditions of political thought – the classical or republican, which drew on the world of classical Greece and Rome, and the liberal with its foundational moment in seventeenth-century England. In nineteenth-century Britain and its Empire there was no legal category 'citizen', although the language of citizenship was frequently invoked in debates over political rights and duties. The claim for citizenship, inflected through the traditions of revolutionary France, was a claim to put limits on subjecthood, to play a part in government, to make authority responsible to 'the people', however that was defined. Political citizenship, the right to vote, was gradually won by most white British men in the nineteenth century and even by some men of colour such as the Maori. White British women did not win it until the twentieth century. Although citizenship was contested, the peoples of the British Isles and the British Empire were formally equal subjects of the Crown, subject to the rule and protection of the law. In practice subjects were differentiated: a white subject in England had a different status from an indigenous subject in Canada or Australia, a white settler in New Zealand or the racialized subjects of India or the West Indies. All subjects were not the same, as Indian rebels learned to their cost in 1857 and Jamaican rebels in 1865.[16] But the differentiations were informal rather than formal, part of the British 'rule of difference', based on practice. It was not until the mid-to-late twentieth century that these differences were legally codified, at a time when decolonization made clarification urgently necessary.[17]

The debates over the nation were framed by empire, for it was impossible to think about the 'mother country' and its specificities without reference to the colonies. 'The nation' existed through the boundaries that were drawn. Boundaries with Europe were also crucial, as Linda Colley argues in relation to France and Maura O'Connor in relation to Italy.[18] But my concern here is with empire – not to deny the significance of traditional enemies, or of deep identifications with aspirant nations, but to insist on the linked histories of metropolis and colonies. Those colonies provided some of the benchmarks that allowed the English to imagine the particular character of the English nation. In 1832 the construction of imagined others in Ireland, that most particular colony that was also a part of the United Kingdom, and in Jamaica, once the jewel in the crown of the British Caribbean, played a part in the temporary settlements, marked by the Reform Acts, as to who was to belong politically to the nation and what other kinds of subjects there were.

Empire/Ethnicity

Two significant events preceded the Reform Act of 1832. The first was Catholic Emancipation in 1829, widely recognized as critical to the formation of a new nation, the second was the slave rebellion which broke out in Jamaica at Christmas, 1831. Each had its aftermath in the new Whig settlement: the Irish Coercion Act of 1833 and the attempt to reform the Irish church, to be followed by the 1836 Commission to Inquire into the State of the Irish Poor in England and the act which abolished slavery in most British colonies from 1 August 1834. What was the place of these dramas in the constitution of the imagined nation?

Relations between England and Ireland had been problematic from the twelfth century. The Act of Union of 1800 meant that Ireland became an integral part of the United Kingdom, different from any other colony in that it was represented in the House of Lords and the House of Commons. Indeed, there were one hundred Irish MPs in the Commons. Ireland was not a colony juridically, yet it was a colony in that Irish Catholics in Ireland were treated as a conquered people and English Protestants in Ireland acted as colonial settlers. Since its invasion by the Anglo-Normans there had been systematic attempts to control and exploit the island on a permanent basis from the sixteenth century, parallel to colonial ventures in north America. Although ruled as a separate kingdom until 1800, anyone born there was regarded as a natural-born subject in

England but this carried with it no notion of common rights. From the earliest days assumptions about the barbaric nature of the Irish were used to justify English rule and anti-Irish racism was based on notions of biological difference, laced with a cultural racism associated with anti-Catholicism.[19] The constitutional union of 1800 was a consequence of the radical and nationalist rebellion of 1798 and the fears that had been generated of an Irish/French alliance, not to speak of the presence of Irish radicals in England. The Union attempted 'a structural answer to the Irish problem, with overtones of "moral assimilation" and expectations that an infusion of English manners would moderate sectarianism'.[20] One of the effects of this junction of a rapidly industrializing economy with an agricultural one was that Ireland became a country supplying cheap food and labour to England and migration increased steadily, swelling the Irish presence in the ports of London, Liverpool and Glasgow and spreading into the new towns.

The question of Catholic emancipation, of the granting of full civil rights to Catholics, was not new in the late 1820s but was given new urgency in England by the Union. Indeed, many Catholics were under the impression that it had been promised as part of the settlement. The Union had resulted in a closeness between Ulster Presbyterians and the Anglo-Irish of the established Church, now committed together to the maintenance of the new status quo. 'Ruling through Dublin Castle', argues historian James Reynolds, 'they still looked upon themselves as England's garrison, withstanding the pretensions of the "mere Irish", potential rebels who protested through a handful of noisy agitators'.[21] But the Union meant that the 'Irish question' had come to Westminster and Irish Catholics had new hopes. The emancipation of Catholics in England would have been relatively unproblematic, they were few in number and mostly quiet in disposition. But Irish Catholics with their majority status in Ireland as an oppressed community, taxed for a state Church that was not their own, were another matter. The idea of religious toleration including civil and political rights had gained support amongst some in England. The year 1828 saw the repeal of the Test and Corporation Act, which had been ineffective for many years but was still on the statute book and excluded Protestant Dissenters from public office. A powerful nonconformist pressure group including Congregationalists, Baptists and Unitarians had campaigned unceasingly for this: it meant the open abandonment of the principle that membership of the state Church was a prerequisite for full citizenship under the British constitution.[22] This had clear implications for Catholics and Jews. In 1830 the question of whether Jews could be admitted to Parliament was to be raised. Were the Jews 'a people', could they become Englishmen?[23] Here was another difficult instance of the relation between religious and political belonging. In a society in which Church and state were intimately connected and the monarch was the head of the Church, what place was there for subjects with a prior loyalty to the Pope? Given their commitment to Rome how could Catholics become *political citizens*?

But Ireland was a very special case and the Catholic question became the most pressing political question of the 1820s. As a correspondent of Peel wrote in 1827, it was 'mixed up with every thing we eat or drink or say or think'.[24] The peculiar relation between Britain and Ireland was at the heart of this. Ireland's geographical proximity to England had always given it a special status and made it a site of danger in times of acute hostility. Irish migrant labour had long played a part in the English economy. The new feature of the post-Union period was that these migrants settled provoking a set of issues about Irishmen in England, just as the settlement of decolonized Afro-Caribbean and South Asian men and women disrupted the balance of the nation in the 1950s and 1960s. Meanwhile there was severe economic unrest in Ireland and a series of crises in public order. Ribbonism, an anti-Protestant secret movement, with nationalist overtones, celebrating tradition and custom and strongly based amongst Dublin artisans as well as the rural poor, caused considerable trouble to the colonial rulers. From 1823 the Catholic Association, an open and accountable mass movement, funded by the 'Catholic rent' of a penny a month, masterminded by the brilliant speaker and publicist Daniel O'Connell, and representing many middle-class Catholics as well as the peasantry, organized on behalf of Catholic tenants, churches and the Catholic community. The movement was 'a colossus of democratic power', argues Reynolds, 'unprecedented in the annals of political organization in the British Isles'.[25]

Mobilizing the Catholic population across parish, town and county, a pyramidal structure commanded from the headquarters at the Dublin Corn Exchange, heavily dependent on the parish clergy to discipline the flock, the Catholic Association constituted the Irish as a Catholic nation, unified by the theme of 'know your wrongs', by the press, that potent medium for national imaginings, and by the determination that emancipation should be won. By 1828 it had a membership of 15,000 and three million associate members in a population of six and a half million. O'Connell's leadership was crucial. A magnificent orator he could move between the pathetic and the savage, the rough and the sublime, the bitter and the funny. Clearly 'native Irish' in his appearance his masculinity was on display. He was, argues Reynolds, 'a master of persuasion'. In the country he was witty, scurrilous, handsome, cocking his eye here and there to 'his boys' as he strode to the platform. As a French traveller commented, 'O'Connell is of the people. He is a mirror in which Ireland sees herself complete, or rather he is Ireland herself'.[26] This manly man, the 'Liberator' as he came to be named, had the capacity to speak for and symbolize the nation, a nation always characterized as feminine. His masculinity could embrace Hibernia, symbolizing the unity of the heterosexual couple, drawing in the ladies and women who attended the Catholic Association meetings in large numbers and supported the demand that Catholic men should be able to sit in Westminster.[27] O'Connell's masculinity was crucial to his leadership for the power of the Association rested on the fear that it generated, the fear of violence, of a people armed, of the anarchy of the Ribbonmen being displaced by a much more widespread mobilization. His favourite quote from Lord Byron:

> Hereditary bondsmen, know ye not
> Who would be free themselves must strike the blow?[28]

depended on the image of the nation arising, a vision that was being pursued vigorously in other parts of the world and that linked Ireland to nationalist and anti-colonial struggles across the globe.

From the later 1820s the Association focused on electoral influence, seeking pledges, vetting parliamentary candidates and utilizing to the full the 40 shilling freeholder vote that existed in Ireland. The spectre behind their influence was that of mass disobedience, of incendiarism and of the loss of authority of the colonial state. Liberal Anglo-Irish Protestants who were afraid of any further destabilization were willing to go along with emancipation and the Whigs supported it in the imperial Parliament. O'Connell, though pre-eminently a Catholic leader, was always cognisant of the importance of Protestant support.

The election of O'Connell himself, in a by-election in County Clare in 1828, brought the issue of emancipation to a head. Catholics were eligible to stand for Parliament but could not take their seats because of the oath that was required. It was clear that there would be major troubles in Ireland if Catholic demands were not met: the spectre of large numbers of Catholics being elected and forming a shadow parliament loomed. The Irish military Commander-in-Chief warned that reinforcements would be necessary if the crisis were not resolved and the government decided to concede. Wellington bit the bullet as a military man and Peel was persuaded to do his duty to his monarch and to take the Bill through the Commons. There was a real possibility that delays would lead to a wider struggle for national rights, the break-up of the Union and a linkage to questions of parliamentary reform in Britain. As O'Connell argued in 1827: 'My object is to make one step at least in the amelioration of mankind by carrying Emancipation. This measure would reconcile Ireland to England. If it is not carried soon these countries will certainly separate.' There were serious worries about the loyalty of the army and Peel, as Home Secretary, was deeply worried about security. As Wellington put it to Peel, the choice was between restraints 'unknown in the ordinary practice of the constitution' and concession. Such restraints, on a white population so close to Britain, were not imaginable. An attempt was made to limit the effects of emancipation by raising the level of the Irish county franchise from 40shs to £10 thus reducing the number of Catholic electors in Ireland from 100,000 plus to around 16,000.[29]

The overwhelming popular sentiment in England was anti-Catholic. Persistent themes in this included objections to the celibacy of the priesthood, to the power of Rome which was seen as inimical to the monarchy and the liberties of the nation and the individual, and to the 'sacrifice of the mass'. Enormous numbers of petitions were organized against emancipation, particularly from the centres of Irish settlement in England, with a high level of participation from women and the poor.[30] Petitioning was one of the ways in which women could claim an engagement with political affairs. They might not be able to vote but they could express their identification with a certain definition of the imagined nation through their hostility to emancipation. For some Protestant men it may have been easier to be tolerant given their acceptance in the public sphere. Brunswick Clubs, similar to the Orange Order and Pitt Clubs, were organized both in England and Ireland, committed to the maintenance of Protestant power. But they were never able to mobilize opinion to the degree that they could prevent government concession. Anti-Catholicism was certainly endemic but according to its historian it was a passive rather than an active force.[31] No sooner was the Act passed than Protestant militants began to exert themselves to revivify their cause. Catholic emancipation, as Best has remarked, far from providing a settlement between Catholics and Protestants, increased conflict and convinced Protestants that they must defend their position.[32]

The attitudes of the governing classes had softened towards Catholics: as Colley notes they had proved their patriotism in the wars, they were no longer a danger and could be included.[33] Nevertheless, the king was deeply reluctant to agree to emancipation given his position as head of the church and his family were even more opposed. But the inclusion was a guarded one. A greatly reduced number of Catholic males could now vote, enter Parliament and hold civil office. They were still excluded from the old universities and from the highest legal office. What was given with one hand was taken away with another: only some Catholics were deemed safe. O'Connell's movement had ensured emancipation but anti-Catholicism was still rife and the figure of the Irish rebel continued to haunt the English imagination. Irish Catholics were both within and without the nation: some were political citizens but their subjecthood was framed by Irishness, their forms of cultural belonging to that nation strictly limited.

This ambivalent relation was played out in the months preceding and following the Reform Act. As George Rudé argues, the worst popular disturbances leading up to 1832 were in Ireland. There were food riots in Limerick and Roscommon, land hunger and tithe wars in the South and West, nightly assaults from Whiteboys, Ribbonmen and followers of Captain Rock.[34] In 1831 Lord Lieutenant Anglesey believed that 'the fate of Ireland hangs upon a thread . . . a false movement may involve us in insurrection'.[35]

Yet the Reform Act for Ireland, as Theodore Hoppen has demonstrated, resulted in a much more limited extension of the franchise than in England. While in England and Wales about one in every 17 town dwellers enjoyed the vote in 1833, the Irish proportion was only one in 26. This disparity was even more marked in the counties.[36] When the first reformed Parliament met, Ireland dominated the agenda. The further deterioration of law and order, described by Halévy as 'a condition of sheer lawlessness', with 9,000 crimes in 1832 including 568 acts of incendiarism, 290 cases of cattle maiming and 242 murders, was causing serious concern.[37] A draconian Coercion Bill, including the suspension of Habeus Corpus, was proposed alongside measures of church reform intended to ameliorate Catholic grievances. Catholic men could now enter some public offices, but many Irish Catholic men had lost the franchise. Catholic Irish women had succeeded in their campaigning on behalf of their men. Protestant women had failed in their petitions but had claimed the right to intervene in the public sphere. It was the 'rule of difference' that articulated these paradoxical instances on the site of the imagined nation.

Empire/Race

The British had colonized Jamaica in 1655. The white settlers soon started to plant sugar, which was already successfully grown in Barbados, and brought in slaves to work the plantations. They won the right to their own form of government, an elected House of Assembly, subject to the authority of the crown and the imperial Parliament in the person of the governor. By the late eighteenth century West Indian planters were very effectively represented at Westminster through their connections in both the House of Commons and the House of Lords, and the West India Committee operated as a powerful and effective pressure group.[38] The emergence of an anti-slavery movement in the 1780s meant that the plantocracy became increasingly concerned about their interests and the Colonial Office, created in 1794, was subject to intense lobbying from both sides.[39]

Following the long struggle over the campaign to abolish the slave trade, which finally succeeded in 1807, the wars had dominated the public mind closely followed by the re-emergence of radicalism in the postwar years. By the early 1820s it was clear that the abolition of the slave trade had not effected an end to slavery and that the policy of amelioration, intended to reduce the harshness of plantation life, was not working either. A new anti-slavery campaign was orchestrated. Led by evangelicals and Quakers the anti-slavery movement had extensive support across classes and organized as a very effective pressure group. It was women campaigners who began to insist on a radical shift in the demands of the movement and a commitment to immediate abolition. Although formally excluded from citizenship, women such as Elizabeth Heyrick identified themselves as political subjects with political responsibilities in the public world.[40] In Parliament a number of the most prominent supporters of anti-slavery, such as Brougham and Macaulay, were also supporters of electoral reform and the opponents of reform tended to be opponents of abolition, as, for example, the Duke of Wellington, Lord Harewood and Viscount Chandos.[41] By 1831 it was clear that, however strong the support for anti-slavery was in the country, it could not succeed in Parliament given the power of the West India interest, the veto of the Lords and the antipathy of the king. Anti-slavery and reform became necessarily intertwined.

Christmas 1831 saw the outbreak of a major slave rebellion in Jamaica. As the largest of the British West Indian islands Jamaica had dominated the debates over slavery since the 1780s. The presence of a very active group of dissenting missionaries on the island in the 1820s ensured that their stories of the horrors of slavery competed in the British press with the West India interest's assurances of the benevolent intentions of the planters and the good conditions in which slaves worked. The rebellion that broke out on 27 December was the largest in the history of the island. All of the western parishes were affected, the sugar harvest was destroyed and more than one million pounds worth of damage was done to property.

The rebellion was organized by men who were Christian converts and who used the established network of the mission meetings, took inspiration from the Bible, and claimed the dissenting missionaries as their allies. Led by the enslaved Baptist deacon Sam Sharpe they were convinced that the Bible taught that slaves were entitled to freedom and they must organize to overthrow the system. They proclaimed the natural equality of man and denied on the Bible the right of white men to hold black men in bondage. Although there was a long history of resistance by black women to slavery, rebellion focused on armed struggle put men in the forefront.[42]

The slaves, as Mary Turner argues, turned Christianity into a revolutionary ideology, which was far from the intentions of the missionaries and which they did their best to disassociate themselves from.[43] The plantocracy, who had been ruling the island since the seventeenth century through the House of Assembly in conjunction with the London appointed Governor, responded brutally to the rebellion and the slaves were summarily dealt with in ways that would have been unthinkable in Ireland. There was particular fury with the missionaries for the planters blamed them for 'the Baptist War' as it was named, assuming that slaves could not have masterminded such an event themselves. The brutality of the revenge exacted on both slaves and missionaries resulted in numbers of missionaries refusing the apolitical stance of their societies and coming out in public in favour of abolition. William Knibb, a Baptist missionary on the island, was sent to England by his brethren to make their case and became a powerful speaker in the cause of abolition both in lecture tours across the country and to the Select Committees of both Commons and Lords on slavery.

The slave rebellion had been preceded by a long period of agitation by free men, both coloured (the contemporary term for mixed-race) and black, who sought civil rights from the House of Assembly in Jamaica. They had been in correspondence with anti-slavery leaders and had sought support from the British government against the Jamaican plantocracy. They eventually received the same rights as white men on the island on November 1830. The plantocracy had hoped to enlist them against abolition by this late concession but their ploy failed and the free men of colour supported slaves and missionaries in the aftermath of the rebellion.[44] This enabled the imperial government to suppress what had become in effect a white planter rebellion, involving the destruction of chapels and attacks on missionaries. Civil war threatened on the island but the Colonial Office decided on a show of strength, white resistance was defeated and the acceptance of emancipation was assured.[45]

The rebellion was crucial to abolition in the imperial Parliament for the events had alerted the Commons to the fear of a successful slave uprising. In April and May of 1832 the news had arrived in England of the persecution of the missionaries and there was increasing awareness of the scale of atrocities in the period of martial law after the rebellion. A great Anti-Slavery Society Convention was held in London, which coincided with 'the Days of May' when the House of Lords had blocked the third Reform Bill and the country rose in protest. The Convention petitioned Parliament and Buxton, the anti-slavery leader in the House of Commons, presented a resolution demanding immediate emancipation and inquiring what the government would do if faced with a general insurrection of the negroes. A parliamentary committee was established to consider the most practical way to free the slaves. In the election campaign of 1832, following the passing of the Reform Act, anti-slavery societies across the country demanded that candidates should commit themselves to emancipation and 104 of the new MPs subscribed to this pledge.[46] Many of the West Indian proprietors had recognized that they could not sustain order and that they would do better to fight for the best compensation deal they could drive through. In the king's speech following the election no mention was made of abolition: again the anti-slavery forces were mobilized and this time slavery was abolished, part of the reforming agenda of the new Whig government that had been elected.

Slaves were freed by the Imperial Parliament and by the colonial Houses of Assembly from 1 August 1834. Male and female slaves were partially freed, named apprentices for a fixed term, to be prepared for full adulthood and free labour, to learn the ways of freedom. The men were welcomed into masculinity, for as slaves they had lacked its key constituent in the English imagination – independence. The women were now to become wives, daughters and mothers, dependents of men, secure within the family.[47] All were to be full subjects of the British empire, no longer subject to the arbitrary power of their masters and with the same rights as other British subjects: to the rule of the monarchy and the law. In 1834 the Colonial Office believed that in due course freed black men, black subjects, would become political citizens.[48] For the moment, however, black men were represented as children, to be educated for adulthood. It was propertied white and coloured men who continued to be represented in the island's House of Assembly and the plantocracy continued to frustrate the feeble efforts of the Colonial Office to introduce even minor reforms that would have improved the opportunities for freed slaves. The 'rule of difference' in Jamaica meant that white men continued to rule over black, that coloured men were politically represented but still marginalized and that black women were now to be the property of their husbands, as one anti-slavery activist put it, rather than of their masters.[49] White women owned property and exercised power over employees and servants, but as women they were judged secondary to men.[50]

Nation/Class/Gender

While the British Parliament debated Ireland and Jamaica its major preoccupation throughout this period was with domestic political reform. Historians have interpreted this history in a number of ways, from the traditional Whig narrative, inaugurated by Macaulay, of the 'young energy of one class against the ancient privileges of another' and the capacity of the English to adapt and reform in time and save the country from revolutionary change, to those Marxist accounts that have focused on questions of class struggle.[51] In E.P. Thompson's magisterial narrative, for example, the level of agitation amongst both middle and working classes in favour of parliamentary reform in 1832 led to a capitulation of the monarchy and landed aristocracy in the face of the fear of revolution. But only the middle classes benefited, a betrayal that led to the development of Chartism.[52] More recently political historians have emphasized that public opinion made reform inevitable, that the Whigs did not legislate out of fear but out of a recognition that the middle classes had to be taken into account. As Lord Grey put it,

> A great change has taken place in all parts of Europe since the end of the war in the distribution of property, and unless a corresponding change be made in the legal mode by which that property can act upon the governments, revolutions must necessarily follow. The change requires a greater influence to be yielded to the middle classes, who have made wonderful advances both in property and intelligence.

The principle of his bill, Grey told the House of Lords, was 'to prevent the necessity of revolution'. Far from this meaning the passing of power from the aristocracy to the middle classes, however, this was in the words of Ian Newbould, 'the magnates' attempt to maintain the territorial aristocracy in greatness'.[53] The new narratives of historians influenced by post-structuralism have questioned such certainties about the categories of class. 'It was not so much the rising "middle class" that was the crucial factor in bringing about the Reform Act of 1832', argues Dror Wahrman, 'as it was the Reform Bill of 1832 that was the crucial factor in cementing the invention of the ever rising "middle class"'.[54] The Reform Act gave the middle class its solidity, provided the endpoint of a social transformation, was 'an important catalyst in the decisive transformation of people's conceptions of their society'.[55]

It was in the summer of 1830 that reform agitation became widespread, linked to the tide of rural protest and violence in Southern England. Revolutions had taken place in France and in Belgium, raising the cry of political liberties across Europe. Agricultural disturbances broke out in Kent. Farmers had tried to replace English labourers with Irish, and English farmhands had expelled the Irish by force, inspired, Halévy argues, by the example of France.[56] In 1831 there were serious revolts in a number of English counties, the Captain Swing riots, with crowds of labourers demanding higher wages, destroying machinery and property. Villages provided the base for these activities and itinerant bands of men were engaged in arson, threatening letters, meetings about wages, attacks on overseers, parsons and landlords and the destruction of machinery. Sometimes the men 'blacked up' and went out at night for cover; at other times the riots were theatrical, public performances of the labourers' demands. In the account of Hobsbawm and Rudé it was a men's movement of primarily young men or those in their early middle age, a high proportion of whom were married and trying to support women and children. The power of their actions depended always on the threat of violence, although very little actual violence took place. The judicial reaction was swift: 19 were hanged, 644 jailed and 481 transported to Hobart and Sydney. Only two women seem to have been included in these figures, both were transported and one was condemned in part on account of her known sexual practices.[57]

The political agitation that was spreading through the country did not make links with these agricultural labourers who remained outside of the reform process and the debates over full membership of the nation. Political unions focused on questions of liberty and freedom as in the slogan of the Birmingham Political Union:

> We raise the watchword, Liberty
> We will, we will, we will be free.[58]

Birmingham was a hotbed of anti-slavery activity as well as of anti-Catholicism and the language of freedom appeared to connect the claims of freeborn Englishmen, enslaved to the aristocracy and corrupt forms of government, with the claims of plantation slaves. They also connected the claims of the reformers with those of the Irish. Thomas Attwood, the leader of the Birmingham Political Union, had learned from the Catholic Association and consulted with O'Connell. But the Irish were not the same as the English and slaves were not freemen: the symbolic condition of slavery, the white slavery of artisans and factory hands, frequently evoked by the radicals, had little connection with the slaves in the British Caribbean. Many radicals were profoundly unsympathetic to the abolitionists who they saw as hypocritical, shedding tears for 'negroes' abroad whilst exploiting their 'slaves' at home.[59] Abolitionists meanwhile, believed that black slaves in the West Indies needed their liberty won for them by freedom-loving Britons.[60] Freedom had many meanings, meanings which were articulated through the rule of difference.

Before long the reform agitation had spread across the country. The radical George Edmonds in Birmingham drew on images of Irishness to characterise the struggle:

> Like the wild Irish of old, the British millions have been too long insolently placed without the pale of social governments ... I now speak the thoughts of my unrepresented fellow millions, the wild English, the free-born slaves of the nineteenth century ...

The claim made by 'the British millions', the 'free-born slaves' was for the equality of citizenship, personal dignity and worth, for a place in the political world, understood by most as a world of men. The right to vote should no longer be associated with property, 'Instead of bricks, mortar and dirt, MAN ought to be represented'.[61]

The great majority of those active were artisans and working men but middle-class reformers were often in key positions of leadership. By May 1831 the Duke of Wellington feared that the revolution had begun. 'I cannot see what is to save Church, or property, or colonies, or Union with Ireland', he wrote.[62] The riots which took place in Nottingham, Derby and the three days of serious disorder in Bristol in October 1831, cast the spectre of revolution even more vividly. There were fears that the army could not be relied on. Alexander Somerville, serving with the Scots Greys in Birmingham recorded in his autobiography the command that they were to 'rough sharpen' their swords on the day of the great gathering of the Unions at Newhall Hill when 2,000 met to demand reform. 'On this memorable Sunday', he wrote, 'we sharpened our swords to prevent these new boroughs from obtaining any representatives'. But a rumour had been industriously spread and conveyed to the highest quarters . . . founded on a well-determined resolution of certain soldiers that the army was not to be relied on, if the constitutional voice of the country was attempted to be suppressed by the unconstitutional use of military power.[63]

In these circumstances the presence of middle-class men offered a potential safety net. The irony was that the public agitation was orchestrated behind Lords Grey and Russell in support of a bill from which the majority had nothing to gain. As the radical Irish editor Bronterre O'Brien put it in relation to Thomas Attwood, the leader of the greatest of the Political Unions in Birmingham: he controlled the Birmingham Political Union with 'such a show of good nature that the Brummagem operatives seemed really to believe that they would be *virtually*, though not actually, represented in the "reformed" parliament'.[64]

In the autumn of 1831 and the 'days of May' of 1832, Thompson argues that Britain 'was within an ace of a revolution', only avoided because of the deep constitutionalism of the Radical tradition, the skill of middle-class radicals and the recognition by the diehard opponents of reform that they would have to concede. It had been the intention of the Whig reformers from the start to 'attach numbers to property and good order'. As Lord Grey put it, 'It is of the utmost importance to associate the middle with the higher orders of society in the love and support of the institutions and government of the country.' An investigation was conducted in Leeds by Baines, the middle-class editor and reformer, to discover how many men would be enfranchised by the proposed £10 householder franchise. His canvassers 'stated *unanimously*' that the £10 qualification did not admit to the exercise of the elective franchise a single person who might not safely and wisely be enfranchised: that they were surprised to find how comparatively few would be allowed to vote. Those who it was safe to include were the solid and rich middle class, 'the genuine depositories', in the words of the radical Utilitarian Brougham, 'of sober, rational, intelligent, and honest English feeling'.[65] Such epithets were those associated with men and the public discussion of middle-class virtues had focused on masculinity, on manly independence and the ways in which it could be contrasted with the feminine traits of the aristocracy. For James Mill, for example, the middle class was represented by men, male participants in various forms of public life and his *Essay on Government* explicitly rejected arguments for the enfranchisement of women on the grounds that they were the dependants of men.[66]

But aristocratic and middle class women were not simply outside of politics. As recent research has shown they were a part of the vibrant political culture outside of parliament. Elaine Chalus demonstrates, for example, that enfranchisement was far from the only prerequisite for political participation. Women of the political elite lived in a world in which it was fully expected that they would be part of familial politics in their widest sense – exercising influence and patronage in a wide range of spheres, electioneering with vigour and enthusiasm.[67] There is evidence that women did exercise the municipal franchise prior to the Municipal Corporations Act of 1835 and as Jane Rendall has noted there is scope for more research in this area.[68] Meanwhile, women had been active in anti-Catholic agitation as we have seen, and middle class women were heavily involved in the anti-slavery movement. Women did identify with the nation, but not as citizens.

In the course of the parliamentary committee meetings on reform a discussion took place that illuminates the gendering of politics at this moment. In the unreformed system of franchise freemen had the vote in some boroughs and in a small number of these boroughs, 'a right existed, by which the daughters of freemen conveyed the right of voting to their husbands'. An amendment was proposed which would have protected this hereditary right for 'the right of the daughter to confer the privilege on her husband ought to be as sacred as the right of the master to confer freedom on his apprentice'. The committee entertained themselves hugely on this topic, telling tales of ladies locked up in rooms in order to secure hasty marriages, of the origin of the right being associated with the lack of personal charms of the ladies of Bristol and an attempt by Queen Elizabeth to secure husbands for them, and with the renowned beauty of these same Bristol ladies meaning that such rights could now be dispensed with.[69] The hilarity provoked and the ridicule associated with the idea of political rights being passed through women suggest the underlying anxieties that men had on the subject. If fears of revolutionary politics underpinned the debates over reform, so, it might be argued, did fears of feminism. The spectre of Wollstonecraft perhaps lurked in the shadows, a woman who had defied sexual conventions and demanded political rights for women. The naming of the vote as a masculine privilege could only have been necessary if at some level it was felt that this could no longer be assumed.

Women were certainly present in the reform agitation. In his struggle against the tide of reform the Duke of Wellington relied on female friends to coax country-bound gentry and aristocrats up to London to vote. Aristocratic women, familiars of the world of politics, gathered in the House of Lords to listen to debates and waited anxiously at home for news from their menfolk.[70] At the other end of the social scale working class women were present in large numbers at reform demonstrations and female political unions were well established.[71] (At present we know almost nothing of the activities of middle-class women on questions of reform.) In August 1832 a petition to the House of Commons from Mary Smith of Stanmore and presented by Orator Hunt, a leader of the reform movement, asked for the vote for 'every unmarried woman having that pecuniary qualification whereby the other sex is entitled to the said franchise'.[72] Smith was a wealthy Yorkshire lady and saw no reason why those who paid taxes should not have a share in the election of their representatives.[73] Matthew Davenport Hill, part of the celebrated radical Unitarian Hill family, even went so far as to endorse women's suffrage in his election campaign in Hull in 1832.[74] But 1832 does not rank as a significant moment in the articulation of feminist demands. While the men entered the political fray as independent subjects fighting for their right to vote, the women were positioned as wives and mothers, supporting the cause of working men. As William Cobbett, the voice of radical culture in the 1820s and 1830s, argued, women were excluded from the right to vote because, 'husbands are answerable in law for their wives, as to their civil damages, and because the very nature of their sex makes the exercise of this right incompatible with the harmony and happiness of society'.[75] By nature, it was claimed, the female sex were unsuited to the public sphere.

Interestingly, two of the historians of feminism of this period have nothing to say about the Reform Act of 1832. Barbara Taylor is concerned with the emergence of different forms of feminism in the period, particularly that associated with Owenism. For these women the movement associated with the reform of Parliament does not appear to have been central.[76] Anna Clark traces the gendered formation of the British working class, and the debates over masculinity and femininity, citizenship and domesticity, which structured working-class political discourse. She argues that the traditional association of masculinity with political power was reworked in the early nineteenth century in the context of radicalism and that despite many challenges and alternative possibilities, 'the fatal flaws of misogyny and patriarchy ultimately muted the radicalism of the British working class'. In her chronology the Reform Act scarcely figures: other events were much more decisive in gender formation, particularly the affair of Queen Caroline in 1820 which marked a moment when radicals admitted that the rights of women were a political issue.[77] The feminist questions raised by radicals such as Wollstonecraft in the 1790s, the Paineite focus on the distinctive arenas of fatherhood and motherhood, the notions of plebeian citizenship that paid attention to the needs of the family, the participation of women in the radical communal based politics of the 1820s, the debates over the double standard in relation to Queen Caroline, the shadowy knowledge and threat of all these could be condensed in the decision to specify that it was men who could vote in elections and be political citizens of the nation. Single women property owners and all married women must remain as subjects.[78] Gender, in other words, was central to the reorganization of the political nation that took place in 1832. New groups of men successfully claimed the right to be included in the body politic, underlining the association of masculinity with political power and certifying that middle-class men in particular could enjoy the fruits of their labour in new ways appropriate to their economic status. As Wahrman argues, the campaign for middle-class suffrage was on the basis of masculine virtues; their manly independence was contrasted with the effeminacy of the aristocracy: it was this that provided the basis for the demand that public opinion – meaning the voices of certain men – should be respected. It was 'the possessors of the wealth and intelligence of the country, the natural leaders of the physical force of the community', who claimed inclusion in the political nation.[79] 'The rule of difference' articulated in 1832 was a masculine form of rule. Property provided the basis of the franchise, except for women. The specific exclusion of women meant that the demand for inclusion would follow: the naming clarified the practice. In the next major set of political debates over the parliamentary franchise the question of women's suffrage was on the agenda.[80]

* * *

Two vignettes provide telling instances of aspects of the operation of 'the rule of difference' in the newly elected reformed Parliament of 1833. A magazine description of the House of Lords arrayed for the king's speech evokes the gendering of the nation with its racialized overtones. The House was 'altogether very brilliant' with the king, the peers and the bishops there in all their splendour, together with the Commons. They were watched by:

> 300 to 400 superbly dressed ladies, all plumed with ostrich feathers, many adorned with costly jewels, and from the elegance of their costume, the surpassing beauty of many of their persons, the intelligent expression of their eyes and lips, and the general air and carriage of graceful motion which characterised them, presenting a sight not often to be witnessed even in England, and certainly not to be seen, in any other country of the world with which we are acquainted, to the same extent and perfection as here. What the

Turkish ambassador, who was among the strangers present, must have thought of such realization of the favourite *houris* of the faithful, as was here portrayed before him, it would be difficult to say; but we conceive his description of this scene of brilliant beauty, when he returns to Constantinople, will be deemed fabulous by many; and if believed at all, will excite in the harems of the seraglio, where it is sure to penetrate, an anxious wish on the part of the sultan's ladies to be admitted to this open display of their beauties now hidden from all admiring eyes, by being immured in the solitude of confinement: and to all it must at least prove this truth, that female loveliness is capable of being greatly heightened, even in its beauty, by intellectual cultivation; and that the dignity of man is never more conspicuous than when woman is made a participator with himself in all the high and refined pleasures which intellectual pursuits afford . . .[81]

The Turkish ambassador had witnessed the rituals of the 'rule of difference': differences that were always in part racially encoded. The black subjects of the empire had no actual presence in the Houses of Parliament, but the West Indian planters who were there in considerable numbers were carrying their shadows. The beauty and intelligence of 'the ladies' gained meaning from their racialized others, not at this point those freed women slaves who were to be won to domesticity but the orientalized figures of the harem. The public participation of 'the ladies' in this ceremonial (though of course they were spectators only) provided the sign of the superiority of British culture and 'the dignity of man': that civilization known in relation to the imagined court and harem of the Islamic sultan, the language of excitement and penetration conveying the exoticized sexuality of the Orient.

If 'the ladies' carried one set of messages about the proper ordering of the nation, the Irish carried another. One of the first items to be debated in the Commons after the king's speech was Ireland. The Irish members behaved true to form as one diarist recorded:

O'Connell's speech, artful and persuasive in a very high degree, made a deep impression. It required a very skilful answer and certainly did not receive it from Stanley . . . Luckily for ministers O'Connell was not satisfied with this moderate success. He must needs shew his strength, or perhaps shew the Repealers in Ireland that they had not sent so many representatives to the House in vain. One after another these Hibernian orators rose to repeat in lengthy and declamatory harangues their complaints of the wrongs of the country and their accusations against the Ministry. Their coarse manners, fierce deportment and baseless assertions, at length heartily wearied the House . . .[82]

The 'coarse manners' and 'fierce deportment' contributed to the acceptance of the terms of the Coercion Bill, for the Irish clearly were not the same as the English. O'Connell's failure to control his followers demonstrated the incapacity of the Irish to manage themselves. The 'rule of difference' was indeed a complex business requiring the regulation of class, ethnic, racial and gender divisions both 'at home' and across the empire, to secure the nation in its imagined homogeneity with subjects and citizens in place.

Notes

1. Many thanks to Jane Rendall for her helpful comments on this piece and to Sally Alexander, Cora Kaplan, Lynne Segal and Barbara Taylor for the discussion we had.
2. It grows out of a piece of research which is fully researched: Hall, C., McClelland, K. and Rendall, J. (2000), *Defining the Victorian Nation: Class, Race, Gender and the Reform Act of 1867,* Cambridge: Cambridge University Press.
3. Woodward, E.L. (1971), *The Age of Reform 1815–1870,* 2nd ed. Oxford: Clarendon, 88; Gash, N. (1970), *Aristocracy and People. Britain 1815–1865,* London: Edward Arnold, 152. The Reform Acts for Scotland and Ireland were separate pieces of legislation with slightly different effects, which I cannot discuss here.
4. An Act to amend the Representation of the People in England and Wales 7 June 1832. *A Collection of Public General Statutes passed in the Second and Third year of the Reign of His Majesty King William the Fourth.*
5. James, C.L.R. (1963), *The Black Jacobins. Toussaint L'Ouverture and the San Domingo Revolution* 2nd ed. New York: Vintage; Fanon, F. (1967), *Black Skin, White Masks* first published 1961, Harmondsworth: Penguin.
6. See, for example, Cooper, F. and Stoler, A.L. (eds) (1997), *Tensions of Empire. Colonial Cultures in a Bourgeois World,* Berkeley and Los Angeles: University of California Press; Stoler, A.L. (1995), *Race and the Education of Desire. Foucault's History of Sexuality and the Colonial Order of Things,* Durham: Duke University Press; Burton, A.

A. (1994), *Burdens of History. British Feminists, Indian Women and Imperial Culture, 1865–1915,* Chapel Hill: University of North Carolina Press. For a different approach to linking Britain and Empire see Bayly, C.A. (1989), *Imperial Meridian. The British Empire and the World 1780–1830* London: Longman.

7. See, for example, Colley, L. (1992), *Britons. Forging the Nation 1707–1837* New Haven: Yale University Press; Kearney, H. (1995), *The British Isles.A History of Four Nations* Cambridge: Cambridge University Press.

8. Bayly, *Imperial Meridian* 3.

9. On this shift particularly in relation to Jamaica see Holt, T.C. (1992), *The Problem of Freedom. Race, Labor and Politics in Jamaica and Britain, 1832–1938* Baltimore: Johns Hopkins University Press.

10. Chatterjee, P. (1993), *The Nation and its Fragments. Colonial and Postcolonial Histories,* Princeton: Princeton University Press, 10. On the inclusionary pretensions of liberal theory and the exclusionary effects of liberal practices, see Mehta, U.S., 'Liberal Strategies of Exclusion', in Cooper and Stoler (eds) *Tensions of Empire.*

11. As yet 'the rule of difference' is a descriptive category rather than anything more but I hope to develop its analytic use in future work.

12. Alexander M.J. and Mohanty, C.T. (eds) (1997), *Feminist Genealogies, Colonial Legacies, Democratic Futures* New York: Routledge, xviii. Virtually all states, as Alexander and Mohanty argue, conflate heterosexuality and citizenship and in the process produce a subordinated class of sexualized, non-procreative, non-citizens. Unfortunately in this essay I cannot explore this argument but it offers rich possibilities for historical analysis. On questions of difference and intersectionality, see also Brah, A. (1996), *Cartographies of Diaspora. Contesting Identities,* London: Routledge.

13. Colley, *Britons.*

14. See, for example, Thompson, E.P., (1993), 'The Making of a Ruling Class?' *Radical History Review* 337: (Summer): 377–82. Thompson argues that Colley's account is of the making of a ruling class rather than a nation.

15. Colley, *Britons,* 359.

16. For a reading of the impact of the 'Indian Mutiny' on England, see Dawson, G. (1994), *Soldier Heroes. British Adventure, Empire, and the Imagining of Masculinities,* London: Routledge; for the Morant Bay rebellion in Jamaica see Heuman, G. (1996), *'The Killing Time'. The Morant Bay Rebellion in Jamaica,* Basingstoke: Macmillan.

17. Cohen R., (1994), *Frontiers of Identity. The British and the Others,*

London: Longman. Paul, K. (1997), *Whitewashing Britain. Race and Citizenship in the Postwar Era*, Ithaca: Cornell University Press.

18. Colley, *Britons*; O'Connor, M. (1999), *The Romance of Italy and the English Political Imagination*, New York: St Martins Press.
19. Hickman, M.J. (1995), *Religion, Class and Identity. The State, the Catholic Church and the Education of the Irish in Britain*, Aldershot: Avebury, 22–8.
20. Foster, R.F. (1988), *Modern Ireland 1600–1972*, Harmondsworth: Penguin, 282.
21. Reynolds, J.A. (1970), *The Catholic Emancipation Crisis in Ireland 1823–1829* 2nd ed. Connecticut: Greenwood, 9.
22. McCord, N. (1991), *British History 1815–1906*, Oxford: Oxford University Press, 40.
23. For Macaulay's response to this see Clive, J. (1973), *Thomas Babington Macaulay. The Shaping of the Historian*, London: Secker & Warburg, 157.
24. Quoted in Machin, G.I.T. (1964), *The Catholic Question in English Politics 1820–1830,* Oxford: Clarendon, 1.
25. Reynolds, J.A. (1970), *The Catholic Emancipation Crisis in Ireland 1823–1829* 2nd ed. Connecticut: Greenwood, 18.
26. Reynolds, J.A. (1970), *The Catholic Emancipation Crisis in Ireland 1823–1829* 2nd ed. Connecticut: Greenwood, 30, 37, 40.
27. As yet we do not have a history of women's involvement in the Catholic Association as far as I am aware. Maria Luddy argues that women were involved in eighteenth and early nineteenth century food riots and electoral disturbances and that upper-class women in Ireland engaged in the same kind of patronage and influence as in England. She suggests that the first formal political organization of women was in the Irish anti-slavery societies. Luddy, M. (1995), *Women in Ireland 1800–1918, a documentary history.* Cork: University of Galway Press, 239–40.
28. Quoted in Reynolds, J.A. (1970), *The Catholic Emancipation Crisis in Ireland 1823–1829* 2nd ed. Connecticut: Greenwood, 17.
29. Reynolds, J.A. (1970), *The Catholic Emancipation Crisis in Ireland 1823–1829* 2nd ed. Connecticut: Greenwood, 135, 165, 168.
30. Colley, *Britons*, 29. This seems to have been the first time in British history that large numbers of women signed petitions to Parliament alongside of men. As Colley notes, the hostility to Catholic emancipation has not as yet been fully investigated.
31. Machin, *The Catholic Question*, 87, 144; Colley, *Britons*, 324–34 on the petitions.

32. Best, G.F.A. (1967), 'Popular Protestantism in Victorian England', in R. Robson (ed.), *Ideas and Institutions of Victorian Britain. Essays in Honour of George Kitson Clark*, London: G.Bell & Sons, 139.

33. Colley, *Britons*, 328.

34. Rudé, G. (1967), 'English Rural and Urban Disturbances on the eve of the First Reform Bill, 1830–1831', *Past and Present,* 37 (July): 87–102.

35. Quoted in Smith, E.A. (1990), *Lord Grey 1764–1845*, Oxford: Clarendon, 135.

36. Hoppen, K.T. (1985), 'The Franchise and Electoral Politics in England and Ireland 1832–1885', *History* 70: 202–29.

37. Halévy, E. (1950), *The Triumph of Reform 1830–1841* vol. 3 of *A History of the English People in the Nineteenth Century* 2nd ed. London: Ernest Benn, 130.

38. Higman, B.W. (1967), 'The West Indian "interest" in Parliament 1807–1833', *Historical Studies*, 13 (49): 1–19.

39. Young, D.M. (1961), *The Colonial Office in the Early Nineteenth Century*, London: Longman.

40. Midgley, C. (1992), *Women Against Slavery. The British Campaigns 1780-1870.* London: Routledge.

41. Blackburn, R. (1988), *The Overthrow of Colonial Slavery 1776–1848*, London: Verso, 445.

42. On the resistance of enslaved black women see Bush, B. (1990), *Slave Women in Caribbean Society, 1650–1838*, Bloomington: Indiana University Press, 1990.

43. Turner, M. (1982), *Slaves and Missionaries. The Disintegration of Jamaican Slave Society 1787–1834*, Urbana: University of Illinois Press.

44. Heuman, G. (1987), *Between Black and White. Race, Politics and the Free Coloureds in Jamaica 1792–1865*, Connecticut: Greenwood.

45. Turner, M. (1982), *Slaves and Missionaries. The Disintegration of Jamaican Slave Society 1787–1834*, Urbana: University of Illinois Press.

46. Blackburn, R. (1988), *The Overthrow of Colonial Slavery 1776–1848*, London: Verso, 453.

47. On the gendering of the new colonial order see, for example, Hall, C. (1993), 'White Visions, Black Lives: the free villages of Jamaica', *History Workshop* 36 (Autumn): 100–32; on the new gender order in the Cape see Scully, P. (1997), *Liberating the Family? Gender and British Slave Emancipation in the Rural Western Cape, South Africa, 1823–1853*, Oxford: James Currey.

48. This viewpoint was to change. See Holt, *The Problem of Freedom*.
49. Quoted in Hall, C. (1992), *White, Male and Middle Class: Explorations in Feminism and History*, Cambridge: Polity, 33.
50. Beckles, H.McD. (1993), 'White Women and Slavery in the Caribbean' *History Workshop* 36 (Autumn).
51. See, for example, Macaulay, T.B. (1889), *Miscellaneous Writings and Speeches*, London: Longmans, Green & Co., 483–92.
52. The paragraph that follows is drawn from Thompson, E.P. (1963), *The Making of the English Working Class*, London: Victor Gollancz, 807–32.
53. Newbould, I. (1990), *Whiggery and Reform, 1830–1841*, Stanford: Stanford University Press, 57–62.
54. Wahrman, D. (1992), 'Virtual Representation: Parliamentary reporting and Languages of Class in the 1790s', *Past and Present*, 136: 113.
55. Wahrman, D. (1995), *Imagining the Middle Class. The Political Representation of Class in Britain c1780–1840*, Cambridge: Cambridge University Press, 18.
56. Halévy, *The Triumph of Reform*, 7
57. Rudé, G. (1976), 'English Rural and Urban Disturbances', 91; Hobsbawm, E., and Rudé, G. (1976), *Captain Swing*, London: Lawrence & Wishart, 211, 219, 248.
58. Quoted in Briggs, A. (1959), *The Age of Improvement 1783–1867*, London: Longman, 257.
59. Hollis, P., 'Anti-Slavery and British Working-Class Radicalism in the Years of Reform', in Bolt, C. and Drescher, S. (eds) (1980), *Anti-Slavery, Religion and Reform: Essays in Memory of Roger Anstey*, Folkestone: Dawson, 1980.
60. On the giving of freedom in the Birmingham context see Hall, *White, Male and Middle Class*, 26–33.
61. Quoted in Thompson, *The Making*, 827.
62. Quoted in Smith, E.A. (1992), *Reform or Revolution? A Diary of Reform in England 1830–1832*, Stroud: Alan Sutton, 72.
63. Quoted in Smith, E.A. (1992), *Reform or Revolution? A Diary of Reform in England 1830–1832*, Stroud: Alan Sutton, 128.
64. Quoted in Thompson, *The Making*, 815.
65. Quoted in Thompson, *The Making*, 817–9.
66. Wahrman, *Imagining the Middle Class*, 387; on the construction of masculinity in this period see Davidoff, L. and Hall, C. (1987), *Family Fortunes: Men and Women of the English Middle Class, 1780–1850*, London: Hutchinson.

67. Chalus, E. (1997), '"That epidemical madness Madness": women and electoral politics in the late eighteenth century', in Barker and Chalus (eds), *Gender in Eighteenth-Century England: Roles, Representations and Responsibilities*, London: Addison-Wesley Longman; Liddington, J. (1998), *Female Fortune. Land, Gender and Authority. The Anne Lister Diaries and other writings 1833–1836*, London: Rivers Oram.

68. Hall, McClelland and Rendall, 'Introduction', in *Defining the Victorian Nation*.

69. *Hansard*, 3rd.Series, vol. 10, February– March 1832, cols. 61–2.

70. Smith, E.A. (1992), *Reform or Revolution? A Diary of Reform in England 1830–1832*, Stroud: Alan Sutton, 88–90.

71. Thompson, D. (1976), 'Women and Nineteenth-Century Politics: A Lost Dimension', in J. Mitchell and A. Oakley (eds), *The Rights and Wrongs of Women*, Harmondsworth: Penguin.

72. I am grateful to Jane Rendall for this reference. (1832), *Journal of the House of Commons* 87: 551.

73. Fulford, R. (1957), *Votes for Women. The Story of a Struggle*, London, 33–4.

74. Hill, R. and F. (1878), *The Recorder of Birmingham. A Memoir of Matthew Davenport Hill*, London: Macmillan, 115.

75. Hall, C., 'The Tale of Samuel and Jemima: gender and working-class culture in early nineteenth-century England', in *White, Male and Middle Class*. Cobbett is quoted on 115.

76. Taylor, B. (1983), *Eve and the New Jerusalem. Socialism and Feminism in the Nineteenth Century*, London: Virago.

77. Clark, A., *The Struggle for the Breeches. Gender and the making of the British working classes*, London: Rivers Oram, 1995, 271; see also, Clark, A (1996). 'Gender, Class and the Nation: franchise reform in England , 1832–1928', in J. Vernon (ed.), *Re-reading the Constitution: New Narratives in the Political History of England's Long Nineteenth Century*, Cambridge: Cambridge University Press.

78. For the European context for this see, Offen, K. (1998), 'Contextualising the Theory and Practice of Feminism in Nineteenth-Century Europe (1789–1914)', in R.Bridenthal, S.M.Stuard and M.E.Wiesner (eds), *Becoming Visible. Women in European History*, 3rd ed. Boston: Houghton Mifflin.

79. The quote is from Buller: Wahrman, *Imagining the Middle Class*, 381, 394.

80. Hall, McClelland and Rendall, *Defining the Victorian Nation*.

81. *Parliamentary Review and Family Magazine,* cited in Smith, E.A. (1992), *Reform or Revolution? A Diary of Reform in England 1830–1832*, Stroud: Alan Sutton, 151–2.
82. Le Marchand's Diary, cited in Smith, E.A. (1992), *Reform or Revolution? A Diary of Reform in England 1830–1832*, Stroud: Alan Sutton, 152–3.

7

The Making of the Egyptian Nation
Beth Baron

Egyptian nationalists start the story of Egyptian nationalism with the 'founder of modern Egypt' Muhammad 'Ali (r. 1805–48), whose 'national' army turned peasants into Egyptians. Yet historians have recently challenged that narrative, arguing that the Albanian Mehmet Ali Pasha (the Turkish version of his name) should be seen as an Ottoman *vali* (governor) who harboured imperial and dynastic ambitions rather than sympathy for an Egyptian 'nation'.[1] Scholars thus tend to point to the 'Urabi Revolt (1881–2), which ended in British occupation – or even the anti-imperialist movement that surfaced in the 1890s – as the earliest stirring of Egyptian nationalism.

Yet one key to understanding the origins of the modern Egyptian nation lies in deeper structural changes of the long nineteenth century. During this period, the dominant social formation – the Ottoman-Egyptian household – unravelled, in great part due to the demise of slavery. I argue that the simultaneity of the end of slavery (and the overwhelming majority of slaves in nineteenth-century Egypt were women) and the emergence of nationalism in Egypt is more than a coincidence. Debates over slavery and its demise in practice played a multifaceted role in the making of the nation. The end of harem slavery helped Egyptianize the Ottoman-Egyptian elite, which increasingly intermarried with the local population. The new elite wrestled with the ethnic boundaries of the nation – including Copts, attempting to incorporate Sudanese in a special relationship, excluding Circassians, Syrians, and others – in a process of homogeniz-ation common in nation-building. At the same time, domestic slavery stood at the centre of Egypt's relationship to the Sudan, which Mehmet Ali's armies had conquered in the 1820s and over which the British and Egyptians later vied for control.

The end of slavery, most specifically harem slavery, also generated a series of debates collectively known as the 'woman question' through which questions about the shape of the household, the 'building block of the nation', were worked out. The new nation would not be built on households that included female concubines from the Caucasus, retainers from Central Asia, eunuchs and female domestic slaves from Africa, and patriarchs from Anatolia or the Balkans, but rather on the bourgeois family. That family – Copt or Muslim – would be grounded in Egyptian territory. The 'woman question' thus became the fault line along which men and women negotiated ethnic boundaries, cultural identity, and social transformations.

Whereas this chapter argues that the end of slavery helped to turn Ottomans into Egyptians, I am neither an Egyptian or an ex-Ottoman. My forebears fled the neighbouring Russian Empire in the late nineteenth century to escape religious persecution. One set of great-grandparents left Russia with four children, beginning an odyssey that would take them across continents and over the Atlantic, and in the process they had seven more children. One daughter was born in Istanbul, and according to family lore, another was kidnapped there in the bazaar. (In the 1880s, demand for harem slaves remained high while the traditional sources in the Caucasus had been cut off.) My grandfather's sister was found and returned to the family. She thus did not end her life in the Sultan's or a pasha's palace but on the shores of America, where I can contemplate what might have been her fate as well as the fate of those who were not returned to their families.

Transformation of the Elite in Nineteenth-Century Ottoman Egypt

Mehmet Ali became recognized as the Ottoman governor of Egypt in the struggle that followed the French withdrawal from Egypt and eventually won the right to pass the position on to his sons. The local Ottoman elite over which he presided remained bound by their loyalty to the house of Mehmet Ali, their commitment to serve in Egypt, and a sense of belonging to an imperial Ottoman tradition. Ottoman was not an ethnic but rather a cultural and supra-ethnic identity. Made up of multiple ethnicities (Albanians, Greeks, Circassians, Kurds, Georgians, Bosnians, and others) and coming from diverse Ottoman territories, this elite spoke Turkish (and thus were often identified as Turks rather than Ottomans) while the Egyptian population they ruled spoke mostly Arabic.[2]

A core component of the Ottoman elite, especially those members of that elite who rose to high positions of power, were *kul* slaves. They had been purchased at a young age and raised in the households of powerful persons, who trained and set them on careers in the army and the bureaucracy. Most prominent among them were Circassians from the Caucasus region who shared ethnic ties and often took pride in their slave pasts, which were seen to provide them with social mobility. Their slave backgrounds bound them to one another as well as to their former owners. In Egypt in the mid-nineteenth century, a government official could think of only two ministers who had not been slaves and predicted that those two might not last long in their positions. Although he may have exaggerated, slaves were clearly quite prominent in the elite.[3]

The Ottoman elite reproduced itself through reliance on the institution of harem slaves and a household structure patterned after that of the Sultan. Just as young boys were purchased and groomed for military or bureau-cratic service in the capital or provinces, young Circassian and Georgian girls were purchased and groomed to serve as concubines or wives in the households of the elite. Some were kidnapped and others taken as prisoners in war; many Circassian girls were also sold by their parents, who were themselves often of the slave class, to improve their lot in life. While they constituted only a minority of slaves imported into the Ottoman Empire (the majority were African women), they served as a linchpin in the elite social system. Through such alliances, Circassians in Egypt and elsewhere could keep their ethnic identity intact, and local Ottomans of other backgrounds could keep their distance from the native population. Sometimes these concubines or slave partners came from the households of Mehmet Ali or his sons, who in this way sought to cement bonds of loyalty. Ismail (r.1863–1879) had bound officers to the court by having them marry slaves from his harem; by the late 1870s, at least fifty officers had been married to Circassian slaves from the palace.[4]

The House of Mehmet Ali was not averse to drawing on Egyptian talent as well. The Pasha incorporated Egyptians trained in languages and other skills into the bureaucracy as technocrats, and his son Said (r.1854–63) allowed the sons of village officials to become army officers up to a certain rank. Moreover, a new group of rural notables, who benefited from the privatization of land and Egypt's entry into the world market as an exporter of cotton, increasingly served in the provincial government. The new rural notables marked their entry into the Ottoman elite by purchasing Circassian slaves and patterned their households after that of the *vali*.

Consider Muhammad Sultan, the 'King of Upper Egypt', who arose to prominence in mid-century as a provincial governor. Serving the viceroys faithfully, he increased his holdings to over 13,000 feddans by 1882, becoming the largest landowner in the region around Minya. He crowned his achievements as president of the Chamber of Delegates (established by Ismail in 1866).[5] His household included a wife, a Circassian concubine (Iqbal), several eunuchs, and Egyptian and Circassian companions for his children. Iqbal bore a daughter (Huda) in 1879 who became one of the leading female nationalists and the founder of the Egyptian Feminist Union in the post-war period. Huda relates in her memoirs that her widowed grandmother left the Caucasus with five children (as part of the Russian-forced migrations of the mid-1850s to mid-1860s) and sent Iqbal to live in Egypt. There Iqbal was raised in the home of a patron and later joined the household of Muhammad Sultan.[6] References to Circassian slave mothers among the elite abound; but only fragments of their lives are revealed in memoirs, court records, police registers, and biographical notes.[7] The female slave experience has generally been suppressed from the collective Egyptian memory along with the Ottoman past.[8]

In the course of the nineteenth century, the elite underwent a transformation in a process that proceeded on two converging paths. On one path, native Egyptians from the rural notability became upwardly mobile, increasing their landholdings and finding new opportunities for government employment as Arabic joined French and Turkish as an official language from mid-century. Egyptian notables and a growing corps of technocrats replaced Ottomans in the administration. On the other path, the entrenchment of the Mehmet Ali dynasty enhanced the sense of Egypt's separateness from Istanbul and along with other factors generated greater local ties on the part of Ottoman-Egyptian officials. The latter set down roots and increasingly intermarried with the local elite, which in turn further diluted Ottoman-Egyptian identity. When Turkish speakers left Egypt, they were not replaced by *kul* slaves, and those who stayed behind (or upwardly mobile Egyptian notables) could no longer import harem slaves. Thus one of the most crucial factors in the transformation of the elite was the abolition of slavery, which cut off the supply of male and female recruits.[9]

The abolition of slavery in the Ottoman Empire occurred piecemeal over the second half of the nineteenth century. In the face of British pressure to eliminate all forms of slavery, Ottoman officials enacted a series of reforms, not all of which immediately worked. Edicts at mid-century in Istanbul and Cairo prohibited the trade in black slaves; but demand remained high, particularly during the cotton boom in Egypt in the 1860s, and these decrees tended to be ineffective. Ottomans resisted tampering with harem slavery in particular, for it touched on religious sensitivities (Islam permits slavery) and sustained the household structure. In 1877 the British and the Egyptian government signed a Convention for the Suppression of the Slave Trade yet delayed the prohibition of the trade in white slaves for seven more years. Harem slavery died out as the sources dried up: it had become almost impossible to procure young white girls after Circassian migrants had been settled in the Ottoman Empire for a few decades.[10]

Dror Ze'evi has linked the abolition of slavery to the dissolution of elite identity and the formation of official nationalism in the centre of the Ottoman Empire:

> Whether or not the *kul* involved in the process realized that they were cutting off the branch they were sitting on, this was the end result of the series of events. By abolishing slavery the core of the Ottoman elite abolished its own definition, its own terms of reference . . . in fact the old elite retracted and made way for a new one . . . the *kul* became a dinosaur, an obsolete remnant of a disappearing way of life.[11]

Ze'evi argues that the new elite that arose to supplant the old one in Istanbul sponsored state nationalism. In a similar process, the new Arabic-speaking elite that arose in Egypt in the second half of the nineteenth century challenged the old Turkish- and Circassian-speaking elite as well as growing European dominance of Egyptian affairs and sponsored an anti-imperialist nationalism.

The 'Urabi Movement, 1881–2

The 'Urabi Movement can be seen as the outcome of stresses created in the process of transformation in elite identity as Arabophone groups on the rise sought a share in power with the older dominant elite.[12] Ahmad 'Urabi (b.1841 – d.1911), the son of a village shaykh from the region of Zaqaziq, emerged as the leader of the Egyptian army officers. These officers had assailed the incompetent strategies of Ottoman-Egyptian officers that had resulted in defeats in African campaigns.[13] But now cuts in the officers corps threatened the Egyptian officers rather than their Ottoman-Egyptian counterparts, as 'Urabi himself later related:

> The practice in Egypt was to tend to discriminate by race. And so all the promotions, decorations and rewards went to those of the Circassian race, since they were from the Mamluks [slaves], the paid retainers of either the Khedivial family, or of the aristocracy who were in turn also Mamluks of the Khedivial family. After this faction came that of the Turks and others who were not Egyptians, along with those of mixed origins. Thereafter came those Egyptian by race . . .[14]

The army's challenge to the government started with military grievances but soon developed wider political content as 'Urabi and his circle became the core around which discontent with Khedive Tawfiq (r.1879–92) and European intervention crystallized. The rural notables, led by Muhammad Sultan, called for a constitution that would give them a greater role in central government and would check the autocratic rule of the *khedive*. The rural notables and army officers thus found common cause, for the moment, under the slogan 'Egypt for the Egyptians!'

'Urabi had little time to launch his reform programme, which apparently included the suppression of domestic slavery. (His own wife was of African slave origin; the daughter of Prince Ilhami's wet nurse, she had grown up in Khedive Ismail's harem.)[15] In March 1882, Wilfred Blunt wrote to the British Anti-Slavery Society on behalf of the 'National Party of Egypt' to explain their views. 'I have received the most positive assurances from Arabi Bey, the Minister of War, that he will cooperate loyally in this work, and he has authorized me to say that he will not rest until the stigma of slavery is entirely removed from the Egyptian community.'[16] Blunt distinguishes between the past promises of 'the Turk' in Egypt, and the proposals of 'the Egyptian'. Yet whether 'Urabi was sincere or could be effective is uncertain, for some of the most prominent nationalists had a mixed record on the slave issue. For example, under 'Urabi, Fawzi Pasha, an Egyptian officer who had a record of slave trading, became police chief of Cairo.[17] And when Mahmud Pasha al-Barudi, a prominent ally of 'Urabi and nationalist poet had been Prefect of Cairo Police, a Circassian slave from his household had applied to the British consulate for a certificate of manumission, complaining that Barudi's wife had her tied and beaten.[18] 'Urabi himself later used the metaphor of slavery to describe the condition of all Egyptians: 'where are those who will free the Egyptians from their slavery?'[19]

As the *khedive*'s autocratic hold slipped, the British and French sent gunboats to Alexandria with a threatening note. Riots broke out in June and the British bombed the city in July. Tawfiq then sought British protection and was joined by a number of Ottoman-Egyptian officials and wealthy rural notables. The bulk of the population, however, supported 'Urabi's stand against the British invasion. 'Arabi found some of his most patriotic and powerful adherents [in Egyptian harems]', his defence lawyer later wrote. 'The National cause, even in its earlier stages, was warmly espoused by the great majority of Egyptian ladies, and they continued to support it till hope was no longer possible.' The lawyer cites interviews and correspondence with female members of the royal family as evidence. 'We saw in Arabi a deliverer, and our enthusiasm for him knew no bounds', said one princess.[20] 'Urabi rallied the population with appeals to *al-din wa'l-'ird wa'l-watan* (religion, honour, and the nation) and by declaring a *jihad* (holy war). Yet he did not frame the contest in strictly religious terms. 'The Egyptian nation,' 'Urabi later wrote, 'for all its variety of religious affiliation, did indeed do its duty in defence of the homeland.'[21] Throughout the conflict, 'Urabi also affirmed his loyalty to the Ottoman Sultan, for in spite of their resentment of many Turkish speakers in their midst, most Egyptians still felt ties to the Ottoman Empire.

The British, however, speedily defeated 'Urabi's forces, initiating an occupation that would last seventy years. The occupation reinforced the territorial integrity of Egypt by effectively cutting the province from the Ottoman Empire and transforming it into a 'veiled protectorate' under the control of Sir Evelyn Baring (later Lord Cromer), British agent and consul general from 1883 to 1907.[22] The occupation therefore accelerated the transformation in elite identity already underway as the Ottoman-Egyptian elite became further Egyptianized. The nationalist movement, having been dealt a sharp blow, remained dormant until the early 1890s when Abbas Hilmi II (r.1892–1914) helped to rejuvenate it as a lever against Cromer.

The Sudan and Egyptian Identity

At about the same time that the British occupied Egypt, the Egyptians lost their grip over the Sudan. Egyptian administration of the Sudan stemmed from the days of Mehmet Ali, whose southern conquests had been technically for the Sultan and who appointed military governors from among the Ottoman-Egyptian elite. Ismail had enlisted British officers to lead Egyptian troops in the expansion and administration of African territory under Egyptian control; and as part of Egypt's 'civilizing' role, Ismail consented to the prohibition of the slave trade in the Sudan. In 1881 as the 'Urabi movement gained momentum in Egypt, a young religious leader in the Sudan, Muhammad Ahmad, rallied followers against Ottoman-Egyptian rule. Among the backers of the Mahdi, or 'rightly guided one' as he became known, were those merchants and clerics who saw the attempts to eliminate the very lucrative slave trade in the 1870s as an assault on Islamic law and their own livelihoods. They also opposed Ottoman-Egyptian taxation policies. By 1885 the Mahdi's forces had seized Khartoum, routed the remaining Egyptian troops, killed the ranking British officer, and established an independent Islamic state.[23]

Egyptian nationalists did not let go of the Sudan so easily, for as Eve Powell convincingly demonstrates, the idea of the Sudan as part of Egypt had become embedded in the nationalist imagination. Herein lay a central paradox: Egyptian nationalists fought European imperialism at the same time that they sought to regain control of their own empire in the Sudan. Powell shows how this battle was fought metaphorically over the bodies of female slaves. In August 1894, government officials intercepted six Sudanese women destined for domestic slavery in the homes of three prominent pashas, one of whom – the president of the Legislative Council, 'Ali Sharif Pasha – had earlier called for the dissolution of the Slave Trade Bureau. The military trial pitted the British defenders of the slave women's right to freedom against the nationalists and their assertion of the pashas' right to buy slaves as an act of 'rescue'. 'Each side fought over these tired women in ragged clothing with the same ideologies and slogans with which they fought over the Sudan itself', writes Powell.[24] The trial ended in the acquittal of two of the pashas, but a convention in 1895 and a special decree in 1896 enacted stiffer penalties for buyers of slaves.[25] A further feature of the elite Ottoman-Egyptian household – African domestic slaves – became obsolete.

British-led Egyptian forces reconquered the Sudan in 1898: Egypt was now both colonized by the British and colonizer of the Sudan. Yet the British quickly sought to erode Egyptian control of the Sudan, and in 1899 they established the Anglo-Egyptian Condominium in the Sudan – a partnership founded on Egyptian funds and British military governors. The linkage of the Sudan and Egypt in a Nile Valley entity nonetheless remained a tenet of the Egyptian nationalists, who did not want to see their empire dismembered.[26] The nationalist lawyer Mustafa Kamil (b.1874 – d.1908) asked, 'who can praise this policy of force and arbitrariness, which has effectively repudiated the rights of Egypt in the Sudan after we had watered it with our blood and expended therein colossal sums of money?'[27] Ahmad Lutfi al-Sayyid, another nationalist, spoke of the Egyptians and Sudanese as 'brothers, or as cousins, all from one mother'.[28]

The Sudan of nationalist rhetoric contrasted with that of nationalist images, for the rhetoric emphasized male bonds while the images showed female bodies. The Sudanese that most elite Egyptians had known best were female domestic slaves, and the Sudan in post-war cartoons often appeared as a highly sexualized, nearly naked black woman with exaggerated facial and sexual features. Egypt, on the other hand, appeared as a light-skinned, modestly dressed and veiled upper-class woman (no doubt of Ottoman-Egyptian descent).[29] Egyptians tried to incorporate the

Sudanese into the Egyptian nation as 'minors', wards of Egypt, to be tamed and civilized. But the British aborted the plan and encouraged the Sudanese to develop their own nationalist aspirations.

Copts and Egypt's Ancient Past

While the issue of the sovereignty of the Sudan forced Egyptians to consider race and culture, the question of the place of the Copts in the national community helped Egyptians to explore and mine the past. At the heart of national identity lies a perception of common descent, of shared lineage, of the relatedness of the community. But which past would nationalists draw from – Pharaonic, Coptic, Islamic, Arab, Ottoman – to craft that lineage and shape national narratives? Copts claimed direct descent from the ancient Egyptians of Pharaonic times, stressing that they were the 'real Egyptians' not latecomers like the Arab tribes who had conquered Egypt. Likewise, Arab tribes in Egypt, many of which had been settled in the time of Mehmet Ali, retained a memory of common lineage. Descent may have been imagined, the actual story quite muddled, but the sense of relatedness, of shared blood, had real power. Egyptian nationalists used various strategies to fuse the lines of Copts and Muslims to create a single lineage of ancient pedigree.

Religious minorities in the Ottoman Empire had been treated as protected peoples, a category of subjects who paid special taxes and faced certain restrictions. They had their own corporate structure as *millet* (religious community) and collectively enjoyed a degree of autonomy: their own religious leaders ran community affairs and administered the religious laws that covered many aspects of life. Anthony Smith suggests that these millets were pre-modern ethnies that had the potential to become separate nations.[30] Indeed, many Christian groups in the empire – from the Balkans to Mount Lebanon – pushed for autonomy or independence in the nineteenth and early twentieth centuries. High concentrations of Copts existed in Upper Egypt – in areas such as Asyut they formed a quarter of the population – and they made up 5 to 20 per cent (depending on who counted) of the population in Egypt. Yet the Copts did not attempt to build a separate state.[31]

Most nineteenth-century Copts were illiterate peasants who shared a spoken language and many customs with Muslims. Coptic women, like Muslim peasant women, were veiled and practised female circumcision, and often venerated the same saints. Coptic men were exempt from the army until the middle of the nineteenth century, when new laws eliminated the special *jizya* tax and introduced compulsory army service. Some Copts

profited from Egypt's changed land tenure laws and her integration into
the world market. Those who accumulated large landholdings formed
part of the rural notability, which became increasingly secularized in the
second half of the century, and Coptic notables and professionals began
vying with the religious hierarchy for political leadership of the
community and control of its institutions. For centuries the Copts had
held a monopoly on positions in finance in the Egyptian administration;
but the dominance of Coptic clerks eroded under the occupation. Different
segments of the Coptic community proved increasingly receptive to the
appeal of nationalism.

Incorporating the Copts into the nation gave contemporary Egyptians
a bridge back to the 'Golden Age' of Pharaonic times and an apparent
physical link to ancient Egyptians. This then enlarged the body of material
from which they could draw their symbols, myths, and models. Some of
the earliest representations of the Egyptian nation – as early as the 1880s
– were of Pharaonic women, and in post-war cartoons such images were
common.[32] 'Egyptian women used to study science, speak from pulpits,
and govern the empire when women in other countries were still in a
state of slavery and misery', wrote Malaka Sa'd, Coptic editor of *al-Jins*

Figure 7.1 *Egypt represented as a pharaonic woman right after the British conquest.*
Print in *Abu Naddara*, No. 3, 1884

al-Latif, of women in the Golden Age.[33] Evidence of Egypt's glorious past was used to advance calls for women's progress together with national revival.

Hoping to fuse ethnies and overcome divisions between Copts and Muslims, male and female nationalists adopted a variety of kin idioms. They spoke of the 'sons of the Pharaohs' and the 'Mothers of the Nation'. The latter identified women as the bearers and rearers of its future citizens: the nation would only advance with women's progress and girls' education. For only educated mothers – Muslim or Copt – would imbue their sons with love for the nation. 'It is upon you, tenderhearted mother, to instil in your son respect for his beloved nation, which has no dignity without him. The glory of this nation and its misery are in your hands', wrote Fatima Rashid in an article on 'Nationalism and Woman'.[34] Writers pointed out the assumed etymological links between *umm* (mother) and *umma* (nation) and stressed their special connection.[35] Depicting themselves as 'mothers of the nation' gave women a moral authority to engage more openly in politics, and they returned repeatedly to that source of authority and unity.[36]

Yet the bonds between Copts and Muslims were not always harmonious. By 1907 competing nationalist visions had crystallized into two major political parties. A secular nationalist version gained currency among a group of landowning provincial notables. Rather than immediate evacuation, this group called for an evolutionary path to independence and cooperation with the British authorities so that reforms could be enacted and limits placed on the *khedive*'s power. The leading ideologues were educated in law or similar subjects in Europe and adopted the model of secular nationalism current in the West. Their Hizb al-Umma (Party of the Nation) attracted Coptic notables, who saw promise in its platform. Mustafa Kamil had galvanized students and others of the urban middle classes in a more popular movement. He called for the immediate evacuation of the British while still preaching loyalty to the Ottoman Sultan/Caliph. His al-Hizb al-Watani (Nationalist Party) combined territorial affinity with religious identity, although he clearly prioritized the former.[37]

Shortly after launching the party, Mustafa Kamil died, and under his successor Muhammad Farid (b.1868 – d.1919), the party's paper became more stridently pan-Islamic and anti-Coptic in tone. In a heated atmosphere, a young Watani Party sympathizer assassinated Egyptian Prime Minister Butrus Ghali, a Copt, in 1910. The crisis in relations between the Muslim and Coptic communities reached a peak. The British subsequently muzzled the press and drove Farid and other leading

Watanists into exile. British policy sought to suppress those they labelled 'fanatic' nationalists while encouraging the 'moderates', the powerful landowners of the Umma Party who spoke a secular language that they could understand.

The 'Woman Question'

Religious and secularly oriented nationalists pitched battles over the cultural content of Egyptian nationalism on different manifestations of the 'woman question'. The bundle of issues touching on education, work, seclusion, veiling, marriage, and divorce that collectively made up the 'woman question' thus became the fault line along which cultural adjustments were worked out in Egyptian nationalism. Which symbols would each side adopt? What meanings would they give them? Whose causes would they support?

These debates have been analysed in the context of nationalism, feminisms, and modernity, and are linked directly to the British occupation. Leila Ahmed, for example, sees the main protaganist Qasim Amin as 'the son of Cromer and colonialism', a vessel for colonialist rhetoric during the British occupation.[38] Yet I would argue that the debates arose as a consequence of transformations in Egyptian society across the long nineteenth century, in particular the unravelling of elite Ottoman-Egyptian households. Thus the Egyptian 'woman question' must be set in the broader Ottoman context, and the debates in turn-of-the-century Cairo should be seen in connection with those carried out in Istanbul. In both cities, and elsewhere in the empire, reformers critiqued elite family structures in order to find solutions to the perceived family crisis. This crisis was in part precipitated by the abolition of harem slavery.[39]

Harem slavery was a defining feature of elite Ottoman households. Its abolition helped speed the Egyptianization of that elite and threw the entire household structure into disarray. Slave or freeborn women of the Ottoman-Egyptian elite may have had different origins but they lived similar lives, secluded within the harem, served by domestic slaves, and often guarded by eunuchs. What would a household now look like in Egypt? The emerging middle classes worked out their own answers in the press from the 1880s and in the women's press in particular from the 1890s. The earliest founders of women's journals were Syrian Christians who geared their monthlies to 'Eastern women' and opened their pages to female writers. Egyptian Copts and Muslims soon began their own Arabic journals, with such titles as *al-Jins al-Latif* (the Gentle Sex, 1908), *Tarqiyat al-Mar'a* (Woman's Progress, 1908), and *Fatat al-Nil* (Daughter of the Nile, 1913). In spite of their diverse ethnic backgrounds, these writers evolved a common format and focused mostly on domesticity. They tended to push a bourgeois family model: a conjugal marriage based on love, a mother dedicated to raising her children, a wife frugally managing her household. Female intellectuals called for girls' education, which stood at the centre of the women's awakening in Egypt, yet they differed on the degree to which they endorsed veiling and seclusion.[40]

The debate became especially vocal at turn of the century with the publication of two books by Qasim Amin (b.1863–d.1908) – *Tahrir al-Mar'a* (*The Emancipation of Woman,* 1899) and *al-Mar'a al-Jadida* (The New Woman, 1900). Amin had stepped right out of the old Ottoman-Egyptian elite. His father, Muhammad Bey Amin Khan, had been Ottoman governor of Kurdistan, and when that region had erupted in revolt, the Sultan had given him a land grant in Egypt. There he married into the family of Ahmad Bey Khattab and became a high officer in Ismail's army. Amin had a secular education, which was capped by a law degree in France. He returned to take up a judicial post, joining the circle of reformers working with the British, and married a daughter of the Turkish admiral Amin Tawfiq.[41] Yet the world he had been born into had become transformed: the Ottoman elite had solidified its local roots and had become increasingly Egyptianized. At the same time, it looked to Europe for political models and social solutions. There Amin found inspiration, and his bourgeois vision closely corresponded with that of the editors of women's journals. He pushed for a package of girls' education, conjugal marriage, unveiling, and an end to seclusion. And he argued that educated women would help the nation develop, echoing a theme articulated in the women's press.[42]

Rebuttals to Amin came from religious nationalists such as Mustafa Kamil, Fatima Rashid, and her husband Muhammad Farid Wajdi. While they endorsed women's education, they opposed some of Amin's other reforms, arguing that Islamic culture should provide the models for women and the family. This group generally came from the middle classes, not the highest ones where harem slavery had been most articulated, and continued to look to Istanbul for models rather than to Europe. The 'Woman Question' illuminated a cultural split and difference in religious orientation between the two nationalist camps, a split that became clearer with the emergence of the Watani and Umma parties.

One of the most contentious aspects of the 'Woman Question' was marriage: Should families arrange marriages? Should the couple be allowed to meet beforehand? Should romantic love have any role in the relationship?[43] In the early 1890s at the age of thirteen, Huda Sultan was married to her cousin and guardian 'Ali sha'rawi (whose children by his first wife were older than her) in order to keep the family lands intact. In the mid-1890s at the age of eighteen, Safiya Fahmi (b.1876–d.1946), daughter of the Ottoman-Egyptian politician Mustafa Fahmi (who had a long record of Cabinet appointments before and after the British occupation), married Sa'd Zaghlul, an ambitious lawyer about twenty years her senior. These marriages followed established patterns of consolidating alliances among elite households. But in 1904 the marriage of Safiya al-Sadat to Shaykh 'Ali Yusuf challenged convention and resulted in a trial that sparked a national debate.

Shaykh 'Ali Yusuf came from a humble background but had risen to national prominence as the editor of *al-Mu'ayyad*, a member of the General Assembly, and a confidant of Khedive Abbas. Having amassed wealth along the way, he sought a new marriage to a woman from a notable household. The youngest daughter of Shaykh 'Abd al-Khaliq al-Sadat, popularly revered leader of the descendants of the Prophet, had caught his eye. Her father agreed to the match but postponed the wedding for years. Safiya then took matters into her own hands and agreed to go ahead with the ceremony in the home of a relative, claiming that she was of age and able to give her own consent to marriage. Upon learning of their contracted marriage, al-Sadat went to a religious court to have it annulled on the grounds that 'Ali Yusuf had tricked her into marriage and that he was of inferior social standing. The court ruled in favour of the father and annulled the marriage. Safiya returned home only when a secret agreement had been worked out that she could marry 'Ali Yusuf in her father's presence after some time had elapsed.[44]

The court case became a national drama, drawing heavy coverage in the press and sparking heated exchanges. Many sided with the father and his right to determine his daughter's fate; others took offence at the personal attacks on the renowned journalist. The controversy also led to a major rift between Mustafa Kamil, who attacked his rival 'Ali Yusuf in the pages of *al-Liwa'*, and the *khedive*, who intervened in support of his propagandist.[45] The case touched at core cultural issues, challenging both social hierarchies and patriarchal authority. The road from ethnie to nation was a rocky one involving the renegotiation of power relations and fundamental social structures.

After the abolition of harem slavery, the harem system slowly and sometimes painfully disintegrated. Patterns of socialization were reworked in the process. Women in elite households had previously been educated within the confines of the harem in 'in-house' schools. Now they went outside to partake of more public forms of schooling, and they often used nationalist rhetoric to justify this and other activities. Gender segregation had been an important feature of Ottoman households with separate spaces (the harem) and special dress (the veil) for women. But fashions changed and many elite women adopted Western dress (which they concealed with long cloaks when they went outdoors). The face veil remained one of the last vestiges and main markers of the old Ottoman order, and it increasingly became a symbol of cultural contention.

In response to foreign critiques and attacks by Egyptian reformers, religious nationalists clung to the veil. 'This veil is not a disease which holds us back. Rather it is the cause of our happiness', wrote Fatima Rashid. 'And we will guard it carefully and do all that concerns us from behind this beloved veil that is our symbol and the symbol of our Muslim grandmothers.'[46] The veil worn by the Egyptian elite in the early twentieth century was a white *yashmak* that had originated in Istanbul. Egyptian peasants had their own style of veiling: they pulled a headscarf across the face when the situation demanded. The Cairene newspaper *al-'Afaf* (Modesty) featured a drawing of a peasant woman standing between a river and palm trees with the pyramids and a sphinx in the background on an early cover in 1910. The woman has a light veil drawn across her face that revealed the contours of her features. That veil was darkened a few weeks later after the journal had come under attack. *Al-'Afaf* and the religious nationalists behind the newspaper supported veiling as a sign of modesty and moral virtue as women became a marker of cultural purity.[47]

The more secularly oriented nationalists adopted the veil as a cultural symbol with a markedly different meaning. From turn of the century, they called repeatedly for unveiling, and, sure enough, a trend toward unveiling had begun: minority women stopped veiling, younger girls never started, and veils became lighter over time. 'Women are not the only ones who are veiled in Egypt', asserted 'Abd al-Hamid Hamdi, the editor of the newspaper *al-Sufur* (Unveiling), founded in 1915. 'We are a veiled nation.'[48] The goals of the paper were 'the creation of a literary awakening aimed at freeing the mind, delivering Egyptian nationalism from weak elements, and freeing woman from the chains of ignorance and unsound traditions.'[49] The veil became a metaphor for both backwardness and virtue as women came to stand for the nation.

Conclusion

Through the long nineteenth century, the elite in Egypt underwent a metamorphosis, from local Ottoman-Egyptian or Egyptian. In the early stages, harem slavery (and the purchase of Circassians in particular) had been crucial in maintaining elite identity for Ottomans or attaining it for ambitious Egyptians replicating the household structure of the khedivial courts. The abolition of slavery and the practice of intermarriage sped the transformation of the ethnic composition of the elite. This meant both that more Egyptians had climbed up into the elite and that Ottomans were becoming more assimilated into the Egyptian population. Their Egyptian-born descendants became Arabic speakers, and although they may personally have been proud of their Turkish ancestry, they publicly renounced the Ottoman past.[50] The nationalist movement arose in part in reaction to ethnic tensions as created in the transition as Arabic speakers pushed for promotions in the army and more power in the central government. While the 'Urabi movement itself was aborted, the under-lying transformation of the elite was completed in the following decades.

But now a British occupation sat perched in Egypt, presenting a new set of overlords. Moreover, that overlord competed with Egypt for control of the Sudan, a source of domestic slaves for elite households. Sovereignty of the Sudan remained a tenet of Egyptian nationalism even as the British edged the Egyptians out. As the bid for restoring the Egyptian empire – or a Nile Valley entity – failed, only territorial Egypt with her own Muslim and Coptic inhabitants remained. Egyptian Copts and Muslims could not literally join in one family, but they could figuratively. Here the familial metaphors produced by male and female nationalists – particularly ones of motherhood – helped the two communities to combine lineages. This gave Egyptians a myth of continuity from antiquity to the present and helped to fuse collective memories. The debate on the cultural content of Egyptian nationalism found its clearest expression in the issues that collectively made up the 'woman question'. Female intellectuals helped to craft some of the symbols and to shape the debates, and women fought in both the religious and secular nationalist camps.

Notes

1. Toledano, E. (1990), *State and Society in Mid-Nineteenth-Century Egypt*, Cambridge: Cambridge University Press, introduction. For a comprehensive critique of the nationalist discourse on Mehmet Ali and his army, see Fahmy, K. (1997), *All the Pasha's Men: Mehmed*

Ali, His Army and the Making of Modern Egypt, Cambridge: Cambridge University Press.
2. Toledano, E. (1990), *State and Society in Mid-Nineteenth-Century Egypt*, Cambridge: Cambridge University Press.
3. Ze'evi, D. (1996), '*Kul* and Getting Cooler: The Dissolution of Elite Collective Identity and the Formation of Official Nationalism in the Ottoman Empire', *Mediterranean Historical Review* 11: 177–95; Toledano, E. (1990), *State and Society in Mid-Nineteenth-Century Egypt*, Cambridge: Cambridge University Press, 58; Toledano E. (1998), *Slavery and Abolition in the Ottoman Middle East*, Seattle: University of Washington Press, chapter.1.
4. Baer, G. (1969), *Studies in the Social History of Modern Egypt*, Chicago: University of Chicago Press, chapter 10; Toledano, E. (1981), *The Ottoman Slave Trade and Its Suppression: 1840–1890*, Princeton: University of Princeton Press, 1982; Toledano E. (1998), *Slavery and Abolition in the Ottoman Middle East*, Seattle: University of Washington Press; Schölch, A. (1981), *Egypt for the Egyptians! The Socio-political Crisis in Egypt 1878–1882*, London: Ithaca Press, 24, 67.
5. Sha'rawi, H. (1981), *Mudhakkirat Huda Sha'rawi*, Cairo: Dar al-Hilal, 10–31; Hunter, F. (1983), 'The Making of a Notable Politician: Muhammad Sultan Pasha (1825–1884)', *International Journal of Middle East Studies* 15: 537–44.
6. Sha'rawi, H. (1981), *Mudhakkirat Huda Sha'rawi*, Cairo: Dar al-Hilal, 32–40; Shaarawi, H. (1986), *Harem Years: The Memoirs of an Egyptian Feminist (1879–1924)*, M. Badran (trans.), London: Virago Press, 1986, 23–6.
7. Sha'rawi, H. (1981), *Mudhakkirat Huda Sha'rawi*, Cairo: Dar al-Hilal; Tugay, E. (1963), *Three Centuries: Family Chronicles of Turkey and Egypt*, Oxford: Oxford University Press; Toledano, E. (1981), 'Slave Dealers, Women, Pregnancy, and Abortion: The Story of a Circassian Slave-girl in Mid-Nineteenth Century Cairo', *Slavery and Abolition* 2: 53–68; Tucker, J. (1985), *Women in Nineteenth-Century Egypt*, Cambridge: Cambridge University Press, 164–93.
8. Toledano, E. (1996), 'Forgetting Egypt's Ottoman Past', in E. Toledano and U. Wokoeck (eds), *Formation and Transmission of Tradition in Muslim Societies*, Tel Aviv: Tel Aviv University, 163–80.
9. Hunter, F. (1983), 'Egypt's High Officials in Transition from a Turkish to a Modern Administrative Elite, 1849–1879', *Middle Eastern Studies* 19: 277–91; Toledano, E. (1990), *State and Society in Mid-Nineteenth-Century Egypt*, Cambridge: Cambridge University Press.

10. Baer, G. (1969), *Studies in the Social History of Modern Egypt*, Chicago: University of Chicago Press, 176–89; Toledano, E. (1993), 'Late Ottoman Concepts of Slavery (1830s–1880s)', in *Poetics Today* 14: 477–506; Toledano, E. (1998), *Slavery and Abolition in the Ottoman Middle East*, Seattle: University of Washington Press, 24–41.

11. Ze'evi, D. (1996), '*Kul* and Getting Cooler: The Dissolution of Elite Collective Identity and the Formation of Official Nationalism in the Ottoman Empire', *Mediterranean Historical Review* 11: 193–4.

12. J. Cole characterizes the movement as a social revolution that sought to overthrow a dual elite of Ottoman-Egyptians and Europeans. He argues that 'a nativist discourse temporarily helps subsume the class differences among the challengers under a broad proto-nationalism'. (Cole, R. (1993), *Colonialism and Revolution in the Middle East: Social and Cultural Origins of Egypt's 'Urabi Movement*, Princeton: Princeton University Press, 283.) Schölch does not see social and political revolution as driving forces but rather a reforming impulse that had no intention of setting up a secular Egyptian national state – Schölch, A. (1981), *Egypt for the Egyptians! The Socio-political Crisis in Egypt 1878–1882*, London: Ithaca Press, 313.

13. Powell, E. (1995), 'Colonized Colonizers: Egyptian Nationalists and the Issue of the Sudan, 1875-1919', Ph.D. thesis, Harvard University, 98–9.

14. 'Urabi, A. (1982), *The Defense Statement of Ahmad 'Urabi the Egyptian*, T. Le Gassick (trans.), Cairo: American University in Cairo Press, 18.

15. Schölch, A. (1981), *Egypt for the Egyptians! The Socio-political Crisis in Egypt 1878–1882*, London: Ithaca Press, 221, 341 n.8.

16. British and Foreign Anti-Slavery Society (BFAAS) Papers, Rhodes House, Oxford, C22/G30, Blunt to Allen, Suez, 17 March 1882.

17. Powell, E. (1995), 'Colonized Colonizers: Egyptian Nationalists and the Issue of the Sudan, 1875-1919', Ph.D. thesis, Harvard University, 102.

18. British Public Record Office, London, Foreign Office (FO), 141/128, Borg to Vivian, Cairo, 3 February 1879.

19. 'Urabi, A. (1982), *The Defense Statement of Ahmad 'Urabi the Egyptian*, T. Le Gassick (trans.), Cairo: American University in Cairo Press, 28.

20. Broadley, A. (1884/1980), *How We Defended Arabi and His Friends*, London: Chapman and Hall, rep. Cairo, 373–6.

21. 'Urabi, A. (1982), *Kashif al-Sitar*, trans. in 'Urabi, A. (1982), *The*

Defense Statement of Ahmad 'Urabi the Egyptian, T. Le Gassick (trans.), Cairo: American University in Cairo Press, 42; Blunt, W. (1907/1967), *Secret History of the English Occupation of Egypt: Being a Personal Narrative of Events*, London: Unwin, rep. New York: Fertig, , appendix 1; Schölch, A. (1981), *Egypt for the Egyptians! The Socio-political Crisis in Egypt 1878–1882*, London: Ithaca Press, 283–4, 288.

22. Al-Sayyid, A. (1969), *Egypt and Cromer: A Study in Anglo-Egyptian Relations*, New York: Praeger.

23. Powell, E. (1995), 'Colonized Colonizers: Egyptian Nationalists and the Issue of the Sudan, 1875-1919', Ph.D. thesis, Harvard University; Nakash, Y. (1988), 'Reflections on a Subsistence Economy: Production and Trade of the Mahdist Sudan, 1881–1898', in Kedourie, E. and Haim, S. (eds.) (1988), *Essays on the Economic History of the Middle East*, London: Frank Cass, 51–69.

24. Powell, E. (1995), 'Colonized Colonizers: Egyptian Nationalists and the Issue of the Sudan, 1875–1919', Ph.D. thesis, Harvard University, 151; see introduction, chapter 3.

25. FO 407/127, No 91 Rodd to Kimberley, Cairo, 31 August 1894, 56-8; FO 407/127, No 98, Rodd to Kimberley, Alexandria, 14 September 1894, 62; FO 407/127, No 121 Rodd to Kimberley, Cairo, 16 September 1894, 72–3.

26. Powell, E. (1995), 'Colonized Colonizers: Egyptian Nationalists and the Issue of the Sudan, 1875–1919', Ph.D. thesis, Harvard University.

27. Moustafa Kamel Pasha (1907), *What the National Party Wants*, Cairo: English Standard, 21.

28. Powell, E. (1995), 'Colonized Colonizers: Egyptian Nationalists and the Issue of the Sudan, 1875–1919', Ph.D. thesis, Harvard University, 180–1.

29. See cartoons in *al-Kashkul* 92 (1923), 1; *al-Kashkul* 132 (1923), 11; *al-Kashkul* 4:162 (1924), 20; *al-Kashkul* 3:153 (1924), 1. See also, Baron, B. (1997), 'Nationalist Iconography: Egypt as a Woman', in J. Jankowski and I. Gershoni (eds.) (1997), *Rethinking Nationalism in the Arab Middle East*, New York: Columbia University Press, 105–24.

30. Smith, A. (1989), 'The Origins of Nations', *Ethnic and Racial Studies* 12, reprinted in G. Eley and R. Suny (eds) (1996), *Becoming National: A Reader*, Oxford: Oxford University Press, 123.

31. For background on the Copts in modern Egypt, see Behrens-Abouseif, D. (1982), 'The Political Situation of the Copts, 1798–1923', in B. Braude and B. Lewis (eds.), *Christians and Jews in the Ottoman*

Empire, New York: Holmes and Meier, vol.1, 185–205; Tamura, A. (1985), 'Ethnic Consciousness and Its Transformation in the Course of Nation-Building: The Muslim and the Copt in Egypt, 1906–1919', *Muslim World* 75: 102–14; Reid, D. (1995), 'Archeology, Social Reform, and Modern Identity among the Copts (1854–1952)', in A. Rousillon (ed.) (1983), *Entre Reforme Sociale et Mouvement National: Identite et Modernisation en Egypte (1882-1962)*, Cairo: CEDEJ, 311–35; Labib, S., 'The Copts in Egyptian Society and Politics, 1882–1919', in G. Warburg and U. Kupferschmidt (eds.), *Islam, Nationalism, and Radicalism in Egypt and the Sudan*, New York: Praeger.

32. See, for example, *Abu Naddara* 7, no.9 (1883), 100; *Abu Naddara* 8, no.3 (1884), 142; *al-Musawwara al-Lata'if* (29 March 1920), 4; *al-Musawwara al-Lata'if* (11 July 1921), 7; Baron, B. (1997), 'Nationalist Iconography: Egypt as a Woman', in J. Jankowski and I. Gershoni (eds.) (1997), *Rethinking Nationalism in the Arab Middle East*, New York: Columbia University Press, 105–24.

33. Sa'd, M. (1908), 'al-Mar'a fi Misr', *al-Jins al-Latif* 1: 38–9.

34. Rashid, F. (1908), 'al-Wataniyya wa'l-Mar'a', *Tarqiyat al-Mar'a* 1: 28.

35. 'J., F.' (1916), 'Kalima 'an Khutbat al-Anisa Victoria Sa'd', *al-Jins al-Latif* 9, (4): 139. B. Lewis suggests that the Quranic word *umma* (the people or the community) is probably a loanword from either Hebrew or Aramaic rather than connected with the Arabic *umm* (mother). Lewis, B. (1988), *The Political Language of Islam*, Chicago: University of Chicago Press, 17.

36. Baron, B. (1991), 'Mothers, Morality, and Nationalism in Pre-1919 Egypt', in R. Khalidi et al. (eds.), *The Origins of Arab Nationalism*, New York: Columbia University Press, 271–88.

37. Kazziha, W. (1977), 'The Jaridah-Ummah Group and Egyptian Politics', *Middle Eastern Studies* 13: 373–85; Goldschmidt, A. (1968), 'The Egyptian Nationalist Party: 1892–1919', in Holt, P., *Political and Social Change in Modern Egypt*, Oxford: Oxford University Press, 308–33; Holt, P. (1982), 'The National Party from Spotlight to Shadow', *Asian and African Studies* 16: 11–30; Lockman, Z. (1988), 'The Social Roots of Nationalism: Workers and the National Movement in Egypt, 1908–19', *Middle Eastern Studies* 24: 445–59; Gershoni, I. and Jankowski, J. (1986), *Egypt, Islam, and the Arabs: The Search for Egyptian Nationhood, 1900–1930*, Oxford: Oxford University Press, 4–10.

38. Ahmed, L. (1992), *Women and Gender in Islam: Historical Roots of*

a Modern Debate, New Haven: Yale University Press, 163. L. Abu-Lughod argues that Amin's vision of conjugal marriage effectively subjected a woman to her husband and children by undermining women's homosocial bonds. (Abu-Lughod, L. (1998), 'The Marriage of Islamism and Feminism in Egypt: Selective Repudiation as a Dynamic of Postcolonial Cultural Politics', in Abu-Lughod (ed.), *Remaking Women: Feminism and Modernity in the Middle East*, Princeton: Princeton University Press, 243–69.)

39. See Kandiyoti, D. (1998), 'Some Awkward Questions on Women and Modernity in Turkey', in *Remaking Women*, 270–87; Kandiyoti, D. (1991), 'End of Empire: Islam, Nationalism and Women in Turkey', in D. Kandiyoti (ed.), *Women, Islam and the State*, Philadephia: Temple University Press, 22–47; Kandiyoti, D. (1998), 'Slave Girls, Temptresses, and Comrades: Images of Women in the Turkish Novel', *Feminist Issues*, 35–49.

40. See Baron, B. (1994), *The Women's Awakening in Egypt*, New Haven: Yale University Press.

41. Hourani, A. (1983), *Arabic Thought in the Liberal Age 1798–1939*, Cambridge: Cambridge University Press, 164–70; Cole, J. (1981), 'Feminism, Class, and Islam in Turn-of-the-Century Egypt', *International Journal of Middle East Studies* 13: 387–401.

42. Amin, Q. (1899), *Tahrir al-Mar'a*, Cairo: Matba'at al-Sharqiyya, 2nd. ed.; Amin, Q. (1900), *al-Mar'a al-Jadida*, Cairo: Matba'at al-Sha'b, rep., Cairo: al-Markaz al-'Arabi li'l-Ba'th wa'l-Nashr.

43. See Baron, B. (1991), 'The Making and Breaking of Marital Bonds in Modern Egypt', in N. Keddie and B. Baron (eds.), *Women in Middle Eastern History*, New Haven: Yale University Press, 275–91.

44. Moyal, E. (1904), 'al-Sayyid 'Abd al-Khaliq al-Sadat wa Karimatuhu', *al-'Aila* 3, (11): 83–4; Baha' al-Din, A. (1954), *Ayyam Laha Ta'rikh*, Cairo: Dar Ruz al-Yusuf, 1: 47–61; Kelidar, A. (1981), 'Shaykh 'Ali Yusuf: Egyptian Journalist and Islamic Nationalist', in M. Buheiry (ed.), *Intellectual Life in the Arab East, 1890–1939*, Beirut: American University in Beirut, 10–20; Rizk, Y. (1997), 'Al-Ahram: A Diwan of Contemporary Life', *al-Ahram* (6–12 February): 9.

45. Farid, M. (1992), *The Memoirs and Diaries of Muhammad Farid, an Egyptian Nationalist Leader (1868–1919)*, A. Goldschmidt (trans), San Francisco: Mellen University Research Press, 19. The saga also inspired fiction, becoming the basis for Out El Kouloub's novel *Ramza*, Nayra Atiya (trans.) Syracuse: Syracuse University Press, 1994, crafted out of stories she had heard in the harem as a child.

46. Rashid, F. (1908), 'Kalima `an al-Hal al-Hadira', *Tarqiyat al-Mar'a*
    1: 76.
47. See frontispieces, *al-'Afaf* 1 (12 May 1911) and (9 June 1911); al-
    Salimi, S., 'Didd al-'Afaf', *al-'Afaf* 1 (29 May 1911): 14. Baron, B.
    (1989), 'Unveiling in Early Twentieth-Century Egypt: Practical and
    Symbolic Considerations', *Middle Eastern Studies* 25: 370–86.
48. Hamdi, A. (1915), 'al-Sufur', *al-Sufur* 1, (1): 1.
49. (1919), *Al-Sufur* 5, (202): 1.
50. See Toledano, E. (1996), 'Forgetting Egypt's Ottoman Past', in E.
    Toledano and U. Wokoeck (eds.), *Formation and Transmission of
    Tradition in Muslim Societies*, Tel Aviv: Tel Aviv University, 163–
    80.

8

The Ambiguities for Feminists of National Belonging: Race and Gender in the Imagined Australian Community

Marilyn Lake

Feminists and the Nation

Feminist scholars have long pointed out that the imagined communities that constitute nations have, as often as not, excluded women. This was especially clear in the Australian case, where national mythologies and histories have defined the Australian nation in terms of the burgeoning of a distinctive national type, a type of man, the Bushman. In the words of journalist Francis Adams, writing in his 1890s book, *The Australians*, the Bushman was 'the one powerful and unique type yet produced in the new land'.[1] In the national imaginary, Australia was a homosocial community – a community of pastoralists, shearers, swagmen, gold-diggers, bush rangers, explorers.[2] It was a fantasy with extraordinary resilience and it resonates powerfully still. For, as if the sustained feminist challenge posed over the last thirty years by feminist history had never occurred, a recent feature article in a weekend magazine on the new *Oxford Companion to Australian History* managed to devote two entire pages to Australian history without mentioning one woman, past or present, neither as historian nor historical subject. Considerable attention was devoted, on the other hand, to the alleged controversy over whether legendary bush-ranger and folk hero, Ned Kelly, was really an extra-ordinary horseman.[3]

In nineteenth-century Australian colonial discourse, national independence from Britain was conceptualized as a coming to 'manhood'. In the first issue of the journal, the *Republican,* founded by Louisa Lawson in 1887, a column called 'Australian independence', declared:

> It is high time that the sensible and self-respecting lifted up their voices for separation and independence. With all due acknowledgment of and respect for that maternal solicitude with which England has watched us in our infancy

and flattered us in our youth, if the outcome of it all has to be abject grovelling to Royal ermine and jewelled heads, the sooner we shake the dust from our knees and hold our heads erect the better. If our loyalty means neither more or less than sacrifice of all our interests, hopes and manhood to English avarice, cupidity and pride, undeniably the time has come to cut the painter ... That there are difficulties in raising a flag of our own as the symbol of our self-hood and independent manhood we readily admit ... But even so we see no valid reason to despair.[4]

Thus was nationhood equated with manhood; but how could women voice a claim to the status of manhood? Lawson was a leading feminist as well as a republican nationalist and her decision to wind up the *Republican* after only one year in favour of *The Dawn A Journal for Australian Women* was undoubtedly a response to the gendered contradictions of these political subjectivities. *The Dawn* was established in 1888 as a journal in which women could 'express their opinions on political and social questions which involve their interest'.[5] Whereas nationalists appealed to the 'brotherhood', Lawson as feminist addressed the 'sisterhood'. In a column in its first issue called 'About Ourselves', *The Dawn* announced:

'Woman is not uncompleted man, but diverse', says Tennyson and being diverse why should she not have her journal in which her divergent hopes, aims and opinions may have representation ...

There has hitherto been no trumpet through which the concentrated voices of womankind could publish their grievances and their opinions. Men legislate on divorce, on hours of labour, and many another question intimately affecting women, but neither ask nor know the wishes of those whose lives and happiness are most concerned. Here then is *Dawn*, the Australian woman's journal and mouthpiece – a phonograph to wind out audibly the whispers, pleadings and demands of the sisterhood.[6]

The main demand of the 'sisterhood' was for representation, in the cultural, artistic, literary and historical discourses that defined the nation and in the political institutions that governed it. 'This most potent constituency we seek to represent', declared Lawson, 'and for their suffrages we sue'.[7]

Lawson herself wrote much nationalist verse and she noted in one poem, 'The Women of the Bush', the tendency for women to be omitted from accounts of nation-building:

Ah how I bless the pioneers
The women lost to fame,
Who braved the bush for strenuous years
To make Australia's name.[8]

To retrieve these pioneer women 'lost to fame' and inscribe them in the historical record as nation-builders, however, was, in the imperial context of Australia's founding, to ignore their part in the dispossession of Aboriginal people that had made the pioneering possible. If white women would thus be written into the national story of land settlement as pioneers proving their national virtue on the land, Aboriginal women would, perforce, be relegated to a mythological past.

The imagined community that was Australia at the turn of the century was racist, as well as masculinist.[9] The upsurge of nationalist sentiment in the late nineteenth century coincided with, and was indeed predicated on, the disavowal of the continuing presence of Aboriginal people. Invoking the Darwinist conceit that Aborigines were 'a dying race', doomed to extinction, nationalists determinedly expelled them from national consciousness. They also sought to expel Asian residents already present and to prevent other non-whites from arriving. The new nation declared itself to be White Australia and the constitution of the Commonwealth of Australia, inaugurated in 1901, specifically excluded Aborigines from being counted in the census. By 1906, the masthead of the nationalist magazine the *Bulletin* changed from 'Australia for the Australians' to the more explicit 'Australia for the White Man'. In the nationalist literature that proliferated from the 1880s, Aborigines, if mentioned at all, were cast as relics from a primitive past with no place in a modern nation-state.

Thus feminist desires to join the nation seemed to collude in the racist oppression on which 'Australia', as both nation and state, was based. A project necessary to the empowerment of white women – the demand for enfranchisement in the nation-state and recognition as nation-builders – rested on the disempowerment and lack of recognition of Aboriginal women. Yet there was more ambivalence among feminists to the exclusions of the national project than a charge of 'complicity' might suggest.[10] Some feminists were oblivious to the fate of Aboriginal women, but some leading suffragists such as Rose Scott explicitly opposed a racially discriminatory franchise. A number increasingly identified with their downtrodden 'sisters'.

The tensions inherent in the relationship forged between Australian feminists and the nation in the late nineteenth century – a nation that was both masculinist and racist – became fully evident by the 1930s, when the place of Aboriginal people in the nation was brought newly into public consciousness, first, by expanding campaigns for Aboriginal rights and second, the commemoration of state centenaries (in Victoria and South Australia) and the national sesqui-centenary of settlement (in New South Wales). Nineteenth-century nation building cast a long shadow over twentieth-century feminists' relationship to the nation. As the nationalist and feminist writer Miles Franklin observed in 1937, Aborigines remained a 'long gone presence' on the Australian scene – their voices were 'almost within hearing'.[11] Nation building was haunted by the original sin of dispossession. For Franklin the only way for white Australians to atone for the founding act of theft was through establishing a spiritual relationship with the land through writing.

Feminists were divided on the issue of how to reconcile their own desire for national recognition with recognition of the prior rights of Aboriginal people. Nationalist feminists became more defensively racist, while those campaigning for Aboriginal rights were often cast as disloyal or sentimental extremists. Others occupied an uncomfortable and shifting middle ground. In exploring the ambiguities and ambivalence that characterised feminism's relation to the nation from the 1880s until the 1930s, this paper will look at three moments of feminist engagement with the national project, highlighted by the activism of three feminists born in successive generations in the nineteenth century: republican suffragist Louisa Lawson born in 1848, nationalist and feminist writer Mary Fullerton, born in 1868 and imperial campaigner for Aboriginal rights, Constance Ternente Cooke, born in 1888.

An Australian Song

Born on a pastoral station near Mudgee in New South Wales, Louisa Albury attended the local 'national' school, but was forced to cut short her education to care for her siblings. Her father was a station hand; she married a gold digger named Larsson, who took up a selection. The family's income was intermittent and they depended on Louisa's earnings from raising cattle, running a store and a post office. She finally left her husband in 1883 and moved with her younger children to Sydney, where she ran a printery and worked as a journalist. Proud and self-reliant, she became a champion of independence, both for Australia and for women.

During the 1880s and 1890s, Louisa Lawson wrote much nationalist verse, hailing in conventional terms Australia's promise as a land of freedom and independence. She wrote *An Australian Song* (two versions), *Australia, Sweet Australia, Australia Felix* and *Women of the Bush*. Typically these poems combined praise for the country's natural beauty with tribute to its democratic promise:

> For we hail from a land that is great and grand,
> And the pride of the Southern Sea;

'Tis a sunny land, 'tis a golden land,
And the home of the brave and free.[12]

The political potential of a democratic Australia was defined precisely in opposition to the social and political hierarchies that characterized Old World Britain. Lawson also made reference in her verse to the country's 'pre-history' and its earlier inhabitants, who were present, for the most part, in spirit form only. Thus in 'Uloola':

> Where the great dividing ranges
> Raise their ramparts bold and blue
> Guarding through th'eternal changes
> Old world landmarks in the New
> There are in its secret places
> Shrined by prehistoric man
> Deities whose imaged faces
> Frown in basalt stygian. [13]

I have written elsewhere about the ways in which the meaning of Australian turn-of-the-century feminism in Australia was forged in a condition of 'double difference'. Differentiating herself temporally from both Old World 'barbarism' and Stone Age 'primitivism', the white Australian feminist self-consciously equated the modernity of the New World with the novel possibilities of women's advancement.[14]

In a poem called 'The Squatter's Wife', Lawson recognized the continuing presence of Aboriginal women in contemporary Australia, representing them in this instance as the cause of the white woman's degradation and humiliation. Lawson had read about the case of Alice Gertler, 'a beautiful and gifted girl', who had accompanied her husband to his pastoral station far away in the bush only to find he already had already installed an Aboriginal mistress and family.

> Lonely hut on barren creek,
> Where the rotting sheep-yards reek,
> Far away from kith and kin,
> None save thee and native gin
> Many a weary mile within – Alice Gertler
> . . .
> Bound to one who loves thee not,
> Drunken off-spring of a sot;
> Even now at wayside inn
> Riots he in drink and sin,
> Mating with a half-caste gin – Alice Gertler.[15]

Whereas the writer's sympathy in 'Alice Gertler' was clearly reserved for the white woman humiliated by the liaison between her husband and the 'half-caste gin', Lawson, anticipating later feminist campaigns for Aboriginal rights in the 1920s and 1930s, would soon come to represent Aboriginal and non-Aboriginal women as equally the victims of the white man's selfishness and lust.

Aboriginal women, Lawson came to argue, were 'wives and mothers like ourselves'. But they were also 'poor remnants of a dying race', to whom white women should 'show consideration and kindness ... sympathising in their troubles, alleviating, as far as possible, their hardships, and honouring their womanhood as we honour our own'.[16] The possible conflict between the nationalist claim to Australia as 'home' and the feminist positioning of white women as deserving of honour as pioneers, on the one hand, and recognition that these processes involved the dispossession and disavowal of Aboriginal women, on the other, was thus obviated by the comforting conceit that the indigenous people were 'a dying race'. They had not been killed by the settlers and removed from their lands by the 'pioneers'. Rather they were doomed to extinction by the impersonal force of evolution that allowed white women to figure as innocents in this saga of inevitable progress.

Lawson stated her feminist project as one of 'representation', but as Judith Butler and others have noted, the very act of representation is itself regulatory, constitutive of the identity 'woman' for whom representation is sought.[17] Lawson sought to represent the interests of 'woman', but the women to whom she gave voice were white women, the victims of men's tyranny, but not themselves the oppressors of other women. In making the feminist case for the agency of pioneer women in building the nation, for recognition of white women's work as settlers, Lawson could not simultaneously acknowledge them as the beneficiaries of other women's dispossession and disempowerment.

Nation-Building as Dispossession and Depravity

In a passionate letter to Sir John Harris of the Anti-Slavery Society in England in 1937, Mary Montgomerie Bennett, a leading campaigner for Aboriginal rights in Western Australia wrote of the declining numbers of 'pure-blood' Aborigines: 'They call it "dying out" but it is "killing out"'.[18] From the 1920s, a group of Australian feminists – Christian in values and imperialist in outlook - became active in campaigns for Aboriginal rights that also began to challenge triumphalist accounts of national progress. While an emergent group of professional historians located in the Universities wrote the first congratulatory histories of the nation, feminist reformers began to construct a very different national history that took as its departure point 'the victimisation of Aboriginal women'.[19] Their identification with the plight of Aboriginal women, sexually abused and robbed of their children, led them to become outspoken critics of Australia, attacking it from abroad and even suggesting that it had no moral right to exist: 'If the present wicked immoral traffic continues...then Australia cannot last and it will be definitely to the good for Australia to disappear.'[20] For these women, Australia was not the home of the brave and the free. Settlement was, rather, an alibi for the gratification of men's lusts, a source not of civilisation, but of contamination. 'The terrible plight of the civilised Aborigines', wrote Mary Bennett, the most outspoken of this feminist network, 'is the logical conclusion of our own dealings with them'.[21] Characteristically, she attributed the spread of typhoid in the outback 'as arising solely from the insanitary habits of so many white men'.[22]

Feminists' relentless criticisms of Australia from abroad rankled with some of their fellow-countrywomen and men and angered the government. 'Public opinion in Australia is very thin skinned about criticism from England', Bennett noted with satisfaction.[23] The network of feminists, active in Britain, Australia and Geneva, included Edith Jones, president in the mid-1920s of the Victorian Women Citizens' Movement, Ada Bromham, a leading member of both the Woman's Christian Temperance Union and the Women's Service Guild in Western Australia, M. Jamieson-Williams and Ruby Rich of the United Associations of Women in New South Wales, Constance Ternente Cooke of the South Australian Women's Non-Party Association and Bessie Rischbieth, president of the Australian Federation of Women Voters, with which the state organizations were affiliated. Many of these women were born in England and some lived in London for long periods of time. Edith Jones, who was married to a Church of England minister returned to the United Kingdom in 1929, when her husband was appointed vicar of Marlborough. In London, she ran the Australian sub-committee of the Anti-Slavery Society.

Jones's friend, Constance Ternente Cooke, delivered the annual address for the Anti-Slavery Society in London in 1927, outlining the appalling conditions of Australian Aborigines. Married to a professor at the University of Adelaide, Cooke convened the Aboriginal Welfare Committee of the South Australian Women's Non-Party Association and was a member of the Aborigines' Protection League. She was also a member of the committee to promote the idea of Aboriginal self-government through the establishment of a Model Aboriginal State. Her address to the Anti-Slavery Society was attended by activist Mary Montgomerie Bennett, a Queensland pastoralist's daughter living in London who had published her loving biography of her father *Christison of Lammermoor* in the same year. When Bennett herself addressed the London based British Commonwealth League in 1929 she faced a hostile reception from the Australians present. Buxton reported to Cooke:

> Mrs Bennett had an opportunity this week of reading a paper at the British Commonwealth League when a resolution was passed. She was not, however, satisfied with her reception; she felt there was a hostile element and the Secretary Miss Collison being an Australian objected to her criticising the Federal Government.[24]

In 1930, Constance Cooke presented another paper to the Pan-Pacific Women's Conference in Honolulu, where she told the assembled delegates that the Australian nation had been built on two great wrongs:

> The first great wrong was when the original inhabitants were deprived of all their lands by the legal device of declaring them the property of the Crown, women as well as men, were relegated thus to the position of serfs . . .
>
> The second great wrong to the race has been the interference of the white man with the native woman . . . The native woman has not had a chance for the strict native morality has been undermined.[25]

Cooke's paper elaborated these charges at some length, specifying the actual conditions of Aboriginal people in each state and in the federal territories. Dismayed at the prospect of this paper being delivered at an international gathering, the Minister for Home Affairs asked that a lengthy government reply also be read at the conference, defending its record in the administration of Aboriginal affairs in north and central Australia. As there was no time for a paper to be read, a copy was printed in the conference proceedings. From the government's point of view worse was to come. The feminists used the British Commonwealth League and the Anti-Slavery Society to attract the attention of the British press to Australia's appalling treatment of Aboriginal people, especially the enslaved condition of women. Edith Jones helped draft Anti-Slavery Society letters to the Australian Prime Minister and the High Commissioner in London.

In a paper by Mary Bennett read to the British Commonwealth League called 'The Aboriginal Mother in Western Australia in 1933', she followed Cooke in presenting the history of Australian settlement as a cause for national shame. Australian settlers were predatory and rapacious. Bennett reiterated Cooke's argument about the two stages in our history: first white men took the land, then they took the women. In Bennett's formulation, the two moral wrongs had become historical 'facts':

> Examination of the circumstances of Aboriginal mothers living in touch with civilisation discloses that their condition has become very much worse, and concerns us much more nearly than the condition of the wild Aborigines, because the terrible plight of the 'civilised' aborigines is the logical conclusion of our own dealings with them . . .Two outstanding facts confront us:
>
> (1) Slow starvation of the natives through our depriving them of all land to live on . . . arising from dispossession...
> (2) Wholesale prostitution of the woman; originally 'property' they have now become merchandise . . .[26]

She pointed out that far from being destined to extinction, the Aboriginal population and culture would survive if their lands were returned to them. The destruction of the indigenous population was not pre-ordained, but rather the result of the actions of greedy white men:

> If the squatters would, as an act of mercy, surrender a small proportion of their thousand mile sheep-walks and cattle runs, or if the Government would as an act of justice, reclaim a small proportion of these vast leases for the natives' use, and at the same time secure human rights to them, the process of extermination of our native race would cease. It pays the white man to dispossess the natives of their land wholesale, because the Government permits them to impress the natives as labour without paying them.[27]

It was argued that the Aboriginal women were the chief sufferers of this history of dispossession and exploitation – that in the north west of Australia it had become 'so much the accepted thing for white men to abuse native women that it [was] the custom of the country'.[28] Aboriginal women were subject to particular abuse as 'sex slaves' and as mothers robbed of their children. As enfranchised women citizens, these feminists believed they had a particular duty to engage in political work on behalf of Aboriginal women, who had no political standing in the new Commonwealth.

In other papers and in correspondence with the Anti-Slavery Society, Bennett accused the Australian government of permitting slavery to exist in the north and north west and from the 1920s she sought League of Nations intervention into the administration of Aboriginal affairs.

Australia, she said, was breaching the 1926 Slavery Convention and the International Labour Organization preamble and Truck Acts. Natives were forced to work without pay and were forcibly removed from their lands and families. Her allegations were prominently aired in the *Manchester Guardian*, prompting denials by the Prime Minister and a rush of official reassurances. The feminist agitation was effective, however, in securing the appointment of the Moseley Royal Commission into the treatment of Aborigines in Western Australia, which began its hearings in 1933.

A number of feminists associated with the Women's Service Guild, together with Aboriginal women with whom they worked, appeared as witnesses before the Royal Commission, testifying to the oppressive conditions in which Aboriginal women and children lived. They spoke especially about the systematic sexual abuse to which Aboriginal women and girls were subjected, often by the police, and the devastating impact of the breaking up of families. 'I want to know', said Aboriginal witness, Emily Nannup, to Royal Commissioner Moseley, 'why my children are being taken away from me'.[29] It was government practice to remove children of mixed descent from their mothers and place them in institutions or with white families. 'Under the law', said Ada Bromham referring to the 1905 Western Australian legislation, 'the mother has no right over the child'.[30] Bromham was vice-president of the Women's Service Guild and leader of the 1926 Australian delegation to the International Women's Suffrage Alliance in Paris. The rights of mothers, Aboriginal and non-Aboriginal, were of major concern to these maternalist feminists between the wars. 'No department in the world can take the place of a child's mother', said Mary Bennett, 'and the Honourable the Minister does not offer any valid justification for the official smashing of native family and community life.'[31] In her extensive evidence, Mary Bennett spoke eloquently of the pain of the hunted ones:

> So mothers with infants and individual children and sometimes families are mustered up like cattle and deported to the remote Government native settlement at Moore River, there to drag out their days and years in exile, suffering all the miseries of transportation for no fault but only because the white supplanters are too greedy and too mean to give them living areas in their own districts.[32]

In a hostile exchange with Chief Protector of Aborigines, A.O. Neville, Bennett charged Neville with being an 'oppressor'. He taunted her with being 'an idealist', to which she replied 'I believe in treating people like human beings. It goes no deeper than that.'[33]

Nationalist Self-justification and Feminist Self-innocenting

The feminist mobilization in support of Aboriginal rights had little immediate effect in improving the condition of Aboriginal women and children, but it created new divisions in the ranks of feminists. At issue was the meaning of feminist identification with the nation. Bessie Rischbieth, the magisterial president of the federal organization, the Australian Federation of Women Voters, had supported the feminist demand for state recognition of Aboriginal mothers' rights over their children and since 1927 had sought an acknowledgement of federal responsibility for Aboriginal affairs, but she deplored Bennett's relentless criticism of the government and disapproved of her tactic of securing adverse publicity for Australia overseas. She criticized Bennett for using the evidence of the Aboriginal women to pursue a personal feud with the Chief Protector of Aborigines, A.O. Neville. Accusations proliferated. Bennett retaliated against Rischbieth's criticism by calling her a 'rotter' and a 'beast' and implied that her worldly ambition was more important to her than the plight of Aboriginal people. She wrote angrily: 'It *is* the business of Women's Societies to reform the condition of Aboriginal and half-caste women in Australia, but if they are too smug and too self-seeking to attempt it then I will seek help from outside wherever I can get it not forgetting Japan'.[34] Rischbieth was prepared, in fact, to raise the issue of Aboriginal reform at the British Commonwealth League in 1935, but considered it inappropriate to do so at the League of Nations, especially under the heading of 'slavery'.

The conflict between feminists like Bennett, Cooke and Bromham, determined to call the nation to account for its treatment of Aboriginal people, and those more concerned to register national achievements was dramatized by the occasion of the centenary of settlement in South Australia in 1936. As a delegate from the Aborigines Protection League to the Women's Centenary Committee, Cooke had urged that the Women's Centenary programme include Aboriginal women. 'I have done my utmost to get our Aboriginal women included', she wrote to John Buxton in 1935.[35] Following a visit to the Point Pearce Aboriginal station where she found Aborigines agitating for 'land of their own', Cooke reported 'I am stressing the need of land for our Aborigines whereever it is possible' and urged the Women's Centenary Committee to recommend to the government that 'a portion of the land that we have taken from the Aborigines be allotted to them in perpetuity'.[36] When this, too, was rejected Cooke left the Committee. At the same time, her suggestion that the collection of women's writing being published to mark the centenary include a chapter acknowledging Aboriginal women as the first pioneers was also refused; instead there appeared a piece on 'pioneer women and Aborigines' by the discredited apologist for the 'dying out' of Aborigines, Daisy Bates.

In 1934 in Victoria, in 1936 in South Australia, and 1938 in New South Wales, centennial or sesquicentennial celebrations of settlement led to the establishment of special committees to produce collections of women's writing that would celebrate 'women's contribution' to Australian history. In Victoria, the *Centenary Gift Book* edited by Nettie Palmer and Frances Fraser specifically honoured those who 'made the great venture and came with their men-folk to this unknown land'. Once in Australia:

> Women did more than cook and sweep. They milked cows, dug for gold, sowed the corn, and even literally put their hand to the plough. They tended the sick and dying, they comforted the homesick and in every way passed down to the women of today their splendid heritage of courage and initiative.[37]

In New South Wales the publication *The Peaceful Army*, edited by Flora Eldershaw, included a chapter by Miles Franklin commemorating the work of New South Wales suffragist Rose Scott and an 'Ode to the Pioneer Woman' by nationalist poet Mary Gilmore who dedicated her tribute to 'the pioneer woman' who with 'endurance and courage' 'made the land':

> For they were women who at need took up
> And plied the axe, or bent above the clodded spade;
> Who herded sheep; who rode the hills, and brought
> The half-wild cattle home – helpmates of men.[38]

The 'working' of this new land was, then, central to the claims made by these nationalist feminists on behalf of white women as national subjects. Nationalist feminist writers also claimed the bush as their own; they defined it as a source of inspiration, nourishment and illumination. Miles Franklin and her friend Mary Fullerton also believed that, in pioneering the bush, settlers were pioneering a superior way of life, built on independence and self-respect – conditions made possible by the democratic social relations (and economic resources) of the New World. As feminists they insisted that this new society was equally the achievement of men and women; it was women who sustained the family farms and bush communities.

On one level the settlers' right to the land was taken for granted; on another, the founding act of dispossession returned again and again to haunt these determined appropriators of land and nation. The need to justify settlement was evident in Fullerton's history of Australia called *The Australian Bush* which was dedicated to the 'memory of the stout-hearted – the Pioneer Women of the Bush'. Fullerton was a feminist and socialist journalist who grew up in a bark hut in the Gippsland bush. In Melbourne before the war, she worked as a writer and political activist (she was secretary of the Women's Political Association) before migrating to England to live with her friend Mrs Mabel Singleton. Writing about Australia from a great distance, her vision of her country was informed by nostalgic longing. As a writer in exile, she was the displaced 'native'. Fullerton's heroes were the white settlers. Commenting on Australia's lack of appreciation for local writing, she wrote to Miles Franklin: 'Settlers I allow free of blame in the matter of failing to say "well done" to the writers of their land. They and such don't have the time to do more than *create* the subject matter, sweat and colour for the true tales of true Aus life.'[39]

In *The Australian Bush*, she observed that as a 'menace to settlement' the Aborigine was 'practically dead', his extinction read as a foregone conclusion:

> he will linger on, a wretched remnant to be cared for by whites, for fifty years or so yet; when he must disappear, leaving hardly a mark of his poor vagrant existence on the face of the land.[40]

Perhaps to ease her bad conscience, the feminist in Fullerton was moved to find implicit justification for the British settlers' appropriation of Aboriginal country in the alleged 'chattel' status accorded to Aboriginal women by their men:

> the female Aborigine, the lubra or 'black gin' as she is called . . . has no status, no right of any sort at any time. From start to finish she is a chattel to be claimed. or disowned, beaten, burdened, or even killed at the discretion of her men-folk. The Australian lubra is veritably the most pitiful being in existence. Her lot is, at best, with the dogs . . .[41]

Fullerton concluded this tirade by pointing to the familiar moral of the story:

> No other point of difference is so marked between the civilized white man and the savage, as the respective treatment of their women. At some cross-road far away, and long ago, the two parted company in this, and civilisation began . . .[42]

This self-justifying nationalist conceit that Aborigines were doomed by evolution to extinction, their historical destiny to make way for Europeans, was elaborated by Fullerton in an extraordinary contribution to the aforementioned collection of women's writing published to mark the centenary of settlement in Victoria called the *Centenary Gift Book*, a piece she named 'A Fantasy'.

In arch and awkward prose, Fullerton imagines the moment when the Yarra Yarra tribe confronted the arrival of the white man. There were early warning signs, portents of change, notably in an Aboriginal woman's defiance of her patriarchal master, her refusal of customary subservience. An 'ebon woman' forgot her place and 'struck back'. The tribe was uneasy:

> That which had never been had happened now; a lubra had rebelled. They felt the dark approach of Change, were silent in the shade of things to be that had not been.[43]

When 'the lubra' returns to the tribe she has a fearful tale to tell of intruders, the arrival of the 'great white men'. While some younger Aboriginal men are keen to defend their land ('The Bush that they would steal is ours; we shall preserve our own'), the king in his wisdom counsels resignation:

> The dark man's kingdom was to pass from his dominion. The great wide bush that their nomadic feet had trod since ocean made it land, would pass to these new lords, these pallid men . . .[44]

The wail of the bunyip confirmed the tribe's doom; they knew the white men 'should henceforth rule their lives, be lord of all the stern, mysterious, well-loved bush'. Thus are the usurpers freed from the responsibilities of historical agency; as Mary Bennett had observed of this nationalist narrative, there is no killing out, only dying out; no act of theft, merely a logical succession.

By the 1930s, then, different feminists found themselves on opposing sides in a dispute over the meaning and implications of national belonging in Australia. In Adelaide, at the triennial meeting of the Australian Federation of Women Voters, Constance Cooke clashed with the president Bessie Rischbieth over a proposal that the platform be extended to include the demand for equality of status for Aboriginal women. Rischbieth insisted that the conference simply reaffirm existing policy requiring the federal government to assume national responsibility for Aboriginal affairs. Mary Bennett reported exultantly to her friend Edith Jones in London:

Now the most wonderful thing has happened at the Centenary AFWV Conference. My darling Mrs Ternente Cooke brought forward a Resolution to give citizen rights to Aborigines, but the Board would not accept it, she was asked to re-affirm the Resolution of the preceding Conference dealing with Aborigines and to do it without comment, as Aborigines were not considered to come within 'Equality of Status' etc!!! However Mrs Ternente Cooke protested against this. To my thinking the truly important thing is that an Australian lady has brought forward a Resolution asking for equality of status for Aborigines. This is something to dream of and work for and those who tried to trample her only cut their own throats . . . Mrs Ternente Cooke . . . has made history.[45]

The writer, Miles Franklin, was less sanguine about the increasing attention paid to Aboriginal rights. In her diary she noted :

There is a movement here to sentimentalise the Aborigine beyond truth and proportion. It would be deleterious if it could succeed, but it cannot . . . We are left to our phantoms, our mirage, our pregnant oblivion to engender new spiritual experience.[46]

The dilemma posed to feminists by nationalist identifications, evident in the 1880s and fully articulated by the 1930s, highlights the ways in which nations were historically constituted in racial as well as gendered terms. The desire to join the nation, to be recognized as national subjects, confronted feminists with the racial exclusions constitutive of Australian nation building. The most ardent nationalists, the writers, opted for denial and disavowal; others more imperial and/or internationalist in orientation sought reforms that would incorporate Aboriginal people into the nation-state as citizens, which would, in the words of activist Ada Bromham, extend to Aboriginal women 'rights common to other women' alongside 'a full measure of protection and encouragement in their own culture'.[47] Bromham's alertness to the significance of cultural difference to political rights was prescient. The challenge of defining women's rights in a national context in ways that do not themselves perpetuate white racial privilege is with us still.

Notes

1. Adams, Francis (1893), *The Australians* , London: T. Fisher Unwin, 144.
2. White, Richard (1981), *Inventing Australia* , Sydney: Allen & Unwin, 85–110.

3. *Weekend Australian* (1998), 12–13 September: 5–6.
4. *Republican* 1, (1), 4 July, 1987.
5. *Dawn*, 1 May, 1888.
6. *Dawn*, 1 May, 1888.
7. *Dawn*, 1 May, 1888.
8. Lawson, L. (1895), 'The Women of the Bush', Scrapbook, vol. 1, Lawson papers, ML MSS A, Mitchell Library.
9. Grimshaw, P., Lake, M., McGrath, A. and Quartly, M. (1996), *Creating A Nation*, Melbourne: Penguin, 191–3.
10. On complicity, see Lake, M. (1987), 'Mission Impossible: How Men Gave Birth To The Australian Nation – Nationalism, Gender and Other Seminal Acts', *Gender and History* , 4, (3); and Curthoys, A. (1993), 'Identity Crisis: Colonialism, Nation and Gender in Australian History', *Gender and History*, 5, (2).
11. Franklin, M., diary, 21 June 1937, 36. Ml MSS 364/4, Franklin papers, Mitchell Library.
12. Lawson, L. (1895), 'An Australian Song', Scrapbook, vol. 1, Lawson papers, ML MSS A, Mitchell Library.
13. Lawson, L. (1895), 'Uloola', Scrapbook, vol. 1, Lawson papers, ML MSS A, Mitchell Library.
14. Lake, M. (1994), 'Between Old World "Barbarism" and Stone Age "Primitivism" : The Double Difference of the White Australian Feminist' in N. Grieve and A. Burns, (eds) *Australian Women Contemporary Feminist Thought*, Melbourne: Oxford University Press, 80–91.
15. Lawson, L. (1895), 'The Squatter's Wife', Scrapbook, vol. 1, Lawson papers, ML MSS A, Mitchell Library.
16. Lawson, L. (1897), 'A Word for the Blacks', *Dawn*, (1 November), 1; Sheridan, S. (1995), *Along the Faultlines Sex, Race and Nation in Australian Women's Writing 1880s–1930s*, Sydney: Allen & Unwin, ch. 9.
17. Butler, J. (1990). *Gender Trouble: Feminism and the Subversion of Identity*, New York: Routledge, 1990, 6–8.
18. M.M.Bennett to Sir John Harris, 7 March 1937, Anti-Slavery Society papers, MS Br.Emp. S22 G377, Rhodes House, Oxford.
19. Hancock, W.K. (1930), *Australia*, London: Ernest Benn; Scott, E. (1928), *A Short History of Australia*, Melbourne and London: Oxford University Press; On the 'victimization' of women, see the evidence given by Bennett to the Royal Commission Appointed to Investigate, Report and Advise upon matters in relation to the Condition and Treatment of Aborigines, Western Australia, 1935, Minutes of

Evidence, 213.

20. Bennett to Harris, 7 March 1937, Anti-Slavery Society papers, MS Br.Emp. S22 G377, Rhodes House, Oxford.

21. Bennett, M.M (1995), 'The Aboriginal Mother in Western Australia in 1933', reprinted in M.Lake and K.Holmes (eds) *Freedom Bound 2 Documents on Women in Modern Australia*, Sydney: Allen & Unwin, 60–3.

22. Bennett to Buxton, 22 August 1936, Anti-Slavery Society papers, MS Br. Emp. S22 G378.

23. Bennett to Buxton, 18 October 1933, Anti-Slavery Society papers, MS Br.Emp. S22 G377.

24. Harris, John to Cooke, Constance 7 June 1929, Anti-Slavery Society papers, Ms Br.Emp. S22 G374, Rhodes House, Oxford.

25. Cooke, Constance Ternente 'The Status of Aboriginal Women in Australia', Anti-Slavery Society papers, MS Br. Emp. S22 G378, Rhodes House, Oxford.

26. Bennett, M.M (1995), 'The Aboriginal Mother in Western Australia in 1933', reprinted in M.Lake and K.Holmes (eds) *Freedom Bound 2 Documents on Women in Modern Australia*, Sydney: Allen & Unwin, 60–3.

27. Bennett, M.M (1995), 'The Aboriginal Mother in Western Australia in 1933', reprinted in M.Lake and K.Holmes (eds) *Freedom Bound 2 Documents on Women in Modern Australia*, Sydney: Allen & Unwin, 60–3.

28. Bennett to *Australian Board of Missions Review* reported in *West Australian*, 19 May 1932. MS 2004/12/351, Rischbieth papers, National Library of Australia.

29. On the 'victimization' of women, see the evidence given by Bennett to the Royal Commission Appointed to Investigate, Report and Advise upon matters in relation to the Condition and Treatment of Aborigines, Western Australia, 1935, Minutes of Evidence, 576.

30. On the 'victimization' of women, see the evidence given by Bennett to the Royal Commission Appointed to Investigate, Report and Advise upon matters in relation to the Condition and Treatment of Aborigines, Western Australia, 1935, Minutes of Evidence, 557.

31. On the 'victimization' of women, see the evidence given by Bennett to the Royal Commission Appointed to Investigate, Report and Advise upon matters in relation to the Condition and Treatment of Aborigines, Western Australia, 1935, Minutes of Evidence, 226.

32. On the 'victimization' of women, see the evidence given by Bennett to the Royal Commission Appointed to Investigate, Report and Advise

upon matters in relation to the Condition and Treatment of Aborigines, Western Australia, 1935, Minutes of Evidence, 225.

33. On the 'victimization' of women, see the evidence given by Bennett to the Royal Commission Appointed to Investigate, Report and Advise upon matters in relation to the Condition and Treatment of Aborigines, Western Australia, 1935, Minutes of Evidence, 299.

34. Bennett to Harris, 20 October 1935, Anti-Slavery Society papers, MS Br. Emp. S22 G377, Rhodes House, Oxford.

35. Cooke to Buxton, 20 November 1935, Anti-Slavery Society papers, MS Br. Emp. S22 G377, Rhodes House, Oxford.

36. Cooke to Harris, 9 July 1933, Anti-Slavery Society papers, MS Br. Emp. S22 G377, Rhodes House, Oxford.

37. Foreword, Palmer, N. and Fraser, F. (eds) (1934), *Centenary Gift Book*, Melbourne: Robertson & Mullens.

38. Eldershaw, F. (ed.) (1988), *The Peaceful Army* (reprint), Melbourne: Penguin, 2.

39. Fullerton, M. to Franklin, M., 26 March 1929, Franklin papers, Ml MSS 364/16, Mitchell Library.

40. Fullerton, M. (1928), *The Australian Bush*, London: Dent, 66.

41. Fullerton, M. (1928), *The Australian Bush*, London: Dent, 68.

42. Fullerton, M. (1928), *The Australian Bush*, London: Dent, 69.

43. Fulleron, M. (1934), 'A Fantasy' in Palmer, N. and Fraser, F. (eds) *Centenary Gift Book*, Melbourne: Robertson & Mullens, 44.

44. Fulleron, M. (1934), 'A Fantasy' in Palmer, N. and Fraser, F. (eds) *Centenary Gift Book*, Melbourne: Robertson & Mullens, 46.

45. Bennett to Jones, enclosed in Jones to Harris, 30 December 1936, Anti-Slavery Society papers, MS Br.Emp. S22 G378, Rhodes House, Oxford.

46. Franklin's notes re 'Foreword' to *The Australian Novel*, Ml MSS 364/4, Mitchell Library.

47. Bromham to editor, *West Australian*, 26 June 1932.

Part 3
National Wars, Military Systems and Gender Relations

9

A Valorous *Volk* Family: The Nation, the Military, and the Gender Order in Prussia in the Time of the Anti-Napoleonic Wars, 1806–15

Karen Hagemann

Translated by Pamela Selwyn

The fatherland is in peril!' said the king to his faithful and devoted subjects, and everyone hastened to wrest it from this danger. Men reached for their swords and tore themselves from the bosom of their families; youth disentangled themselves from the tender embraces of their mothers . . . But we women, too, must do our part to help promote victory, we, too, must unite with men and boys to save our fatherland.

These words introduce the 'Appeal to the Women of the Prussian State' of 23 March 1813, which was composed by twelve princesses of the house of Hohenzollern under the leadership of Marianne of Prussia, sister-in-law of King Frederick William III. With this text, the female members of the royal family took the initiative and, in response to the king's declaration of a 'war of liberation' against Napoleonic France one week earlier, called upon women to found a 'Women's Association for the Good of the Fatherland'. The aim of this association was to collect donations of money and materials to help arm, equip and clothe the 'defenders of the Fatherland' and to organize food and nursing care for the wounded and sick, so that they could be returned as quickly as possible to the 'grateful fatherland'. The appeal's objective was thus to integrate women into the 'Prussian nation's' community at war.[1]

In his appeal 'To My People' ('An Mein Volk') of 18 March the king had already called upon the men of Prussia to take up arms in 'the final decisive battle' for the existence, independence and prosperity of Prussia. The only alternatives were 'an honourable peace or a glorious downfall'.[2] The Prussian monarchy needed its people in order to re-establish the sovereignty of the state, and at least for the duration of the war, male 'citizens', as civilian members of a community of subjects, had to become at once 'citizens of the state'[3] with a sense of responsibility for the 'nation' and 'warriors' prepared to defend its interests. To this end on that same day a 'universal militia' *(Landwehr)* – de facto universal conscription without substitution – was introduced in Prussia for the duration of the war. The new military programme was confirmed by the announcement, together with this ordinance, of the creation of a territorial reserve *(Landsturm)*. The military law of September 1814 later codified this form of universal conscription.[4]

These two appeals were among the most widely distributed official calls to arms of the period of the Prusso-German Wars of Liberation of 1813 to 1815, and caused an extraordinary sensation. Not only did the appeal 'To My People' represent the first direct appeal from the monarch, as 'father of the country', to his – in the call to arms exclusively male –

Figure 9.1 *Two Volunteer Riflemen Bid Farewell to their Parents,* Johann Friedrich Jügel. Auqatint after a drawing by Heinrich Anton Dähling, undated (Staatliches Museum Schwerin)

'*Volk*' – the 'sons of the fatherland' – asking them to participate in its 'rescue'. It also explained the reasons for the war – something absolutely unheard-of up until then. The complementary 'Appeal to the Women of the Prussian State' caused a similar stir. For the first time, princesses of the royal family, led by Marianne of Prussia, who had assumed the role of 'mother of the country' after the death of Queen Luise in July 1810, made a public political statement and called upon women to participate in public life. The 'entire nation' – men and women, young and old, single and married, poor and rich – were to take part in the struggle which Christian and patriotic rhetoric styled a 'holy war'. The Prussian-Saxon debacle of 1806–7, like the Austrian defeat of 1809, had, after all, shown that the French nation could only be defeated in a national 'people's war' *(Volkskrieg)* conducted on the basis of a universal 'arming of the people'. To this end Prussia had to be recast as a 'valorous nation' capable of leading the German 'struggle for liberation'. In the face of a mighty opponent and the prevailing crisis of state and society, this model appears to have appealed equally to many male 'patriots'[5] – mainly enlightened aristocrats and members of the educated middle classes, including numerous state officials and reform-minded military officers – and their female partners. It promised a state order that was harmonious and stable within and ready to defend itself against any attack from outside. The necessary preconditions appeared to be a reform of the Prussian state and army and the recasting of the territorial state as a modern 'monarchical nation'. Shaping an appropriate gender order was part of this project.

Until now, the abundant scholarship on Prussia and Germany during the period of the wars against Napoleon,[6] which is considered the era when 'modern German nationalism' arose,[7] has paid little attention to the outstanding significance of gender images for the discursive construction of national myths and ideologies, the constitution of national movements or the mobilization of military preparedness.[8] This is surprising when we look at the sources: unlike most historians, educated contemporaries, at least, recognized and discussed the close connections between the nation, war and the gender order. A central theme of topical literature was the relationship between 'patriotism' (understood as an automatic and self-sacrificing 'love of country'),[9] 'valorousness' *(Wehrhaftigkeit)* and 'manliness' *(Mannlichkeit)* on the one hand and 'morality' *(Sittlichkeit)* and 'womanliness' *(Weiblichkeit)* on the other. Research in women's history and gender history has also scarcely addressed this phenomenon. In their analyses of the cultural construction of gender difference, studies of the change in gender images and relations in the late eighteenth and early nineteenth centuries have rarely reflected upon the fact that the 1789 French Revolution ushered in not merely an epoch of far-reaching social and political transformation, but also a phase of national formation between 1792 and 1815, marked by long periods of war in Europe and beyond.[10]

The following will undertake a closer analysis of the discourse on the nation, war and the gender order in the years of the German uprising against Napoleon. The investigation will focus on the connections among three historical phenomena that have heretofore been conceived of and examined separately: firstly, the construction of a national identity and advent of a patriotic national[11] mobilization that involved broad segments of the population for the first time; secondly, changes in the structure of the military and the conduct of war, not least as a result of the introduction of universal conscription; and thirdly, the reformulation of a polar and hierarchically organized gender order, which was justified for the first time in anthropological terms, thus claiming universal validity.[12] The geographical focus will be on Prussia, which aside from Austria was the largest German territorial state at the time. This focus make sense both because Prussia was a centre of increasingly intense public discussions of the nation, the military and the gender order after 1806–7, accompanied by a broad-based journalistic campaign to mobilize for war, and because it played the leading role on the German side in the Wars of Liberation themselves.[13]

The analysis is based on publications by well-known propagandists in the cultural and political discourse of the time such as Ernst Moritz Arndt, Johann Gottlieb Fichte and Friedrich Ludwig Jahn. These men were important participants in the common project of the cultural creation of a German national myth *(Nationalmythos)*,[14] defined as the construction of a national 'reality', which condensed and simplified the real or imagined traditions of a social community in narrative form and in this way created cultural norms and social conventions that no longer required evidence or justification. The objective of this myth was the constitution and stabilization of a social community as a 'nation'. At its heart was the creation of a national identity – of a national unit conceived of and experienced as a collective self, which rested on factors such as history, language, culture, ethnicity, and territory, which were referred to as 'primordial' and were apparently acceptable to broad strata of the population.[15] In order to determine how widespread national myths and stereotypes were, and thus chart their reception and acceptance in broader segments of the population, the whole range of contemporary topical literature was examined alongside the works of well-known authors. This included newspapers and magazines as well as official proclamations, army bulletins and newspapers, pamphlets, appeals, sermons, poems and songs. The most important function of these patriotic national media, whose main addressees were men, appears to have been to provide 'pathetic phrases' (*Pathosformeln*) – emotionally catchy images and stereotypes as well as symbolic words – for use in the process of collective self-understanding.[16] Appeals and lyric poetry were particularly able to serve this function not only because – unlike political newspapers, periodicals and brochures – they had a strongly appellative quality and spoke in particular to the emotions, but also because they were published in significantly larger editions, were distributed relatively cheaply and frequently even free of charge, not least through the army, and could also be read or sung aloud. Because of their specific forms and their wide dissemination they were able to formulate a common patriotic project for a broader public than the other media of similarly oriented topical literature. They sought to convey a sense of national identity and at the same time provided patriotic, nationalist models of feeling, conduct, and values. The 'pathetic phrases' they offered were formulated throughout in gender-specific terms. They thus contributed significantly and lastingly to the cultural creation of a German national mythology. Their authors were mainly educated men of the nobility but above all of the middle classes.[17]

National Identity and Gender

Among scholars of German history, the period of the late-eighteenth and early nineteenth century is generally regarded as an extremely crisis-ridden phase of historical upheaval accompanied by numerous wars, in which contemporaries experienced, within a brief space of time, the extensive reorganization of territorial and political conditions, the dissolution of the old Holy Roman Empire, secularization in the Rhineland the states of the Confederation of the Rhine, which now belonged to France, and an increasing tendency towards secularization more generally, the initiation of programs of modernization and reform in the individual states, the collapse of Napoleonic hegemony and, finally, the reordering of Europe at the Congress of Vienna.[18] This transformation was accompanied by long-term changes in the economic and legal system of the household and family[19] as well as in gender images and relations. The French Revolution was of extraordinary significance here. It not only made it conceivable that men's demand for political equality and individual liberty might also apply to women – it also demonstrated that women could intervene actively, radically, and violently in the making of public opinion, an arena of action and power with genuinely masculine connotations.[20] Women's demands and activities during the Revolution were followed with interest in Germany and perceived as a serious threat to the gender order there as well.[21] Educated men[22] were apparently the first people to experience this multiply accelerated establishment of a bourgeois social order as mental disorientation and sociocultural insecurity, causing them to search for new individual and collective models and values in all areas of the economy, society and politics. The growing group of educated middle-class men was particularly deeply involved in the discourse on a necessary reformulation of the reigning canon of norms and values. Their educational and professional careers, which were oriented towards change and geographical mobility, appear not merely to have predisposed them to think in terms broader than the particular interests of the individual territorial states, but also to have compelled them to reflect upon questions of social identity and position as well as the perspectives for economic, social and political change.[23]

The words 'people' *(Volk)* and 'nation',[24] which were used largely synonymously, became central notions in the cultural construction of a new individual and collective identity. In the context of the discourse on 'patriotism', which had been conducted with increasing intensity since the late eighteenth century, the initially very vague ideas took on clearer contours and increasingly moved in the direction of a 'cultural nation' *(Kulturnation)* or 'folk nation' *(Volksnation)*. By the beginning of the nineteenth century, the common core of the various models was already the idea of an 'innate', specifically 'German national character', which expressed itself in authentically German traits and virtues, in the German language, culture, customs and history.[25] The most important 'German' character traits, according to the topical literature of the day, were 'vigour', 'uprightness', 'straightforwardness', an 'abhorrence of tricks', 'honesty' and 'earnest good intentions'.[26] These attributes followed traditional national stereotypes, to be sure, but in the altered context of the age of revolution (the reference to the *'Volk'* and the 'nation' as a unified active subject) they assumed a new quality.[27]

The tendency of the patriotic national discourse, which was to exclude those outside and integrate those inside its parameters – a basic pattern now acknowledged in the literature – became much stronger in Prussia during the period of the wars against Napoleon. After 1806 'patriots' were primarily concerned with using a national myth to make Prussia, the intended 'head' of the 'German nation', into a national community capable of bearing arms, which could lead the struggle for liberation. The construction of an integrative Prussian-German identity was central here.

In the course of the increasingly intense ideological mobilization for the struggle against French rule, this national identity, whose core was the presumed existence of a specifically German national character, was not merely presented as a counterimage to and bulwark against the national enemy,[28] France, but also differentiated socially and in terms of gender – a circumstance that has been largely ignored by scholars. The cultural constructions of national, social and gender identities were tightly intertwined. Viewed in relation to the French counterimage, which developed ever more clearly into a national concept of the enemy, the 'German nation' as a whole came to be described in terms of traits with middle-class associations and masculine connotations: Contemporary political writers generally referred to 'the Germans' as 'virtuous', 'introspective' and 'hearty', 'loyal', 'simple', 'honest' and 'just', but above all as 'honourable' and 'valorous'. 'The French', in contrast, were presented as 'trivial', 'clever' and 'refined', 'slick', 'false', 'superficial', 'lascivious' and 'indecent' and thus characterized in terms of qualities generally associated with effeminacy[29] and attributed to the court nobility.[30]

Internally, this model of the 'German nation' was further differentiated by gender. The 'German national character', which was presented to the outside world as middle-class and manly, was complemented by middle-class feminine counterparts to the masculine 'national virtues'. According to contemporary writers, the most important 'character traits' of 'German women' were 'solicitousness' and 'domesticity', but above all 'morality'.[31] In keeping with the late-Enlightenment 'anthropologization' of thought, these national character traits were deduced from 'nature'. 'Anthropology as a universal science' continuously nourished social and political attitudes.[32]

An analysis of the discourse on *'Volk'* and 'nation' in these years that integrates gender as a 'sociocultural category'[33] thus shows the high degree to which patriotic national visions and concepts were steeped in notions of a femininity and masculinity appropriate to the 'German national character'. Contemporaries conceived of national identity in gender-specific terms and of gender identity, in its concrete cultural incarnation, in national terms. This created national identity was fundamentally rooted in a doubly 'dualistic basic structure' of self- and other-definition by means of national and gender stereotypes: it was determined by a national self- and counter-image, which was differentiated along both social and gender lines. 'German' masculinity and femininity were defined on the one hand by the complementary image of the other sex, and on the other through distancing from their same-sex counterimages of 'non-German' masculinity or femininity. Thus constructed, 'national identity' as the core of the cultural national myth was, in a much more complex way than scholars of nationalism have assumed up until now, structurally at once inclusive and exclusive – potentially aggressive towards all that was considered other or alien.

The internal integrative function of the new national myth was promoted significantly by a persistent vagueness – social and gender-specific differentiations notwithstanding – in the definition of the terms *Volk* and 'nation'. This was advantageous, given the need for broad mobilization against French domination, as it prevented political controversy and thus had a unifying effect.[34] In the contemporary discourse, *Volk* and 'nation' encompassed a broad range of political ideas, which can only be hinted at here: regional-state patriotism *(Landespatriotismus)*, in which the individual German territorial state was considered a 'nation' that claimed the loyalty of its inhabitants, remained far more widespread than the earliest models of so-called modern German nationalism *(deutscher Nationalismus)*, with their goal of a unified German nation state. Loyalty to the individual state certainly could correspond to a German cultural ideal conceived in nationalist terms, but it could also be pitted against calls for national unification.[35] The Prussian brand of regional patriotism – religious, devoted to king and native soil and tradition-conscious – went hand in hand with the vision of a German *Kulturnation*. In this model, Prussia itself was conceived of as a 'monarchical nation' with the king as the 'father' of the *Volk* at the top. 'Monarchical nationalism' of the Prussian type was a specific variant of the generally more traditionally oriented regional-state patriotism. The Prussian monarchy was conceived of as a 'nation-state' under which various ethnic groups in the population were subsumed.[36] The at once exclusive and integrative effect of the constructed national myth was decisively strengthened between 1806 and 1815 by changes in the structure of the army and conduct of warfare, in the context of which the models of 'the nation' were masculinized by militarizing and at the same time familializing them.

The Military, War and Masculinity

The militarization of the notions of *Volk* and 'nation', already apparent among opinion-leading intellectuals at the turn of the century as a reaction to the Revolutionary wars with their far-reaching consequences for domestic and foreign policy, not only intensified markedly after 1806, but also attained a remarkably widespread influence at least in middle-class circles, above all during the Wars of Liberation.[37] Prussian military reforms and the journalistic and pamphlet campaign focusing on promoting military preparedness for the 'struggle for liberation' that accompanied them were an important impetus here. A broad consensus existed among educated 'patriots' and reform-minded officers that Prussia could only stand up to the French foe if the 'nation' were militarized and the military bourgeoisified along the French model. The aim was a rapprochement between the 'citizens of the state' and the army as a precondition to the necessary introduction of universal conscription. The military needed to be reorganized to make it better conform to the notions of freedom and political consciousness of these 'citizens', who were averse to the traditional standing army with its drill and duress. The most important measures of Prussian military reform were undertaken in this spirit. At the same time, intensive propaganda was required to overcome the aversion to all things military and to create a broad patriotic national willingness to fight, particularly among the men who were to be mobilized for military service for the first time by universal conscription. The broad exemptions contained in the cantonal law of 1792, which remained in force until the beginning of the Wars of Liberation, meant that these included not only aristocrats, civil servants and members of the educated and propertied middle classes, but also the male inhabitants of entire regions and large towns.[38]

The idea of an 'uprising against Napoleon', and with it the acceptance of universal conscription, was greatly reinforced by the experience of extreme economic exploitation and permanent existential threat during the French occupation. Broad sections of the country had become deployment and transit zones and supply areas for the Grande Armée. Without this 'formative experience' we can understand neither the 'momentum of the uprising of 1813' nor the broad impact of this patriotic mobilization.[39] Growing segments of the population no longer saw war against France as a 'war between monarchs' but as a national 'war of liberation' against the 'Napoleonic usurper'. The mobilization for war in the press and pamphlets, which heated up after the French defeat in Russia in the autumn and winter of 1812–13, heightened this change in mood.

Its effectiveness appears to have rested in part on a preference for using traditional religious concepts and Christian symbols. The Prussian-Saxon debacle of 1806 was interpreted as 'divine judgement' and the French occupation of large parts of the country as 'God's beneficial punishment', a 'salutary' step away from the path of 'slackness' and 'cowardly sloth' and towards the knowledge that what people needed was 'action with weapons', and 'manly sacrifice' for the 'fatherland'.[40] The disaster of the Grande Armée in Russia was styled 'God's terrible judgement'. 'Piety' and 'the fear of God' had bolstered the 'mighty courage' of the Russian people and led to victory over Napoleon, 'the bloody and pitiless monster'. The 'German nation' should finally emulate the Russians and rise up with God like true men.[41] In the course of this campaign, the 'nation' was increasingly conceived of as a military fighting unit, which had to be motivated to pursue a 'holy war' against the 'detestable French' and their 'godless Emperor'.[42]

It is also likely that the war propaganda was successful with one of its main target groups – middle class men – not least because it was at the same time a campaign to make men more 'manly'. Even before the war, topical literature had been gripped by a veritable 'mania for manliness' *(Männlichkeitsrausch)*,[43] which further escalated during the war.[44] During the uprising against Napoleon, the patriotic national discourse was always also a discourse about masculinity, since a new 'valorous' *(wehrhafter)* man was needed if – as the 'patriots' intended – the *volk's* war against France were to proceed successfully. Thus, at least in the topical literature of the years 1812–15, manliness was the central theme when authors came to reflect upon the sexes. Following the literary tradition of the heroic era and soldiers' songs, patriotic national lyric became a central site for the definition of masculinity.[45]

It seems likely that the striking development of the discourse on masculinity in these years was not merely the result of the necessary mobilization of male military preparedness, but also a reaction to the fundamental unsettling of (chiefly) middle-class men's self-esteem by women's participation in the French Revolution, which they saw as a threat to male dominance in society and the state. The discourse may thus also be interpreted as the expression of a cultural crisis of masculinity. The campaign of patriotic military mobilization doubtless contributed significantly to the 'resolution' of this crisis, as it propagated a strong, virile image of maleness well suited to boosting men's self-confidence. Two motives – one political and national and the other gender specific – thus reinforced each other and contributed to the intensity of the discourse on masculinity.

The militarization, and thus also masculinization, of ideas about the 'nation' continued to increase during the Wars of Liberation, not least as a consequence of the introduction, with the Prussian military law of September 1814, of universal conscription without substitution for both wartime and peacetime. Now every man, regardless of his social position and actual political rights, could potentially be enlisted to defend the fatherland as a 'citizen of the state'. In monarchist Prussia, as in revolutionary America and France, universal conscription became an important basis for the building of the nation state. Only wars fought by the *Volk*'s armies' could (re)establish and defend national sovereignty.[46] This changed the character of war; the *ancien régime* 'prince's war' between states became a 'people's war' justified by 'national interests'. The Wars of Liberation were the first in Prussian history to be fought by a 'peoples's army' *(Volksarmee)*.[47]

At the same time, regardless of political system, the introduction of universal conscription intensified women's exclusion from the centres of political power and opinion and thus also promoted the hierarchization of the gender order. With universal conscription, the status of a 'full citizen' in a 'nation' became tied to the bearing of arms.[48] Since only male 'citizens of the state' were given the right and duty to bear arms and conduct war, women could be denied citizenship status. The 'nation-state' thus developed into a military-influenced, male-dominated space. On the new level of the nation state, women were structurally excluded from the community of 'state citizens' and thus from broad segments of the political public sphere, and were to remain so in the long term.[49]

The hierarchical order of gender relations was ideologically under-pinned by the designation of arms-bearing man as the protector of weak and defenceless woman. This image attained great popularity in topical literature during the Wars of Liberation, as it transported the widespread opinion that only a man who valorously defended the fatherland was a 'real' man capable of fulfilling his duty as 'protector of home and hearth' – and thus as a husband. By participating in the 'liberation struggle', which was a sort of initiation phase, 'youths' also proved their fitness for marriage; grown men demonstrated their masculine potency through their 'capacity to bear arms'.[50]

In Prussia, as in Revolutionary France, the introduction of universal conscription changed not merely the character of war and the gender order but also the image of the soldier. While soldiers of the *ancien régime* did not need to concern themselves with the causes of a particular war, the 'warriors' of the 'national armies' had to identify with the war aims propagated by their governments. Mere unconditional obedience and soldierly courage no longer sufficed: the motto 'victory or death' symbolizes the passionate self-sacrifice for the 'nation' that was now expected of them.[51] This image of the soldier, which was broadly propagated in Prussia for the first time immediately before and during the Wars of Liberation, was the core of a new romanticized manly heroism, which culminated in the national myth of the 'hero's death for the fatherland'. This myth, which had already been successfully invoked in the French Revolution under different political circumstances, appeared in ever new variations in the topical literature of the day, particularly in lyric. It made use of the old Christian pietist notion of the sacrificatory death.[52] The 'warrior' was recast as a Jesus-like martyr who sacrificed himself on the 'altar of the fatherland'.[53]

The myth of the freely chosen patriotic hero's death was about the reciprocal creation of meaning between death and the fatherland. The ultimate sacrifice confirmed the reality of the fatherland, which had to be liberated (or created in the first place). The fatherland, in turn, invested death in battle with a higher meaning, sanctifying it, and promised the men who fought eternal life in the glorious memory of those they left behind. It was no accident that the veneration and commemoration of heroes attained great significance in the period of the Wars of Liberation. With the introduction at the very beginning of the war of two symbols of Christian patriotic heroism, the 'iron cross' (the first medal to be bestowed for 'military valour' regardless of social rank) and the 'plaque of honour' in all churches (which was to mention by name every 'warrior' who had died a 'hero's death'), the Prussian state took account of the general mobilization. Now that every man of military age was supposed to be a 'ready defender of the fatherland' who might die in battle, 'death on the field of honour' had to be made socially acceptable by means of a glorification that encompassed all soldiers. The veneration and commemoration of heroes had to be democratized if men's willingness to fight and sacrifice, and not merely conscription, were to become universal.[54]

A new patriotic and valorous model of masculinity centred on the terms 'honour', 'love of liberty', 'piety', 'strength', 'comradeship', 'discipline', 'bravery', 'glory', 'loyalty', but above all 'patriotism' and 'valorousness' attained a dominant significance in Prussia for the first time within the context of changes in the military structure and conduct of war and the accompanying patriotic national mobilization. This model combined the old values of Prussian soldierly honour, aristocratic officers' virtue and Christian middle-class ethics with new notions of male state citizens' participation and romantic heroism. The model was adapted to different generations and social strata in order to achieve as wide an influence as possible.[55] Three main motifs run through this new model of masculinity, regardless of social and ideological distinctions. Firstly, it was strongly marked by the notion that the readiness and capacity to fight were preconditions for the right to participate as a 'state citizen'. This new pairing secured male power in the emergent nation state in the long term. Secondly, the new model of masculinity established the image of the 'valorous' man ready and able to protect 'home and hearth' as a 'truly manly' and at the same time 'truly German' man. What was new in this motif was above all the equation of 'valorous', 'manly' and 'truly German'; the three adjectives formed an inseparable complex of concepts in contemporary discourse. Thirdly, this model was dominated by the motif of the 'hero's death for the fatherland'. The cult of heroes was not new, of course, but its democratization and nationalization were. All three motifs lastingly influenced notions of masculinity and contributed greatly to investing them with violent and belligerent connotations.

The Nation, War and Femininity

Parallel to the masculinization of models of the 'nation' and the militarization of concepts of masculinity, women's place in the 'German nation' was also more precisely defined and an image of 'German femininity' elaborated discursively as part of the intense efforts at redefining gender differences that had been underway since the late eighteenth century. The process of constructing a gender order appropriate to the times, which established the hierarchy of political power relations between the sexes and defined at once universal and complementary national 'sex-specific characters' from which allegedly 'natural' gender-specific spheres of activity were derived, was embedded in the process of shaping Prussia and Germany into a 'valorous' nation. In short, the production of a new hierarchical and complementary gender order was a basic component of this development. The two projects mutually formed and reinforced each other. The dichotomic juxtaposition of the sexes assumed a new quality within the context of the anthropological redefinition of gender differences in this period. Whereas gender differences had previously been conceived of largely as social differences – the differences between men and women had been derived from their respective positions and duties within a society of estates[56] – they were now anthropologized, justified in terms of anatomical differences between men and women and their respective functions in the reproductive process.[57] This new version of the dichotomous view of gender, which, in its anthropological incarnation, claimed universal validity for the first time, provided an excellent basis for the politically desired militarization of notions of masculinity after 1806.[58] After all, the masculine virtues contained in this gender image were, in their essence, already defined by military and active qualities and intended to apply to all men. The feminine virtues were intended as their complement. The militarization of the complementary gender images in turn intensified and rigidified the notion of the 'polarity' of the sexes. 'Valorousness' became the masculine, and 'morality' *(Sittlichkeit)* the feminine 'character trait' *par excellence.*[59]

The new gender image enjoyed growing popularity among the educated middle classes and the enlightened aristocracy after the turn of the century.[60] Women came to be associated increasingly exclusively with the so-called 'privacy' of household and family.[61] The relegation of women to the space of 'domesticity' was the reverse side of their exclusion from the arms-bearing 'brotherhood of state citizens'[62] and thus from the ruling centre of the 'nation', now conceived of essentially as a community of those prepared to fight. This in turn strengthened the exclusion of the female sex from the power centres of politics and public life. Nevertheless, women did have important public tasks to perform, but primarily in the so-called 'domestic private' space: they bore significant patriotic responsibility as wives, housewives and mothers, since the family was considered the 'nursery of the nation'.[63]

In both peacetime and wartime, 'honourable German women's' foremost 'patriotic duty' was to fulfil their domestic and familial responsibilities in a manner in keeping with 'national honour', culture and customs. Women were expected to 'keep their womanly honour pure', instruct their children in 'German national customs' and cultivate 'German culture' in language and dress.[64] They were also, however, expected to make considerable personal 'sacrifices for the fatherland' during the period of national crisis. As the 'mothers of heroes', and sweethearts or wives of soldiers, they were supposed to motivate their sons and men to fight, to 'inspire their courage' and assure them that they would maintain 'discipline and morality' during their absence. If their menfolk died a 'hero's death' they were to mourn the dead with dignity and treasure the memory of the fallen man's 'glory'.[65] Queen Luise of Prussia was portrayed as the ideal German woman.[66] The topical literature of the day elevated her 'capacity for suffering and love' in the 'years of national humiliation to the status of a 'patriotic female virtue'. Women's love and solicitousness for their own 'warriors' were constructed as a mirror-image of men's hatred of the enemy, and women's 'sacrificial courage' on the home front was contrasted with men's heroic 'warrior courage' at the front in battle.[67]

The topical literature of the years 1813–15 also called upon women to prove their patriotic attitudes by acts of 'patriotic charity'. Their 'natural' maternal love should be expanded into patriotic motherliness. The many women who left the home to work together in 'patriotic women's associations' accordingly met with broad approval. Following the example of the Prussian 'Women's Association for the Good of the Fatherland' and other groups, at least 600 women's associations were active between 1813 and 1815. Apart from the abovementioned collection of donations on behalf of the troops and nursing care they also made bandages and assisted the impoverished families of disabled and fallen 'warriors'. For the first time, large numbers of women, particularly from the propertied and educated classes, were willing to commit themselves to the cause of the 'fatherland'. This was also repeatedly emphasized in the contemporary press and cited as proof that broad segments of the population had been gripped by the 'sacred urge of patriotism'.[68]

As long as women's patriotic activities did not overstep the propagated hierarchical and complementary gender order, it was perfectly acceptable to honour it publicly. The 'female heroism' of fighting women, in contrast, could be accepted as an exception at best. The small number of so-called 'heroic maidens' – the literature has counted twenty-three – did not conform to the image of the 'peaceable and weaker sex'. Their activities, regarded by some as the expression of the extraordinary spread of patriotism, and by others as a sign of the decay of morals, customs and order, could be accepted at most if they maintained their 'female honour' and returned after the war to the expected gender role of spouse, housewife and mother, or better yet, if they died a 'hero's death'. It is no accident that Eleonore Prochaska, daughter of a disabled Prussian non-commissioned officer who fought with the Lützow Freicorps and fell in September 1813, became the most popular 'heroic maiden'. Her death in battle made it safe to style her the German Joan of Arc.[69]

In Germany, as in Revolutionary France, any female initiative to arm women collectively, and deploy them on an equal basis in the 'national war', met with outrage.[70] The majority of men and women alike rejected this suggestion because it called women's 'femininity' into question and threatened the 'natural' gender order. Women's patriotic engagement was not permitted to challenge the model of the hierarchical and complementary gender order. It was supposed, instead, to stabilize society and the state.[71]

The Nation as a '*Volk* Family'

In the long term, the designation and acceptance of a 'specifically female space' within the nation strengthened the sexual division of labour by universalizing women's familial and domestic tasks as national women's tasks. The image of the 'nation' as a sort of patriarchally and hierarchically organized '*Volk* family' *(Volksfamilie)* with a complementary gender-specific division of labour was taking shape. The journalist and political thinker Adam Müller, who belonged to the conservative circle of so-called 'political Romantics', formulated this idea in pointed terms. Like most of his educated contemporaries, Müller regarded the family as the foundation of the nation and the basic unit of the state. This unit, founded on 'trust in God', 'love', and 'loyalty' was an 'organic' union and contained the fundamental 'natural' opposites and inequalities of human existence – masculinity and femininity, youth and age – from which all others derived.[72] This image was transposed onto the 'nation' in the political dicourse of the era. Like many people of his time, Müller too understood the 'nation' as a '*Volk* family', an anthropological unit whose cohesion rested on the same basic values as the individual family. These values were used in the topical literature to describe the relationships between all the 'members' of the 'nation': the head of the '*Volk* family' was the 'royal household', whose every act, great or small, was embued with 'piety', 'morality' and 'true domesticity'. At the top was the monarch as the 'father of the country', at his side the queen as 'mother of the country'; both were as lovingly and caringly devoted to each other as they were to their children/subjects. The 'father of the country' led the 'brotherhood' of 'valorous' male citizens as their 'supreme commander'. The 'mother of the country' served as an 'example' and 'educator' to the 'fatherland's daughters', who like her had to fulfil their patriotic duties in the domestic and familial sphere.[73] This model of the nation as an extended family was formulated prototypically for Prussia. The topical literature of the years between 1806 and 1815 increasingly portrayed the royal family around Frederick William III and Luise of Prussia as a model 'bourgeois' patriotic family, in every respect worthy of emulation.[74]

The concept of the state as an extended family was not new. The antique and Christian traditions were now merely modified to suit contemporary needs and ideas.[75] The old notion of a dualistic relationship based on fear and love between the 'father of the country' and his 'children' was replaced by the idea of a relationship based primarily on love and loyalty. The modern middle-class ideal of the family, and with it the new hierarchical and complementary model of the gender order, with its claims to universal validity, were integrated into models of the nation. The emotionalization of political concepts was intended to help overcome (conceptually) the dualism of monarch and subjects and integrate the people into the 'monarchical nation', not least in order to motivate them to make the 'patriotic sacrifices' necessary for the war effort. What made the model of the '*Volk* family' (which we find under other political circumstances and in other forms in Revolutionary France as well as the British Empire)[76] so generally attractive was its potential for connotations that crossed estate and class boundaries and its emotional content oriented towards individual experience and Christian tradition, which rendered it comprehensible to broad segments of the population.

The familialization of the concept of the nation did not contradict the simultaneous tendency towards militarization and masculinization, but rather was a necessary part of it. The image of the nation as a '*Volk* family', like that of the individual family, was male- and patriarchally dominated with strong military influences under the conditions of universal conscription. In periods when the 'fatherland' was imperilled by war, the entire '*Volk* family' had to become a 'military fighting community', in which all members had to fulfil specific 'patriotic duties' according to their social position, gender, age and marital status and make the necessary 'sacrifice on the altar of the fatherland'. In both peacetime and wartime, the army, conceived of as a 'community of brothers' – as relatively equal, emotionally closely connected men of the same descent and culture with the monarch as their commander – was a power-political centre of the 'valorous nation'. The 'brothers" equality was established primarily by means of their equal freedom to offer themselves for the 'fatherland' – to die a hero's death in the national struggle for liberation. Women had no access to this brotherhood of patriotic martyrs, to be sure, but it could not function without them. The hero depended upon the suffering, mourning woman who could express and preserve his own amputated feelings, allowing him to repress the reality of death in battle and with it the fear of dying, thus rendering him capable of fighting in the first place. For this reason women were charged with the 'patriotic duty' of mourning the fallen 'heroes' and preserving their 'glorious memory'. Women were expected to accept wholeheartedly all of the 'sacrifices' that the 'valorous nation' demanded of them. This was the necessary precondition for both men's individual 'valour' and the nation's collective capacity to conduct war.

A Gendered Order of the German Nation

The analysis of the Prussian discourse on the nation, war and the gender order at the time of the wars against Napoleon between 1806 and 1815 shows that in this period, significantly promoted by military interests – the necessity of conducting a 'people's war' – two historical processes central to the later national development became inextricably linked: the construction of the basic pattern of the modern myth of the German 'nation', and the basic structures of a new hierarchical and complementary gender order that corresponded to the altered political and military requirements of the emerging system of nation states and, for the first time, claimed validity across estate lines. With the model of the '*Volk* family', this gender order integrated men and women into the 'nation' in specific ways depending upon their social origins, marital status and age. On the one hand, it ensured the military preparedness of the 'nation' by committing every man as a potential or actual 'citizen of the state' to the 'defence of the fatherland' and at the same time demanded specific patriotic duties of all groups in the population who were ineligible for military service. In this context, German nationalism was formulated for the first time as a 'national religious' sacrifactory myth, which made the 'nation' as a collective active subject the highest divinely ordained context of meaning and emotionally associated the national with the military in a way that would have a lasting effect. On the other hand, even under the emerging conditions of a 'national society of state citizens',[77] the model promoted continued male dominance in the state by linking military service and (state) citizen's rights. The period of the wars against Napoleon was a kind of catalyst that accelerated and intensified the mutually influential processes of the nationalization of the gender order and the gendering of the 'nation'. This was the first key period in the process of national formation. In it the basic characteristics of national 'political culture'[78] took shape in Prussia and Germany. The logic of patriotic national thought, sentiment and action that developed at this time retained its relevance far beyond the years 1813–15. This applies both to the patriotic national discourse's basic repertoire of pathos formulas and to the basic stock of national myths, symbols and rituals. Over the course of the long nineteenth century these linguistic and pictorial models were merely adopted, reshaped and refined by various political and social groups to suit the respective concrete historical circumstances.

Notes

1. (1813), 'Aufruf an die Frauen im Preußischen Staat' in *Vossische Zeitung,* no. 39.
2. Aufruf 'An Mein Volk,' in Spies, H.-B. (1981), *Die Erhebung gegen Napoleon 1806–1814/15,* Darmstadt, 254 f.
3. In the discourse of the early nineteenth century, the term 'citizen' (*Bürger*) essentially encompassed the private individual on the one hand and the public, political 'state citizen' (*Staatsbürger*) on the other. Between the two was the 'citizen of the state' (*Bürger des Staates*). It

is also in this sense that I employ the terms. Cf. Riedel M. (1972), 'Bürger, Staatsbürger, Bürgertum', in *Geschichtliche Grundbegriffe* (=GGr.), Stuttgart, vol. 1, 672–725, 700ff.

4. On the reform of the Prussian military see: Stübig H. (1994), 'Die Wehrverfassung Preußens in der Reformzeit. Wehrpflicht im Spannungsfeld von Restauration und Revolution 1815–1860', in Foerster, R.G. (ed.) *Die Wehrpflicht: Entstehung, Erscheinungsformen und politisch-militärische Wirkung* Munich, 39–53; Frevert, U. (1997), 'Das jakobinische Modell: Allgemeine Wehrpflicht und Nationsbildung in Preußen-Deutschland,' in Frevert, U. (ed.) *Militär und Gesellschaft im 19. und 20. Jahrhundert*, Stuttgart, 17–47.

5. Cf. Giesen, B. (1993), *Die Intellektuellen und die deutsche Nation. Eine deutsche Achsenzeit,* Frankfurt a.M., 122ff.

6. On the historiography, see Berding, H. (1987), 'Das geschichtliche Problem der Freiheitskriege 1813–1815,' in Von Aretin, K.O.F. and Ritter, G.A. (1987), *Historismus und moderne Geschichtswissenschaft: Europa zwischen Revolution und Restauration, 1797–1815,* Wiesbaden, 201–15; Marion W. Gray (1986), The Rise of German Nationalism and the Wars of Liberation (1803–1814), in Horward, D.D. *Napoleonic Military History: A Bibliography*, New York and London, 435–78.

7. Following Dieter Langewiesche's terminology, 'modern nationalism' will be defined here functionally as 'all behaviours' that have as their aim 'the creation or preservation of a nation-state'. Langewiesche D. (1992), 'Reich, Nation und Staat in der jüngeren Deutschen Geschichte', *Historische Zeitschrift* 254: 341–81.

8. For an overview of international research on nationalism, see Eley, G. and Suny R.G. (1996), 'Introduction: From the Moment of Social History to the Work of Cultural Representation', in Eley, G. and Suny R.G. (eds) *Becoming National. A Reader,* New York, 3–37; Langewiesche D. (1995), 'Nation, Nationalismus, Nationalstaat. Forschungsstand und Forschungsperspektiven,' *Neue Politische Literatur* 40, (2): 181–236; Haupt, H.-G. and Tacke, C. (1996), ' Die Kultur des Nationalen. Sozial- und kulturgeschichtliche Ansätze bei der Erforschung des europäischen Nationalismus im 19. und 20. Jahrhundert,' in Hardtwig, W. and Wehler, H.-U. *Kulturgeschichte Heute. Zwölf Beiträge*, Göttingen, 78–110. An overview on the German national movement is provided in Breuilly, J. (ed.) (1992), *The State of Germany. The national idea in the making, unmaking and remaking of a modern nation-state,* London; Dann O. (1993), *Nation und Nationalismus in Deutschland. 1770–1990,* Munich.

9. 'Patriotismus,' in Brockhaus, F.A. (ed.) (1817) *Conversationslexikon oder Enzyclopädisches Handwörterbuch für gebildete Stände*, Altenburg and Leipzig, vol. 6., 306 f. See Vierhaus, R. (1980), "Patriotismus' – Begriff und Realität einer moralisch-politischen Haltung,' in Vierhaus, R. (ed.) *Deutsche patriotische und gemeinnützige Gesellschaften*, Munich, 9–30.

10. Exceptions include Lipp, C. (1992), 'Das Private im Öffentlichen. Geschlechterbeziehungen im symbolischen Diskurs der Revolution 1848/49', in Hausen, K. and Wunder, H. *Frauengeschichte – Geschlechtergeschichte*, Frankfurt a.M., 99–118; Frevert, U. (1996), 'Nation, Krieg und Geschlecht im 19 Jahrhundert', in Hettling, M. and Nolte, P. (ed.) (1996), *Nation und Gesellschaft in Deutschland. Historsiche Essays*, Munich, 51–170; Hagemann, K. (1996) 'Nation, Krieg und Geschlechterordnung. Zum kulturellen und politischen Diskurs in der Zeit der antinapoleonischen Erhebung Preußens', in *Geschichte und Gesellschaft* (= GG) 22: 562–91; and, 'Heldenmütter, Kriegerbräute und Amazonen: Entwürfe 'patriotischer' Weiblichkeit zur Zeit der Freiheitskriege,' in Frevert, *Militär*, 174–200; and, 'Of 'Manly Valor' and 'German Honor': Nation, War and Masculinity in the Age of the Prussian Uprising against Napoleon,' in (1997) *Central European History* 30: 187–220; Reder, D.A. (1998), *Frauenbewegung und Nation. Patriotische Frauenvereine in Deutschland im frühen 19. Jahrhundert (1813–1830)*, Cologne.

11. Following Miroslav Hroch, I use the terms 'national' or 'patriotic national' here for this early phase of German nationalism instead of the English term 'nationalist', which is more common in this context but, at least to German ears, negatively connotated. 'National' also has the advantage of being more open and better able to encompass the ambivalence and multi-layered quality of contemporary conceptions. Cf. Hroch, M. 'From National Movement to the Fully-Formed Nation: The Nation-Building Process in Europe', in Eley, G. and Suny R.G. (eds) *Becoming National. A Reader,* New York, 60–77, 62.

12. What I will not discuss here is the question of 'race', which is also important for this subject. Not by accident the appearance of the early German nationalisms and the early form of modern antisemitism were closely connected. But interestingly the intensive public debate about the so-called 'Jewish question' ('Judenfrage'), i.e. the possibilities and limits of the emancipation of the (male) Jews, started not earlier than 1815, when Napoleon was beaten for the second time and the question had to be discussed concerning what the political and cultural

order of Prussia and Germany should look like. Because of the limited space I will not go deeper into this difficult problem here. But the reader will find a chapter in my forthcoming book. Important new books on the early antisemitism in Germany are: Erb, R. and Bergmann, W. (1989), *Die Nachtseite der Judenemanzipation. Der Widerstand gegen die Integration der Juden in Deutschland 1780–1860,* Berlin; Hortzitz, N. *'Früh-Antisemitismus' in Deutschland (1789–1870/72). Strukturelle Untersuchungen zu Wortschaft, Text und Argumentation* (Tübingen, 1988); Katz, J. (1980), From Prejudice to Destruction. Anti-Semitism, 1700–1933, Cambridge, Mass., Part II. Interesting for the discussion about of the duty and right of male jews to bear arms (since 1813) and their possibility to get equal political rights: Fischer, H. (1968), *Judentum, Staat und Heer in Preußen im frühen 19. Jahrhundert. Zur Geschichte der staatlichen Judenpolitik,* Tübingen. The research on the early German national movement is till now not very much interested in the early anti-semitism, which is interpreted as an extremism of some radical German thinkers like Johann Gottlieb Fichte and Ernst Moritz Arndt. Only Paul Lawrence Rose stressed the shared anthropological basis of the argumentation of early nationalism and antisemitism. Important was mainly the idea of anthropologically justified 'national charakters'. But his book is problematic for other reasons. See Rose, P.L. (1990), *Revolutionary Antisemitism in Germany from Kant to Wagner,* Princeton, and the comments from: La Vopa, A.J. (1993), 'Jews and Germans: Old Quarrels, New Departures', in *Journal of the History of Ideas* 54 (1993): 675–95; Menges, K. (1995) 'Another Concept in the "Sonderweg" Debate?' P. L. Rose's 'Revolutionary Antisemitism' and the Prehistory of the Holocaust'.,*German Studies Review* 18: 291–314.

13. See Ibbeken, R. (1970), *Preußen 1807–1813. Staat und Volk als Idee und in Wirklichkeit,* Berlin; Von Münchow-Pohl, B. (1987), *Zwischen Reform und Krieg. Untersuchungen zur Bewußtseinslage in Preußen 1809–1812,* Göttingen.

14. See, among others, Giesen, B. (1994), 'Vom Patriotismus zum völkischen Denken: Intellektuelle als Konstrukteure der deutschen Identität,' in Berding, H. (ed.) *Nationales Bewußtsein und kollektive Identität. Studien zur Entwicklung des kollektiven Bewußtseins in der Neuzeit 2,* Frankfurt a.M., 45–393.

15. Cf. Giesen, B. (1994), 'Vom Patriotismus zum völkischen Denken: Intellektuelle als Konstrukteure der deutschen Identität,' in Berding, H. (ed.) *Nationales Bewußtsein und kollektive Identität. Studien zur*

Entwicklung des kollektiven Bewußtseins in der Neuzeit 2, Frankfurt a.M., 86–162; James, H. (1989), *A German Identity 1770–1990,* London, chaps. 1 and 2; Wülfing, W. et al. (eds) (1991), *Historische Mythologie der Deutschen 1798–1918,* Munich. On the problem of the term 'national identity' see Suny, R.G. (1993), 'Rethinking Social Identities: Class and Nationality', in: Suny, *The Revenge of the Past: Nationalism, Revolution and the Collapse of the Soviet Union* (Stanford), 3–19; Smith, A.D. (1991), *National Identity,* Reno; Verdery, K. (1993), 'Whither "Nation" and "Nationalism"?' *Daedalus,* Summer: 37–46.

16. On the significance and construction of nationalist 'pathetic phrases' (Pathosformeln) see Link, J. and Wülfing, W. (eds) (1991), *Nationale Mythen und Symbole in der zweiten Hälfte des 19. Jahrhunderts. Strukturen und Funktionen von Konzepten nationaler Identität,* Stuttgart; François, E. et al. (eds) (1995), *Nation und Emotion. Deutschland und Frankreich im Vergleich im 19. und 20. Jahrhundert,* Göttingen.

17. The article is one result of my research project on 'Nation, Krieg und Geschlecht in Preußen in der Zeit der antinapoleonischen Kriege, 1806–1815', financed by the German Research Foundation. Cf. more general: Hofmeister-Hunger, A. (1994), *Pressepolitik und Staatsreform. Die Institutionalisierung staatlicher Öffentlichkeitsarbeit bei Karl August v. Hardenberg,* Göttingen, especially pp. 181–328; Schäfer, K.-H. (1974), *Ernst Moritz Arndt als politischer Publizist. Studien zu Publizistik, Pressepolitik und kollektivem Bewußtsein im frühen 19. Jahrhundert,* Bonn; Weber, E. (1991), *Lyrik der Befreiungskriege (1812–1815): Gesellschaftspolitische Meinungs- und Willensbildung durch Literatur,* Stuttgart.

18. Cf. Wehler, H.-U. (1987), *Deutsche Gesellschaftsgeschichte,* vol. 1: *Vom Feudalismus des Alten Reiches bis zur Defensiven Modernisierung der Reformära. 1700–1815* (Munich) 347–548.

19. Cf. Koselleck, R. (1981), 'Die Auflösung des Hauses als ständischer Herrschaftseinheit. Anmerkungen zum Rechtswandel von Haus, Familie und Gesinde in Preußen zwischen Französischer Revolution und 1848', in Bulst, N. et al. *Familie zwischen Tradition und Moderne. Studien zur Geschichte der Familie in Deutschland und Frankreich vom 16. bis zum 20. Jahrhundert,* Göttingen, 109–124.

20. On the literature, see Claudia Opitz (1991), 'Auf der Suche nach den vergessenen Töchtern der Revolution. Neuere Forschungen über Frauen und Frauenrechte im revolutionären Frankreich 1789–1795', in Fieseler, B. and Schulze, B. (eds) *Frauengeschichte: gesucht –*

gefunden? Auskünfte zum Stand der historischen Frauenforschung, (Cologne), 146–63; Offen, K. (1990) 'The New Sexual Politics of French Revolutionary Historiography,' in *French Historical Studies* 16 (Fall): 909–22.

21. See, most recently, Kuhlbrodt, P. (1990) 'Die Französische Revolution und die Frauenrechte in Deutschland', in *Zeitschrift für Geschichtswissenschaft* 38: 405–21.

22. At the beginning of the nineteenth century, what contemporaries referred to as the 'educated estate' *(Stand der Gebildeten)* encompassed both the educated middle class *(Bildungsbürgertum)* in the narrower sense and the educated aristocracy. Cf. Bödeker E.H., (1989), 'Die gebildeten Stände im späten 18. und frühen 19. Jahrhundert: Zugehörigkeit und Abgrenzungen. Mentalitäten und Handlungspotentiale', in Kock, J. (ed.) *Bildungsbürgertum im 19. Jahrhundert,* part IV, Stuttgart, 21–52.

23. Cf. Frevert U., '"Tatenarm und gedankenvoll"? Bürgertum in Deutschland 1780–1830,' in Berding, H. et al. (eds) *Deutschland und Frankreich im Zeitalter der Französischen Revolution.*

24. Cf. Koselleck, R., (1992), 'Volk, Nation, Nationalismus, Masse,' in *GGr.,* vol. 7, Stuttgart, 141–431, 315 ff.

25. Cf. 'Nation', in (1806) *Johann Georg Krünitz's ökonomisch-technologische Encyklopädie [. . .]*vol. 101 (Berlin), 393–415, 393.

26. Cf. Jahn, F.L. (1810) *Deutsches Volkstum,* Lübeck, in Jahn, F.L., *Werke,* (new ed. by Carl Euler), vol. 1 (Hof, 1884), 143–380, 155.

27. On the differences between early modern forms of national prejudice and modern national stereotypes, see Jeismann, M. (1995), 'Was bedeuten Stereotype für nationale Identität und politisches Handeln?,' in Link, *Mythen,* 84–92; Winfried Schulze, (1995), 'Die Entstehung des nationalen Vorurteils. Zur Kultur der Wahrnehmung fremder Nationen in der europäischen Frühen Neuzeit,' *Geschichte in Wissenschaft und Unterricht* (= GWU) 46: 642–65.

28. Cf. Jeismann, M. (1992), *Das Vaterland der Feinde. Studien zum nationalen Feindbegriff und Selbstverständnis in Deutschland und Frankreich 1792–1918* (Stuttgart), 27–102.

29. Contemporary discourse distinguished between the positively connoted *weiblich* (feminine) and the negatively connoted *weibisch* (effeminate). See 'Wahrheiten und Zweifel II,' in *Tageblatt der Geschichte* (=TG), no. 51, 13.3.1815.

30. Cf. 'Wie viel zu gründlicher Befreiung von der fremden Herrschaft zu thun noch übrig ist,' in *Deutsche Blätter* (=DB), 1815, vol. 2: 513–527, 517f.

31. Cf. 'Wahrheiten und Zweifel I, II und III,' in *TG* no. 47, 7.3.1815, no. 51, 13.3.1815, no. 52, 14.3.1815.

32. Cf. Honegger, C. (1991), *Die Ordnung der Geschlechter. Die Wissenschaften vom Menschen und das Weib,* Frankfurt a.M., 107–125; Riedel, W. (1994), 'Anthropologie und Literatur in der deutschen Spätaufklärung. Skizze einer Forschungslandschaft,' in *Internationales Archiv für Sozialgeschichte der Literatur*, 6. Sonderheft: Forschungsreferate, 3. Folge, Tübingen, 93–157. On organic thinking in politics, see also Kaiser, G. (1961), *Pietismus und Patriotismus im literarischen Deutschland. Ein Beitrag zum Problem der Säkularisation,* Wiesbaden, 139–59.

33. Bock, (1988), 'Geschichte, Frauengeschichte, Geschlechtergeschichte' in *GG* 14: 364–91, 373ff.

34. Only after the military objective of liberation had been achieved in 1814 did public discourse begin, parallel to the negotiations at the Congress of Vienna, to further refine the terms, rendering them more precise, a process which was accompanied by a rapid increase in political differences. Cf. Dann, *Nation*, 85 ff.

35. Cf. Wehler, *Gesellschaftsgeschichte*, vol. 1, 506ff; Berdahl, R.M. (1985), 'Der deutsche Nationalismus in neuer Sicht', in Winkler, H.A. (ed.) *Nationalismus*, 2nd ed., Königstein/Ts., 138–54, 140.

36. See Harnisch, M. (1989), 'Nationalisierung der Dynastien oder Monarchisierung der Nation? Zum Verhältnis von Monarchie und Nation in Deutschland im 19. Jahrhundert', in Birke, A.M. et al. (ed.) *Bürgertum, Adel und Monarchie. Zum Wandel der Lebensform im Zeitalter des bürgerlichen Nationalismus*, Munich, 71–92.

37. Cf. Dann, O. (1990), 'Der deutsche Bürger wird Soldat: Zur Entstehung des bürgerlichen Kriegsengagements in Deutschland,' in Steinweg, R. (ed.) *Lehren aus der Geschichte? Historische Friedensforschung,* (Frankfurt a.M.), 61–84; Kunisch, J. (1992), 'Von der gezähmten zur entfesselten Bellona: Die Umwertung des Krieges im Zeitalter der Revolutions- und Freiheitskriege,' in Kunisch, J. *Fürst – Gesellschaft – Krieg. Studien zu bellizistischen Disposition des absoluten Fürstenstaates* (Cologne), 203–26.

38. Cf. Wohlfeil, R. (1964), *Vom stehenden Heer des Absolutismus zur Allgemeinen Wehrpflicht (1789–1814),* Frankfurt a. M.), 86f.

39. Münchow-Pohl, *Reform*, 397.

40. *Der Preußische Correspondent*, no. 1, 2.4.1813: 1.

41. Ernst Moritz Arndt, 'An die Preußen,' [January] 1813, in Spieß, *Erhebung*, 224–8.

42. Koselleck, *Volk*, 332.

43. Schulz, G. (1989), *Die deutsche Literatur zwischen Französischer Revolution und Restauration. Zweiter Teil: Das Zeitalter der Napoleonischen Kriege und der Restauration 1806–1830,* München, 76.

44. There has been little research thus far on the relationship among the military, war and masculinity. On the period around 1800, see Frevert, U. (1996), 'Soldaten, Staatsbürger. Überlegungen zur historischen Konstruktion von Männlichkeit', in Kühne, T (ed.). *Männergeschichte-Geschlechtergeschichte. Männlichkeit im Wandel der Moderne,* Frankfurt a.M, 69–87; and, 'das Militär als 'Schule der Männlichkeit'. Erwartungen, Angebote, Erfahrungen im 19. Jahrhundert,' in Frevert, *Militär,* 145–200; Karen Hagemann, *Valor.*

45. Cf. Hagemann, *Valor:* 190ff and 209ff.

46. Finder, S.E. (1975), 'State- and Nation-Building in Europe: The Role of the Military', in Tilly, C. (ed.) *The Formation of National State in Western Europe,* Princeton and N.J., 84–163, 134ff.

47. According to the official figures on the size of the Prussian army in August 1813, 107,800 men out of a total of 227,900 troops in the first line were militia men; 92,900 were soldiers of the standing army; 18,300 were volunteers in the detachments of riflemen; and 8,900 were members of various volunteer corps. Cf. *Das preußische Heer der Befreiungskriege,* 3 vols, Berlin: Großer Generalstab, Kriegsgeschichtliche.

48. This connection becomes particularly clear when one examines the significance of conscription for the political emancipation of Jewish men in Prussia. See Fischer, *Judentum,* 63 ff.

49. Cf. Frevert, U. (1995), '"Unser Staat ist männlichen Geschlechts". Zur politischen Topographie der Geschlechter vom 18. bis frühen 20. Jahrhundert,' in Frevert, *'Mann und Weib, Weib und Mann'. Geschlechter-Differenzen in der Moderne,* Munich, 61–132.

50. Cf. Hagemann, *Valor,* 214 ff.

51. Cf. Howard, M. (1981), *War in European History,* London, 75–93; Rothenberg, G.E. (1980), *The Art of Warfare in the Age of Napoleon,* Bloomington; Esdaile, C.J. (1995), *The Wars of Napoleon,* London and New York.

52. Cf. Mosse, G.L. (1990), *Fallen Soldiers. Reshaping the Memory of the World Wars,* New York and Oxford, 15–52.

53. Kaiser, *Pietismus,* 124ff.

54. Jeismann, *Vaterland,* 95ff.

55. Cf. Hagemann, *Valor.*

56. Wunder, H. (1992), *'Er ist die Sonn', sie ist der Mond'. Frauen in der Frühen Neuzeit* (Munich), 261 ff.

57. Honegger, *Ordnung*, 186–99.
58. Cf. Frevert, U. (1981), 'Geschlecht – männlich/weiblich. Zur Geschichte der Begriffe (1730–1990), in Frevert, *Mann*, 13–60, Karin Hausen, 'Family and Role-division: The Polarisation of Sexual Stereotypes in the Nineteenth Century – An Aspect of the Dissociation of Work and Family Life,' in Evans, R.J. and Lee, W.R. *The German Family: Essays on the Social History of the Family in 19th- and 20th-century Germany*, London, 51–83.
59. See 'Wahrheit und Zweifel I,' in *TG* no.47, 7.3.1815.
60. Cf. Frevert, Geschlecht, 31 ff.
61. On the problem of the conceptual pair 'public sphere' (*Öffentlichkeit*) and 'private sphere' (*Privatheit*), see Davidoff, L. (1993), '"Alte Hüte". Öffentlichkeit und Privatheit in der feministischen Geschichtsschreibung,' *L'Homme* 4: 7–36; Hausen, K. (1993), 'Öffentlichkeit und Privatheit. Gesellschaftspolitische Konstruktionen und die Geschichte der Geschlechterbeziehungen,' in Hausen, K. *Frauengeschichte*, 81–8; Elshtain, J.B. (1993), *Public Man, Private Woman: Women in Social and Political Thought*, 2nd ed., Princeton, N.J.; Pateman, C. (1989), *The Disorder of Women, Democracy, Feminism and Political Theory*, Cambridge.
62. 'Anrede an die Landsturmmänner der kurischen Nehrung,' in *TG*, no. 8, January 1814.
63. (1826), 'Nation,' in *Rheinisches Conversations-Lexikon oder Enzyklopädisches Handwörterbuch für gebildete Stände,* Cologne, 74–9.
64. 'Einige Worte über das Verhältnis der deutschen Frauen zu den Weltbegebenheiten', in *DB*, 1814, 2. vol.: 310–15. Cf. Hagemann, Heldenmütter.
65. 'Ein Wort an Deutschlands Frauen und Jungfrauen', in *DB*, 2. vol., 1813: 65–75; Jahn, *Volksthum*, 352–69.
66. Cf. Wülfing, W. (1984), 'Die heilige Luise von Preußen. Zur Mythisierung einer Figur der Geschichte in der deutschen Literatur des 19. Jahrhunderts,' in Link, J. and Wülfing, W. *Bewegung und Stillstand in Methaphern und Mythen. Fallstudien zum Verhältnis von elementarem Wissen und Literatur im 19. Jahrhundert*, Stuttgart, 233–75.
67. Cf. 'Deutsche Hülfsvereine,' in *DB*, 1815, 2. vol.: 209–14.
68. Cf. 'Ueber eine deutsche Ehren- und Hausangelegenheit' in *Schlesische Provinzialblätter* (= SP), 3. Stk., March 1815: 238–53.
69. See, for example, 'Leonora Prochaska', in *Feld-Zeitung*, no. 37 (1813).
70. Cf. Opitz, C. (1989), 'Der Bürger wird Soldat – und die Bürgerin . . .? Die Revolution, der Krieg und die Stellung der Frauen nach 1789,'

in Schmidt-Linsenhoff, V., *Sklavin oder Bürgerin? Französische Revolution und neue Weiblichkeit 1760–1830,* ed., Frankfurt a.M., 38–53.

71. Cf. Hagemann, Heldenmütter, 192ff.
72. Cf. Müller, A. (1810) *Über König Friedrich II. und die Würde und Bestimmung der preußischen Monarchie,* Berlin), 70–1.
73. Cf. *Denkmal der Preußen auf ihre verewigte Königin Luise, durch weibliche Erziehungsanstalten,* ed. by W. A. Klewitz, Halberstadt, 1814, 6–7.
74. Cf. 'Chronik. Breslau,' in *SP,* no. 3, March 1813; See Wülfing, Luise, 236ff and 248ff.
75. On the history of the topos of the *Landesvater* (father of the country) more generally, see Münch, P. (1982) 'Die 'Obrigkeit im Vaterstand' – Zu Definition und Kritik des 'Landesvaters' während der frühen Neuzeit,' *Daphnis* 11: 15–40.
76. Hunt, L. (1992), *The Family Romance of the French Revolution,* Berkeley, XIV ff and 79 ff; Colley, L. (1992), *Britons: Forging the Nation 1707–1837,* New Haven, 237 ff; Wienfort, M. (1993), *Monarchie in der bürgerlichen Gesellschaft. Deutschland und England von 1640 bis 1848,* Göttingen, 183 ff.
77. See Brubaker, R. (1992), *Citizenship and Nationhood in France and Germany,* Cambridge, especially chapter I.
78. On the term see Hunt, L. (1984), *Politics, Culture, and Class in the French Revolution,* Berkeley and Los Angeles, 12 f; Lipp, C. (1996), 'Politische Kultur oder das Politische und Gesellschaftliche in der Kultur,' in Hardtwig and Wehler, *Kulturgeschichte,* 78–110.

–10–

Regendering Afrikanerdom: The 1899–1902 Anglo–Boer War

Helen Bradford

If someone had told me in the 1980s, that I would analyse Afrikaner nationalism, I would have laughed. I was a white, English-speaking, South African historian. Political virtue resided in exploring African resistance. The point was not to understand Afrikaner nationalism but to end it. But as apartheid fades into history, preoccupations change. I write, then, as an outsider, producing partial, situated knowledge, of the single most significant event fuelling modern Afrikaner nationalism: the 1899–1902 Anglo-Boer war.

In 1899, South Africa did not exist; the region consisted of two British colonies (the Cape and Natal) and two Boer republics (the Transvaal and Orange Free State). The war turning these republics into British colonies stimulated Afrikaner nationalism throughout the region: hardly unusual from a comparative perspective. Yet viewed through a gendered lens, this war-forged nationalism was distinctive. The *volk* was largely gendered as male in the late nineteenth century, but many men mobilized as 'brother Africanders' surrendered and deserted the *volk*. Barely a decade after conquest, ex-Boer generals fought World War I on the British side. Boer women, however, acquired an 1899–1902 reputation for being more irreconcilable than men. Between 1902 and 1914, nationalists formed women's organizations, erected a women's monument, celebrated Women's Day, promoted the 'mother tongue'. Women – 'the strongest element in our nation' – had gatecrashed into a homosocial *volk*.[1] The Anglo-Boer war was the single most significant event fuelling not merely modern Afrikaner nationalism, but a regendered Afrikaner nationalism, transferring its weight from its (weak) male to its (strong) female leg.

It is futile to scan the academic landscape for explanations. Despite a small body of feminist literature, the hegemonic gender identity of 'Afrikaner nationalist' is male. Moreover, most analysts have stressed the creation of ethnic nationalism and Afrikaans: the 'invented community of the *volk* required the conscious creation of a single print-language . . . and a literate populace'.[2] Consequently, a war when printed Afrikaans did not exist, and many Afrikaners spoke English, has also been neglected. What follows explores these two lost worlds: of national identities tied to fighting for fatherlands rather than reading the mother tongue, and of semi-literate women proving themselves the better patriots, the better men.

Pre-War Nationalist Discourses

The Transvaal and Orange Free State were carved out from land inhabited by an African majority. Whites escaping British rule in the Cape and Natal – and British introduction of formal racial equality – invaded the region. Here 'Boers' ('farmers'), speaking the *taal* (the language), proved their own colonial credentials. The 'time-honoured privileges of our calling' as men, wrote a Transvaaler, where ten wars were fought against Africans between 1860 and 1899, were to 'dare any man, take as much property as we are able to remove, set fire to any village, lay any natives under tribute.'[3] Guns, citizenship and land were institutionalized attributes of republican manhood. White men alone could bear arms on commando, vote and be granted huge farms (although black men, forbidden arms, could be conscripted.)

As in many societies with gender-differentiated incorporation into the body politic, nascent nationalist discourses, drenched with references to countrymen, brothers and fatherlands, both marginalized women and emerged, above all, in response to war. In particular, in 1895–6, after gold was discovered in the Transvaal, and after the first (1880–1) Anglo-Boer war against colonization of this republic had already been fought, a botched invasion of the Transvaal was sanctioned by London and bankrolled by the Cape premier, Cecil Rhodes. 'Let us stand manfully by one another', responded one, calling upon 'Africanderdom' throughout South Africa; 'the foundation of a wide-embracing nationalism must be laid.'[4]

Africander/Afrikander/Afrikaner (variants existed in a polyglot region) was less a cultural than a racialized geopolitical identity. Africans were 'kaffirs'; only whites who identified with Africa could become Africanders. Elite men squabbled over this identity. Rhodes had promised an 'Afrikander government' in 1890, countering those who claimed 'Africander should be interpreted as Transvaaler'.[5] But 'Africander' acquired strong anti-imperialist connotations after his invasion. To be a 'true Afrikaner and an upright Englishman' remained possible, but 'Rhodes, the Afrikaner, has become an impossibility'.[6]

If Rhodes was now outside the fold, the issue of 'manfully' uniting Afrikanerdom remained. Winning male support for republican, let alone broader nationalism, had long been problematic. Poverty and parochialism undercut republican loyalties. Boer men often failed to heed callups. In 1896, 41 per cent of Transvaalers liable for commando duty did not own guns. 'To every man his own home is the capital'; 'every father laid down the law for his own wife and children, without troubling himself about the rest of the community'.[7] Typical missionaries of Afrikaner nationalism – anglicized male urbanites – had limited success in converting patriarchs identified by their occupation. Boers lived on farms, a Transvaal visitor was told; Afrikaners lived in towns, and were mainly educated at the Cape's (aptly named) Victoria College.[8]

After Rhodes's invasion, as republican budgets poured into Mausers for white men, notables invoked gender to aid the transformation of farmers into Afrikaners. Phenomena ranging from agriculture and religion to ethnonyms were packaged with masculine connotations. Land loss to Englishmen meant sons would become tenants on fathers' farms; manliness was (or should be) a defining feature of the Afrikaner character and culture; the Boer was the world's best fighter; men's defence of their fatherland was blessed by the God of their fathers. Yet in 1899, with London again threatening war against the Transvaal unless gold-rush immigrant men obtained the vote, it remained unclear whether 'sons of Africa' would fight – or would lurk on farms, heeding warnings that war between whites threatened white supremacy. They should 'stand as men not with big gobs and then run away . . . plies do not forget the mousser', urged one anxiously.[9] '*Broeder-Afrikaners*!' exhorted a Free State manifesto; 'let us stand side by side and do our holy duty as men!'[10] 'Brother Africanders!' began a Transvaal tract, outlining a century of suffering at British hands, and juxtaposing 'defenceless women' with 'men capable of resistance'.[11]

Pace these middle class men subscribing to Victorian gender norms, Boer women, economically indispensable in rural households, were not known for their pacifism. Most had folk or personal memories of waging war against African men: loading male rifles, firing female revolvers, hacking off black male hands. Their 'intense hatred of the Englishman', too, was notorious.[12] Many drove men into the first Anglo-Boer war; in 1899, 'Afrikaner Boer women' threatened to fight themselves, impatiently demanding of their men 'prove yourself to be a man!'[13] Anti-imperialism probably had a gender gap long predating this war.

Yet in October 1899, women were banned from war zones; imperial aggression was to be met with male, not female, militarism. The close links between guns, masculinity and nationalism, noted in societies ranging from Australia and Britain to Palestine and Zimbabwe, were also evident here.[14] Attempts to unify white men divided by class, ethnicity, region and history, threatened on the male terrains of war and the vote, centred on rifles, commandos, male-only spaces and nationalist discourses stressing virility. 'Brother' invoked male comradeship. 'Afrikaner' provided a racialized identity broader than ethnicities or states; many an English Afrikaner, a Cape or Natal Afrikaner, joined the cause. As *broeder-Afrikaners*, farmers were urged to invade British colonies, as two petty republics declared war on the world's greatest empire.

The 'Hands-Up' Time

Generals soon learned that many men were unwilling or unable to be *broeder-Afrikaners*. On the first day of war, only 54 per cent of men from eight Transvaal districts had arrived on the Natal front; many were not fully equipped. Moreover, men volunteered for any battle – and a great majority often refused to fight. They did not want to get up so early, explained a commandant arriving for battle with only three men. The Free State Commandant-General declined to participate in an attack coinciding with a cattle sale.[15] Enthusiasts certainly won victories, but gender attributes rooted in rural patriarchy also undercut militarism.

Preventing Boers from taking home leave, a task so hard that the Transvaal Commandant-General proposed peace barely a month after the war's start, was almost impossible when the republics were invaded. Homesteads were plundered from the first day the huge imperial army invaded the Free State in February 1900, marching north on Pretoria. Boer men were now at the receiving end of a type of war they were more accustomed to inflicting. They were being routed. Property was being seized – this would allegedly cease if they surrendered. Black civilians were welcoming the enemy of their own oppressors.

Republican forces melted away. The 'great majority thought more of their farms, their families and their private affairs than of the fate of the Republics'.[16] Forty per cent of the white men who had initially been mobilized surrendered between March and July. Most black men – and thousands of white men – simply fled home. It was almost impossible to hear a patriotic word, noted a Dutch volunteer; every man seemed only too glad to go home. 'Rumours again did the rounds that the approaching enemy respected neither family members nor private property', reported a Transvaler as his commando retreated into its home district. 'Now that the enemy was almost on the farms, patriotism faded away.'[17]

Generals could not stem the haemorrhage. Transvaal forces were almost non-existent in early June. Their President, urged to end the war, asked President Steyn, his Free State counterpart, how many men remained. 'I have knocked the bottom out of "the Great Afrikaander nation" forever and ever', rejoiced the High Commissioner for South Africa, days after the Free State was annexed, days before Pretoria was occupied.[18]

He had not. Latter-day historians have offered a 'great man' theory of history as an explanation for this: the new Free State Commandant-General, Christiaan De Wet, led a guerrilla-based revival from March. The same month, a contemporary historian provided a less masculinist reading. This was not a European war, he stressed; '*women* are the fiercest advocates of war to the bitter end. For independence the Boer women will send husbands and son after son to fight to the last'.[19] '[S]o many women in the land are content their men (!) should be away', noted a Free State minister's wife; some were 'so afraid any of theirs may come back!'[20]

War had altered gender power relations. A conflict threatening Boer manhood – military prowess, property, arms – spawned female household heads, female activists, female farmers. Consequently, a husband could be bluntly told to fight: his wife could run the farm. The maleness of God, among one of the most Bible-reading people in the world, reinforced female autonomy. Many women infused God the Father, the 'Master', God who 'promised to be a husband to me', into spaces vacated by patriarchs.[21] Men flooding home were met by women enjoying an intimate relationship with a male Almighty. Nationalism and religion were fused in His scriptures; Boer women had in Him an 'unconquerable faith'.[22]

Deserters were not merely faithless: they were accomplices to murder, cried one woman to her republican 'sisters'. The imperial army was about to lay waste to 'our country, our houses and also us and our daughters'.[23] Warfare targeting homes also aroused fears of proletarianization for women familiar with war's consequences for Africans. Deserters were murdering the *volk* and its dearly bought land, stated one. 'We shall have to work for the English just as the Kaffirs work for us and . . . shall hardly be treated as whites'.[24] In addition, female Boer supporters, seemingly much more than men, spoke in horror of the internal enemies of racial privilege: Africans jeering at Boers 'after the manner of blacks under the English government'; armed African men intimidating Boer women; African farm workers spying for the British and threatening rape.[25] Conquest meant equality between black and white, and miscegenation, declared some Transvaal women in a mass petition for armed Afrikaner women to replace deserters.[26] An unholy alliance of British and black men allegedly threatened republican women with loss of white privileges, antagonistic sexuality and colonization of their intimate spaces.

Consequently, many tried to drive men back to commandos. They practised gender politics in public and private domains; they inserted women into the male terrain of citizenship, commandos and nationalism. In the press, in women-only meetings, in Pretoria's Parliament itself, elite urbanites urged 'sisters and female burghers' to drive back to war men evading 'the call of manhood and patriotism'. Cowards could wear dresses and care for children; an 'Amazonian Corps of Afrikander Women' would replace them.[27] Boer women used their domestic power, refusing to feed men, taunting them. Tales circulated about wives' injunctions. 'Go and fight. I can get another husband, but not another Free State.' 'Remain and do your duty . . . I can always find another husband, but not another Transvaal.'[28] Men placing farms and families above independent states were met by women opposed to exchanging their fatherland for a man at home. Deeply shamed by female kin, enough men left their homes to affect the war. By the time Transvaal generals were urging peace, 'sisters' had helped create the Free State revival.

Some women, however, resigned themselves to male defeat, and began sowing female seeds of cultural nationalism. This war 'has taught us what we are – has brought out the Africanderism' declared one of German descent in the occupied Free State capital. Searching for what separated 'us' from 'Englishmen' she came up with history, republicanism, the *taal* and 'race hatred' as the 'traditions, which alone can make a nation'.[29] Boer mothers, not fathers, would transmit the hatred, she predicted. Boer mothers' hatred was profound, confirmed a soldier, telling of one bereaved of her son, swearing to kill her infant daughter rather than have her marry an Englishman.[30]

In the Cape, elite women dramatically entered politics, outstripping men in overt anti-imperialism. At women-only meetings, some politicized language, refusing to speak English. Many more politicized maternity. 'Give us the children, and we have the *volk.*' This lay at the heart of their strategy. The fate of the *volk* depended on them; by teaching children the *taal*, patriotism and love of the Dutch Reformed Church, they could achieve 'England for the English . . . and *Africa for the Africanders*'.[31] They were placing mothers and homes centre stage in a political project.

Clearly, these projects differed among white female supporters of the Boer cause. Men – black, British, and Boer deserters – haunted women, constituting 'others' excluded from the imagined 'us'. Some, often urban and middle class, responded by giving mothers centrality in creating an ethnicized *volk*. Others, both rural and urban, tried to feminize deserters, invade male spaces and militarize masculinity, elevating love of father- lands above love of men. Boer women were 'Amazonian', warned an officer. 'The Boer woman – strong, fierce, and uncompromising – is a force to be reckoned with in the future settlement of South Africa.'[32]

A '*Volk* of *Broeders*': June–December 1900

By September 1900, the central event of the war had allegedly occurred: the birth of 'a *volk* of *broeders*'.[33] The emergence of a nationalist fraternity was closely connected to an assault on Boer patriarchy.

Initially, remaining on commando was punished by selective farm burning. As victory remained elusive, the imperial commander declared his intention to 'starve into submission' guerrillas and their families.[34] The Transvaal was annexed in September. The army simultaneously embarked on its prime task until the end of the war: laying waste two British colonies. To 'lay waste' meant to gather 'all food, wagons, Cape carts, sheep, oxen, goats, cows . . . Destroy what you cannot eat or remove . . . burn all houses . . . destroy or remove everything.'[35]

Destroying or removing everything – including people, by increasingly interning all Boers, and ultimately extending to demolishing 30,000 settler homesteads – had an unexpected result. It increased Boer men's willing- ness to fight. A colonel imprisoning civilian men was his best recruiter, rejoiced one leader; his commando rose from twenty-five to some one thousand men over two months. Arson, exulted a guerrilla, aided the Boers' cause: the homeless could not flee home. Laying waste farms, raged a British officer, meant 'every Dutchman' was inspired by 'thirst for revenge'.[36] This was not confined to 'Dutchmen'. An English speaker held the Transvaal flag aloft when one commando celebrated the holiest day of the nationalist calendar. Some black men adopted the Boer cause as their own.[37]

Arson and internment, however, hit Boers hardest. Tensions between patriarchy and brotherhood, class and nation, were now being forcibly resolved. 'The private and individual ties so dear to the Boers' hearts were loosened in order that they might cling with all the more disinterested devotion to their national ideal.'[38] They were losing the farms and families underpinning patriarchal worlds; fighting for fatherlands now had more appeal. Men calling themselves 'wild Boers' began following women's route, overtly prioritizing their country over marital ties. When a woman told Transvalers that unless they surrendered, women would be captured, she was told to tell the khakis that wives were replaceable, countries were not. 'We shall not hand over the country for a woman', they shouted.[39] De Wet drummed home the same message: 'you can always get a wife, but if you have lost your country, you never get it back.'[40]

Women, too, continued to invest in a national rather than familial romance. An officer reported that he had never seen such patriotism before, after two months of farm burning. Without exception, the women's message was the same: 'we shall go on fighting'; 'God sooner or later will see us through.'[41] If, 'in so many countries, it was religion that first converted peasants into patriots, long before the onset of modernisation', it was also Boer women's faith that unnerved modern men.[42] More intelligible was the response of Isabella Steyn, of Scottish descent, house arrested after declining to ask her husband, the President, to surrender. 'We women' would continue the war to the end, she declared. Asked how long she thought this would be, she replied: 'I expect and hope till our last cartridge is shot.'[43]

There were variations on these themes. Some women urged surrender; many fled before arsonists came, sometimes tagging along with commandos. Total war was still geographically restricted; many men had yet to be wrenched from their homes. Nonetheless, British imperialism, by eroding the material basis of Boer patriarchy, was undoubtedly forging a *volk* of *broeders*. Unity between Transvalers and Free Staters grew; numbers on commando soared; vengeance linked private concerns to patriotic concerns. Moreover, in a war now popularly seen as a war against women, by Englishmen, more barbarous than almost all blacks, republican women were enhancing their *bittereinder* reputations: as 'more bitter and irreconcilable than the men', an 'amazon', a 'fighter' of 'bloody inclination' who 'outshines the primary product', possessing qualities that 'many men might well envy'. How, an imperialist was asked, did he intend to rule 'thousands of Joans of Arc'?[44]

Concentration Camps

Women, wrote the imperial commander in December 1900, outstripped men in their bitterness and fuelled the war. Removing 'the worst class to . . . a camp' would 'bring them to their senses'.[45] By October 1901, most republican Boer women and children had, after their farms had been burned, been transported to a concentration camp. These camps also housed 'hands-uppers' and black servants, although most 'black Boers', as one called himself, were deported to segregated camps.[46]

Of every 100 whites who died on the republican side, 11 were men killed in action. 82 died in the camps; 13 were women; 65 were children.[47]

Grossly inadequate food and shelter decimated infants and those too poor to supplement rations. The only remaining issue was whether what was termed a holocaust – in October 1901, the annual death rate in white camps peaked at one in three people – would starve women into submission.

Even in the darkest days, women protested. Hundreds of demonstrators cried of dying thirty a day. They sang the Free State anthem. Their leaders, wearing republican colours, were jailed. More typically, failure to keep people alive drove many not into defiance, but into despair. A pregnant woman, a dead child in one side of her tent, her four remaining children all ill, her husband and sons in the veld, was utterly forlorn. Disease, malnutrition and heartbreak often just generated prayers 'that the Lord come quick to fetch me', and skeletal children longing for heaven where there was no more hunger, no more Khakis.[48]

Yet most women with men on commando clung to one tenet. Male surrender improved children's life chances. But most refused to ask their own menfolk to 'hands-up'. They mobilized gender differences to denounce traitors who 'did not deserve the name of *man*'.[49] Unlike black women during the Kenyan Mau Mau rebellion, when quasi-concentration camps broke the back of resistance of women deemed more fanatical than men, most settler women – pass-carrying, servile, doing back-breaking labour, separated from the African poor by little but religion and history – found a way of accommodating concentration camps.[50]

Their faith in divine deliverance was crucial. Utterly reliant on God for political ends – 'Forgive me all my sins . . . and give us our land back', ran a typical prayer – many decided He was chastizing them.[51] Ethical and sometimes sexual norms eroded in camps; grim fights over resources erupted; there was so much sin, wrote an elite Afrikaner, that 'I cannot think that we will soon be dilivered [*sic*] – no we will still have to go through warmer furnaces till we also come out pure'.[52] If sinful women had to be purified, then virtue resided in stoic, even grateful acceptance of pain. '[W]e dare not murmur . . . God has been so good to us', wrote an orphan of her brother's death.[53] Hymns praising God for permitting suffering for their land, Bible readings about child sacrifices demanded of Hebrew heroes, did not, admittedly, prevent faith from faltering. 'Have I *still* not brought enough sacrifices?' cried one, three of her remaining children dying. 'Why doesn't the Lord God give victory to our men, then an end will indeed come to all this misery!' She struggled with the creed of 'real Afrikaners': that the *volk*'s deliverance depended on personal purification through pain.[54]

Nonetheless, there were many *bittereinders*. Some Afrikaners had submitted, stated one, but her husband had to fight on. If but two men remained, 'if he is left alone, while he can hold a gun he must fight on'.[55] They prayed for peace, recalled another, but 'naturally' the thought of surrendering their country 'never, never, came up among us, because what were we suffering and fighting for then?'[56] Let 'our husbands fight, fight', cried a third; 'even if I too have to give up two children many mothers have sacrificed four to five children for our fatherland.'[57] With few exceptions, messages smuggled out to men urged them to fight to the death. In other words, the lives of children were now also being placed on the altar of the fatherland.

From late 1901, white camps improved. Rations were better; over-crowding decreased, since women whose homes and farms had been burned were now left in the veld (unless they persuaded men to 'hands-up'); those already in the camps, whose men were still *bittereinders,* were exiled to Natal. A new energy began flowing through camp politics. On nationalist or religious holy days, thousands of flag-waving children and women, singing republican anthems, marched through two Natal camps. 'Hands-uppers' were forced to cede their republican flag to women: the icons of male-only nation states were being appropriated by women and children, and denied to men who had compromized their manhood and nationality simultaneously.[58] Murderous sentiments were now openly shouted: the General Superintendent of Transvaal Camps noted that many Boer women were bitter enemies of the British. A 'hands-upper' simply called them 'the anti-British sex'.[59] 'Anti-British' could have sweeping connotations for women defining men's nationality by whether and for whom they fought: 'all the Kaffirs became britons [*sic*]', recalled one of a war where 10,000–30,000 black men fought for the imperial army.[60] 'The camps have alienated her from us for ever', mourned a British politician.[61]

In the veld, however, famine loomed. African men, over 50,000 armed independently of Britain, were waging their own wars against Boers. Imperialists, trying to trap guerrillas in cordons, were wearing down morale. One asked what was his most 'manly' option: fighting a war consisting largely of hiding, or surrendering, and perhaps rejoining his family?[62] With a rag-tag army and a mounting toll of landless Boers fighting *for* imperialists for cash or loot, men's war was drawing to an end.

Colonial Masculinities and Conquest

In mid-1902, republican men met to decide on war or surrender – and to struggle over gender. 'Everything else is of minor importance', declared De Wet, acting Free State President, compared to an unarmed future where they were 'no longer men' and 'all stand as women'. It was 'more manly to conclude the peace' than to 'show our manliness by continuing the struggle', argued his Transvaal counterpart.[63]

Those urging brothers to surrender their guns had to reframe manhood. They promoted paternalism: men regaining the right of caring for wives, children, orphans and widows. Consequently, women were now central as imagined victims, needing male protection. They were also scapegoats. In this as in many lost wars, 'women lose, men don't.'[64]

One of their worst problems, noted Transvaal Commandant-General Louis Botha, was the plight of women linked to commandos. In the Transvaal, there were 7,520 mounted men, and some 2,540 families attached to them; in a Free State district, there were 80 fighters and 200 families. In other words, white children and women in the veld often outnumbered men. '[W]e did much of our Coemando's work', recalled two, referring to manufacturing clothes, matches and soap.[65] The husbands of most of these women had already been killed or captured – and the remaining men were no paternalists. When they broke through the cordons, they often abandoned the women. Some women fled to Africans, but many 'were attacked and raped by the Kaffirs'. They were 'a prey to the Kaffirs, because the British will not receive them.'[66] Some husbands were threatening surrender to save them, but most men were unwilling, not being their 'natural protectors'. The plight of these 'helpless victims' was thus forcing leaders to accept British terms, although '[w]e men' could fight on.[67]

Camp women figured less in discussions: one was only too pleased if wives were in the concentration camps, noted Botha. Yet they too had to be saved by surrender, either because they were 'innocent, helpless women and children', or because they threatened the nation, dead or alive.[68] '[O]ver 20,000 have already died, and there is another more important matter, viz., the immorality in the Concentration Camps', noted one. The female sex, he argued, under enemy influence, was deviating from forefathers' morals; this was 'the worst cancer' attacking 'our national existence'.[69] Claims that women were dying a 'moral death', while men died a 'national death', left the source of male disquiet unclear.[70] Yet the tropes spoke eloquently of male sexual insecurities when 'enemy' men ruled 'their' women.

These reconstructions of gender were opposed by advocates of war: largely young men, unmoved by paternalism, and mainly Free Staters, for whom African resistance was less significant. But senior Transvaal men insisted they met not as an army, but as a *volk*. To fight on meant elevating male ambition above the whole *volk*, including the unborn; 'from the womb of the future, they call on us to decide wisely'.[71]

Male wisdom was of more concern to women of the present. Four days before the war ended, a guerrilla noted they met not one (white) woman in the veld who did not urge them to fight on. Those in the veld were among the toughest *bittereinders*, claimed Steyn; he had received not one request for peace without independence from women; they were unconquerable. But a different view dominated discussions. Most women in the camps 'are indeed full of courage, but if they knew how matters stood in the veld, they would think otherwise.'[72] War-weary men were interpreting the will of the *volk* – and inaugurating the gender backlash common after war. The image of Boer woman as heroine was being replaced by woman as womb, as cancer, as sexually soiled. *Bittereinder* men were being portrayed as nationalist heroes defeated not on battle-fields, but by their concern for the prostrate, feminized *volk*.

Men who had talked gender to think peace, had declared hopes for reconciliation, had signed a deal according them £3 million compensation – for a loss variously estimated at £20–£80 million – then had to sell surrender to the women's camps.

At the Natal camp where leaders' families were primarily located, many thought the news one more English lie. What of 'all the misery in hope and confidence in a *certain* deliverance?' asked one.[73] Their 'brave heroes would not *thus* have sold out us, our country . . . and our holy dead', another assured others; 'if we should lose, then it would be over the bodies of us and our burghers.'[74] The acting Transvaal President came to confirm that men preferred to live. A vast crowd of women, having paid for their politics in the only currency many possessed, voiced anguished antag-onism. 'Is it for *this* that I sacrificed my husband, my son, my child?'[75] 'Why did you give the country away', they shouted at another camp; 'we had it hard for so long we would still have held out'.[76] She would have preferred to see her husband's grave, stated Cornelia De Wet. Women in concentration camps were more dismayed than anyone else, noted the acting Transvaal President.[77]

Many were not merely dismayed. Unlike veterans, who increasingly engaged in the fraternal politics of race, creating an Anglo-Afrikaner alliance to subordinate black men, many white women moved in the direction prefigured during men's seeming 1900 defeat. Middle class, women-only organizations were established; female cultural nationalism took off. De Wet's wartime instructions for women – 'draw a line between our *volk* and the enemy', 'hold ourselves apart' – were being fulfilled.[78] The writing or speaking of the *taal* or Dutch was turned from a custom to a cause: a woman who kept her camp diary in English switched to

Dutch the day she was told she was a British subject. The war was also interpreted in a way very difficult for defeated men: as nationalist *progress*, creating one people from Afrikaners in four countries.[79] A male war ending in defeat, turning men into women, was different from a female war turning women into Amazons. A conquest of Boer men, opening public male-only spaces to white veterans from both sides, was different from a conquest of Boer women, who could enshrine 'race hatred' and the 'mother tongue' in homes. Promoting reconciliation through Boer men was deeply flawed, noted a politician: 'he is a secondary factor to his wife and daughter ... the woman rules ... She it is who returns forgetting nothing and forgiving nothing.'[80] Women who had turned men into a secondary factor and had gatecrashed into the *volk*, women with a proven ability to elevate racist nationalism above life itself: such women were not the least legacy bequeathed by British imperialism to South Africa and the world.

Conclusion

Forged under threatened or actual war, *fin de siècle* Afrikaner nationalism was a profoundly gendered project. It centred not on people's ethnic peculiarities, but on the ideal Afrikaner man. For able-bodied white men, gender and nationalism fused. Their task was be 'sons of Africa', 'brother Africanders', displaying 'manhood and patriotism', wielding the rifles symbolizing both identities.

This task was massively rejected by Boer men early in the war. They chose farms and families over *volk* and fraternity. Some rejoined the cause when women extruded them from their homes. Many more rejoined when imperialists, destroying the material base of class and patriarchal orders, made revenge a personal concern. Once this proved a chimera, and private and nationalist interests again diverged, the patriarchal ideal with which fraternity was always in competition was reinstated. Older men, with a new-found ability to sacrifice their fatherland for wives, dreamed of restoring patriarchal authority: over white women, over black men.

For republican women erased from most nationalist discourses, patriotic duties and symbols were not well defined. They created their own, fuelled by fierce anti-imperialism and racism. Barred from the arms or vote reserved for white men, many turned to the iconography of male-only states. National flags, national anthems invoking freedom and *volk*, republican icons, rallies on red-letter nationalist days: these oral and visual ways of conveying political messages were extremely significant. The languages available to women sewing images of their President onto men's hats, or to a girl playing a national anthem on a piano as troops prepared to burn her home, or to women wearing republican flags in concentration camps, extended way beyond those figured in words. For semi-literate Boer women, as for Egyptian and Tanganyikan women, the print culture of Westernized men was not the only vehicle for disseminating nationalism.[81] There were other ways – often linked to feminine skills – for conveying political messages in this era.

Politics, however, was traditionally linked to settler manhood – and many white women invaded this domain as well. At first, they appropriated men's work and authority. Then, as men retreated from war, they laid claim to public speech, politics, citizenship and arms. Then, as they and their homesteads became imperialists' prime targets, they acquired a reputation for being more *bittereinder* than men. Then most republican women were made prisoners of war. Having died with their children in numbers perhaps double those of men killed in action on both sides; having borne the brunt of a war in which 30,000 homesteads were razed and over 27,000 white and 14,000 black concentration camp deaths occurred; having waged war against 'hands-uppers' in camps; having remained 'on commando' to the point where they and their children often outnumbered men; having adopted so many valued masculine attributes, bar the rifles repeatedly refused – then, in mid-1902, republican women learnt that men had handed their guns to barbarians, in order to look after them.

After the war, facing conquest, a gender backlash and a desperate need to erase the camps, women shifted from masculine to maternal domains. The 'phenomenal rise' in birth rates of *taal*-speakers in the ex-republics was accompanied by women swearing that their life task was to bring up children: '*they* must win back our freedom'.[82] Women and children, not defeated patriarchs and male-only domains, were also the focus of postwar nationalism. Unlike prewar nationalists, who mobilized English-speakers into a *volk* equated with men, postwar nationalists promoted the feminized, ethnicized *taal* ('mother tongue', 'Afrikaans'). They stressed women's political agency ('[w]ho has greater interest in politics than the woman?')[83] They sought to save white children from Anglicization, to alleviate the poverty of Dutch/Afrikaans women, to elevate white women who had died in the camps into iconic representatives of the *volk*. This nationalism was partly constructed by and accorded very well with the sentiments of the 'anti-British sex'. Women had been more manly than many men in supporting *fin de siècle* masculinist Africander nationalism – which had betrayed them. Many members of the most irreconcilable sex now advanced into the twentieth century under the banner of ethnically defined, maternalist Afrikaner nationalism – which promptly idealized them not as amazons, but as mothers of the *volk*. Yet whether they were gendered as masculine or maternal, one constant remained. As De Wet noted of women's prominence in resurgent Afrikaner nationalism during World War I, 'it was always a foregone conclusion that the national feelings of the woman were more powerful than those of the man.'[84]

Notes

1. *De Zuid-Afrikaan*, 23 March 1905, quoting ex-Commandant-General Louis Botha.
2. McClintock, A. (1993), 'Family Feuds: Gender, Nationalism and the Family', *Feminist Review*, 44: 68.
3. Schikkerling, R. (1964), *Commando Courageous*, Johannesburg: Kaartland, 354.
4. Reitz, F. (1900), *A Century of Wrong*, London: Review of Reviews Office, 50.
5. Giliomee, H. (1989), 'The Beginnings of Afrikaner Ethnic Consciousness, 1850–1915', in L. Vail (ed), *The Creation of Tribalism in Southern Africa*, London: James Currey, 40; Gordon, C. (1970), *The Growth of Boer Opposition to Kruger 1890–1895*, Cape Town: Oxford University Press, 10.
6. Tamarkin, M. (1996), *Cecil Rhodes and the Cape Afrikaners*, Johannesburg: Jonathan Ball, 299, 245.
7. Pakenham, T. (1995), *The Boer War*, London: Abacus, 378; van Jaarsveld, F. (1961), *The Awakening of Afrikaner Nationalism*, Cape Town, Human & Rousseau, 130. See also Pretorius, F. (1991), *Kommandolewe Tydens die Anglo–Boereoorlog 1899–1902*, Kaapstad: Human & Rousseau, 26.
8. 'Dagboek van Oskar Hintrager', *Christiaan De Wet–Annale* 2, 1973, 28.
9. Malan, S. (1982), *Politieke Strominge onder die Afrikaners van die Vrystaatse Republiek*, Butterworth: Durban Woburn, 299–300.
10. Breytenbach, J. (1969), *Geskiedenis van die Tweede Vryheidsoorlog 1899–1902*, 5 vols., Pretoria: Staatsdrukker, vol. I, 140.
11. Reitz, *Century*, 1, 93.
12. van Heyningen, E. (1991), 'Women and the Second Anglo-Boer War', unpublished paper given at Conference on Women and Gender in Southern Africa, University of Natal, 27.

13. Vis, W. (1902), *Tien Maanden in een 'Vrouwenkamp"*, Rottterdam: Daamen, 45; Neethling, E. (1902), *Should we forget?*, Cape Town: HAUM, 3. See also Davitt, M. (1902), *The Boer Fight for Freedom*, New York: Funk & Wagnalls, 77; Hillegas, H. (1900), *With the Boer Forces*, London: Methuen, 276.

14. Dawson, G. (1994), *Soldier Heroes*, London: Routledge, 290; Kesby, M. (1996), 'Arenas for Control, Terrains of Gender Contestation: Guerilla Struggle and Counter-Insurgency Warfare in Zimbabwe 1972–1980', *Journal of Southern African Studies* 22, no. 4, 569; Sherwell, T. (1996), 'Palestinian Costume, the Intifada and the Gendering of Nationalist Discourse', *Journal of Gender Studies* 5, 300–1; Lake, M. and Damousi, J.(1995), 'Warfare, history and gender', in J. Damousi and M. Lake (eds), *Gender and War*, Cambridge: Cambridge University Press, 2.

15. Seiner, F.(1902), *Ervaringen en Herinneringen van Een Boeren-strijder op het Slagveld van Zuid-Afrika*, Rotterdam: J.C. van Scenk Brill, 77; Reitz, D.(1968), *Commando*, London: Faber & Faber, 93; Breytenbach, *Geskiedenis*, vol. I, 160–4.

16. Hancock, W. and van der Poel, J. (1966), eds., *Selections from the Smuts Papers*, 7 vols., Cambridge: Cambridge University Press, vol.1, 565.

17. Mangold, W. (1988), *Vir Vaderland, Vryheid en Eer*, Pretoria: RGN, 180, 186. See also ver Loren van Themaat, H. (1903), *Twee Jaren in den Boerenoorlog*, Haarlem: H. D. Tjeenk Willink, 86.

18. Denoon, D. (1973), *A Grand Illusion*, London: Longman, 59.

19. University of Cape Town (hereafter UCT), James Stewart collection, pamphlet 29 (1900) of South African Conciliation Committee, 5 (my emphasis.)

20. Marquard, L. (1967), ed., *Letters from a Boer Parsonage*, Cape Town: Purnell, 48, 61.

21. Rijksen-van Helsdingen, J. (1918), *Vrouweleed*, Kaapstad: De Bussy, 48; Rothmann, M.E. (1939), comp., *Tant Alie van Transvaal*, Kaapstad: Nasionale Pers, 206. See also Hobhouse, E. (1924), *War Without Glamour*, Bloemfontein: Nasionale Pers, 49.

22. UCT, Stewart collection, pamphlet 29 (1900) of South African Conciliation Committee, 5.

23. JAD to 'Myne Zusters in de Z.A.R. en O.V.S', *Standard and Diggers' News* (hereafter *S&DN*), 5 May 1900.

24. A. du Plessis to Ed., *S&DN* 23 May 1900.

25. Van Heyningen, 'Women', 20; see also Rothmann, *Alie*, 177; Raal, S. (1938), *Met die Boere in die Veld*, Kaapstad: Nasionale Pers, 8.

26. Petition from Mev. H. Bosman and 500 others to Generals, *S&DN* 21 May 1900.
27. A. du Plessis to Ed., *S&DN* 23 May 1900; *S&DN* 12 May 1900.
28. Rankin, R. (1901), *A Subaltern's Letters to His Wife*, London: Longmans, 98; Schikkerling, *Commando*, 311–2.
29. van Heyningen, 'Women', 26.
30. Abbott, J.(1902), *Tommy Cornstalk*, London:Longmans, 247–8.
31. EJM, 'Een krachtig beroep op de moeders van ons land', *De Zuid-Afrikaan* 21 August 1900; 'De Vrouwen-vergadering te Kaapstad', pamphlet reprinted from *Ons Land*, 10–12 July 1900. See also du Toit, M. (1996), 'Women, Welfare and the Nurturing of Afrikaner Nationalism: a Social History of the Afrikaanse Christelike Vroue Vereniging, c.1870–1939', University of Cape Town, unpublished PhD, 58–68.
32. Rankin, *Letters*, 97, 99.
33. 'Dagboek van Hintrager', 142.
34. Pakenham, *War*, 458.
35. Spies, S. B. (1977), *Methods of Barbarism?*, Cape Town: Human & Rousseau, 122.
36. March Phillipps, L.(1902), *With Rimington*, London:Arnold, 188. See also Badenhorst, C.(1903), *Uit den Boeren–Oorlog 1899–1902*, Amsterdam: Höveker & Wormser, 77, 79, 80; 'Dagboek van Hintrager', 72.
37. Pretorius, *Kommandolewe*, 265, 310–12.
38. Hancock and van der Poel, *Smuts*, 565.
39. Rothmann, *Alie*, 219.
40. Van Schoor, M., Malan, S. and Oberholster, J. (1954), eds., *Christiaan Rudolph De Wet, 1854–1912*, Bloemfontein: Nasionale Vrouemonumentekommissie, 88.
41. Phillipps, *Rimington*, 203, 208.
42. Colley, L. (1992), *Britons*, New Haven: Yale University Press, 369.
43. Schoeman, K. (1983), *In Liefde en Trou*, Kaapstad: Human & Rousseau, 40.
44. Spies, *Barbarism?*, 153; Badenhorst, *Boeren-oorlog*, 95; Schikkerling, *Commando*, 179; Oberholster, A., (1978), ed., *Oorlogsdagboek van Jan F.E. Celliers, 1899–1902*, Pretoria: RGN, 151; van Reenen, R.(1984), ed., *Emily Hobhouse*, Cape Town: Human & Rousseau, 37.
45. Spies, S.B. (1980), 'Women and the War' in P. Warwick (ed), *The South African War*, Harlow:Longman, 168.
46. Pakenham, *War*, 573.

47. Balme, J. (1994), comp., *To Love One's Enemies*, Cobble Hill: Hobhouse Trust, 474.

48. A.D.L. (1904), *Women's Endurance*, Cape Town: South African Newspaper Co., 39. See also Transvaal Archives (hereafter TA), P. van Zyl collection, vol. 1, M. Els testimony about a women's demonstration on 25 Nov. 1901; Brandt-van Warmelo, J. (1905), *Het Concentratie-Kamp van Iréne*, Amsterdam, HAUM, 69.

49. TA, van Zyl collection, vol. 1, 'Mev. Greyling en de Handsuppers'.

50. Presley, C.(1992), *Kikuyu Women, the Mau Mau Rebellion, and Social Change in Kenya*, Boulder: Westview, 157, 165, 169.

51. Phillipps, *Rimington*, 208.

52. TA, Janie Kriegler collection, diary entry for 7 July 1901.

53. TA, Kriegler collection, diary entry for 21 February 1902.

54. Vis, *Vrouwenkamp*, 153, 175.

55. Hobhouse, E. (1902), *The Brunt of the War and Where it Fell*, London, Methuen, 311.

56. TA, van Zyl collection, vol. 1, testimony of Hester Jacobs, 13 Dec. 1903.

57. TA, Carolina Historiese Komitee, vol. 6, unsigned memoirs headed 'Dit is October 1899'.

58. TA, Kriegler collection, entries for 25 December 1901, 1 January 1902; see also Postma, M. (1939), *Stemme uit die Verlede*, Johannesburg: Voortrekkerpers, 9.

59. Grundlingh, A. (1978), *Die Hendsoppers en Joiners*, Pretoria: HAUM, 142. See also Otto, J. (1954), *Die Konsentrasie-Kampe*, Kaapstad: Nasionale Boekhandel, 147.

60. Neethling, H. (1917), *Vergeten?*, Kaapstad: Nasionale Pers, 250.

61. Ramsay Macdonald, J. (1902), *What I saw in South Africa September and October 1902*, London: Echo, 24.

62. Oberholster, *Oorlogsdagboek*, 295, 302.

63. Kestell, J.D. and van Velden, D.E. (1912), *The Peace Negotiations between the Governments of the SAR and the OFS, and the Representatives of the British Government*, London: R. Clay & Sons, 167–8, 178.

64. Theweleit, K. (1993), 'The Bomb's Womb and the Genders of War', in M. Cooke and A. Woolacott (eds.), *Gendering War Talk*, Princeton: Princeton University Press, 284–5.

65. TA, van Zyl collection, vol. 1, testimony of Allie and Annie Venter; Kestell and van Velden, *Negotiations*, 55, 74.

66. Kestell and van Velden, *Negotiations*, 54, 71.

67. Ibid., 180, 201.

68. Ibid., 196. See also De Wet, C. R. (1902), *De Strijd Tusschen Boer en Brit*, Amsterdam: Hoveker & Wormser, 493.
69. Kestell and van Velden, *Negotiations*, 198–9.
70. De Wet, *Strijd*, 485.
71. De Wet, *Strijd*, 497.
72. De Wet, *Strijd*, 433. See also Oberholster, *Oorlogsdagboek*, 380; Kruger, N.(1949), *Rachel Isabella Steyn*, Kaapstad: Nasionale Pers, 41.
73. *Tant Miem Fischer se Kampdagboek Mei 1901 – Aug. 1902*, Kaapstad: Tafelberg, 1964, 120.
74. TA, Kriegler collection, diary entry for 1 June 1902.
75. Kestell and van Velden, *Negotiations*, xvi.
76. TA, Caroline Historiese Komitee collection, vol. 6, testimony of Zannettha Joubert.
77. Kruger, *Steyn*, 143; Kestell and van Velden, *Negotiations*, xvi.
78. ver Loren van Themaat, *Boerenoorlog*, 318–9. See also Butler, J.(1989), 'Afrikaner Women and the Creation of Ethnicity in a Small South African Town, 1902–1950, in Vail (ed.), *Tribalism*, 71.
79. Neethling, *Forget?*, 128; TA, Kriegler collection, entry for 1 June 1902.
80. Macdonald, *What I Saw*, 23–24.
81. Baron, B.(1993), 'The Construction of National Honour in Egypt', *Gender and History* 5, no.2: 244; Geiger, S. (1996), 'Tanganyikan Nationalism as "Women's Work": Life Histories, Collective Biography and Changing Historiography', *Journal of African History* 37, no.2: 473.
82. O'Meara, D. (1983), *Volkskapitalisme*, Johannesburg: Ravan, 82; TA, Kriegler collection, diary entry for 13 July 1902.
83. Kruger, *Steyn*, 86–7.
84. Kestell, J.D. (1920), *Christiaan De Wet*, Kaapstad: Nasionale Pers, 243.

Part 4
Nations in Social and Cultural Practice – Gender-specific Participation in National Movements

–11–

The Ladies' Land League and the Irish Land War 1881/1882: Defining the Relationship Between Women and Nation
Margaret Ward

As an Irish historian whose initial researches arose from a need to understand why women in Ireland occupied so marginal a place in public life, my analysis of the past is intertwined with a hope that this knowledge will help to shape the future. I am also a feminist, motivated by the desire to contribute to women's empowerment, so that in constructing a narrative, political agency rather than discourse analysis is emphasized. Events that took place in the nineteenth century may appear remote from current preoccupations, but once the political repercussions of what became known as the 'Land War' are understood, it becomes apparent that the origins of the fragile relationship between Irish feminism and nationalism are embedded in that period. The backlash against women's participation in the campaign for tenant rights foreshadowed their exclusion from the task of nation building. The history of the Ladies' Land League possesses a dual importance in that it also serves to demonstrate the extent to which women were determined to assert their right to an independent political existence, regardless of the opposition of church leaders and some politicians. I would, however, argue that it is possible to be critical of nationalist movements for their deliberate gendered exclusion of one half of the population, while remaining sympathetic to the political aims of such a movement.

There is another tendency within Irish feminist historiography – one which prefers to equate feminism with the supposedly more progressive attitudes associated with evangelical protestantism and women's move into the public sphere of philanthropy. This is contrasted with the restrictions on Catholic women's lives, as religious females in convents assumed roles that would otherwise have been an avenue of emancipation for many Irish women. It is more than an academic dispute on the origins of the authentic feminist impulse. Discursive forms of interpretation are mirrors of the political divisions that for generations have shaped civil and political society in Ireland, and there is an underlying political agenda here. To contend that 'Most women who took part in specifically feminist politics during the nineteenth century supported the Union'[1] is to make an implicit equation between 'progressive' politics and possession of a pro-British political outlook that requires interrogation. To emphasize this point, one need only consider the views of the Anglo-Irish born Frances Power Cobbe, a feminist best known for her pioneering publication *Wife Torture in England*, published in 1878. Elizabeth Steiner-Scott's study of Cobbe reveals the extent to which her indictment of wife beaters revolved around a stereotype of the brutal Irish labourer.[2] Barbara Caine goes further in her discussion of Cobbe's article 'Women in Italy in 1862', where Cobbe's 'hatred of Catholicism dominates her discussion, providing the basis for her view of the degradation and limitations of Italian women.'[3] Furthermore, to argue that the demand for the franchise had its roots in evangelical philanthropy is to ignore the experiences of Catholic women in Ireland.[4] To what extent did involvement in nationalist political movements generate awareness of gender oppression? Were they empowered to move out of the domestic sphere into the public world? Such competing narratives, products of a society divided by religion and politics as well as by class and gender, are given shape by the ideological imperatives of the historian. They cannot be integrated while the divisions in the wider society remain unreconciled, but we can begin the process by accepting that the notion of 'parity of esteem', the fundamental bedrock upon which the peace process in Ireland is being constructed so painstakingly, must also extend into academic life.

An unwillingness to look with understanding at the historic efforts of women in Ireland to fight for their right to participate in public life has repercussions for women today. Partition and the partial achievement of independence in 1922 led to the development of a confessional state where the primacy of women's domestic responsibilities became enshrined in the Irish constitution. Analysis of the forces that led to this gendered conception of citizenship is a task that assumes great urgency now that an opportunity for 're-inventing' the nation has presented itself. A first stage in the development of a genuinely inclusive history requires recognition of the extent to which our identity (as Irish/British/feminist etc.) is mediated through our relation to a variety of variables. When we consider what is relevant to a discussion on the historical origins of Irish feminism, those underlying theoretical and political differences gain a clarity that must be welcomed by all those concerned with advancing the future status of women.

The models of 'relational feminism' and 'individualist feminism' put forward by Karen Offen are useful tools for determining how different groups of women can be considered feminist while simultaneously maintaining political views at variance with each other.[5] Women who operated as individuals, with the sanction of their communities, exemplified relational feminism in that they regarded their contribution to society in terms of their responsibility to a broader collective, rather than as a means to achieving greater individual autonomy. Most significantly, relational feminists sought to 'equalize the power and authority of women and men in society . . . without eroding or eliminating distinctive, and, to them, desirable gender differences.'[6] A relational feminist view was clearly expressed by Fanny Parnell, originator of the Ladies' Land League in America, whose political career was rooted in a belief that womanly qualities needed to be brought into the public sphere. In her participation in the American Ambulance while nursing those wounded in the fighting to save Paris during the Franco-Prussian War of 1870, in her later patriotic poetry, and in her appeal for women to bring their 'women's attributes of compassion and enthusiasm' to the cause through joining the New York Ladies' Land League, Parnell never viewed women's rights in isolation from their responsibilities to the nation.[7]

Relational feminism, rooted in terms of attachment to a collectivity, also provides a means of understanding why the feminism of Protestant philanthropists in Ireland could not encompass support for their contemporaries in the Ladies' Land League. During this period, the small numbers of female philanthropists who had formed an Irish section of the British Ladies' National Association (LNA) to campaign against the implementation in Ireland of the Contagious Diseases Acts (CDAs), were forced by the turmoil of the land war to suspend their activities. It has been assumed that Catholic women did not become involved with the LNA because the organization openly questioned the double standards of sexual morality inherent in the victimization of prostitutes.[8] However, the Acts, as they were implemented in Ireland, were targeted at women who consorted with British soldiers, and some acknowledgement of this political reality, in the context of British imperial rule over Ireland, is essential. The unresolved national question in Irish political life has served to distort many ostensibly straightforward political causes. From a nationalist-feminist perspective it might have been permissible to have argued against the CDAs on the grounds that such regulations were designed to protect the health of British imperial troops at the expense of the Irish women they patronized. Feminists used this approach to oppose state regulation of prostitution in Egypt.[9] However, when thirteen women of the Ladies' Land League were arrested for their activities and (unlike their male colleagues, who were considered by the state to be political prisoners) imprisoned under statutes designed to keep prostitutes off the streets, the Irish members of the LNA did not protest on the women's behalf. On the contrary, the feminist journal the *Englishwoman's Review* carried an article which welcomed the introduction of repressive measures: 'since they were necessary they ought to be systematically and resolutely carried out'.[10] Political opposition to the objectives of the Land League determined attitudes and overrode any prospect of feminist solidarity. As nationalist confidence increased and calls for home rule strengthened, the feminists involved in the LNA formed the Dublin branch of the women's Liberal Unionist Association in order to counteract advances in the independence movement.[11] The relational feminism of the Anglo-Irish philanthropists gave priority to the maintenance of class relations and the link with Britain. Placed in this context, the conflation of feminism with support for the union appears in a less progressive light. For Catholic women, antipathy towards the British presence in Ireland was a crucial determining factor explaining their indifference towards the introduction of the Contagious Diseases Acts. For both, feminism was rooted in a specific collectivity, a reminder that feminism cannot be viewed in isolation from its social and political context.

The experience of the Ladies' Land League helps to reveals the extent to which class and religion determined political choices, thereby limiting cooperation on feminist issues. It must, however, be emphasized that, in England, there were those who supported the Irish nationalist ideal while they worked to achieve feminist ends. Josephine Butler, founder of the LNA, had praised the political campaigning of home rule advocates when she spoke at a LNA conference in Dublin.[12] Some radical suffragists in England, sympathetic to the Irish nationalist position, gave considerable support to the Ladies' Land League. Scots woman Jessie Craigen, a paid worker for the LNA, gave up that position in order to work for the Ladies' Land League. Helen Taylor, president of the Ladies' Land League of Great Britain, attended evictions and organized the Political Prisoners' Aid Society.[13]

Within the ranks of the Ladies' Land League there were women who could be defined as relational feminists and those who were clearly individualist feminists. However, as events progressed, many found themselves moving away from the collectivity of relational feminism as their right to existence was challenged by men they had regarded initially as colleagues. Anna Parnell, organizing secretary of the League, a close friend of Helen Taylor (whose stepfather, John Stuart Mill, was the best-known advocate of individual liberties), openly encouraged the development of individualist feminism within the organization. A great-aunt by marriage was an executive member of the American Women's Suffrage Association, and in her earliest writings Anna Parnell voiced criticisms of women's lack of voting rights. In 1885 she would speak on behalf of Helen Taylor during her attempt to be selected as Liberal-Radical parliamentary candidate. As a political activist she insisted that women should develop their own methods of organization in order to begin the process of transforming their lives: 'You cannot alter your stature, the scripture says, but you can mould your course of life anyway you please.'[14] This determination to develop an autonomous role for women was to increase the gender-based conflict between the two leagues.

Political agency for peasant women in rural Ireland was confined to defence of land and home from the demands of the landlord. That agency was a product of their domestic role and community acceptance of their participation was rooted in that understanding. The Irish system of land tenure, based upon conquest and expropriation, and defined by penal laws intended to eliminate the Roman Catholic religion, denied Catholics the right to own their land. While the penal laws no longer applied, Catholics remained subjected to excessively high rents. Many lived on small, uneconomic holdings, continually threatened by eviction. The peasant community considered it to be a woman's traditional responsibility not only to take care of the home, but also to preserve it. While their resistance to evictions was expected (and could take the form of physical attacks and rioting) there was never any suggestion that the gendered separation of spheres was being breached. Female militancy was an 'offspring of male agency and . . . structural necessity'.[15]

A land war began in 1879 with the establishment of the Land League, an amalgam of Fenians (physical force advocates) and members of the Irish Parliamentary Party, intended to carve out a 'new departure' in Irish political life. Women in possession of the family farm (usually widows) were recognized as heads of household by the rural community and therefore eligible for league membership.[16] Farmers' wives and daughters were classified as non-productive workers by government census and Irish politicians – a lack of status that was reflected in their subordinate political role. However, as Tebrake has demonstrated, female members of the league were forbidden from speaking at meetings and restricted to standing at the back, far away from the platform. As the objective of the League was to fight for a reduction in rents through the tactic of paying only 'at the point of a bayonet' if the landlord refused to accept the offer of a 'reasonable rent', women's importance lay in the fact that they constituted an important element in a community's resistance. One technique of passive resistance against those who did not support the aims of the Land League was that of 'boycotting': social and economic ostracism. The economic boycott reinforced the importance of women's domestic role for the wellbeing of the whole community. Some women also imposed a 'marriage boycott' on those who broke ranks. This did not, however, challenge the separation of public and private worlds, and even those possessing outspokenly conservative views on the role of women could tolerate it. It was a public role of a kind, but not one that threatened the traditional gender order.

The success of the Land League in confronting the British government reached crisis point in late 1880. After the government decided to introduce a Coercion Act, which would make the Land League illegal and its leaders liable to arrest without trial, the latter were faced with two options: either to allow the land agitation to die down for lack of leadership, or to devise an alternative form of leadership. With the precedent of the successful fundraising of the New York Ladies' Land League, which had stimulated the formation of numerous other female American branches, Michael Davitt, the founder of the Land League and a supporter of women's political participation, argued that a woman's organization in Ireland would keep up the appearance of continuing the battle. The other leaders feared 'public ridicule' and agreed to the 'most dangerous experiment' only because no one could think of an alternative.[17] From the beginning, therefore, there was considerable unease at the idea of women taking part and their contribution was conceived solely as one of dispensing charitable relief to those evicted. Women were expected to remain within these parameters.

The woman asked to take the role of organizing secretary was Anna Parnell, sister of Charles Stewart Parnell, leader of the Irish Party. As members of the Protestant land-owning class, with an American mother, Delia Tudor Stewart Parnell, daughter of an American naval hero responsible for a famous victory over the British in 1812, the Parnells were very different from their contemporaries within the Anglo-Irish élite. Crucially, as their biographer has stressed, the death of their father opened a door to freedom for the youngest children in the family, who were to enjoy physical and intellectual liberties denied to their older siblings. This Irish American heritage and exposure to different lifestyles in America, France, Britain and Ireland, meant that there was little pressure to conform to conventional expectations. The sisters were well read, familiar with the latest economic and political theorists and radical in their analysis of the oppressive nature of class society. In *The Hovels of Ireland* Fanny explained for an Irish American audience the exploitation of the Irish peasant. She rejected rule by a privileged élite in favour of a democracy ruled by a 'natural aristocracy' of the educated and able. Côté considers her 'profound disdain and contempt for her own class . . . almost aggressive' in its outspokenness.[18] Charles Stewart Parnell admired Anna's intellectual powers, despite the fact that the two did not agree on issues: 'My sister knows all about Irish politics. She is never at a loss and never is mistaken in her judgment.'[19] Anna was very much a 'new woman' in her lifestyle and in her attendance at art colleges in Dublin and London. Despite being a member of the Irish gentry she had little personal income and resented the financial dependency of herself and the other female members of her family. The terms of their father's will left only small annuities for the sisters, paid out of the estates bequeathed to their brothers. Her condemnation of landlordism might have been rooted in personal bitterness ('if the Irish landlord had not deserved extinction for anything else, they would have deserved it for the treatment of their own women') but it did not end there.[20] She dismissed them as a 'worthless class'. At the height of the agrarian agitation, the executive of the Ladies' Land League sent a donation to Durham miners evicted from their cottages by the colliery owners, an expression of political solidarity that would have been incomprehensible to their philanthropic contemporaries.[21] Parnell's later account of events, *The Tale of a Great Sham*, is a penetrating analysis of the deficiencies of the male leadership's programme. Once she realized that preparations for a rent strike had not been made because there was no intention of escalating the campaign, the basis for conflict between the two leagues was established. The mass movement of the Land League was part of a tactical calculation by her politician brother to put pressure on the British government to grant home rule to Ireland. He was much less concerned to achieve a radical solution to the land question. For the women, however, 'the programme of a permanent resistance until the aim of the League shall be attained, was the only logical one.'[22]

Anna Parnell wanted national self-determination for Ireland, but the political disabilities suffered by her sex moved her towards advocacy of a mass movement independent of parliament as the only means by which women, as a disenfranchised group, could be involved in politics. She had no belief in the promises of any British government to pass legislation unless they were forced to by pressure from the Irish: 'Had a conviction existed in England that a spirit prevailed in Ireland which would probably ensure its people taking, not Home Rule, but independence, at the first opportunity, then Mr Gladstone could have passed Home Rule.'[23] She believed the Land League was unable to force the English 'to relax their murderous grip' because it capitulated too soon. By 1905 she was predicting that the failure of the Land League, followed by the failure of the home rule movement, would lead, once again, to armed rebellion.[24]

While it is unlikely that the Ladies' Land League would have taken the direction it did without her guidance, Anna Parnell did not dictate events. Much of what happened took place because ordinary women from both the Catholic middle class and the peasantry were empowered to take responsibility for the political direction of a mass movement. Apart from Parnell herself, executive members came from the small Catholic middle class, primarily from the commercial class and from strong farming backgrounds. One ran a successful general store, another ran a hotel and others supported themselves through governessing in Spain and France. Two would become well known writers. From memoirs of the period there was no sense that Parnell regarded herself as a member of an élite. Her obvious pleasure in working with her executive (manifested in frequent small gifts to the young women in the office), reveals a woman who found in her colleagues: 'a comforting sense of belonging (which) dulled for a time the pain of self-imposed isolation from which she suffered during most of her adult life.'[25] Her dedication was obvious, she seldom left the office before midnight, walking unescorted to her lodgings. Martha Vicinus has described the challenge posed by the suffragists – 'Unescorted upper-class women on the streets spoke of political and sexual independence' – in terms that have equal force in Anna Parnell's disregard of convention.[26]

Although most branches included townspeople and relatives of tradesmen amongst the membership, some were exclusively peasant in composition. Women now had a 'public function and public visibility' that was in marked contrast to their usual lives, as League membership gave even peasant women 'power and influence independent of male control'.[27] The reversal in gender roles at public meetings was not achieved without a struggle. The first speeches of Anna Parnell made it plain that she expected men to respect the women's organization by staying away from meetings. She showed her anger when young men from villages continued to attend the women's public meetings, using language replete with expressions of gendered hostility. Previously, women had: 'only been able to stand at the outskirts of your meetings, at a respectful distance, and pick up the crumbs from your table.'[28] The men were urged to move back from the platform to enable women to come forward. At a public meeting a few months later Parnell remarked:

'I observe that we have succeeded today in getting rid of the men nearly entirely – and I am sure that we all feel much more comfortable in consequence.'[29] The gender difference between a Land League and a Ladies' Land League meeting was immediately apparent: 'the ladies thronged around the platform instead of as formerly, viewing the proceedings at a respectful distance.'[30] Holding a political meeting in order to rally support was in itself to transgress boundaries: 'When respectable women sold newspapers or stood on a soapbox and spoke in public, traditional male privileges were called into question.'[31] When women began to challenge male colleagues from within a shared political movement, the danger was that 'male privileges' would prove as delusive as the emperor's new clothes.

There was a significant difference between male and female methods of conducting political campaigns in that the women disliked mass meetings, which they felt encouraged irresponsible speeches. Anna Parnell maintained that the most effective method of putting across a message was by holding meetings at the scene of an eviction, where discussion could be generated and a common policy agreed upon. As she began to understand the situation her criticisms of the men became more outspoken. Women were to work independently of men to whom they had been

Figure 11.1 The Royal Irish Constabulary entering a meeting of the central branch of the Ladies' Land League. Print in *Illustrated London News,* 24 December 1881

accustomed to 'trust and to look for help', and she exhorted them: 'learn to depend upon yourselves and to do things for yourselves and to organize yourselves.'[32] She was uncompromising in her refusal to be characterized in a traditional female role. When a resolution applauded her for being 'prepared to work as well as weep', she retorted that they would leave the weeping to the men. The traditional gendered assumptions of passive female and active male were challenged. Women were in the position of being able to use their domestic role for definite political ends. They were urged to pay for groceries with cash so that their men folk would not use the money to pay the rent to the landlord. Domesticity could incorporate defiance of male control of household finance as well as political resistance to landlordism. The public/domestic distinction collapsed into a political movement where women were empowered to use their traditional role for political ends and the leadership of the movement – middle class urban women – challenged all the conventions. In opposing this new departure, Protestant and Catholic alike were in agreement. Archbishop McCabe of Dublin issued a pastoral letter: 'the daughters of our Catholic people, be they matrons or virgins, are called forth, under the flimsy pretext of charity, to take their stand in the noisy streets of life. The pretext of charity is merely assumed . . . They are asked to forget the modesty of their sex and the high dignity of their womanhood by leaders who seem reckless of consequences'.[33] Ecclesiastical condemnation of the Ladies' Land League extended to the Irish American community, where several bishops denounced the participation of their parishioners. They too understood that women in political clubs constituted 'an infringement upon the sacredness of the home'.[34] The editor of the Protestant *Belfast Newsletter* applauded such condemnation: 'the only function of women in a political meeting was the dispensing of the refreshment of tea at the beginning of the meeting'.[35]

As Anna Parnell travelled the countryside she made it plain that women would be doing more than distributing relief to the evicted. She did not want them to be 'threatened, frightened or deterred to do anything they had a right to do under the law', but she was clear that as the law 'especially in Ireland was not the same as right' they would very likely soon be offering resistance to its implementation.[36] Applications for relief were refused unless accompanied by evidence that eviction had been a consequence of resistance rather than inability to pay rent. Parnell's argument was that: 'One estate that was not paying rent, but going into Land League houses when the evicting "army" arrived, would have constituted a much more alarming object lesson to landlords than fifty estates paying Rent at the Point of the Bayonet'. When attempting to implement this strategy the women clashed with the men. The latter preferred to give grants to those in need while the women argued for the erection of huts. This was not because they took a traditional female role of arguing for the primacy of domestic space, but because they saw the existence of such shelters, which would also enable the evicted to ward off potential landgrabbers, as 'a permanent sign and symbol that all power did not lie with the foreign enemy in possession of the country.'[37]

By October 1881 all the male leadership had been arrested, and the women were left on their own for the next seven months to continue to support evicted tenants, to encourage resistance, to channel funds to the needy, and to ensure that the newspaper *United Ireland* was still published, although its editor was in jail and possession of it was an imprisonable offence. Their voluminous dresses became hiding places for contraband literature. It was a unique situation, and a great deal of international interest was aroused. The *Times* commented that the women's rooms 'are lighted brilliantly in contrast with the darkness visible in the apartment in which the men's land league was wont to assemble.' However, despite this shining defiance the women, dismissed as 'petticoats and pinafores', were not expected 'to do much mischief.' Neither were the men expected to look to them 'for real advice and guidance'.[38] They were correct in this latter assessment. The imprisoned men did not consult their female colleagues over changes in policy. Once in jail they issued a 'No Rent Manifesto' which had huge implications for the conduct of the campaign. There would no longer be 'rent at the point of a bayonet', so the women found themselves coping with increasing numbers of evictions. Anna Parnell's assessment was that this new manifesto had come too late. In August the government had passed a Land Act to deal with the question of fair rents. Only the wealthier farmers could benefit, but they began to apply for a re-evaluation of their rent and started to leave the ranks of the league. Those who could not pay any rent because their holdings were too small to be economic remained as supporters of the league, and for them the need was land redistribution rather than rent reduction. In the latter stages of the struggle the natural allies of the women were those most marginal in Irish society.

Women continued to join the resistance. By the start of 1882 there were five hundred branches, some with between one and two hundred members. On 16 December 1881 the Inspector General of Constabulary announced that: 'where any females are assembled – such meeting is illegal.' Anna Parnell responded by arguing that only an Act of Parliament could outlaw the organization and all branches mobilized in defiance. Simultaneous mass meetings were held around the country on 1 January.

This resistance had the effect of shaming men for not having displayed the same determination. A long editorial of self-reproach in *United Ireland* admitted that this reversal of roles was a humiliation: 'We only wish the men had done [their business] as stoutly, as regularly, and as fearlessly . . . Is it easier to cow a nation of men than a handful of women?'[39] The women also stressed the difference in determination between the two leagues. One organizer, arguing against an attempt to close a meeting of a local branch, joked: 'I will speak to those ladies as long as I like; the law which took the men's arms could not touch the women's tongues.'[40]

The situation was approaching crisis point. There were almost one thousand men in jail, at a cost to the League of £400 a week in food bills. The programme of resistance was an expensive one. A total of £70,000 would be spent by the Ladies in various forms of relief. The charge of undue extravagance, made when the men were released, was no more than an excuse to find fault with the manner in which they had conducted their campaign. Agrarian crimes like the burning of haystacks and mutilation of animals were becoming widespread – not authorized by the women but understood by them as a symptom of despair. The imprisoned Parnell was concerned that the League was being used, as Davitt phrased it, 'not for the purposes he approved of, but for a real revolutionary end and aim'.[41] The growing alarm of both Parnell and the British government led to the start of negotiations culminating in what was later dubbed the 'Kilmainham Treaty' of May 1882. By this, the government agreed to release the prisoners and to amend the provisions of the Land Act. In return, Parnell promised to use his influence to prevent further 'outrages'.

At first, the men had hoped that the Ladies would stay in existence, under their control, to carry on the work of deciding on suitable cases for relief. They would, in the bitter words of Anna Parnell, be no more than: 'perpetual petticoat screens behind which [the men] could shelter not from the government but from the people.'[42] This they refused to do. They had strong objections to a policy of doling out relief unlinked to a programme of resistance, and argued that they wanted release from their 'long and uncongenial bondage'. Jessie Craigen wrote to Helen Taylor: 'I made great sacrifices for the Irish cause . . . but it was to fight for the liberty of the people and not to put political tricksters into power.'[43] There were many who testified to the women's refusal to cooperate. Henry George, the American agrarian radical, also wrote to Helen Taylor: 'The women really feel bitter towards the parliamentary men. They have been treated badly and their obligations have not been kept, and on several occasions the men got a very frank piece of their minds'.[44] Although

Parnell and Dillon complained to George that the women had been 'too extravagant and were not controllable' George disagreed, telling Patrick Ford, the influential editor of the Irish-American paper *Irish World:* 'I am inclined to think they have done a great deal better than the men would have done'.[45] He was not the only one to hold this position. Andrew Kettle, a founder of the Land League, believed: 'Anna Parnell would have worked the Land League revolution to a much better conclusion than her great brother.'[46] While some men admitted their disagreements with their leader they were not prepared to pursue this further, afraid of provoking a split in the parliamentary party.

After several months of wrangling, during which the men declared that they would refuse to honour the financial commitments of the Ladies' Land League if the women did not sign a declaration promising that they would agree to disband their organization but continue to 'consider all applications for grants made to the Land League, and make recommendations on them for that body', the women finally manoeuvered their dissolution without incurring any obligation to the men. They altered one word on the agreement, making themselves responsible only for cases of applications to the Ladies' Land League, not the Land League. It was likely that the men realized the subterfuge but decided it provided everyone with an 'escape from an untenable position'.[47] There was no reason why women should have agreed to a limited role of relief provision divorced from policy making. Accounts of this period have stressed this forcible dissolution while failing to acknowledge the desire of the women to sever their relationship with their former colleagues. Fanny Parnell, still in America, had died suddenly of heart failure on 19 July and her sister, distraught and disillusioned, withdrew from these negotiations. She would no longer contemplate cooperation with men: 'However long I might live, I knew that it would never again be possible for me to believe that any body of Irishmen means a word of anything they said.'[48]

The eventual disbandment of the Ladies' Land League, on 2 August, was presided over by an American woman, one of a group sent over to add to the small number of full-time organizers. Several members of the Ladies' Land League later moved to America (which had experienced harmonious relations between male and female branches of the League), and maintained prominent positions in Irish American political circles. In Ireland, however, to paraphrase Cynthia Enloe, women were denied access to the 'front' so that men could claim a superiority that justified their dominant position.[49] Parnell had threatened to leave public life if the women were not disbanded. The stakes were high. In May 1882 he and Gladstone were on the threshold of an agreement to ensure limited political independence would be granted to Ireland by means of a home rule bill.[50] This goal was to be pursued through male alliances that would perpetuate female exclusion through the reimposition of separate spheres within Irish nationalism. A new campaigning body was formed to take the place of the Land League. This organization – the Irish National League – was composed of male politicians and was described as 'an open organisation in which the ladies will not take part'. Disenfranchized women were irrelevant to the calculations of politicians. Only the history of gender relations within the land movement provides an adequate explanation for the exclusion from all nationalist organizations of an entire generation of women.

Although memoirs of the period were published, the full story of the Ladies' Land League remained unknown to outsiders. Discourses of national struggle are constructed by those who control the writing of history, and when it came to the writing of histories of the Land War, with women disillusioned and out of the public sphere, the former male leadership had unrivalled scope to construct their narratives without fear of contradiction. Representations of the Ladies' Land League mirrored contemporary attitudes towards women's political participation. In 1905 they were patronized as 'sweet girl graduates',[51] but twenty years later, memories of women's role in the war of independence and the ensuing civil war prompted denounciations of the 'fanaticism' of 'Miss Parnell's band of harridans'.[52] Only with Anna Parnell's 70,000 word manuscript, *The Tale of a Great Sham,* was there a full account of the embittered relations between the two groups. Her narrative, written after 1904, was a riposte to Michael Davitt's *The Fall of Feudalism in Ireland.* Davitt's sympathy for the Ladies' Land League, coupled with his rejection of the Irish Party's new strategy, had led him to remark that the women had been more successful than the men because they had less scruples in encouraging violence. At the same time, his overall thesis claimed a primacy for the role of the men. Anna Parnell denounced it as 'one of the most blackguardly books ever written, containing the most impudent libels on me, and specially constructed for concealing the fact that the Land League ran away.'[53] Her account avoided personalities to the extent that even her brother was described only in terms of his political position: 'Not that an individual's actions are unimportant only that it does not matter what particular individual does them, except in so far as he or she represents a number of persons'.[54] This approach did not encourage publishers, yet it could also be argued that no publisher would have agreed to produce a work possessing such a potential to destabilize the restored gendered hierarchy. Harper's, publishers of Davitt's work, refused to consider the manuscript even before she had written it, no doubt fore-warned by her outspoken comments. Despite the efforts of a new generation of nationalist-feminists in Inghinidhe na hEireann, she failed to find a publisher before her death in 1911. The manuscript disappeared after a police raid, coming to light only in 1959. It was published by an Irish feminist publisher in 1986, but is now out of print.[55] Anna Parnell had recognized the gendered nature of political power. She had not agreed with the political direction taken by the movement and, realizing that women were unable to influence policy, removed herself from the public sphere: 'If the men of that country have made up their minds it shall not be done, the women cannot bring it about.'[56] She supported the formation of Inghinidhe na hEireann and spoke on behalf of the fledgling Sinn Fein, but would not return to live in Ireland.

Membership of the Ladies' Land League had conferred identity, status and real power upon women. Its formation signalled an acceptance (albeit temporary) of women's right of entry into the public sphere. They were no longer sporadic participants in the defence of community and home, but members of a movement that included women from different class and religious backgrounds, united in a shared identity. Once they gained an independent political existence they began to develop a radical critique of patriarchal structures. The re-assertion of male dominance ensured that those binary oppositions that defined male-female relations were reconstituted through the establishment of a gendered order that heavily circumscribed the future participation of Irish women in political move-ments. The Land War was therefore a defining moment in the future negotiation of the relationship between women and the Irish nation. Once the traditional gendered order was restored, women's ability to participate in the political sphere was restricted.

The next generation of female activists, feminist and nationalist, applauded the achievements of the Ladies' Land League while they criticized politicians for their lack of interest in the contribution of women. In the period leading to the Easter Rising of 1916 the struggle by nationalist women for inclusion, conceptualized in terms of women's relation to the nation, revived the conflicts of the Land League era. Those who accepted the primacy of woman's domestic role imagined political participation as an extension of those responsibilities: 'each rifle we put in their hands will represent to us a bolt fastened behind the door of some Irish home to keep out the hostile stranger',[57] yet many agreed that women should be encouraged to: 'get away from wrong ideals and false standards of womanhood, to escape from their domestic ruts, their feminine pens'.[58] Women played a significant role in the war of independence of 1919–22, but after the split over the treaty with Britain in 1922, and the formation of the Irish Free State, that patriarchal and conservative nationalism, so evident in the Irish Parliamentary Party of the late nineteenth century, regained dominance. Individualist feminists still remained within the ranks of feminist and nationalist groups, but oppositional forces had little influence. As Louise Ryan has demonstrated, women's exclusion from the public sphere was based, not only on positive images of domesticity, but also on 'demonised images of the deviant non-domestic woman.'[59] Women were excluded from the task of nation-building because their former male colleagues resurrected fears of disorderly women (the 'furies'), in order to create an independent state based upon masculine authority and feminine domesticity. A gender-based negotiation of tradition and modernity continued to determine a central part of Irish social and political life over the succeeding decades, thereby ensuring that a postcolonial identity remained elusive.

Notes

1. Côté, J. and Hearne, D. (1995), 'Anna Parnell' in M. Cullen and M. Luddy (eds), *Women, Power and Consciousness in 19th Century Ireland,* Dublin: Attic Press, 286.
2. Steiner-Scott, E. (1997), '"To Bounce a Boot Off Her Now and Then . . . ": Domestic Violence in Post-Famine Ireland', in Maryann Gialanella Valiulis and Mary O'Dowd (eds) *Women and Irish History,* Dublin: Wolfhound Press, 1997, 128.
3. Caine, B. (1997), *English Feminism 1780–1980*, Oxford: Oxford University Press, 125.
4. Luddy, M. (1995), *Women and Philanthropy in Nineteenth Century Ireland,* Cambridge: Cambridge University Press. Historians have taken Luddy's work as a central reference point for an analysis of feminism that concentrates upon the contribution of unionist women.
5. Offen, K. (1998), 'Contextualising the Theory and Practice of Feminism in Nineteenth Century Europe (1789–1914)' in Bridenthal, R., Mosher Stuard, S., and Wiesner, M.E. (eds) *Becoming Visible: Women in European History*, Boston and New York: Houghton Mifflin, 327–55.

6. Offen, K. (1998), 'Contextualising the Theory and Practice of Feminism in Nineteenth Century Europe (1789–1914)' in Bridenthal, R., Mosher Stuard, S., and Wiesner, M.E. (eds) *Becoming Visible: Women in European History,* Boston and New York: Houghton Mifflin, 332.

7. See Côté, J. (1991), *Fanny and Anna Parnell: Ireland's Patriot Sisters*, Dublin: Gill & Macmillan, for biographical details.

8. Luddy, M. (1995), *Women and Philanthropy in Nineteenth Century Ireland,* Cambridge: Cambridge University Press, 139–141.

9. Badran, M. (1995), *Feminists, Islam and Nation: Gender and the Making of Modern Egypt,* Princeton: Princeton University Press.

10. *Englishwoman's Review,* 14 January 1882, in Luddy, M. (ed.) (1995), *Women in Ireland 1800–1918, a documentary history,* Cork: Cork University Press, 177.

11. Cullen, M. (1995), 'Anna Maria Haslam' in Cullen, M. and Luddy, M. (eds) *Women, Power and Consciousness in 19th Century Ireland,* Dublin: Attic Press, 177.

12. Sixsmith-James, L. (1998), *Prostitution in 19th Century Ireland,* M.A. thesis, Bath Spa University College.

13. Holton, S.S. (1996), *Suffrage Days,* London: Routledge, 59–60.

14. Côté, J. (1991), *Fanny and Anna Parnell: Ireland's Patriot Sisters*, Dublin: Gill & Macmillan, 167.

15. McClintock, A. (1995), *Imperial Leather,* New York: Routledge, 366.

16. Tebrake, J. (1992), 'Irish Peasant Women in Revolt: the Land League Years', *Irish Historical Studies* xxviii, No.109, 63–80.

17. Davitt, M. (1904), *The Fall of Feudalism in Ireland,* London: Harper & Row, 299.

18. Côté, J. (1991), *Fanny and Anna Parnell: Ireland's Patriot Sisters*, Dublin: Gill & Macmillan, 114.

19. Kettle, A.J. (1958), *Material for Victory*, Dublin: Fallon, 48.

20. Parnell, A. (1986), *The Tale of a Great Sham,* ed. Dana Hearne, Dublin: Arlen House, 85–86.

21. Foster, R.F. (1976), *Charles Stewart Parnell: the Man and his Family,* Sussex: Harvester, 275.

22. Parnell, A. (1986), *The Tale of a Great Sham,* ed. Dana Hearne, Dublin: Arlen House, 55.

23. Parnell, A. (1986), *The Tale of a Great Sham,* ed. Dana Hearne, Dublin: Arlen House, 165–166.

24. Parnell, A. (1986), *The Tale of a Great Sham,* ed. Dana Hearne, Dublin: Arlen House, 178.

25. Côté, J. (1991), *Fanny and Anna Parnell: Ireland's Patriot Sisters*, Dublin: Gill & Macmillan, 162.
26. Vicinus, M. (1998), 'Fin-de-Siecle Theatrics: Male Impersonation and Lesbian Desire', Melman, B. (ed.), *Borderlines*, New York and London: Routledge, 179.
27. Tebrake, J. (1992), 'Irish Peasant Women in Revolt: the Land League Years', *Irish Historical Studies* xxviii, No.109, 70.
28. Côté, J. (1991), *Fanny and Anna Parnell: Ireland's Patriot Sisters*, Dublin: Gill & Macmillan, 167.
29. Ward, M. (1983), *Unmanageable Revolutionaries: Women and Irish Nationalism*, London: Pluto Press, 16.
30. *Belfast Newsletter,* 15 March 1881.
31. Vicinus, M. (1998), 'Fin-de-Siecle Theatrics: Male Impersonation and Lesbian Desire', Melman, B. (ed.), *Borderlines*, New York and London: Routledge, 179.
32. Ward, M. (1983), *Unmanageable Revolutionaries: women and Irish nationalism,* London: Pluto Press, 16.
33. Luddy, M. (1995), *Women and Philanthropy in Nineteenth Century Ireland,* Cambridge: Cambridge University Press, 263.
34. Côté, J. (1991), *Fanny and Anna Parnell: Ireland's Patriot Sisters*, Dublin: Gill & Macmillan, 168.
35. *Belfast Newsletter,* 18 March 1881.
36. Côté, J. (1991), *Fanny and Anna Parnell: Ireland's Patriot Sisters*, Dublin: Gill & Macmillan, 168.
37. Parnell, A. (1986), *The Tale of a Great Sham,* ed. Dana Hearne, Dublin: Arlen House, 151.
38. *Times*, 24 October 1881.
39. Ward, M. (1983), *Unmanageable Revolutionaries: Women and Irish Nationalism,* London: Pluto Press, 28–9.
40. Ward, M. (1983), *Unmanageable Revolutionaries: Women and Irish Nationalism,* London: Pluto Press, 24.
41. Davitt, M. (1904), *The Fall of Feudalism in Ireland,* London: Harper & Row, 349.
42. Parnell, A. (1986), *The Tale of a Great Sham,* ed. Dana Hearne, Dublin: Arlen House, 155.
43. Jessie Craigen to Helen Taylor, 19 August 1982, Item 71, Vol. XVIII, Mill-Taylor Collection, London School of Economics and Political Science.
44. Henry George to Helen Taylor, 1 October 1982, Item 81, Vol. XVII, Mill-Taylor Collection, London School of Economics and Political Science.

45. Côté, J. (1991), *Fanny and Anna Parnell: Ireland's Patriot Sisters*, Dublin: Gill & Macmillan, 217.
46. Kettle, A.J. (1958), *Material for Victory*, Dublin: Fallon, 48.
47. Parnell, A. (1986), *The Tale of a Great Sham,* ed. Dana Hearne, Dublin: Arlen House, 157.
48. Parnell, A. (1986), *The Tale of a Great Sham,* ed. Dana Hearne, Dublin: Arlen House, 164.
49. Enloe, C. (1983), *Does Khaki Become You? The Militarization of Women's Lives,* Boston: South End Press, 15.
50. See Bull, P. (1996), *Land, Politics and Nationalism,* Dublin; Gill & Macmillan, particularly Chapter 4, 'Land as Metaphor', 94–101.
51. O'Brien, W. (1905), *Recollections,* London; Macmillan, 382.
52. St John Ervine, quoted by Hearne D. (1983), 'Rewriting History: Anna Parnell's "The Tale of a Great Sham"' in Gallagher, S.F. *Women in Irish Legend, Life and Literature*, Gerrards Cross.
53. *Gaelic American*, 29 December 1906, report of correspondence between Anna Parnell and Maire de Buitleir, reprinted from the *Irish Peasant.*
54. Anna Parnell to Helena Moloney, 7 July 1910, in Ward, *Unmanageable Revolutionaries,* 265.
55. See Côté, J. (1993), 'Writing Women in Irish History: the Biography of Fanny and Anna Parnell', in Noonan, J. (ed.) *Biography and Autobiography – Essays on Irish and Canadian History and Literature,* Ottawa: Carleton University Press, 60; introduction by Dana Hearne to Parnell A. (1986), *The Tale of a Great Sham,* (ed.) Dana Hearne, Dublin: Arlen House, 9–34.
56. Parnell, A. (1986), *The Tale of a Great Sham,* ed. Dana Hearne, Dublin: Arlen House, 173.
57. O'Farrelly, A. (1995), in Ward, M. (ed.). *In Their Own Voice: Women and Irish Nationalism,* Dublin: Attic Press, 40.
58. Constance de Markievicz, in Ward, M. (ed.). *In Their Own Voice: Women and Irish Nationalism,* Dublin: Attic Press, 47.
59. Ryan, L. (1998), 'Negotiating Modernity and Tradition: newspaper debates on the "modern girl" in the Irish Free State', *Journal of Gender Studies* 7 (2), 181–97.

12

Women in a Nation of Men: The Politics of the League of German Women's Associations (BDF) in Imperial Germany, 1894–1914

Angelika Schaser

Translated by Pamela Selwyn

The leading members of the Bund Deutscher Frauenvereine (BDF), the umbrella organization of German women's associations founded in 1894, were recruited mainly from the upper middle classes and urban strata. Like the male educated middle classes, the BDF supported national unity, and it sought to deploy the concept of the 'cultural nation' as an emancipatory strategy on women's behalf. Although the BDF initially conceived of itself as part of an international as well as a national movement, like Wilhelmine society more generally, it underwent an increasing nationalization after the turn of the century and came to identify with the imperialist aims of the German nation-state. Only in the Weimar Republic did the BDF return to a greater emphasis on the internationalism of the women's movement.

German scholars of nationalism only discovered the category of gender in the 1980s,[1] and the field remains 'inadequately explored'.[2] Women have either been left out or subsumed under the term nation, and not studied in their own right. After all, women had no 'fatherland'; they were incapable of bearing arms and were thus excluded from civil rights – the nation-state was composed of male individuals. On the other hand, though, the common 'mother tongue' constituted an essential character-istic of the nation, and it was largely passed down by women. Thus it is not surprising that issues of gender history have seemed most pressing for the study of the creation of a national identity.[3] Only in times of external and/or internal threat did the 'nation's second half' capture the spotlight. Women thus come to the attention of women's and gender history at historical moments in which the nation needed reassurance –

in times of war, revolution or violent upheaval.[4] Such events, however, merely represented eruptions of a 'female nationalism' that also revealed itself in peacetime and contributed to German society's national search for itself. If we move beyond the question of women's participation in and specific contribution to national uprisings, the study of the obvious gender imagery transported by the image of the nation as an 'extended family', and of its significance for the constitution of the German nation is only just beginning.[5] International comparisons in the field of gender and the nation are also almost wholly lacking in German scholarship.[6]

In what follows, I will show how an expanded definition of the 'German women's movement' can afford us glimpses of a large number of previously ignored women's associations that, although they were at first indifferent or opposed to women's emancipation, came with the increasing nationalization of the women's movement to be mobilized by the BDF. The associations, often organized within the German Red Cross (DRK), devoted themselves to national tasks and had connections with BDF member organizations on the local level. The second section will draw attention to the fact that it was the division of labour within the BDF that enabled women's associations inside and outside the BDF to develop closer ties. Until the outbreak of the First World War, the BDF's heterogeneity permitted a very functional approach to nationalism and opened it to accusations of internationalism, which was understood as tantamount to socialism. The final section will show, using the example of the Nationaler Frauendienst (National Women's Service, NFD) founded by the BDF at the beginning of the First World War, and the discussion of 'female compulsory service', how the BDF attempted to portray all of women's areas of activity as 'national tasks'. It was thanks to the BDF's successful 'enclosure policy' before 1914 that the majority of women's associations accepted the BDF's leadership role after the outbreak of war, and that the BDF managed to use this broad support in order to promote women's equality and integration into the nation while still emphasizing gender difference.

The Range of Women's Associations in Germany

Thus far, women's historians have focused on certain bourgeois-liberal, Protestant-influenced women's associations, proceeding from the assumption that there was a sharp polarization between the middle-class and proletarian women's movements.[7] More recent work shows that there were numerous contacts between the personnel of the proletarian women's associations and of BDF member organizations, particularly on a local level.[8]

Because of the frequent dominance of male board members, charitable organizations such as the Prussian Patriotischer Frauenverein (Patriotic Women's Association), whose members were drawn from upper middle class and aristocratic circles, have been described by historians as lacking any autonomous (female) associational life.[9] This assessment is valid only for certain of these associations, however. It also ignores the potential dynamism within such organizations, a result of the partial collaboration and frequent overlapping memberships of women in charitable and denominational associations and/or women's educational associations.[10]

Because they have tended to equate the middle-class women's movement with the large national women's organizations, such as the BDF, and one of the oldest and most important women's association, the Allgemeiner Deutscher Frauenverein (General German Women's Association, ADF, founded 1865 in Leipzig), scholars initially overlooked the fact that in contemporary perceptions, the women's movement extended far beyond the umbrella of the BDF. In an entry on 'women's associations', the 1905 Meyer's Lexikon gives a detailed list of the 'Red Cross women's associations' and lumps all others together under 'other women's associations'.[11] Helene Lange, a member of the BDF executive and a well-known representative of the middle-class women's movement, also distinguished between two groups of women's associations: the one pursued 'purely humanitarian aims', while the other dedicated its efforts to 'promoting women's interests'.[12] At the beginning of the twentieth century, before the 1908 reform of the Prussian act regulating associations, which allowed women to become members of political associations, charitable associations constituted the largest group. The number of charitable patriotic women's associations rose sharply in the early years of the Wilhelmine era: there were 400 in 1877, and almost 800 in 1891.[13] The wars of 1864 and 1866 had led throughout Germany to the spontaneous creation of women's associations that placed themselves in the tradition of the Frauenverein zum Wohle des Vaterlandes von 1814 (Women's Association for the Good of the Fatherland), which had been founded after the occupation of Prussia by Napoleon. On 11 November 1866 Prussia's Queen Augusta founded the Vaterländischer Frauenverein (Patriotic Women's Association) in order to 'ensure that those female contingents who, regardless of religion or rank, did such truly selfless and magnificent work during the war, may continue their successful joint activities in peacetime as well'. The association was placed under the aegis of the Red Cross and was supposed to 'seek, in a patriotic spirit as well, to offer immediate assistance in general or local calamities such as wars, conflagrations, floods and epidemics, and to alleviate suffering as

Figure 12.1 A Meeting of the Board of the Patriotic Women's Association under the Chairwomanship of Empress Augusta in 1880. Woodcut after a drawing by E. Henseler. (Bildarchiv Preussischer Kulturbesitz.)

much as possible.'[14] When the precursor to the German Red Cross, the Gesamtorganisation der Deutschen Vereine zur Pflege im Felde verwundeter und erkrankter Krieger (General Organization of German Associations for the Care of Wounded and Sick Soldiers in the Field) was founded in 1869, it only included men's associations. The question of their relationship to the women's associations remained open. Apparently, however, the latter did not simply allow themselves to be subsumed. The Verband deutscher Frauenvereine (Federation of German Women's Associations) was founded on 12 August 1871.[15] The largest member group, the Patriotic Women's Association, alone counted 1,050 branch and auxiliary associations and a total of 274,741 members' in 1902.[16]

The second group of women's associations served 'the promotion of women's interests' in one way or another. Most regarded themselves as professional or educational organizations and only a minority – above all the ADF, which was founded in 1865 – was primarily dedicated to women's emancipation.[17] These heterogeneous associations came together in 1894 in the BDF, which could thus claim to represent the middle-class women's movement in Germany. Even if the members of a more radical wing founded the Verband fortschrittlicher Frauenvereine (Federation of Progressive Women's Associations) in 1899 as an alternative to the BDF, the gesture remained temporary and demonstrative, as the founding associations did not leave the BDF but remained members.[18] In 1907 the entire Federation of Progressive Women's Associations joined the BDF. What all of these associations of the middle-class women's movement had in common was that they defined themselves as unaffiliated to any political party, as a 'cultural movement'. We have no reliable figures, but we may conclude from the growing membership in the BDF that this second group also enjoyed increasing membership: founded in Berlin in 1894 by 34 women's associations, the BDF had 193 member associations in 1907, und 52 member federations in 1914 (which together represented 2,362 associations) plus 289 groups that joined directly.[19]

The BDF had close ties to the national-liberal tradition, which sought to overcome the cultural pessimism of the post-unification period with the help of a 'New Idealism'. Before the outbreak of the First World War proponents of this tendency had clearly decided 'the competition between power-political expansionism and foreign cultural and economic policy ... in favor of "peaceful imperialism".' [20] This did not, however, prevent the BDF and its member associations from supporting the Wilhelmine program of warship construction at the turn of the century or propagating the acquisition of colonies.[21] At a rally held by the ADF, one of the most influential organizations within the BDF, in the run-up to the new Navy Act of 1900, a speaker called for naval construction as a peacekeeping measure: 'We do not want Germany to be even fractionally weaker than other nations should it ever, despite its love of peace, be compelled to defend its national independence in a war thrust upon it.'[22] The BDF, too, considered military and economic strength the indispensable basis for maintaining peace and increasing German influence abroad. The main tool should, however, be the 'dissemination of the German idea' in the form of economic and cultural exports. It was in this spirit that the BDF, which repeatedly emphasized that the women's movement was primarily a women's educational movement, participated directly and indirectly as a 'cultural imperialist' institution. The numerous new German schools founded abroad after 1870 with vigorous support from the Allgemeiner deutscher Schulverein zur Erhaltung des Deutschtums im Auslande (General German School Association for the Preservation of Germanness Abroad)[23] were also carefully registered and approved by the BDF. Women were probably very active in this field, even if their activities are seldom explicitly mentioned. When, for example, the address book of German schools abroad was published in 1904, the chairman of the

General German School Association for the Preservation of Germanness Abroad, which included women's and girls' groups, could report that the Association's central board of directors had compiled the material 'mostly at the expense of our hard-working local women's group in Darmstadt'.[24] This work was first centralized in the Auslandsbund Deutscher Frauen, which was founded in 1915 as the central body representing the interests of German women abroad.[25]

This enumeration only partly takes account of the parallel organizations and women's auxiliaries of men's associations, such as the Deutscher Frauenverein für die Ostmarken (German Women's Association for the Eastern Provinces) founded in 1895, the Flottenbund deutscher Frauen (German Women's Naval League) founded in 1905 and the Frauenbund der Deutschen Kolonialgesellschaft (Women's League of the German Colonial Society, FBDKG) founded in 1907. The women active in these groups supported the nationalist course of the men's associations to which they had attached themselves and sought to make their own specifically feminine contribution. Some, including the women's league of the Deutscher Flottenverein (German Naval Association) and the Frauenbund der Deutschen Kolonialgesellschaft belonged to the BDF.[26] Historians have shown little interest in these women's associations, regarding them as mere insignificant appendages of the male organizations. Yet even in these organizations women apparently pursued their own agendas, which could differ markedly from those put forward by the 'mother association' founded by men.[27] Thus shortly before the First World War there was an intense debate in the commission of the German Colonial Society (Deutsche Kolonialgesellschaft) over collaboration with the Frauenbund der Deutschen Kolonialgesellschaft. The latter's feminist stance was the reason for the lack of collaboration, as all those present agreed. The fact that there had been an attempt to elect 'a Miss Gertrud Bäumer to the committee of the women's league' was considered proof positive of the Frauenbund der Deutschen Kolonialgesellschaft's emancipatory ambitions. This episode shows the depth of the mistrust between men and women in the Deutsche Kolonialgesellschaft and the degree of the rapprochement between the Frauenbund der Deutschen Kolonialgesellschaft and the chairwoman of the BDF.[28]

However these women may have viewed woman's role, gender polarity and 'female' and 'male' tasks in society, they expanded their own sphere of action through their associational activities. Most of the 'purely charitable' organizations had formed spontaneously during the Revolution of 1848–49 and the wars of the second half of the nineteenth century. Many outlived their original purpose and regrouped in peacetime. This was connected in part with the attempts of governments to put women's auxiliary activities on a more regular basis, but also shows that in times of war women could acquire new spheres of action and competence that they did not relinquish voluntarily once the conflict was over.

Woman's 'Cultural Duty' in the German Cultural Nation

Before the First World War, the nation and nationalism were rarely problematized. For the German educated middle classes, national feeling was an extension of family feeling and 'tribal spirit'.[29] The sense of belonging to the German nation, which was defined as a cultural nation, was considered a sort of inevitable outgrowth of common descent, language and culture, which according to the contemporary view was what constituted the unique 'character' of every nation. In this interpretation, in the case of the German 'cultural nation', the sense of solidarity was thus not based on a declared belief in a particular form of state, but rather arose 'naturally' out of descent.[30]

This sort of cultural nationalism must have been considered mere common sense among women of the German middle classes and was accepted as a given by the BDF and its member associations. The most important founding members of the BDF were the large national organizations the ADF and the Allgemeiner Deutscher Lehrerinnenverein (General German Association of Women Teachers, ADLV). These two associations played a pioneering role and strongly influenced discussions within the BDF. Helene Lange (1848–1930) assumed a key position in all three associations. A founding member and chairwoman of the Allgemeiner Deutscher Lehrerinnenverein since 1890, she participated in the founding of the BDF as a member of the executive board in 1894 and was also elected chairwoman of the ADF after the death of Auguste Schmidt in 1902. Her partner in life and work, Gertrud Bäumer (1873–1954), was chairwoman of the BDF from 1910 until 1919. With the journal *Die Frau*, which she began publishing in 1893, Helene Lange also succeeded in creating a central organ of the middle-class women's movement, in which she exercised major influence in the choice and treatment of topics as editor.[31]

Distancing itself from the materialist view of history, the middle-class women's movement in Germany had always emphasized that it represented a 'cultural movement' shaped far more by intellectual motivating forces than visible economic causes. The BDF, most of whose leadership at the turn of the century was close to the national liberal circle around Friedrich Naumann, hoped that women would gain an acknowledged and 'equivalent' participation in the nation state. 'Equivalent' did not sound quite as radical as 'equal'; it emphasized gender, did not recall socialist 'levelling' and contained the notion of a fundamental reform of society that was supposed to render revolution superfluous.

The BDF's 'lack of a programme', so often lamented by scholars, proved to be an advantage in this respect. It enabled the BDF to unite the women's movement's various wings and thereby integrate numerous associations 'that had not yet been consciously influenced by these ideas, but nonetheless served them.'[32] All associations worked together in the BDF on the basis of a minimum consensus: only such objectives 'as all can heartily agree upon' were to be set.[33] In this way the individuality of the member groups could be maintained and the BDF leadership could divide important tasks among the different associations. While the ADF, as a sort of spearhead of the BDF, sought to prepare women for political equality through political education, other groups devoted their efforts to specific educational and professional issues as well as social and charitable work. The close interlocking between the BDF executive and the ADF leadership ensured that the BDF did not lose sight of the goal of women's emancipation. At the same time, its deliberately apolitical stance left sufficient room for associations that opposed women's political equality. Paragraph 2 of the national statutes stated that: 'Through organized cooperation, women's charitable associations should be strengthened in order to work successfully for the good of the family and the nation, to combat ignorance and injustice and strive for a moral foundation for the way of life of all.'[34] In order to remove 'social defects in all areas', the BDF set itself the following tasks in its founding assembly:

> 1. To incorporate after-school facilities for children into all elementary schools, 2. To introduce health education (including information on the harmful effects of alcohol) . . . 3. Protective legislation for women workers . . . 4. To disseminate knowledge of all of the laws affecting women . . . 5. To admit women to state examinations for the medical profession and secondary education, 6. To train women for, and admit them to, the profession of public poor relief.[35]

In this programme, the BDF clearly placed the common good of the state and family before women's individual demands and thus paved the way for the integration of welfare associations. The BDF programme emphasized not better educational and professional opportunities for women (the aims of the educational and professional associations) but rather women's special responsibility within the social reform process: 'woman's

cultural task'. Women were to rid male-dominated society of the deform-
ations of modernity, class hatred, pauperism, monotony and indifference,
and to initiate a return to the 'lasting values' of German culture, thus
contributing to the creation of a nation that transcended class, gender
and religion.

This orientation towards the common good did not, however, mean
that the BDF had lost sight of political equality for women. The BDF
succeeded as early as 1902 in passing a resolution recommending that
'the member associations [should] strongly promote understanding of
the idea of women's suffrage because only women's suffrage could ensure
the lasting success of all of the League's efforts'.[36] For tactical reasons
the demand for suffrage was not placed at the forefront of the BDF's
work, but mainly left to the ADF. In 1910, on the initiative of its
chairwoman Helene Lange, the ADF stated its objectives more clearly. It
now called itself the Allgemeiner Deutscher Frauenverein. Zugleich
Verband für Frauenarbeit und Frauenrechte in der Gemeinde (General
German Women's Association and Federation for Women's Work and
Rights in the Local Community).[37] Comparisons with countries where
women already had the vote made Lange sceptical. She recognized that
formal equality alone could not bring about the hoped-for radical social
change that 'female cultural achievements' might effect. For that reason,
she wanted to prepare women through training in citizenship and intensified participation on the micro level of the municipality 'to bring women's
cultural influence to a full inner development and social efficacy.'[38]

The transformation of the ADF into a 'joint national representative
body' for all of the women's associations active in local politics did not
cause an abandonment of broader objectives. It merely bowed to the
growing division of labour within the BDF and offered an umbrella
organization to groups that had previously held aloof from the BDF. Many
of these were local and regional federations of women's associations
working in the field of municipal policy, which belonged to the charitable
and patriotic spectrum. This further advanced the BDF's enclosure policy,
for from this point onward the ADF 'no longer made its organizational
advancement dependent primarily on the founding new local branches...
but above all on the membership of existing women's associations in the
area of municipal policy.'[39] This 'practical politics' helped the ADF to
attract the interest of mothers and non-professional women.

Although by the turn of the century the BDF increasingly characterized
the women's movement as a national movement, it maintained a sober
and functional approach to nationalism and accusations of internationalism up until the First World War. After the Anti-Socialist Law was

revoked in 1890 the women's movement strengthened its international contacts. Helene Lange received the decisive inspiration for her call for a reform of girls' schooling from the US and England, and she couched it in her usual ironic terms.[40] The founding of the BDF itself had, of course, followed in 1894, inspired by the 1893 congress of the International Council of Women (ICW) held on the occasion of the World's Fair in Chicago, which had been attended by German delegates. In 1897 the BDF became the third national women's organization to join the ICW after its American and Canadian counterparts. These international contacts and sources of inspiration were soon to be played down.

Leading educational policymakers' and educators' idea that 'education' and 'culture' should be regarded not simply as individual but rather as 'national guarantors of identity'[41] also influenced the BDF. Beginning around 1900, the national significance of women's 'cultural work' began to be writ large. The invocation of the nation proved an ideal catchphrase for expanding women's sphere of influence without appearing to be too radical. Both men and women were fascinated by nationalist patterns of thought because they seemed to leave the future open. The 'purely charitable activities' such as (field) nursing that were allotted to women were viewed as a 'complementary counterpart to male military service'[42] and, beginning with the Wars of Liberation, had become a mass phenomenon that united women from monarchists to radical democrats. While some groups sought to use their 'genuinely feminine activities' to establish or solidify the traditional sexual division of labour, others deployed nationalism as an emancipatory ideology and hoped that it would provide women with more education, access to new occupations or more political influence, and even complete political equality.

At the turn of the century, the accelerated expansion of the navy accompanied by a public propaganda campaign and an hysterical international policy led to the increasing nationalization of Wilhelmine society. The growing sense of crisis and increased domestic conflicts after 1905 unleashed a wave of defamation of anything international. Those forces that rejected change and clung to the status quo equated the downsides of modernity with internationalism. Socialism, feminism and 'world Jewry' appeared to be mere variants of the same basic evil.

Helene Lange reacted to this trend not merely by emphasizing the national traits of the German women's movement, but also by using the accusation of internationalism as an opportunity to take the offensive. She asserted that the German women's movement had developed from the nationalism of its origins to internationalism and that it held the 'lack of rights and of a deeper relationship to the cultural life of their own people in the past and present' responsible for women's 'irredeemable' alienation from their own nation. 'Where did this tendency towards internationalism in the German women's movement, which is actually foreign to the German national character and to female nature, come from?' she asked, only to answer 'that German men have forced women who wanted to fulfil their national duties into internationalism'.[43]

Although the BDF's actions acknowledged the prevailing overheated nationalism and took every possible opportunity to emphasize the women's movement's national stance, it was accused by the Deutscher Bund zur Bekämpfung der Frauenemanzipation (German League to Combat Women's Emancipation, founded in 1912) of working towards the demise of the German nation. The anti-feminist League did not attack women's organizations wholesale, but rather offered to support all those women's associations 'that wished to participate in a national and truly feminine spirit in uplifting female life'. The BDF immediately took up this accusation and countered that the German women's movement fulfilled 'a national duty in everything it does' and had 'demonstrated that it placed national unity above the fragmentation of partisan opinion, and that it possessed the strength to express this unity to the outside world as well'.[44] The reference to the unifying character of the women's movement, which the BDF managed to strengthen with its 'non-partisan' stance, was skilfully directed at the distinction, commonly made in Germany, between the 'partisan squabbling' in (male-dominated) political life and the aspirations of a 'female politics' that rose above these differences. The exclusion of the Social Democratic women workers' organizations at the founding of the BDF, regretted by some women who wanted to mediate between the bourgeois and socialist women,[45] meant that in the years that followed the spectrum of women active in the BDF expanded from the traditionally bourgeois liberal groups to those in national conservative circles. The BDF's reply to its enemies was thus not merely supported by its member federations and associations, but also met with the approval of nationalist conservative organizations such as the Lübeck Patriotic Women's Association.[46] In this case, the anti-feminist League's massive attacks did not produce the intended effect of driving a wedge between the charitable patriotic women's associations and those that called for women's emancipation. The enlargement of the BDF facilitated not only its movement in a more national conservative direction, but also gave the BDF board the chance to win over wholly new groups of women to the idea of emancipation.

In its campaign of defamation, the anti-feminist League continued to deploy accusations of internationalism. At this period, though, the successes of the women's movement were so apparent that Gertrud Bäumer could confidently assert that: 'It is in the nature of certain intellectual movements not to be contained by national boundaries.'[47] Internationalism and nationalism were not mutually exclusive, and the German women's movement, 'which has set up a cultural ideal, is by this very fact tied in its personification to the national character'.[48]

The Nationalization of the BDF at the Outbreak of the First World War

Whenever it claimed civil rights for women, the BDF was reminded of the connection between citizenship and the capacity to bear arms, which appeared in the eyes of many to represent the last insurmountable barrier to women's equal participation in the German nation-state. The women's movement was thus occupied with the search for an equivalent to military service that women could perform.[49] It was in this context that the idea of compulsory service for women, a topic discussed with increasingly intensity after 1900, was born.[50] At the much talked-about congress that accompanied the 1912 exhibition on 'Woman in Household and Profession' Elisabeth Gnauck-Kühne called for a 'female service year'. Gnauck-Kühne sought to portray this service year not as an innovation, but as an 'organic extension' of home economics instruction in the schools. Girls should be introduced to their domestic duties just as men were to their military duties. That same year the BDF entered the public debate with a resolution that presented the 'female service year' in a different light – one that emphasized the arena of public welfare work rather than the domestic sphere. To be sure, girls with an elementary school-leaving certificate were to receive obligatory instruction in home economics that would be equivalent to the 'female service year'. The actual 'female service year' for the higher social classes, however, should be spent in women's social work schools under female administration. The BDF argued for the establishment of more such schools, but believed that the female service year should not become obligatory before women had attained political equality.[51]

When the First World War broke out, these plans for compulsory female service were not merely taken up; women's every activity was now declared a 'national task'. The German troops marching off to war were juxtaposed with the 'home army' of women.[52] On the day of mobilization the BDF sent its members an organizational plan for the immediate establishment of a National Women's Service (Nationaler Frauendienst,

NFD). According to Gertrud Bäumer, the basic demands for the implementation of the plan were: '1. Coordination with the Red Cross and the Patriotic Women's Associations; 2. Coordination with the authorities; 3. Consultation with the welfare associations outside the Red Cross [DRK]'.[53] The Nationaler Frauendienst's activities followed in the footsteps of the 'Women's Association of the Fatherland of 1814' and its successor organizations in the German Red Cross. In order to avoid conflicts, the Nationaler Frauendienst clearly distinguished its activities from those of the German Red Cross and emphasized that the German Red Cross alone was responsibility for nursing in the field. The slogan of 'home service', which the Nationaler Frauendienst adopted for its work, was declared to be the 'wartime translation of the term "women's movement"'.[54] Women's municipal welfare work, so strongly encouraged by the ADF in the years before the war, now proved very useful. The women's associations in the cities now joined forces, organizing cooperation with local authorities to secure food supplies and aid families whose breadwinners had been conscripted or made unemployed by the war. The Nationaler Frauendienst also helped women to find employment and set up information centres to assist them in coping with everyday problems. In the nationalist fever of early wartime, it became clear that the BDF could rely upon previously neutral or even hostile groups of women. The war was a great mobilizer of women.[55] Although at the current stage of research it is not yet clear to what extent individual women's associations or women Social Democrats who had previously kept their distance worked with the *Nationaler Frauendienst*.[56] The BDF, or the Nationaler Frauendienst, which it had initiated, appears to have met with a high degree of cooperation among women of all milieus, at least at the beginning of the war. There is much evidence that it was the long-standing if selective collaboration on the local level that now permitted relatively smooth cooperation among Social Democratic, national conservative and liberal women.[57]

During the war Helene Lange emphasized once again that women's duty to serve must not exhaust itself in motherhood. She pointed to 'the analogy between female compulsory service and man's military service ' in order to define women's duties in a future peacetime.[58] She noted that, strictly speaking, men were doubly bound to serve: in wartime they were liable for military service and in peacetime their duty as citizens obliged them to accept honorary posts. In her analysis of this 'double male compulsory service' she set up a parallel between the introduction of universal conscription and the expansion of communal self-administration in order to derive from women's wartime duty to serve a peacetime duty to perform volunteer work.[59] Helene Lange called for obligatory citizenship instruction for girls – a 'female service year' – to help them to fulfil these tasks satisfactorily. The core of this programme would be instruction in home economics and basic economics along with physical education. Here Helene Lange took up a notion developed by the ADF, that girls and women should be given a national education in a Fichtean spirit.[60]

The idea of compulsory service for women sparked a lively public debate. Gertrud Bäumer, however, noted with annoyance in 1916 that most authors who expressed an opinion on women's service treated the women's movement's idea of 'women's duty to serve society in peacetime in a wholly inadequate and dilettantish manner'.[61] Women's compulsory service was generally regarded as a mere wartime stopgap measure, whereas in peacetime women were to be relegated to voluntary, purely charitable activities. Bäumer expressly warned against hastily introducing the compulsory service year on the basis of 'such an underdeveloped consciousness', as it might prove to be a 'Trojan horse of the worst kind'.[62]

Conclusions

Various segments of the population used nationalism as a legitimation strategy for the most diverse objectives. In their demands and actions, proponents and opponents of women's emancipation alike invoked the nation and national obligations. The BDF and ADF were so successful in deploying nationalism as an emancipatory strategy even before the First World War that the anti-feminist opposition came to view this apparently 'moderate' wing of the women's movement as its main enemy.[63] No matter how the activities of the different women's associations were accentuated, and whatever their extent, women's arenas and radius of action expanded clearly beyond the domestic sphere. In other words, even women who opposed emancipation were busy emancipating themselves. This led to the absurd situation after 1918 that women who opposed the suffrage were elected to the National Assembly as deputies of the conservative Deutschnationale Volkspartei. At the beginning of the First World War it became apparent that, in this extreme situation, broad segments of the population were quite willing to accept women's informal and largely unpaid performance of 'national tasks'. As soon, however, as women demanded a concrete participation in the state that went beyond the vague sentiments of national community, 'female national tasks' were quickly restricted to volunteer and charitable activities. This finding substantiates Ute Planert's thesis 'that the restrictive national conception of femininity as a complement to the masculine already contained, inherently, as it were, the seeds of change, without ever truly being able to overcome its intrinsic limitations and embrace gender-political equality.'[64]

Notes

1. See the brief sketches of the state of research in Schaser, A. (1996), '"Corpus mysticum". Die Nation bei Gertrud Bäumer', in Frauen and Geschichte Baden-Württemberg (ed.) *Frauen and Nation*, Tübingen: Silberburg, 118–20, and Planert, U. (1999), 'Zwischen Partizipation und Restriktion. Frauenemanzipation und nationales Paradigma von der Aufklärung bis zum Ersten Weltkrieg,' in Langewiesche, D. and Schmidt, G. (eds), *Deutsche Nation – zeitgenössische Vorstellungen seit dem 16. Jahrhundert* (forthcoming).

2. Bock, G. (1995), Afterword to Duby, G. and Perrot, M. (eds) *Geschichte der Frauen, 5: 20. Jahrhundert*, Frankfurt, New York and Paris: Campus, 635–44, 641.

3. Confino, A. (1993), 'The Nation as a Local Metaphor: Heimat, National Memory and the German Empire, 1871–1918', *History and Memory* 5, (1) (1993): 42–86; Sandkühler, T. and Schmidt, H.G. (1991) '"Geistige Mütterlichkeit" als nationaler Mythos im Deutschen Kaiserreich,' in Link J. and Wülfing W. (eds), *Nationale Mythen und Symbole in der zweiten Hälfte des 19. Jahrhunderts. Strukturen und Funktionen von Konzepten nationaler Identität*, Sprache und Geschichte, 16, Stuttgart: Klett-Cotta, 237–55; Wülfing, W. Bruns, K. Parr, R. (1991), *Historische Mythologie der Deutschen 1798–1918*, Munich: Wilhelm Fink.

4. See Möhrmann, R. (ed.) (1973), *Frauenemanzipation im deutschen Vormärz. Texte und Dokumente,* Stuttgart: Reclam; Lipp, C. (ed.) (1986), *Schimpfende Weiber und patriotische Jungfrauen. Frauen im Vormärz und der Revolution 1848/49*, Moos and Baden-Baden: Elster; Chickering, R. (1988), '"Casting their Gaze more Broadly": Women's Patriotic Activism in Imperial Germany', *Past and Present* 32, no. 188: 156–85; Paletschek, S. (1996), 'Frauen im Umbruch. Untersuchungen zu Frauen im Umfeld der deutschen Revolution von 1848/ 49', in Fieseler, B. and Schulze, B. (eds*) Frauengeschichte: Gesucht – Gefunden?* Cologne, Weimar, Vienna: Böhlau; *Frauen und Nation*,

Tübingen: Silberburg; Frevert U. (1996), 'Nation, Krieg und Geschlecht im 19. Jahrhundert,' in Hettling, M. and Nolte, P. (eds), *Nation und Gesellschaft in Deutschland,* Munich: Beck, 151–70; Frevert, U. (ed.) (1997), *Militär und Gesellschaft im 19 Jahrhundert,* Stuttgart: Klett-Cotta; Hauch, G. (1998), 'Frauen-Räume in der Männer-Revolution 1848', in Dowe, D., Haupt, H.-G., and Langewiesche, D. (eds), *Europa 1848. Revolution und Nation,* Bonn: Dietz, 841–900; Kienitz, S. (1998), 'Frauen', in Dipper, C. and Speck, U. (eds), *1848. Revolution in Deutschland,* Frankfurt a.M., Leipzig: Insel, 272–85; Reder, D. (1998), *Frauenbewegung und Nation. Patriotische Frauenvereine in Deutschland im frühen 19. Jahrhundert (1813–1830),* Cologne: SH-Verlag, and the contribution by Karen Hagemann in this volume.

5. See Lipp, C. 'Liebe, Krieg und Revolution. Geschlechterbeziehung und Nationalismus in der Revolution 1848/49,' in *Schimpfende Weiber,* 353–84.

6. See Planert, U. 'Zwischen Partizipation und Restriktion.'

7. Evans, R.J. (1976), *The Feminist Movement in Germany, 1894–1933,* Sage Studies in Twentieth Century History, 6, London and Beverly Hills: Sage; Greven-Aschoff, B. (1981), *Die Bürgerliche Frauenbewegung in Deutschland 1894–1933,* Kritische Studien zur Geschichtswissenschaft, 46 Göttingen: Vandenhoeck & Ruprecht, 1981.

8. Christiane Eifert, 'Der zählebige Topos der "feindlichen Schwestern". Bürgerliche und proletarische Frauenbewegung von der Jahrhundertwende bis zur Revolution von 1918/19,' in Mütter, B. and Uffelmann, U. (eds) (1992), *Emotionen und historisches Lernen. Forschung, Vermittlung, Rezeption,* Studien zur internationalen Schulbuchforschung. Schriftenreihe des Georg-Eckert-Instituts, Frankfurt a.M.: Diesterweg, 311–24; Epple, A. (1996), *Henriette Fürth und die Frauenbewegung im Deutschen Kaiserreich. Eine Sozialbiographie,* Forum Frauengeschichte, Pfaffenweiler: Centaurus.

9. Daniel, U. (1989), 'Die Vaterländischen Frauenvereine in Westfalen', *Westfälische Forschungen* 39: 158–79, 158.

10. The case of the chairwoman of the Patriotic Women's Associations (*Vaterländische Frauenvereine*), Selma von Groeben (1856–1938), demonstrates the shakiness of such assessments. She was the deputy chairwoman of the *Deutsch-Evangelischer Frauenbund,* directed welfare work in Hannover during the First World War within the framework of the *Nationaler Frauendienst* and remained until her death in close contact with Gertrud Bäumer. See also Heinsohn,

K. (1997), *Politik und Geschlecht. Zur politischen Kultur bürgerlicher Frauenvereine in Hamburg*, Beiträge zur Geschichte Hamburgs, Hamburg: Verlag Verein für Hamburgische Geschichte; Klausmann, · C. (1997), *Politik und Kultur der Frauenbewegung im Kaiserreich. Das Beispiel Frankfurt am Main*, Geschichte und Geschlechter, 19 Frankfurt a. Main and New York: Campus.

11. (1905), *Meyers Großes Konversationslexikon*, 7, 6th ed., Leipzig, and Vienna: Bibliographisches Institut, 45 ff.
12. Lange, H. (1905), 'Frauenvereine', in Rein, W. (ed.) *Encyklopädisches Handbuch der Pädagogik*, vol. 3, 2nd ed., Langensalza: Verlag von Hermann Beyer & Söhne, 109–15, 110.
13. Chickering, '"Casting their Gaze More Broadly"', 162.
14. Quoted in Von Grüneisen, F. (1939), *Das Deutsche Rote Kreuz in Vergangenheit und Gegenwart* Potsdam-Babelsberg: Verlagsabteilung des DRK, 67.
15. Grüneisen, *Das Deutsche Rote Kreuz*, 75–6. For the statutes see 257–8.
16. Lange, 'Frauenvereine', 111.
17. Lange, 'Frauenvereine', 109–15.
18. Evans, *The Feminist Movement*, 149.
19. Bäumer, G. (1921), 'Die Geschichte des Bundes Deutscher Frauenvereine', in Elisabeth Altmann-Gottheiner (ed.), *Jahrbuch des Bundes Deutscher Frauenvereine*, Leipzig and Berlin: B.G. Teubner, 15–64, 23.
20. Kloosterhuis, J. (1994), *'Friedliche Imperialisten'. Deutsche Auslandsvereine und auswärtige Kulturpolitik, 1906–1918*, 2 vols, Frankfurt a.M.: Peter Lang, 1: 75.
21. See the ADF appeal for support of the naval movement in *Die Frau* 7 (1899/1900): 322–3 and Evans, *The Feminist Movement*, 209–10.
22. ADF appeal, *Die Frau*, 322–3.
23. Müller, J.P. (1901), *Deutsche Schulen und deutscher Unterricht im Auslande*, Leipzig: Selbstverlag.
24. (1904), *Handbuch des Deuschtums im Auslande*, Berlin: Reimer, viii.
25. Kloosterhuis, *'Friedliche Imperialisten'*, 2: 349 ff.
26. Greven-Aschoff, Die bürgerliche Frauenbewegung, 259 n. 45 and 286.
27. Venghiattis, C. (1997), *Mobilizing for Nation and Empire: German Women's Patriotic Activism through the Frauenbund der Deutschen Kolonialgesellschaft, 1907–1945*, unpublished paper; Chickering, 'Casting Their Gaze more Broadly', 181 ff. See also Wildenthal, L. (1993), '"She is the Victor": Bourgeois Women, Nationalist

Identities and the Ideal of the Independent Woman Farmer in German Southwest Africa', *Social Analysis* 33: 68–88, and (1997), 'Race, Gender and Citizenship in the German Colonial Empire', in Cooper, F. and Stoler, A. (eds) *Tension of Empire: Colonial Cultures in a Bourgois World,* Berkeley, Los Angeles, London , 263–83.

28. Bundesarchiv Koblenz, Abt. Berlin, 61 Ko 1 (Deutsche Kolonial-gesellschaft), Akte 163, 87. I thank Claire Venghiattis for drawing my attention to this source.

29. (1906) *Meyers großes Konversations-Lexikon,* vol. 14, 6th ed., Leipzig and Vienna, 444.

30. In his French-German comparisons, Rogers Brubaker describes this as a central characteristic of German nationalism. See his (1989), 'Einwanderung und Nationalstaat in Deutschland und Frankreich,' *Der Staat* 29: 1–30 and (1992) *Citizenship and Nationhood in France and Germany,* Cambridge, Ma. and London.

31. Helene Lange was the sole editor of *Die Frau* until 1916, when Gertrud Bäumer joined her. In 1921 *Die Frau* became the official organ of the BDF.

32. Bäumer, 'Geschichte des BDF', 17.

33. This motto was borrowed from the National Council of Women of the United States, which had been founded in 1891.

34. Bäumer, 'Geschichte des BDF', 17.

35. Bäumer, 'Geschichte des BDF', 18.

36. Bäumer, 'Geschichte des BDF', 23.

37. On the history of the ADF see Stoehr, I. (1990), *Emanzipation zum Staat? Der Allgemeine Deutsche Frauenverein – Deutscher Staats-bürgerinnenverband (1893–1933),* Pfaffenweiler: Centaurus.

38. From the ADF's fourth leaflet of 1907, Helene-Lange-Archiv in the Landesarchiv Berlin, 5-29/2.

39. Stoehr, I. (1990), *Emanzipation zum Staat? Der Allgemeine Deutsche Frauenverein – Deutscher Staatsbürgerinnenverband (1893–1933),* Pfaffenweiler: Centaurus, 51.

40. See Lange, H. (1893), *Erziehungsfragen,* Berlin: L. Oehmigke's Verlag, 16–17.

41. Bollenbeck, G. (1994), *Bildung und Kultur. Glanz und Elend eines deutschen Deutungsmusters,* 2nd ed., Frankfurt a.M. and Leipzig: Insel, 165.

42. Lipp, 'Liebe, Krieg und Revolution', 369.

43. Lange, H. (1900/1901), 'National oder International. Ein Frage-zeichen zur Frauenbewegung,' *Die Frau* 8: 1–4, 3.

44. (1911/1912), 'Erklärung des Bundes Deutscher Frauenvereine zur

Organisation der Gegner', *Die Frau,* 19: 630–1.

45. On this see the declaration by BDF chairwoman Auguste Schmidt, in (1900/1901), *Die Frau* 8: 180 and Helene Lange's 'little study of the women's movement' in (1900/1901), *Die Frau* 8: 180 ff.

46. Planert, U. (1998), *Antifeminismus im Kaiserreich. Diskurs, soziale Formation und politische Mentalität,* Kritische Studien zur Geschichtswissenschaft, Göttingen: Vandenhoeck & Ruprecht, 354, n. 34.

47. Gertrud Bäumer (1912/13), 'Frauenbewegung und Nationalbewußtsein', *Die Frau* 20: 387–94, 387.

48. Gertrud Bäumer (1912/13), 'Frauenbewegung und Nationalbewußtsein', *Die Frau* 20: 388.

49. Dammer, S. (1988), *Mütterlichkeit und Frauendienstpflicht. Versuche der Vergesellschaftung "weiblicher Fähigkeiten" durch eine Dienstverpflichtung (Deutschland 1890–1918),* Weinheim: Deutscher Studien Verlag.

50. As early as January 1912 Lange could no longer locate the originator of the 'old' demand for a female service year. Lange, H. (1911/12), 'Die Dienstpflicht der deutschen Frau', *Die Frau* 19: 214–17.

51. (1912/13), Resolutions of the 10th Annual General Meeting of the BDF, *Die Frau* 20: 118–19.

52. Guttmann, B. (1989), *Weibliche Heimarmee. Frauen in Deutschland 1914–1918* (Weinheim: Deutscher Studien Verlag.

53. Bäumer, G. (1913/14), 'Nationaler Frauendienst,' *Die Frau* 21: 714–21, 714.

54. Bäumer, G. (1916), 'Zur Einführung', in Elisabeth Altmann-Gottheiner, (ed.) *Heimatdienst im ersten Kriegsjahr. Jahrbuch des BDF* Leipzig and Berlin: iii.

55. See also Fritzsche, P. (1998), *Germans into Nazis,* Cambridge, Mass. and London: Harvard University Press.

56. See the differing assessments of the participation of women Social Democrats in the *Nationaler Frauendienst* made by Wurms, R. (1982), '"Krieg dem Kriege" – "Dienst am Vaterland". Frauenbewegung im ersten Weltkrieg', in Hervé, F. (ed.), *Geschichte der deutschen Frauenbewegung,* Cologne: Pahl-Rugenstein, 84–118, 115, n. 34 and Weiland, D. (1983), 'Nationaler Frauendienst,' in her *Geschichte der Frauenemanzipation in Deutschland und Österreich. Biographien, Programme, Organisationen,* Düsseldorf: Econ, 178–82, 180.

57. See Guttmann, *Weibliche Heimarmee.*

58. Lange, H. (1914/15), 'Die Dienstpflicht der Frau', *Die Frau* 22: 577–91, 579.

59. Lange, H. (1914/15), 'Die Dienstpflicht der Frau', *Die Frau* 22: 581.
60. Lange, H. (1914/15), 'Die Dienstpflicht der Frau', *Die Frau* 22: 582.
61. Bäumer, G. (1915/16), 'Phantasien und Tatsachen in der Frage des weiblichen Dienstjahrs', *Die Frau* 23: 321–9, 328.
62. Bäumer, G. (1915/16), 'Phantasien und Tatsachen in der Frage des weiblichen Dienstjahrs', *Die Frau* 23: 328.
63. Planert, U. (1998), *Antifeminismus im Kaiserreich. Diskurs, soziale Formation und politische Mentalität*, Kritische Studien zur Geschichtswissenschaft, Göttingen: Vandenhoeck & Ruprecht, 17.
64. Planert, U. 'Zwischen Partizipation und Restriktion. Frauenemanzipation und nationales Paradigma von der Aufklärung bis zum Ersten Weltkrieg,' in Langewiesche, D. and Schmidt, G. (eds), *Deutsche Nation – zeitgenössische Vorstellungen seit dem 16. Jahrhundert,* 2, forthcoming.

Part 5
National Symbols, Rituals and Myths – Gender Images and Cultural Representations of Nations

13

Political Camp or the Ambiguous Engendering of the American Republic

Carroll Smith-Rosenberg

I

This chapter is about representation, gender and the republican nation state. It focuses on the relation of representation to that which is represented – the relation of metaphorical to actual figures, of political representatives to citizens, of money to real estates and labour. It seeks to trace the ways the processes of representation empower and disempower the represented. As gender is the handmaiden of power, it explores as well the ways in which both the representative and the represented are engendered.

In a collection of chapters on the engendering of the nation state, why include one on representation? For two interrelated reasons. First, modern nation states represent themselves, or seek to, as representative republics. It is through the processes and practices of representation that republics govern themselves and seek to legitimate their claims to be governments 'of and by the people'.[1] Second, the process of representation involves asymmetries of power. Either it is a mimetic practice, in which case the representative is a transparent conduit and power resides with the represented, or the process is opaque, one sees the represented only through the representative and power rests with the representative. Figurations of gender, themselves asymmetrical, mark asymmetrical flows of power. Power is associated with virility, its absence with emasculation and the feminine.

And so one must ask, in modern republics, is political representation a mimetic or an opaque practice? Who do the political representatives represent – the people to the state or the state to the people? How do representations of gender mark the flow of power between representatives and those they represent? In a capitalist economy, how do the practices of representation inherent in fiscal capitalism effect the empowerment and engendering of the republican nation state? To explore the fiction and practice of representation, to better understand the engendering of the modern republic, I have turned to the first modern representative republic – the United States of America – and the bitter contestations over representation that marked its founding.

II

All that glisters is not gold
Often have you heard it told
(Merchant of Venice, II. vi, 65–66)

Shakespeare staged his concerns about representation – the deceitfulness of language, the theatricality of appearance, the difficulties inherent in representations of self, gender or value, the complex relation representation in general bears to that which is represented – among the commercial classes of the Venetian Republic.[2]

Like commerce, concerns about the nature of representation followed the Renaissance north, abetted by political and economic revolution.[3] In England, a bloody civil war forced British political philosophers and practical Puritan parliamentarians, alike, to formulate principles legitimating representative government. In the process, they invested the English people with political sovereignty and constituted the modern forms of political representation.

Together, popular sovereignty and political representation constitute the twin poles of the modern republican state, points of oppositional tension that structure our political world. Popular sovereignty empowers citizens, investing them with the right of self governance. Political representation alienates that right, transferring the citizen's right of self-governance to the political representative.[4] The relationship between them structures the deployment of power within the republican state. Fictively, political representation signals 'the marriage of true minds' – as well as a contractual relation between equals, that is, the voter and the representative. Like so many other marriages, however, the fiction of political representation may cloak a relation of dominance and submission. The degree to which the relation of representative and citizen is an interactive one will determine the degree to which the citizen's inalienable right to self-governance is preserved or alienated, confirmed or emasculated.

Political representation was not the only form of representation to trouble Englishmen in their ongoing encounter with modernity. The seventeenth and eighteenth centuries' commercial and financial revolutions,

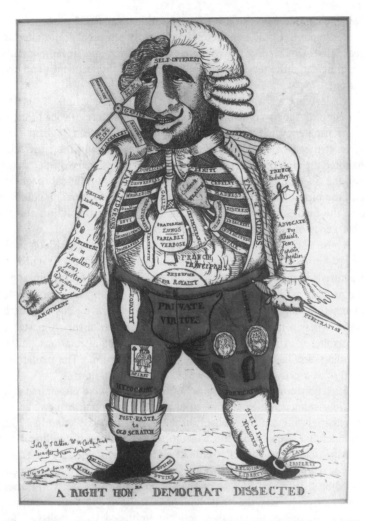

Figure 13.1 *A Right Hon. Democrat Dissected.* Lithograph by W. Dent, 15 January 1793. (Privately owned by the author.)

abstracting market places into the modern 'market', necessitated fiscal innovations: the founding of the Bank of England, the invention of interest-bearing government bonds, the proliferation of bank notes and commercial stock issues.[5] The varying value and uncertain reliability of this paper, wed to desire and hope, gave birth to speculation. Speculation, along with the spectacular display of wealth that speculation enabled, became a modern way of life – fusing political and fiscal concerns about representation. Could commercial paper truly represent real estates and real value? Could speculative commercial paper ground the representative republic's and the republican subject's political independence and civic virtue?

Underlying all was the problem of self representation. If, as Jean Christophe Agnew argues, 'questions about the nature of social identity ... transparency and reciprocity' had bedevilled Jacobean England – and, at least theatrically, the Venetian Republic, so, newly inscribed, they haunted the eighteenth century.[6] This was not only the age of speculation and the *Spectator*. It was the age of revolution – of political revolution and the birth of republican governmental forms, of national revolutions and the birth of post-colonial states, of economic revolution and the emergence of bourgeois cultures and identities.

These varied revolutions intersected in the 1770s and 1780s in the newly formed United States of America. Identities forged over a lifetime fractured, alternative personas multiplied. Men who grew up thinking of themselves as deferential subjects of a British King now represented themselves, successively (or simultaneously) as brave Sons of Liberty, slave owners, white 'American' heirs to British imperialism in the western hemisphere.[7] Alarmingly fluid, identities and social relations, indeed meaning itself, appeared to float free of established order. The exhilaration born of new possibilities fused with fears of the unknown.

Such concerns and confusions, hopes and fears were disseminated by the flourishing commercial print culture that arose among the new nation's increasingly literate and well-off urban populations. By the mid 1780s, Philadelphia, New York, and Boston boasted of monthly political and literary magazines modelled after London's *Gentlemen's Magazine*.[8] Graced with engravings, featuring polished meditations on the great events and men of Western history or the varied peoples of the world, these magazines cultivated the refinement of their urban and would-be urbane readers. At the same time they actively embraced a nationalist — and elitist — political vision and passionately championed the ratification of the new federal constitution. Their publishers and editors were spokesmen for and ardent defenders of a Federalist political vision. Playing off the trope, 'the founding fathers,' I denominate them the new nation's 'urban fathers'.

Determinedly, the new magazines worked to inscribe a forceful and coherent American identity. The changing and uncertain times, however, did little to encourage ideological or discursive coherence. Contradictions and confusions appeared on the new magazines' every page. Closely reading the essays in these magazines, I will explore the multiple ways political, fiscal and rhetorical representations fused with and hopelessly confused one another, in the process engendering political representatives, citizens and the civic state.

III

I do not use the phrase 'engender' lightly.[9] As the gendering of the body is always political, so the political body is always engendered. A patchwork figure, the work of divergent, at times antithetical political discourses, the eighteenth-century Anglo-American republican political body was always emphatically male. Minimally three discordant political discourses interacted to constitute him a virile and manly subject.[10] Classical republican rhetoric endowed him with agency, autonomy and martial vigour. Commercial republicanism, fusing economic and political subjectivities, made him an industrious producer whose manly self-reliance and hard work secured his own and his nation's independence.[11] Liberal humanism, in its turn, endowed him with inalienable rights and political sovereignty, with reason and judgment.[12] United in empowering the virtuous republican subject male, the new urban magazines invoked these same political discourses to represent actual women, the feminine and the effeminate, as irrational and corrupt – that is, as degenerate threats to the pure male space of republican politics. Women thus became the rhetorically invoked negative other who defined and centred the male republican subject.[13]

Nothing could have been easier. Classical republicanism had doubly banished women from the political arena. Not only did women lack the physical strength and martial skills to defend their nation's and their own honour, when married (and most women married) they lacked the economic independence that made manly civic virtue possible. The very antithesis of the independent and virtuous political actor, as femme couverts, their bodies, wills and earthly goods were their husband's property. He represented them within the country's legal and political spheres. Actual women, in contrast, represented all that would corrupt the virtuous republic and republicans – fashion, luxury, commerce, passion, sexual desire itself. Embodying the feminine, they symbolized the political degeneracy of states that had lost their manly virtue.[14]

Commercial republican attitudes towards women were more complex. The new men of commerce, merchants and shopkeepers, along with the even newer men of financial capitalism, had long been represented within classical republican discourses as effeminate. Like women, it was charged, they depended upon credit, desire and the opinion of others. To distance themselves from classical republican charges that their association with women and the feminine belied their claims to manly civic virtue, men of commerce and finance insisted that their civic virtue rested on their manly industry, productivity and frugality. How could they, strong, self-reliant and forceful, be (con)fused with economically dependent, unproductive, passionate and irrational women?[15]

Nothing, however, logically prevented women's incorporation into the liberal vision of man as politically sovereign and endowed with natural rights to life, liberty, and property.[16] Yet eighteenth-century social contractarians, while freeing sons from the bonds of patriarchy, continued to represent wives as incapable of legal and economic subjectivity and hence of civic virtue.[17] As with Locke, they confined women within the pre-political space of the family, subject to her husband's domestic governance. As with Rousseau, they constituted them Sophies in the service of virtuous Emiles, or, in a more Anglo-American hue, republican mothers nurturing heroic sons for the new nation.[18]

Positioned as the protectors and representatives of politically subject (and suspect) wives and daughters, Euro-American men appeared secure in their virile political and economic subjectivities. But how independent, how autonomous and, hence, how virile could their self-image be as it depended always on their own visions of women, whom they represented as disorderly, duplicitous and dangerous? Complicating matters of gender and identity still further, the urban press repeatedly fused male and female subjectivities, refusing the male political subject virility, virtue and power.

IV

The nature of political representation lay at the very heart of these fusions and refusals, as, indeed, it lies at the heart of all discussions of republican government and, most tellingly, of the constitution of the new United States. Classical British republicanism constituted the virtuous political subject an active participant in the legislative functions of the state.[19] Puritan New England came close to enacting this classical republican dream. Not only did every town send representatives to the Massachusetts General Court, by the opening decades of the eighteenth century, but the towns had established their right, through town meetings, to 'instruct' their legislative representatives how to vote on specific issues – indeed to act as if these representatives were their 'agents' or 'deputies'. Cries of 'no taxation without representation', protests against British insistence on virtual, rather than literal, representation generated broad support for the practice of instructing legislative representatives.[20] By the time of the American Revolution, the practice of instructing legislative representatives had spread from Massachusetts to South Carolina. Even in that elitist, slave-owning state voters insisted that the right to instruct their legislative representatives was 'the most invaluable right of a free people'. To deny that right, they continued tellingly, 'will at one stroke transform us into legal SLAVES to our lordly SERVANTS.'[21]

It was precisely this empowerment of the average voter that the 'urban Fathers', through their new constitution, hoped to contain. Indeed, the relation of political representative and political elector constituted one of the principal issues in the debates over the ratification of the new federal constitution.

In three distinct moves, the 'urban Fathers'' magazines rejected popular representations of the political representative as an agent or 'servant' of his politically active and empowered constituents.

First, the magazines rhetorically impugned the competency of those constituents to participate actively in their own governance, depicting the average American political subject as ill prepared for self-government. 'The opinions of the people at large are often erroneous,' the author of *Maxims for Republics,* complained at the height of the debates over the ratification of the Constitution.[22] 'Large collections of people are turbulent, tumultuous, led by clamorous demagogues', another added, concluding that the people were 'not capable of that cool deliberation that is required in choosing legislators.'

Second, having denigrated the political subject, Federalist rhetoric proceeded to idealize the political representative. Urban political magazines represented the political representative as a man of education, blessed with breadth of vision and rational, considered judgement. Independent of his constituents, he was a 'statesman', who based his decisions 'upon facts . . . after faction has ceased to distort and enthusiasm to adorn them.' 'It is otherwise with the public', that is, the electors, a Federalist writer commented with bitter irony, for 'Their judgment is formed . . . while the rage of party gives an acumen to their penetration.'[23] 'There is a wide difference between power being derived from the people and being seated in the people', yet another Federalist essay insisted. 'The former proposition cannot be too often inculcated in a free country. Disorder and tyranny must ensue from all power being seated in the bulk of the people.' On the pages of the nationalist political magazines, governing had become too complex a task for the average voter. 'A science . . . it relates to that most complicated of all God's works, the mind of man,' another essay advised the 'Freemen of America.' 'It requires abilities and knowledge of a variety of other subjects, to understand it.'[24] 'It is true', another essayist insisted, 'that every man has the right of judging, but it not true that every man has the power; and without power, what is the right but a dangerous weapon, that may wound the best of governments?'[25]

No one made this point more forcefully than New York editor and educator, Noah Webster. 'That a legislature should have unlimited power to do right, is unquestionable' Webster argued. 'But such a power they cannot have unless they have all the power of the State' he continued, insisting that 'the liberty of a people does not rest on any reservation of power [for the people] . . . it rests singly on this principle, a union of interests between the governors and the governed.'[26] Repositioning political representatives as the governors and American political subjects as 'the governed', Webster's argument went on to deny American political subjects the rights of active political participation and thus political subjectivity. 'Their delegates . . . stand in their [the people's] place – possess all their powers', Webster's explanation continued. 'Representatives are therefore . . . master of the people.'

One of the most articulate of the new nation's new conservatives, Webster had founded New York City's first political magazine, entitled *The American Magazine,* as part of his campaign to secure ratification of a strong national (and elitist) constitution. In the years following ratification, Webster published the relentless stream of dictionaries, spellers, geographies and histories that have made his name a standard reference in the United States. The goal of all his publications was not simply to grammatically inform successive generations of his fellow citizens, but to rhetorically form them into strong (and inherently conservative) Americans. To understand the 'urban Fathers'' political and constitutional vision, it behooves us, therefore, to read Webster's arguments concerning representation closely and with care.

Webster's argument depended on the assertion that what I am calling a 'mimetic' relationship between the political elector and his political representative. I understand 'mimetic' to mean the precise copying or 'mimicking' of a particular figure in another form. In this case, mimetic representation would refer to the assertion that the political or legislative representative precisely represents the individual political subject or elector. Webster argued that the political representative represented the political subject or elector absolutely, transparently. To adopt his own rhetoric, there was 'a union of interests between the governors and the governed.' No difference existed between the one and the other. It was precisely this transparency that authorized the political representative to act in the political subject's name, to assume his, that is, 'the People's' sovereign powers to legislate and to govern — just as the 'Founding Fathers' in Philadelphia spoke for 'We the People of the United States,' in writing their constitution – a constitution that undoubtedly did not command the support of the majority of the American people, or even of those white men constituted voters. It was precisely because no difference existed between the political representative and the political subject that the political subject was obligated to obey the laws his representative enacted in his name. It went almost without saying, moreover, that advocates of the Federalist constitution insisted that the political subject needed no bill of rights to protect himself from a representative who was but his other self. 'The people chose their Legislature from their own body', Webster proclaimed. 'That Legislature will have an interest inseparable for that of the people'. It then followed on the pages of Webster's *American Magazine,* that 'The acts of these deputies are in effect the acts of the people — and the people have no right to refuse obedience.'[27]

Having so forcefully asserted a mimetic representation, however, Webster then repudiated it. He proceeded to transform the political representative from being an absolute look-alike of the political subject into a 'governor,' a 'master,' other than and independent of those he represented – and emphatically more powerful. How did Webster accomplish this transformation?

Let us step back from our close inspection of Webster's argument momentarily to take a longer and broader view. Edmund Morgan claims that Euro-American understanding of political representation rests upon the Lincolnian assertion that the US government is 'a government of, by and for the people.'[28] The US government, as a representative republic, roots its claim to sovereignty in the sovereignty and the consent of 'the people' whom, as Webster so forcefully argued, legislative representatives represented. But this assertion of representativeness and consent, Morgan continues, was a fiction originated by members of Britain's Long Parliament who 'invented the sovereignty of the people in order to claim it for themselves'. 'In the name of the people,' Morgan continues, 'they became all powerful in government, shedding as much as possible the local subject character that made them representatives of a particular set of people . . . In this transformation, government . . . [became] something other, something external to the local community.'[29]Using the fiction of mimetically representing the people, within representative republics, 'the People's' representatives assume the right to govern in the name of the people. But in the act of assuming such governmental powers, they become radically unlike – and more powerful than – the people they claim to represent. Indeed, as we saw in Webster's arguments, they proceed to assert their right not only to govern for, but, absolutely, to govern their constituents. The people, in their turn, from being sovereign political subjects become subject to the sovereign political power of the representative legislative assembly. Mimetic representation thus slides into metaphoric representation — a form of representation in which the representative (or signifier, to adopt the earlier semiotic vocabulary of Roland Barthes) is decidedly different from that which is represented (the signified). Yet for a metaphor to work, the signifier, by its nature not what it represents, must be made to seem to be like what it represents. It must be able to stand in its place, to appear to represent it. The success of the fiction that Lincoln's quote invokes, and which Morgan seeks to disclose, rests on being able to absolutely maintain the coexistence of mimetic and metaphoric forms of representation, or rather on the ability of the mimetic to cover and obscure the underlying and empowering metaphoric form.[30]

Thus it is that, while within Webster's argument a mimetic relation between political representatives and political subjects is asserted, those political representatives are already different from and superior to those they claim to represent. Like so many other of his fellow Federalist editors, Webster insisted that political representatives, far from perfectly representing the political subjects who elected them, must be their superiors in education, wealth, breadth of vision and political experience.[31]

But even more tellingly, by the act of being elected legislators, political representatives became capable of initiating and passing legislation, that is, of governing. They thus became doubly unlike those they represented and now governed. 'The right of election,' Webster's argument insisted 'is . . . not merely one, . . . it is the only legislative or constitutional act, which the people at large can properly exercise.' Once political subjects as electors had chosen their representatives, they must submit to be governed by them. 'Possess[ing] all their powers,' the political 'representatives are therefore master of the people.' Representatives subsume, take over, cover that which they represent – in late-eighteenth-century Federal political theory, as in late-twentieth-century post-structuralist theories of language and representation.

Federalist spokesmen, such as Webster, adamantly denied the electors' right to instruct or otherwise influence the votes of their representatives. The representative's claim – and hence the representative republic's claim – to civic virtue rested on the representative's absolute independence from 'pressure' from his constituents. Indeed, Federalist concepts of political representation transformed the legislative representative from being his

own constituents' representative to the state to being the state's representative to those constituents. 'I am sensible', Webster expostulated in a
January, 1788 essay in his *American Magazine*,

> that it is a favorite idea in this country, bandied about from one demagogue
> to another, that rulers are the servants of the people . . . The truth is, a
> Representative . . . as a Representative of a State, . . . is invested with a share
> of the sovereign authority, and is so far a Governor of the people. In short,
> the collective body of Representatives . . . are . . . masters, rulers, governors . . .

Judicious and well-informed, seeing beyond the special interests of his
constituents, invested in the powers of the sovereign state, the political
representative must guide and govern his political subjects as the
paterfamilias governed his wife and children.

It is interesting that, having condemned women as the ultimate
corruptors of the pure male republic because they lacked independence
and rational agency (we must remember that women are effaced in all
the US's founding documents – the Declaration of Independence, the
Constitution), political representation, as represented by the 'founding
fathers', combined mimetic and metaphoric forms of representation in
the very way that the eighteenth-century Anglo-American marriage
contract did – and to precisely the same end, to empower the representative
in relation to the figure represented. In fact, striking parallels exist between
political representation and marriage relationships. In marriage, the
husband and wife became one and that one was the husband; so, as the
result of political elections, the political subject and the political
representative became one and that one was the representative. As the
wife, once married, lost her legal subjectivity, so the political subject after
the election relinquishes his political sovereignty and power to his
representative. As the wife could not resist the authority of the husband,
who had the right to discipline her, so the political subject cannot resist
the authority (and legislation) of his representative who has the right
through that legislation to discipline him. Husband and political
representative were positioned as master and governor, the political subject
and wife, subject to their rule.

Seen from this perspective, the act of participating in a political election
becomes the analogue of the act of participating in the marriage contract.
Both constitute contracts that the participants enter at least fictively as
equals. The woman, as a femme sole, possesses legal and economic
autonomy and, hence, subjectivity. She and the man she chooses as her
husband are both free agents contracting to form a family. At the time of

the election, the political elector and the man he chooses as his political representative, are also, fictively, at least, equal. They are both free agents contracting to form a government. Both the marriage and the election contract establish relations of subordination. As that subordination is the product of contractual agreements, as Carol Pateman argues, it masquerades as freedom. The masquerade is furthered by the fact that both contracts presume the consent of all the contractors, and prescribe and thus limit the type of power that can be exercised and the degree of subordination imposed in terms of kind and time. The husband's powers end with the end of the marriage, the political representative's with the end of his term in office and the new election. But now we see that the woman is in fact positioned more powerfully than the elector is. If she does not remarry, as a widow, she regains her legal and economic subjectivities. But the elector will never regain his political sovereignty. He always loses it again with the next election – whether he chooses to vote (contract) or not. He can never become a political widow. Within the representative republic, as constructed by Federalist rhetoric, the political subject must always be governed – otherwise democracy and hence anarchy would ensue. Nor should we forget that the Anglo-American marriage contract, just described, ceased to exist some time during the nineteenth century. Federalist construction of the representative process still governs us.

V

As it made the political subject subject to his political representative, so Federalist rhetoric subjected the political state to its economic, that is, capitalist, subjects. In doing so, Federalist rhetoric again challenged classical republican understanding of the power relations between the state and its subjects. The virtuous republican subject devoted himself to the honour of his republic, sacrificing his self-interest to the general good. Informed by liberal humanist concepts of both the legal and the social contract, Federalist rhetoric inverted this power relationship, making the political state like its private subjects — and subject to their example. Rhetorical analogies make Federalist inversions of classical republicanism explicit. Phrases such as 'Honest nations, like honest men', 'contracting nations . . . like individuals', 'contracts between nations like contracts between individuals' abounded in Federalist magazines. The result? The repositioning of 'nations as . . . individuals.' If 'honest nations' were 'like honest men', then the Federalist state must govern its behaviour upon that of its subjects. As another author explained: 'Societies, Sir, become respectable on the same principle by which the character of an individual is maintained. Dishonesty in either is equally opposed to wisdom.'

As these quotations indicate, the Federalist political state was not only like and, consequently, subject to the example of its private subjects – it was subject to and modelled upon specific kinds of private subjects, its economic subjects — men of commerce, merchants, shopkeepers and speculators in public credit, fundholders, stockjobbers.[32] These subjects, figured as suspect and potentially corrupting within earlier classical republican discourses, on the pages of the new urban press emerged as empowered and idealized figures, exemplars for the new federal government. As merchants were bound by their private contracts, so the new nation was bound by its public contracts, quite literally, that is, by its bonds. 'The duty . . . perhaps even the existence of a country, are involved in the performance of its contracts', a member of the Massachusetts General Court argued. The author of an essay 'On the Redemption of Public Securities' made the demand that the state model itself on contracting subjects unmistakable. 'In private life,' he wrote, 'the man who avails himself of artifice and fraud will soon find his character blasted, and himself the object of contempt, while he who, encompassed with difficulties, maintains an honest course, may hope for the friendship of man, and the favour of heaven.' 'The same,' he continued pointedly, 'will be the case in states . . . so long as "Righteousness exalteth a nation."'[33]

Three radical and interrelated changes follow this initial inversion of the classical republican power relation between the political state and its economic subjects. The first was to privilege the maintenance of public contracts above every other form of state responsibility. Honouring its private contracts became the highest form of public good and responsibility. The second was to reposition a particular class of economic subjects, merchants and fiscal speculators as 'the public'. A third parallel move repositioned the political state as a private economic contractor. Let us look at each in its turn.

'When [a state] . . . makes grants or contracts,' Noah Webster, always willing to lecture his readers, explained to New Yorkers in the midst of the New York State's ratification debates,

> it acts as a party, and cannot take back its grant or change the nature of its contracts . . . A state has no more right to neglect or refuse to fulfill its engagements, than an individual . . . Bargains, conveyances, and voluntary grants, where two parties are concerned, are sacred things – they are the supports of social confidence and security – they ought not to be sported with . . . – they should be religiously observed.[34]

The state 'cannot hesitate a moment about . . . [rendering] justice to the public creditors' a Massachusetts state legislator argued similarly about his own state's Revolutionary War debt.

As this last quotation makes explicit, Federalist rhetoric had repositioned speculators, fundholders and stockjobbers as public creditors, or even more generally, as 'the public', whose faith the commercial state must constantly court. Another Federalist writer, making the implicit shift in power relations between commercial state and economic subject explicit, denominated public creditors, 'the barometer, Mr. Speaker, of modern power; . . . [they] explain the strength of a community beyond the calculations of arithmetic' – or, presumably, of individual political subjects/electors.

Having repositioned private investors, as 'the public' – indeed, as the very barometers of state credibility and credit-ability – Federalist rhetoric repositioned the new nation as a 'private' contractor. As a commercial state, that is, the new federal government had to solicit its private economic subjects for their venture capital. It had, in short, become the object of the evaluating and appraising gaze of its private speculating subjects. As such, it was required to (re)present itself to the public gaze of those speculating subjects as desirable and, yes, desiring (of credit). At the same time, it had to present itself as above reproach, its fiscal virtue intact, its credit, credit-able.

In all these poses, the Federalist state, consciously or unconsciously, mimicked the traditional behaviour of a respectable woman – and found itself positioned as a respectable woman was positioned. The respectable woman, like the commercial state, had to represent herself to the male (public) gaze as a desirable and desirous object. And, like the commercial state, she also had to represent herself as above public (male) reproach, her virtue intact. In both the respectable woman's and the commercial state's complex juggling acts, everything – virtue, honour, credibility and credit-ability – depended upon (re)presentation, appearance and opinion.

In constituting a credit-conscious political state, Federalist rhetoric endowed the political state with what Frances Ferguson has called 'a derived identity', an identity that depended more upon the reception its public/private subjects gave it than upon intentions or even actions of its statesmen. The new nation's legitimacy thus no longer rested simply on the consent of its political subjects, but upon its capitalist economic subjects' 'repeated gesture of imagining the government as if it were an individual whose credit-worthiness one were continually assessing' – assessing as we have seen eighteenth-century men continually assessed the credibility of the virtue of a middle-class woman who had entered the marriage market, in the same way as that woman's identity as virtuous depended upon appearances and the opinions those appearances inspired.[35] This was, as John Agnew so aptly reminds us, the age of the spectator.

Not only did Federalist rhetoric position the political state as subject to and object of the evaluating gaze of its male economic subjects – it ensnared that state in an impenetrable web of economic dependencies. The credibility and value of the Federalist political state was now dependent upon the opinion of its creditors, men of paper and commerce, fancy and speculation. These men were, in their turn, dependent on their creditors, as credit was dependent on appearances and appearances, on acts of presentation. The chain of dependencies stretched on interminably. And all eighteenth-century political theory had made manly independence and self-reliance key to civic virtue, while associating dependency with corruption, degeneracy – and the feminine.

As the representative republic lived within a world of fiction and masquerade, so the commercial state played its roles upon a theatrical stage where speculation and the spectacular met in the gaze. Within this world, appearance, presentation, opinion, fantasy, the spectacular – in short all that had traditionally been defined as feminine – became pre-eminent. Martial courage, manly independence, self reliance, industry – the watchwords of earlier republican male discourses – were marginalized, indeed rendered irrelevant and old fashioned. Of course sovereignty rests ultimately with the state. The state can choose not to court its capitalist subjects. Or can it? Within a capitalist economy, does a state have that choice?

Money, paper money, stocks, bonds, securities, the fiscal revolution and innovations of the long eighteenth century, were central to this theatrical world of speculation and the spectacular. Indeed, money became the ultimate form of representation and credit became its ultimate problematization. 'Money is a mere representation of property', Noah Webster had argued. A form of representation, it cannot be what it represents. It is not wealth, Webster noted, for 'the wealth of a country is its products . . . [and] its industrious inhabitants . . . The laboring men are the support of the nation' – as they are the representative republic's root source of political sovereignty. In this way money's function within a system of economic representation parallels the legislative represent-ative's function within a system of political representation. Both stand for actual subjects — the political subject and the industrious economic subject. But as objects of representation within Federalist political and economic rhetoric, both the virtuous political subject and the industrious economic subject lose their subject status, their capacity for agency, indeed the right to represent themselves. Indeed, we find them slipping into the role of negative other. Federalist rhetoric represents both as passionate, self-interested, lacking self-control, prone to extravagance and demagoguery. Both, therefore, must be prevented from exercising undue influence upon their political representatives and their economic representatives, that is money, credit and commercial paper.

Upon the pages of the Federalist press, popular efforts to secure state passage of paper money bills epitomized the threat the fused political subject/labouring man could pose to the orderly processes of metaphoric representation. We have seen Federalist rhetoric deny the political subject's right to influence his political representative. So did Federalist rhetoric seek to restrain the industrious subject from uniting with his other self, the political subject/elector, to secure legislation that would regulate his economic representative, money. 'Money will go where it is wanted' Webster insisted. 'Hence the mistaken policy of those people who attempt to increase the medium of trade by coinage or by paper money' — both legislative acts. 'They can add to the quantity . . . but not to the value' of money. Popular demands for land banks and state-authorized paper money to deal with the severe fiscal crises and depression of the 1780s had to be resisted – if necessary suppressed with force, as Shay's rebellion illustrates. Within Federalist discourse, money, like political sovereignty, floats above the power of those who are its source.

VI

Federalist rhetoric presents us with a decentred world of sliding dependencies – a world, as well, of interchangeable and hence of exchangeable subjectivities and genders. Just as commerce and paper money made value and property exchangeable and interchangeable, they had made a sovereign state's credit and honour interchangeable and hence exchangeable. Indeed, in this theatrical world of spectacles and spectators, as in Shakespeare's *Merchant of Venice,* all was interchangeable and exchangeable. As actors were men of commerce, so men of commerce had become actors.[36] The political state became a private contractor, just as its private subjects became its 'public'. And as a private contractor, the political state became as well the feminized object of private subjects' 'public' gaze. In its turn, that 'public' became both audience and consumers of the political state – as the political state was subject to its subjects. Now civic virtue – that bastion of martial vigour and manly independence – had become dependent upon performance and display, opinion and reception – just as women were. In short, public and private, political and economic, male and female, virtue and presentation, appearance and perception fused and confused with one another in a theatrical, spectacular world in which all the old certainties were gone. Federalist rhetoric during the debates over the constitution had indeed, as Gordon Wood phrased it, inscribed 'The End of Classical Politics'.

Notes

1. This is obviously a reference to Abraham Lincoln's Gettysburg Address and to Edmund Morgan's (1988) play on that address in his book *Inventing the People. The Rise of Popular Sovereignty in England and America*, New York: W.W. Norton. See discussion later in this essay.

2. Cultural approaches to discursive and symbolic systems of representation make significant contributions to the historian's understanding of theories of political representation. The vanishing point in perspectival art, the cohesive subject/viewer who perceived that point, the rational political subject, imaginary money (that is, commercial paper) — all constituted interdependent building blocks in the development of modern systems of representation. Crucial to that development was the introduction of the concept of 'zero' into European representational systems during the thirteenth century — an introduction that was itself the result of trade between the merchants of Venice and the Arab world: Rotman, B. (1987), *Signifying Nothing. The Semiotics of Zero,* New York: St. Martin's Press, 4–5. I am indebted to Phyllis Rackin both for bringing Rotman's study to my attention and, more generally, for introducing me to the intricacies of Renaissance representation. For an overview of recent critical analyses of representation see Mitchell, W.J.T. (1995), 'Representation,' in Lentricchio, F. and McLaughlin, T. (eds), *Critical Terms for Literary Study* Chicago: University of Chicago Press, 11–22.

3. See Joyce Appleby's (1978), classic, *Economic Thought and Ideology in Seventeenth-Century England*, Princeton: Princeton University Press; Dickson, P.G.M. (1967), *The Financial Revolution in England: A Study of the Development of Public Credit,* London: Macmillan; Hirschman, A.O. (1977), *The Passion and the Interests. Political*

Arguments for Capitalism before Its Triumph, Princeton: Princeton University Press; and MacPherson, C.B. (1962), *The Political Theory of Possessive Individualism. Hobbes to Locke,* Oxford: Clarendon.

4. The subordination of the individual citizen to state governance and to community cohesion is critical to all classic republican theorists from Hobbes, through Locke to Rousseau. For a particularly perceptive exploration of Rousseau's thoughts along these lines see Wingrove, E. (1996), 'Republican Romance', unpublished manuscript, Center for the Study of Social Transformation, University of Michigan.

5. Agnew, J.-C. (1986), *Worlds Apart: The Market and the Theater in Anglo-American Thought, 1550–1750* Cambridge and New York: Cambridge University Press, 1986, see, especially, the prologue and chapter 1.

6. Let me again refer to Agnew's highly suggestive examination of the problematics of exchange in commercializing British and American societies. For an analysis of the constitution of a new American subject on the pages of the American popular press see my essay (1992), 'Discovering the Subject of the "Great Constitutional Discussion", 1786–88', *Journal of American History*, 79 (December): 841–73.

7. For a discussion of the emergence of a public print culture, see Michael Warner, *Empire of Letters*

8. Six political magazines were published during the ratification debates: *American Museum* (Philadelphia), Columbia Magazine and *Monthly Miscellany* (Philadelphia), *American Magazine* (New York City), *New Jersey Magazine* (New Brunswick), Worcester Magazine (Worcester, Massachusetts, *Massachusetts Magazine* (Boston).

9. For the classic study of the engendering of the republic see Carol Pateman, *Sexual Contract*. Although my essay focuses on the engendering of the Euro-American national identity, issues of race at all times hovered in the shadows. As Evelyn Brooks Higginbotham has so persuasively argued, race and gender must always be studied interactively. When race seems most absent from discourses on gender it is of course most present. Higginbotham, E.B. (1992), 'African-American Women's History and the Metalanguage of Race', *Signs*, 17, (2): 251–74. See also Morrison, T. (1992), *Playing in the Dark. Whiteness and the Literary Imagination* Cambridge: Harvard University Press.

10. For a discussion of the multiple discourses that made up late eighteenth-century Euro-American political rhetoric see Kramnick

(1988), '"The Great National Discussion"; The Discourse of Politics in 1787', *William and Mary Quarterly*, 45, (January), 3–32; Nash, *Urban Crucible*, 219–24; Smith-Rosenberg, 'Dis-covering the Subject of "The Great National Discussion"'; Rogers M. Smith, 'The Tocquevillian Thesis Reconsidered,' work in progress.

11. For a summary of commercial republicanism see Kramnick, '"The Great National Discussion"'.

12. Appleby, *Capitalism and a New Social Order*. For critiques of liberal political and legal theory see Pateman, *Sexual Contract* and Braidotti, R. (1991), *Patterns of Dissonance*, trans. Elizabeth Guild, London and New York: Routlege.

13. Smith-Rosenberg, 'Dis-covering the Subject', 855–7. For a general discussion of women's discrediting within eighteenth-century Euro-American political discourses see Kerber, L. (1980), *Women of the Republic: Intellect and Ideology in Revolutionary American* Chapel Hill: University of North Carolina Press; Block, R. (1985), *Visionary Republic: Millennial Themes in American Thought, 1756–80,* Cambridge: Cambridge University Press.

14. Smith, R.M. (1989), '"One United People": Second-Class Female Citizenship and the American Quest for Community', *Yale Journal of Law and the Humanities,* I, (2): 229–93, especially 241–48. For a comparison with European political thought see Landis, J.B. (1988), *Women and the Public Sphere in the Age of the French Revolution* Ithaca: Cornell University Press; Hunt, L. (1991), 'The Many Bodies of Marie Antoinette: Political Pornography and the Problem of the Feminine in the French Revolution', in Hunt, L. (ed.) *Eroticism and the Body Politic*, Baltimore: Johns Hopkins University Press, 108–30; Fraisse, G. (1994), *Reason's Muse. Sexual Difference and the Birth of Democracy,* Trans. Jane Marie Todd Chicago: University of Chicago Press; Linda M.G. Zerilli (1994), *Signifying Woman. Culture and Chaos in Rousseau, Burke, and Mill.* Ithaca: Cornell University Press.

15. For a discussion of the tensions issues of gender engendered within America's emergent middle-class discourses see Smith-Rosenberg, C. (1988), 'Domesticating Virtue', in Elaine Scarry, ed, *Literature and the Body Essays on Populations and Persons* Baltimore: Johns Hopkins University Press. It is critical to note that middle-class spokesmen shifted classical republicanism's grounding of political virtue from landed estates to economic productivity at precisely the same time that ideological changes associated with an emergent middle-class culture increasingly stressed respectable women's

domesticity. A family's claim to middle-class respectability increasingly required married women not to be economically employed. Unmarried women might well lose status if employed as midwives, tavern keepers, even as printers, although these had been highly respected employments for women in the early and mid eighteenth century. Middle-class women could turn to writing and *lower* middle-class single women to teaching, shopkeeping, even to work in the Lowell Mills or domestic weaving, but true middle-class gentility demanded a woman live a life of leisure or benevolent volunteerism. Far more central, married women's earnings and inheritance belonged to her husband except in those relatively rare instances where a premarital contract had been drawn up placing the woman's money in trust. See Linda Kerber, *Women of the Republic*, Marylynn Salmon, *Women and the Law of Property in Early America* Chapel Hill: University of North Carolina Press, 1986; and Kenneth Lockridge, 'Colonial Self-Fashioning: Paradoxes and Pathologies in the Construction of Genteel Identity in Eighteenth-Century America', work in progress.

Some women complained bitterly of their loss of economic autonomy. See letters and diary entries by Annis Boudinot Stockton, her daughter, Julia Stockton Rush and Marian Alexander Williams in the Rush-Williams-Biddle Family Papers, Rosenbach Museum and Library.

16. Rogers Smith makes this point forcefully both in his essay 'One United People' and to me in a private letter.
17. Certainly this is the heart of Pateman's argume in *Sexual Contract*. See, as well, Landis, *Women and the Public Sphere* and Linda Hirshman in 'The Rape of the Locke: Race, Gender and the Loss of Liberal Virtue,' *Stanford Law Review*, 44.
18. See Locke, J. (1988), *Two Treatises of Government*, ed. with an introduction and notes by Peter Laslett Cambridge: Cambridge University Press, Book I, no. 48, 49, 67. See, also Kerber's germinal concept of 'Republican Motherhood', *Women and the Revolution*.
19. Pocock, *Machiavellian Moment*, chapters XI and XII.
20. Wood, *Creation of the American Republic*, chapter V, especially 162–88.
21. Cited by Wood, 168–94.
22. (1787), 'Maxims for Republics', *American Museum*, (11 July): 80–2.
23. (1787), Camillus, 'Letter II,' *American Museum*, (11 October): 381–21.

24. (1787), 'Maxims for Republics,' *American Museum*, (11 July): 81.
25. The *Improver*, No. LXX. (1787), 'Ludicrous thoughts on money' *Columbian Magazine*, 1 September 1787, 646–49.
26. Hickory, G. (1788), [Noah Webster], 'Government', *American Magazine*, (1 January), 75–80. Significantly having insisted that while possessing all the power of the state gave legislators an unlimited power to do good, Webster also admitted in this same paragraph that it also gave them 'an unlimited power to do wrong'.
27. Hickory, G. [Noah Webster] (1787), 'On Bills of Rights', *American Magazine*, (1 December), 13–15 and Hickory G. (1788), 'Government,' *American Magazine*, (1 March), 204–10.
28. Morgan, *Inventing the People*, 56–8 and Chapter 3, *passim*.
29. Morgan, *Inventing the People*, 49–50, 267.
30. Roland Barthes discusses the relation of the signifier and signified at length in his early semiotic essay, 'Myth Today' in his *Mythologies*. He does so in ways that greatly empower the signified in contrast to the ways current post-structuralist discussion of representation disempower that which is represented or signified.
31. Hickory, G. (1788) [Noah Webster], 'Thoughts on the political situation of the United States, etc.', *American Magazine*, 1 October, 804–9 and Hickory, 'Government,' 204–10.
32. 'On Public Faith,' 405–12; 'Circular Letter transmitted by the United States in Congress Assembled, to the Governors of the respective states, April, 1787','397–401; 'On the Redemption of Public Securities,' 415–17; 'On Establishing a Sinking Fund in Pennsylvania . . .', 487–91; 'Thoughts on the Present Situation of Public Affairs,' 306–10.
33. At times this fusion of governmental and mercantile identity became absolute, as when the author of 'Remarks and facts relative to the American paper-money', wrote admiringly of Holland, as a responsible businessman dealing in paper money and manipulator of credit. 'Holland, which understands the value of cash . . . would never part with gold and silver for credit . . . if they did not think and find the credit a full equivalent.'

By subjecting the state to its own subjects, Federalist rhetoric not only refused time-honoured civic humanist assumptions of subject deference, it began to confuse the equally time-honoured fusion of 'the people' as the abstracted source of political sovereignty with the public and the government. Let us look at a comment made in passing by the author of 'On the Redemption of Public Securities'. 'If individuals be defrauded to save money for the public', he warned, 'jealousy will spread among the people, government will fall into contempt and anarchy ensue.' This sentence distinguishes four separate actors: defrauded individual contractors, 'the public', 'the people', 'the government'. It then refuses the relations traditionally assigned these actors. Rather than associating 'the people' with 'the government', as republicans had done since the parliamentary protests of the 1640s, and which the new constitution's evocation of 'We, THE PEOPLE', so emphatically did, this sentence associated 'the people' with defrauded individuals and made 'the people' contempt-uous of a government which sought to save money for 'the public'. Thus it not only separates 'the people' from the representative legislature, it presumes 'the people' with interests separate from, indeed, at odds with, 'the public's'. At the same time, it also disting-uishes 'the public' as a separate socio/economic entity, separate from 'the government,' by representing 'the government' as seeking to save 'the public's' money.

34. American [Noah Webster] (1787), 'Principles of Government and Commerce', *American Magazine,* (1 December): 9–12.

35. Frances Ferguson, unpublished comments on an early draft of this essay, University of Pennsylvania Seminar on the Diversity of Language and the Structure of Power. This invocation of the sexual and the feminine in analysing Federalist repositioning of the male political subject are supported by the magazines' rhetoric. See, for example, the language one advocate used to couple the adoption of the constitution with the redemption of the government's paper money: 'When the promise is once plighted [paper money, bonds issued], government that moment descends to the rank of an individual and all it has to do, is to fall on some effectual measures to fulfill its engagements.' 'Political Sketches inscribed to his excellency John Adams . . .', 230; 'Speech of a member of the General Court of Massachusetts . . .', 'On the Question whether the Public Securities should be redeemed at their Current Value', *American Museum,* 1, 22–45, 412–17.

36. Franklin, B. (1987), *Autobiography* in the Franklin volume of the Library of America, ed. J. A. Leo Lemay, New York: Viking.

–14–

Nationalizing Women and Engendering the Nation: The Czech National Movement*

Jitka Malečková

Our nation is democratic in its character and filled with love of justice. The whole course of Czech history shows the fine character of Czech women, their goodheartedness, their fine relations to the men, the esteem and hearty collaboration between both sexes. We have a number of mythical and historical women-characters showing this kernel of the people; so the three mythical daughters of Krok: Libuša, princess and prophetess in one person, who is believed to have founded Prague; Teta, a priestess and Kazi, a physician [sic] . . .[1]

Claiming that 'esteem and hearty collaboration between both sexes' was a distinct feature of the Czech nation, Františka Plamínková, one of the most prominent and radical representatives of the Czech women's movement, expressed a view which, by 1920, had long roots in Czech national discourse. Her reference to history, to the status of women as proof of the democratic character of the nation, and to mythical heroines in connection with both, was similarly symptomatic of this discourse.

Today, historians in the Czech Republic are not concerned with the relationship between women and nationalism. While Western scholars emphasize the strong impact of nationalism on the emerging Czech women's movement,[2] recent studies of the Czech national movement usually completely neglect the aspects related to gender.[3] The emerging discourse on gender issues in the Czech Republic is not based on the study of history. Yet, feminists and their opponents tend to agree in their identification of a tradition of gender equality as a characteristic feature of Czech society. This view, echoing Plamínková's claim, undoubtedly

* The chapter is part of a research project supported by a grant from the Research Support Scheme of the Open Society Institute/Higher Education Support Program.

deserves closer attention, the more so because, despite a lack of historical evidence, it forms a part of the Czechs' self-perception.

The aim of this chapter is not to deconstruct the myth of gender harmony, but to show its origins in the way images of women and of gender relations were constructed and used in the early Czech national movement. This is manifested by the example of two mythical heroines: princess Libuše, the founder of Prague and of the ruling medieval dynasty,

Figure 14.1 Vlasta, the leader of the women's revolt. Drawing by Mikoláš Aleš from 1899. (In: Mikoláš Aleš, Fatherland and Nation: Pictures from History, Prague 1940.)

and Vlasta, the leader of a women's revolt against male rule. Czech national discourse employed other female images as well, but as mythical heroines Libuše and Vlasta were particularly suited to nationalist invention and reinterpretation. The changing representation and gradual incorporation of the two figures, potentially contradictory to each other, into Czech national mythology demonstrates how the construction of femininity was adapted to the needs of the national movement.

This chapter focuses on the constitutive period of the Czech national movement, from the 1780s to the 1880s. After a brief introduction to Czech history, it follows the nationalization of the mythical heroines in the first half of the nineteenth century, and their popularization between the 1860s and 1880s, when their images spread in the national culture and were adopted by the women's movement. The following years brought further differentiation and new emphases into the interpretation of women's images. The myth of gender harmony, however, was well established by the late 1880s.

Women and the Czech National Movement

In 1526 the Bohemian Crown-Lands, Bohemia, Moravia and Silesia, which had formed the medieval kingdom of Bohemia, were incorporated into the Habsburg Empire. The autonomy of the land's institutions and the power of its elites were curtailed, particularly after the defeat of the uprising of the Bohemian estates in 1620. The strengthening of Habsburg rule after the uprising was accompanied by the persecution and emigration of non-Catholic Czech elites, intellectuals and nobility, and the re-Catholicization of the rest of the population. The following period was marked by an enhancement of the position of the German language in culture, particularly among the upper and middle classes, and in towns.

The Czech national movement thus emerged in the late eighteenth century within a non-dominant group in a multinational empire, lacking a national nobility. Like other movements in similar circumstances, it paid special attention to culture. The first phase of the national movement, from the late eighteenth century to the second decade of the nineteenth century, was characterized by a new enthusiasm for and scholarly interest in Czech language, culture and history. The role of history remained essential throughout the nineteenth century. The construction of a national history, starting with the mythical early Slavic past, through the independent medieval Bohemian Kingdom, and up to the Hussite movement – regarded as the peak of national history – was meant to show the Czechs as well as the outside world the advanced character and achievements of the Czech nation and its right to determine its own fate. From the 1860s, historical arguments (particularly references to the medieval state) were often used in political programmes.

In the second phase of the national movement, from the late 1810s to the 1840s, the growing group of patriots saw their mission in 'awakening' the nation and tried to spread national awareness. The 1840s witnessed an increasing interest in political aspects of nationalism, and in notions of civil liberties and equality as well as a widening of the social basis of the national struggle. The development of patriotic activities was interrupted by the reimposition of absolutism following the revolution of 1848. Thus, the third phase of the national movement, characterized by mass participation, began only in the more liberal 1860s, after the proclamation of a constitution. Czech political life was then led by the (increasingly conservative) liberal Old Czechs and their more radical opponents, the Young Czechs. Further political diversification occurred in the late nineteenth century, starting with the founding of the Social Democratic Party in 1878.

The early patriotic activities of the late eighteenth century were limited to a small group of men – scholars and literati. In the nineteenth century, the urban middle and lower-middle classes, liberal professionals and civil servants, and, from the 1860s also entrepreneurs, were best represented among the national leaders. Students, artisans, tradesmen and peasants joined the movement in the 1840s, and the 1860s were marked by a growing participation of the rural population and of the working class.[4]

Women increasingly attracted the attention of male patriots in the second stage of the national movement, from the 1820s on, when national activists tried to win over their compatriots to the national cause. Facing the success of Germanization, particularly among the urban population, patriotic men discovered the potential of women in their role of mothers. Women were to educate their children as Czech patriots and teach them to speak Czech and to take pride in their Czech origin. Especially in this period, when the number of active patriots was still rather limited, it seemed essential to draw in women as partners in the national struggle.

This was also the period when individual women started to become involved in cultural life, participating in amateur theatrical performances and publishing poems. The first woman who earned her living through writing, however, was the novelist Božena Němcová, towards the mid-nineteenth century. Efforts to improve women's education aimed to prepare patriotically minded mothers as teachers of a new generation. In the 1840s, the scope of women's activities and interests widened, and in the revolutionary atmosphere of 1848, the first two Czech women's associations were founded.

The more influential associations that emerged since the 1860s had similar goals: to prepare girls from the lower-classes for gainful employment and members of the middle-class, for housework and family life. Yet, while the more conservative branch, led by Marie Riegrová (whose father, František Palacký, and husband, František Ladislav Rieger, were both renowned Czech politicians) did not want to go beyond philanthropy, more radical women believed in women's right to education, employment and participation in public life. Even the latter branch of the women's movement, represented from 1865 by the American Ladies' Club and by the Czech Women's Trade Association founded in 1871, was not united in its views on women's roles. The differences among the women, however, were often revealed in literary works rather than in the activities of their organizations. Some writers and active members of the women's groups, like Žofie Podlipská, saw women primarily as mothers and emphasized their probity and their obligations towards the nation. The heroines in the novels of her sister, Karolína Světlá, a leading figure in both the Ladies' Club and the Trade Association, were more complex. They were similarly patriotic and willing to sacrifice themselves for men or for higher principles, but, at the same time, they were active, often stronger than men and occasionally independent.

Writers had an exceptional place among publicly active Czech women as well as in the organized women's movement. In the 1880s, another writer, Eliška Krásnohorská, daughter of a craftsman, led women's efforts for access to higher education and for equal professional opportunities. In 1890, the former resulted in the founding of the first girls' 'gymnasium', a secondary school preparing its students for university, in the Habsburg Empire.

From its very beginnings, the social basis of the women's movement consisted almost entirely of middle-class women from Prague and a few other major towns. The late 1880s, which form the chronological endpoint of this chapter, were also a turning point in the women's movement. The 1890s were marked by the spread of women's associations around the country, the involvement of women from wider social strata and the emergence of working-class women's organizations. The spectrum of women's activities widened and so did their aims, ranging from the moral elevation of women to suffrage. Although representatives of women's organizations as well as of the new generation of writers, both men and women, held different views on women and femininity, they all drew upon and had to come to terms with concepts established in the constitutive period of the national – and women's – movement.

From Mythology to National Myth: Libuše and Vlasta

After Father Czech had brought his people to the Czech lands, the traditional tale tells us, there was a wise man named Krok whose opinion was respected by all. Krok had no sons, but three exceptionally talented daughters. When he died, the youngest of them, the prophetess Libuše, was elected judge – or princess – of her people. She ruled fairly and was loved by everyone until a man, resenting her verdict in a property suit, denounced the rule of a woman over men. Libuše then agreed to cede the throne to a strong man, proposing to marry whomever the people might choose as their prince. She predicted that this would be a plough-man, Přemysl (hence, the origins of the ruling Přemyslide dynasty). Libuše also foretold the founding of Prague – or, in some versions of the story, founded it herself. After her death, women, accustomed to freedom, challenged male rule and, like ancient Amazons, launched a war against men. Led by Vlasta, they fought successfully for many years before they were defeated.

At the beginning of the national movement, nothing suggested that Libuše and Vlasta were to become national heroines. Their story was well known from medieval and early modern chronicles and from later, mainly German, literary adaptations, but it did not seem particularly useful for national needs. The early male patriots of the late eighteenth century were not yet concerned with the role of women in the national movement. More importantly, the way Libuše and Vlasta were treated in the sources seemed to offer little opportunity for their patriotic glorification.

The early twelfth-century chronicle of Kosmas paid particular attention to Libuše due to her connection to the emergence of the Bohemian state and its ruling dynasty. For Kosmas, Libuše was 'an adornment and glory of the female sex, giving orders with as much foresight as if she were a man' but, at the same time, a somewhat problematic figure because of her prophesying or 'witchcraft', as he called it. Kosmas only briefly mentioned a war between young women and men, relocating the famous story of Amazons as well as the abduction of Sabine women to Bohemia.[5] Later chroniclers were more intrigued by the women's revolt. They enriched the legend with a number of male and female characters (including Vlasta as the leader of the revolt), additional stories (like that of Šárka outwitting Ctirad), violent images and male-female dichotomies. Through the fifteenth-century Czech history of Aeneas Silvius (Pope Pius II) and the popular sixteenth-century chronicle of Václav Hájek, which was translated into German in 1596 and published again in the seventeenth century, these elaborations made their way into European culture.

From the seventeenth century, the story served as a basis for several Italian and a number of German operas, dramas, novels and poems. It inspired even such authors as Herder, Brentano and Grillparzer. In most literary works, the original narrative was trivialized and rendered as an adventurous love or chivalrous story where neither the Czechs nor the female heroines were depicted in a particularly favourable light: Libuše and Vlasta took and sometimes even murdered numerous lovers.[6]

Such were the images with which the Czech audience became acquainted by the end of the eighteenth century. Half a century later, Libuše and Vlasta had been integrated into the Czech national culture. The process of nationalization, however, did not consist of a simple spread of a new, unified narrative. Different images of Libuše and Vlasta which were created both under the direct impact of earlier sources, and in explicit contradiction to them, coexisted in the emerging Czech national culture.

The first type of image was presented in works that drew on the earlier literary tradition and used the story merely for entertainment, without any moral or nationalistic overtones. In the late eighteenth and early nineteenth centuries, the women's revolt appeared in early Czech literary production by well-known, though not leading representatives of the first phase of the national movement – Václav Thám, Prokop Šedivý and Šebestián Hněvkovský. Similar works continued to appear in the following stage. In the 1820s and 1840s, the comedies of Václav Kliment Klicpera and Josef Kajetán Tyl transferred the plot from Czech pre-history to a more recent past, changed the names of the heroes and heroines and generally preserved very little from the original story.[7] The character of Vlasta in particular was connected with farce and subject to ridicule. The misogynistic elements expressed in the plot were also traditional, rather than reflecting new views about gender relations. If there were any patriotic motifs in these works they were definitely not embodied by the heroines.

The second phase of the national movement, however, also witnessed the emergence of a new approach to the mythical heroines. It was influenced by the alleged discovery of the so-called *Manuscript of Zelená Hora* in 1817. This forgery was important for the development of women's images for several reasons. First, it depicted Libuše's judgement in the property suit that led to the establishment of the Přemyslide dynasty. In the trial, young women acted as Libuše's assistants and played a role in the proceedings. Thus, it incorporated Libuše, portrayed as a respected and respectable national heroine, into the narrative of the beginnings of Czech history. Moreover, it presented this early period as a time when women had an important place in society. This would have been just an interesting episode if the *Manuscript* had not been accepted as genuine and the oldest source on early Czech society. Indeed, it was held up as proof of the antiquity and high standard of Czech literary culture. As such it was to influence Czech culture, historiography and national discourse for the rest of the nineteenth century.

Together with the Kosmas *Chronicle*, the forged *Manuscripts* served as a major source in the construction of a master narrative of Czech national history. Historians were generally not concerned with the place of women in contemporary society. They tried to identify and emphasize positive features of Czech history, particularly those that contrasted with the German past. In this context, they also mentioned the characteristics and position of women. This was relevant due to the substantial role played by history in the Czech national movement. The images of ancient women, whether directly or through the mediation of popular literature, thus contributed to the creation of the ideals of Czech womanhood and femininity.

Already, in the late eighteenth century, František Martin Pelcl's *Geschichte der Böhmen* emphasized the exceptional education and knowledge of Libuše and her sisters and Libuše's wisdom and popularity.[8] In 1824, Václav Hanka, one of the authors of the forged manuscripts, elaborated in his *Czech History* in much more detail upon Libuše's rule and particularly upon the women's revolt after her death. It is worth noting that Hanka did not depict Vlasta as a negative figure, but rather saw her as Vlasti-Sláva, 'Glory of the Country'. Despite the cruelties committed by both sides, Hanka appreciated the women's courage. More interestingly, he did not draw any moral lesson from the war; he did not claim, for example, that after their defeat, the women were sent back to their female duties. Hanka's role in the construction of Czech gender relations has been neglected thus far. Apart from the impact of the *Manuscript*, his historical work glorified the early period of Czech history as a golden age, 'filled more with goddesses than gods, more with Libuše and her sisters than with a half-historical, half-mythical man.'[9]

František Palacký, the most famous and influential nineteenth-century Czech historian, called the women's revolt the 'strangest legend' and judged that it was difficult to determine whether it had any basis in fact. He preferred to interpret the revolt as a personal conflict between Vlasta and Přemysl rather than a war between the sexes. Despite his doubts, he referred to 'the brave and noble-minded Vlasta'. He did not question the existence of princess Libuše and cited her rule as proof that personal qualities and not age determined the ruler among the ancient Slavs. Palacký also described family life and the position of women among the early Czechs in the most positive terms, implying that these demonstrated the democratic principles prevailing among the ancient Slavs, in contrast with the Germans.[10]

Although both Libuše and Vlasta were mythical heroines, Libuše, at least, was typically presented as a historical figure. Starting with Pelcl, historians increasingly emphasized that Libuše was elected princess for her character and abilities. They appreciated her knowledge, wisdom and fairness no less than her virtue, modesty and kindness. Even after her marriage with Přemysl, Libuše was not depicted as a mother and keeper of the house, but as a princess who participated in ruling justly over the Czechs and in founding Prague.

Vlasta was accepted by historians with some hesitation. Yet, they did not exclude her historicity *a priori*, which is interesting in itself. The view prevailed that it was impossible to decide whether the women's revolt was a poetic invention or a historical fact. Particularly from the *Manuscript,* historians deduced that during Libuše's reign, women gained various privileges and they might have fought for the preservation of these after Libuše's death.

Libuše appeared as an unquestionably positive figure and Vlasta, despite some doubts about her existence, not as an entirely negative one. Rather, implicitly, both of them were used as evidence of the admirable qualities of the Czech nation, of its democratic spirit, education, or courage, which were manifested even by its women. Both Libuše and Vlasta thus played a significant role in the historical master narrative.

At the same time as their incorporation into national history, new images of Libuše and Vlasta appeared in patriotic literature of the second phase of the national movement, the period in which wider support was sought for the national cause. In 1818, Josef Linda, one of the two scholars linked to the forged *Manuscripts*, published his novel *Light over Heathendom* about the beginnings of Christianity in the Czech lands. In the novel, overshadowed by the celebrated *Manuscripts*, Libuše, Vlasta and Šárka appeared only in one episode, but as clearly positive figures, 'heroic and proud foremothers' and examples for contemporary women.[11]

In the following decades, Libuše and Vlasta got further engrained in the patriotic context, and by the 1840s they figured in national allegories. Libuše embodied Prague,[12] which she had founded, and, more implicitly, the land the glory of which she had predicted. In Jan Kollár's influential *Daughter of Sláva*, Vlasta entered Slavic mythology. The Slavs were represented by mythical female figures, the Germans by a male God. Moreover, as Vladimír Macura has shown, the female principle stood here for the Slavs in general, in contrast to the masculine principle identified with the Germans.[13]

These images were not limited to literature. Josef Navrátil, one of the most famous Czech painters of the first half of the nineteenth century, depicted Vlasta in the early 1840s in a cycle of murals about the women's revolt at the Liběchov castle, and together with Libuše on the frescoes of a Prague house. Although Navrátil's romantic heroines were later sometimes criticized for departing from the national artistic tradition, the context of the paintings was undoubtedly patriotic. It was understood as such by contemporaries who appreciated the works and helped to popularize the theme among the public.[14]

Leaving aside literary and artistic goals, the images of Libuše and Vlasta were used in celebrations of the Czech nation and its glorious past and to encourage national pride. At the same time, they played yet another role, symptomatic of the agitational period of the national movement. As newly established national heroines they were to serve as examples for contemporary women in efforts to gain their support for the national cause. This was manifested particularly in poetry in which male patriots 'expressed our wish for you, our sisters, to favour, in your activities, the Fatherland as well as us.'[15]

Although the reference to Libuše as a princess of the Czechs seemed logical enough,[16] the case of Vlasta was less straightforward. She remained a martial symbol, but her fighting spirit was brought into line. Contemporary Vlastas, it was claimed, were not using their magical power in armed combat but could subdue men by the combination of their female charms and their Czechness, which no Czech man could resist. Yet, the 'proud daughters of Vlasta and Šárka' should only grant their favours to the Czech men who fought for freedom.[17] Even more striking is the image of Vlasta as a symbol of the unity of Czech men and women: Vlasta has proven that among the Czechs even women had courage equal to a man's; therefore, both men and women should serve the common homeland, and women should become men's sisters and allies in this struggle.[18]

Women wrote in the same context and apparently in the same spirit. To be sure, the goal of their works was unquestionably patriotic. The mythical heroines, however, could have a deeper meaning for the first women in patriotic circles than they had for their male comrades. Libuše and Vlasta served as immediate models with whom they could identify and who, showing how important women had been and could be for the nation, gave additional relevance to their activities. This identification offers a possible interpretation of a private act of Magdalena Dobromila Rettigová, a prominent figure of the first generation of women writers.

When dying in 1845, she asked to be put on the floor 'like Libuše' who was said 'to have lain down on the floor and died'.[19]

The poem *To Czech Women* by Božena Němcová, the most famous Czech female writer, is usually quoted today, as it was by her contemporaries, as an example of women's patriotism. The message 'to Czech women' was quite clear: while (strong) men fought with arms, (weak) women should contribute to the national cause by educating their children for the country. Yet, in another poem from 1845, Němcová created a somewhat different image of women – more active, independent and even belligerent. She called on women to rise and create 'regiments of warriors' even if men themselves would not fight, in the name of their famous ancestresses Vlasta and Libuše. 'The country was founded by a woman, let the country be defended by women again.'[20]

During the revolution of 1848, the image of a fighting woman gained a more topical dimension. A young woman was reported to have fought alongside men on the barricades, and she was celebrated in the press of the time. An anonymous song referred to the example of the mythical heroines asking Czech women to 'live and die for freedom' like Libuše and Vlasta whose 'blood boils in their veins'.[21] After the revolution, however, the images became more peaceful again and the call to arms less literal.

Popularization of the Images (1860s–80s)

In 1881, the National Theatre in Prague was opened with the opera *Libuše* by the 'most national' Czech composer Bedřich Smetana.[22] Smetana had saved the opera for more than a decade for this exceptional event, which was seen as a culmination of the Czech national movement. The selection of the story of Libuše for this solemn occasion clearly manifested its place in the national culture and the role of Libuše as a national symbol. The opera was not a unique example. By the 1880s, Libuše and Vlasta had indeed become popular heroines and had made their way into new spheres of cultural life, accessible to a wider audience, such as popular journals, exhibitions, and national festivals. In the sculpture and painted decoration of the National Theatre, whose construction was the major artistic enterprise of the time, Libuše figured both in the Přemyslide myth and independently, together with Vlasta and other heroines of Czech mythology.

Smetana's work was composed as a dynastic opera expressing hopes for the reestablishment of Bohemian statehood and corresponded to the arguments about Czech historical rights used then in the political struggle against Vienna.[23] Libuše was not celebrated as a talented woman but, more than before, as a key figure in the formation of the Bohemian state. The man who offends her, criticizing the rule of a woman over men, is forced to apologize for this 'disgrace', and the opera ends with a happy reconciliation and Libuše's prophecy about the glorious future of the Czech nation. Vlasta, who often appeared in nineteenth-century literary works as Libuše's friend and/or relative, is conspicuously absent.

While in the earlier periods of the national movement Libuše and Vlasta were often connected in literature (though less in historiography) in the second half of the nineteenth century the approach to the two figures was more differentiated. Libuše had become an entirely positive, almost untouchable national heroine and even a sacred national symbol. Vlasta, due to her connection with the women's revolt, was more complex and ambivalent. In poetry, drama and occasionally in the arts and music, the women's revolt continued to appear, as in the early period of the national movement, as a vague background story without an ideological message, as an exotic story or a romantic farce. A new impetus was added by the modern interest in psychology.

An anonymous romantic novel *Vlasta and Šárka, Leaders of the Czech Amazons* from 1864 presented the heroines of the revolt as cruel man-haters.[24] The incorporation of Vlasta into the national mythology, however, had some impact on the cultural production of the second half of the nineteenth century. The negative features of the women's revolt now tended to be represented by the originally marginal figure of Šárka. In the 1850s and 1860s, Šárka appeared as the embodiment of the treachery of the women warriors in several paintings.[25] In the two following decades, Bedřich Smetana, Jaroslav Vrchlický and Julius Zeyer, all prominent Czech cultural figures, depicted Šárka as a passionate, jealous and cruel woman and as the main heroine of works symptomatically entitled *Šárka*.[26] Vlasta was either rendered as an ambivalent figure or did not appear at all, although the marginal Vlasta in Vrchlický's poem was a despotic ruler (and called a monster).

More explicit evidence of the effort to create or affirm the myth of gender harmony is presented, for example, by Josef Václav Frič's dramatic poem *Libuše's Trial* from 1861. His Libuše is both beloved and loving, Šárka is a rebel, while Vlasta, the latter's sister in the drama, is more moderate and understanding and respects Libuše's love for Přemysl, though she does not approve of it. Frič intentionally limited his work to Libuše's rule and omitted the women's revolt in order to be able to conclude the story with a happy ending.[27]

With the popularization of the images beginning in the 1860s, Libuše and Vlasta were also increasingly points of reference for women. The use of the mythical heroines in the names of (mostly quite moderate) women's organizations or journals, reflected the popularity of both figures in contemporary Czech society rather than a struggle for women's civil rights. At the same time, however, the images were used to support claims for women's emancipation.

In the concept of the golden age, which was important in the Czech national movement, modern considerations were reflected significantly. The early national society was not seen merely as a distant and outdated stage of history, but it was directly connected with the contemporary national community and was even to serve as a model for its future relations. Images of women in ancient Czech society thus were of immediate concern to nineteenth-century women. The way they treated the mythical heroines reflected their different understandings of the place of women in contemporary society.

Two novels by the prolific writer Žofie Podlipská, intended for young people, represented a moderate approach that saw a woman mainly as a mother and supporter of her husband. Compared to Smetana/Wenzig's opera, the Libuše in her first novel, from 1889,[28] was less a stateswoman than Podlipská's ideal of womanhood. She was wise, talented, peaceful, honest, faithful, modest and beloved by everyone because she preferred to listen and did not take centre stage. She was elected by men, but respected men's power and views.

Vlasta, in Podlipská's second novel, on the women's revolt,[29] was influenced by the old pagan habits and rites connected with the cult of the cruel goddess Děvana. She loved and respected Libuše and hated men not because she was deceived by a man (a motif in many contemporary works), but because of the cult and her jealousy of Přemysl and his influence over Libuše. She was brave and sometimes well-intentioned, but in her struggle against men became absolutely unfeminine. In this context, Podlipská compared her to a monster. Her most positive qualities appeared when she showed motherly feelings toward Libuše's son after Libuše's death. Šárka was even more cruel, less womanly, and less Czech, being a child of the ancient druids, though even she evinced some 'human' feelings towards Ctirad, whom she had betrayed. In fact, Podlipská came closer to portraying Libuše and Vlasta as contrasting images of womanhood than most of her male compatriots. Unlike Podlipská, who saw Vlasta as the embodiment of an outdated pagan past, a novel by a lesser-known male writer presented Vlasta as a rebel who criticized the backwardness of the early Czech society and expressed new, progressive ideas.[30]

In the emerging debate on the woman question from the late 1860s and especially in the 1880s, both men and women represented images of Libuše and Vlasta and of gender equality and the prominent position of women as characteristic features of the Czech nation, and used them to promote women's rights.[31] While in the previous stages of the national movement these images had been used to prove the quality of the nation, now the equality and achievements of women in ancient society served as a model – and argument – for the present-day reform of women's position.

In this sense Eliška Krásnohorská, one of the leading and more radical representatives of the women's movement and author of libretti for several of Smetana's operas, wrote in her *Czech Woman Question* in 1881 that among pagan Czechs women had never been subordinated to men. She did not even have to mention the names, so clear it was for every contemporary reader that the 'noble and just ruler, wise and noble-minded prophetess' was Libuše and the 'female-fighter and heroine' Vlasta. Women, Krásnohorská argued, should regain the high standing and equality known from old sources in order to be able to benefit the nation again.[32] For Krásnohorská as well as for her successors at the turn of the century, however, the contribution of women to the national cause was not limited to supporting men but included participation in education, employment, and later in politics as well. In the struggle for suffrage in the early twentieth century, women did not generally use the images of Vlasta and Libuše, but they often referred to the idea of gender equality which had been created by the earlier discourse.

Conclusion

The example of Libuše and Vlasta shows how the Czech national movement managed to adapt women's images for national goals. At the beginning of the national movement, both Libuše and Vlasta presented marginal, and especially in the case of Vlasta somewhat ridiculous or even negative, figures. Once they were included into the national context, however, the heroines gained both importance and patriotic or positive features. The traditional, non-national images of Libuše and Vlasta existed throughout the nineteenth century side by side with the new, patriotic ones. In the mainstream – male – national discourse, the latter dominated and were spread with the advent of mass culture in the second half of the nineteenth century. By then, Vlasta embodied national courage and Libuše had become a symbol of Czech statehood and of a better future for the Czech nation.

The development of the images of the mythical heroines reflected a more general approach to women and history. Almost from the beginning of modern national historiography and culture, Libuše and Vlasta were included in the national myth. Arguments about the equality and positive qualities of women were to prove the democratic and advanced character of the Czech nation. Libuše and Vlasta in their new patriotic garb were also held up as models for contemporary women in order to gain their support and participation in the national movement. In the process, the militant and anti-male characteristics of Vlasta were suppressed or rather channelled into the fight against national enemies, at the side of men.

The myth of gender harmony emerged in the second period of the national movement rather as a by-product of the image of women's equality among the early Czechs presented in historiography, and of the perception of women as men's companions in the national struggle. From the 1860s on, the idea was strengthened in a more deliberate effort for unity that pervaded the national society in the period of emerging political and social differentiation. The idea of friendly relations between the sexes had its parallel in the emphasis on the peaceful and egalitarian character of the relations between classes.

The way women perceived the mythical heroines was influenced by the mainstream national discourse. The interpretations, however, oscillated between two types of images: that of mothers and supporters of men, and the more independent and active ones, representing women's equal abilities and rights. Even the latter were not used to fight against men, but rather against the Habsburg rule and legislation which were seen as the major obstacle for women's emancipation. While earlier men referred to the mythical heroines calling for women's support in the national struggle, from the 1860s, women cited them when asking Czech men to support their emancipation.

Notes

1. Plamínková, F. (1920), *Economic and Social Position of Women in the Czechoslovak Republic*, Prague: Politika, 5. Quoted from the English original.
2. See Evans, R.J. (1977), *The Feminists: Women's Emancipation Movements in Europe, America and Australasia 1840-1920*, London: Croom Helm – New York: Barnes & Nobles, 96–8; Freeze, K.J. (1985), 'Medical Education for Women in Austria: A Study in the Politics of

the Czech Women's Movement in the 1890s', in S.L. Wolchik and A.G. Meyer (eds), *Women, State and Party in Eastern Europe*, Durham: Duke University Press, 51–63; Nolte, C.E. (1993), '"Every Czech a Sokol!"': Feminism and Nationalism in the Czech Sokol Movement', *Austrian History Yearbook* 24, 79–100; David, K. (1991), 'Czech Feminists and Nationalism in the Late Habsburg Monarchy: "The First in Austria"', *Journal of Women's History* 3, (2): 26–45.

3. A noteworthy exception present works by Vladimír Macura who pays substantial attention to gender in his literary analysis of Czech nationalism. See, for example, (1998) *Český sen* [The Czech Dream], Praha: Lidové noviny.

4. See Kořalka, J. (1992), 'The Czechs, 1840–1900', in A. Kappeler (ed.), *The Formation of National Elites: Comparative Studies on Governments and Non-Dominant Ethnic Groups in Europe*, VI, New York: New York University Press, 77–103. On the phases of the national movement see Hroch, M. (1985), *Social Preconditions of National Revival in Europe: A Comparative Analysis of the Social Composition of Patriotic Groups among the Smaller European Nations*, Cambridge: Cambridge University Press.

5. On the origin of the myth and its treatment in Czech chronicles see, for example, Spunar, P. (1995), "Dívčí válka v českých středověkých kronikách' [The Women's Revolt in Medieval Czech Chronicles], *Tvar* 6, (19): 16–17.

6. See Kraus, A. (1902), *Stará historie česká v německé literatuře* [Old Czech History in German Literature], Praha: Bursík a Kohout, 6–163; Grigorovitza, E. (1901), *Libussa in der deutschen Litteratur*, Berlin: A. Duncker; Graus, F. (1969), 'Kněžna Libuše – od postavy báje k národnímu symbolu' [Princess Libuše - From a Mythological Figure to a National Symbol], *Československý časopis historický* 17, no. 6, 817–44.

7. See Tureček, D. (1996), 'Amazonky na hranici humoru a travestie (České veselohry a vídeňská fraška)' [Amazons at the Borderline between Humour and Travesty (Czech Comedies and the Viennese Farce)], *Divadelní revue* 7, (1): 36-41.

8. Pelzel, F.M. (1817), *Geschichte der Böhmen*, Prag: k.k. privil. Zeitungs- und Intelligenz-Comptoir, 4th edition, 27–8.

9. Hanka, V. (1824), *Dějiny české v kamenopisně vyvedených obrazech* [Czech History in Pictures], Praha: Antonín Machek, 11, 31–3 and *passim*.

10. Palacký, F. (1850), *Dějiny národu českého v Čechách a v Moravě* [History of the Czech Nation in Bohemia and Moravia], Praha: J.G.

Kalve, vol. 3, 106–9, 193–4 and 218–19. In 1868, Jan Erazim Vocel took this latter idea even further emphasizing that, in contrast to the German habits, the Slavic family was based on principles of equality. This, he claimed, could be proved by their attitude to women which was reflected in law and which survived until the Middle Ages.

11. Linda, J. (1949), *Záře nad pohanstvem nebo Václav a Boleslav: Vyobrazení z dávnověkosti vlastenské* [Light over Heathendom or Václav and Boleslav: A Picture from Patriotic Antiquity], Praha: ELK, 46–58.

12. On the image of Prague in the early national culture see Macura, V. (1983), 'Obraz Prahy v české obrozenské kultuře', [The Image of Prague in Czech Revivalist Culture], in *Město v české kultuře 19. století* [Town in Nineteenth-Century Czech Culture] Praha: Národní galerie, 154–67.

13. Macura, V. (1983), *Znamení zrodu: české obrození jako kulturní typ* [A Sign of Emergence: The Czech Revival as a Cultural Type], Praha: Československý spisovatel, 105–6.

14. See Blažková, J. (1946), *Žena věčná inspirace umění: Žena ve výtvarném umění od doby kamenné až po Picassa* [Woman – Eternal Inspiration of Arts: Woman in Arts from the Stone Age to Picasso], Praha: Symposion, xxxi; Lébl, V. and Ludvová, J. (1981), 'Dobové kořeny a souvislosti Smetanovy Mé vlasti' [The Roots and Context of Smetana's Má Vlast], *Hudební věda* 18, (2): 110.

15. Villani, D.M. (1862), *Spisy* [Collected Works], Praha: H.Dominicus, 85.

16. See, for example, Jablonský's poem "To Czech Daughters" (Dcerám českým) in Jablonský, B. (1864), *Básně* [Poems], Praha: Jar. Pospíšil, 4th edition, 224.

17. Nebeský, V.B. (1913), *Básně* [Poems], Praha: J.Otto, 61 and 76. The poems are from the early 1840s.

18. Villani, K. (1940), quoted in Kleinschnitzová, F., 'Podíl ženy na národním obrození' [Women's Contribution to the National Revival], in *Česká žena v dějinách národa* [The Czech Woman in the History of the Nation], Praha: Novina, 123.

19. Macura, *Český sen*, 88.

20. See the poem "Glorious morning" (Slavné ráno) in Němcová, B. (1957), *Básně a jiné práce* [Poems and Other Works], Praha: SNKLHU, 23–4.

21. See Macura, *Český sen*, 83.

22. To this day, the opera is performed on festive occasions. The libretto was written for Smetana by Josef Wenzig, a German writer from

Prague, in German. It was translated into Czech by Wenzig's student Ervin Špindler who further emphasized the patriotic purport of the text. Smetana himself intervened in the process. Interestingly, already in 1836 Wenzig had written a dramatic poem 'Wlasta'. For details on the opera see Očadlík, M. (1939), *Libuše: Vznik Smetanovy zpěvohry* [Libuše: The Origin of Smetana's Opera], Praha: Melantrich.

23. Střítecký, J. (1988), 'Tradice a obrození. Bedřich Smetana' [Tradition and the Revival. Bedřich Smetana], in *Povědomí tradice v novodobé české kultuře (Doba Bedřicha Smetany)* [The Awareness of Tradition in Modern Czech Culture (Bedřich Smetana's Time)], Praha: Národní galerie, 65–76.

24. (1864) *Vlasta a Šárka, vůdkyně českých Amazonek: Romantický příběh z dávné starověkosti* [Vlasta and Šárka, Leaders of Czech Amazones: A Romantic Story from Antiquity], Pardubice: V. Pospíšil.

25. For example "Šárka outwits Ctirad" by P. Maixner from 1856 or "Ctirad and Šárka" by K. Svoboda from 1868. See Stich, A. (1988), 'Tradiční romantické motivy v české hudbě a poezii druhé poloviny 19. století (Šárky)' [Traditional Romantic Motives in Czech Music and Poetry of the Second Half of the Nineteenth Century (Šárkas)], in *Povědomí tradice,* 109, note 6.

26. Vrchlický, J. (1949), *Mýthy* [Myths], Praha: Melantrich, 30–2. In Zeyer's drama, Šárka deceived Ctirad, but later regretted it and decided to be burned with him at the pyre. See Zeyer, J. (1906), *Dramatická díla* [Dramatic Works], vol. 2, Praha: Unie, 201–3. For Smetana's Šárka see Stich, 'Tradiční motivy', 88–90.

27. Frič, J.V. (1861), *Libušin soud* [Libuše's Trial], Geneva: Pfeffer i Puky. See also the postscript for the author's motivation.

28. Podlipská, Ž. (1889), *Přemysl a Libuše* [Přemysl and Libuše], Praha: Štorch.

29. Podlipská, Ž. (1890), *Dívčí boj v Čechách* [Women's Revolt in Bohemia], Praha: Štorch.

30. See Řezníček, V. (1908), *Vlasta: Román z české dávnověkosti podle bájí lidových* [Vlasta: A Novel from Czech Antiquity According to Folk Tales], Praha.

31. See Dvorský, F. (1869), *Staré písemné památky žen a dcer českých* [Old Written Monuments of Czech Women and Daughters], Praha: Fr. Dvorský, v–viii; Jonáš, K. (1872), *Žena ve společnosti lidské, zvláště v Anglii a v Americe* [Woman in Human Society, Particularly in England and in America], Praha: J.Otto, 109.

32. Krásnohorská, E. (1881), *Ženská otázka česká* [The Czech Woman Question], Praha: Dr. Grégr, 4–6.

Constructing National Identity in Latvia: Gender and Representation During the Period of the National Awakening

Irina Novikova

Latvia is among those states and cultures that, despite their European identity, have been shaped by forces of exclusion and marginalization, as well as by the shared peripherality between empires and power such as Great Britain, France, Germany and Russia. The category of gender must be investigated in order to theorize nation-building and nationalism in the Baltic cultures and societies, their plots of modernity, their movements into the contemporary period in which 'transitional' identities are written and new nationalist scripts of exclusion are performed. The theme of gender and representation in the Baltic/Latvian developments of belated modernity requires an analysis of how a new historical subject was constituted and stabilized as a national subject. In what ways did people experience, perceive and represent 'difference(s)'? How was gendered social and political agency as 'a form of knowledge production'[1] constructed in cultural representations of masculinity and femininity?

I do not pretend to present a comprehensive analysis of different phases in gendered representation of Latvian nationhood. Emancipation of the nation as a discourse of difference in belated modernity claimed accessible forms of representation for its gender order, constitutive of 'the subjective and collective meanings of women and men as categories of identity'.[2] What I will try to show is how the ambivalence of simultaneous appeal to tradition constructed out of archaic forms and its emancipation in social movement towards 'nation' shaped 'not simply social roles for women and men, but the articulation in specific contexts of social understandings of sexual difference'.[3]

I will address some aspects of gender and representation appropriated from Latvian folk songs called *daina* (singular, feminine gender) and from the religious movement in Vidzeme and Kurzeme known as Herrn-huters' congregations. I will discuss some aspects of how this ethnographic and religious legacy was converted into gender symbolism at the All-Latvian Folk Song Festival and the epic work *Lāčplēsis* of the Latvian writer Andrejs Pumpurs (1841–1902). Both the event and the narrative will be discussed in terms of their constitutive role in oral and written representations of a new gender order in Latvia.

The Festival tradition as well as publication and spreading of Pumpurs' epic narrative in the emerging national literature were seminal to the politics of gender and representation in the nationalizing process. The nationalizing process started in Latvia in the middle of the 1850s. The 1860s became the time when a publicly conspicuous Latvian-speaking urban elite was created. The establishment of the Song Festival tradition (1873, 1881, 1888) was central to the nation-building phase in the 1870s. The epic narrative of Andrejs Pumpurs was a landmark text indicative of historical changes in understanding and representing gender relations in the nationalizing process of the 1880s.

The Baltic Provinces in the Nineteenth Century

The argument needs to be placed in its historical background. For various reasons, the Baltic region had special status in the Russian Empire. Parts of the Baltic territories had previously belonged to Germany and Poland, or had been under the influence of Denmark and Sweden. This historical legacy helped to shape regional images of religious, economic, cultural and social differences in this largely agricultural territory.[4]

The Baltic Germans were a traditional premodern elite in the Baltic region. A historian Michael H. Haltzel has succinctly written that 'approximately 125,000 Germans completely dominated politically, economically, and culturally the nearly one million Latvians and Estonians of Livland, Estland, and Kurland. German guilds governed the Baltic cities, while corporations of the German nobility (*Ritterschaften*) ruled the countryside. What industry the Baltic provinces possessed was largely owned by Germans, and the rural economy rested on the manors of the few hundred Baltic nobles. Based on the privileges granted them by Peter the Great, the Baltic Germans still retained their ancient judicial system and estate self-government, most of which functioned in the German language, as did the imperial offices in the three provinces. The Baltic school system from the rural elementary schools to Dorpat (Tartu) University, one of the premier institutions of higher schooling in Eastern Europe, was thoroughly German.'[5] Peasant laws of the first half of the nineteenth century, in particular the decrees abolishing serfdom in Estonia (1816), Kurland (1817), and in Livonia (1819) transformed the status of

Baltic peasantry bringing in historical changes in their social and national identification.

This process resulted in the emergence of a Latvian elite and the Latvian 'national awakening' from the mid-1850s. The ideas of the French Revolution influenced the emancipatory views of Latvian literati of the late 1850s and the 1860s in their attempts to construct 'Latvianness' as a return of the 'awakened' nation into the modern family of European nations. Unlike Finland, Latvia did not have a tradition of constitutional autonomy and parliamentary activity when it came to the point of nation building in the Russian autocratic regime. The process of becoming a 'new Latvian citizen' excluded wider political horizons. Self-governing authority was delegated by the Russian autocracy to the *Landtag*, which represented the interests of Baltic German landowners – the traditional, pre-industrial elite.[6]

By the mid-nineteenth century, capitalism began to move slowly toward the East. Latvian society changed considerably between the 1850s and the 1880s thanks to investments in modernization, the construction of railways, and slowly progressing industrialization. Modernization and land reform brought new dynamics into the traditional agricultural economy. Free but landless peasants migrated eastward, to Russia proper. Others moved into cities and mixed into various urban strata.

It was also a period when the relationship between the centre and the margins, as well as the definitions and categorizations of 'centre' and 'margin', came into clearer focus. Both German and Russian imperial projects and realignments of their boundaries in the second half of the nineteenth century contributed significantly to shaping emancipatory ideas in the Latvian national movement. In the 1860s, Otto von Bismarck envisioned a concept of 'Mitteleuropa', to be dominated by the German cultural nation. In the early 1870s, Germany saw itself as an imperial power, with the founding of the German Reich in 1870–1. The Baltic region was becoming a contested political and cultural territory in terms of Germany's colonizing appetites. Earlier ethnographic and linguistic markers gave way to the political marker of the Baltic Germans' belonging (*jus sanguinis*) to the united and militarist German power. Consequently, Russian Imperial paternalism had to define Baltic marginality as a territorial entity through centralized legal reforms that were introduced gradually. Administrative reforms were equally significant in terms of rebalancing power relations between the Baltic German gentry and Latvian peasants.[7]

In the 1860s, the peasantry started a massive campaign to purchase their farmsteads. Parish councils and courts of law tackled major local problems. At the same time, local choirs, associations, orchestras were established.

The role and influence of Slavophiles in Russia, with their anti-German rhetoric, were particularly significant and attractive for Latvian national ideologists. As historian David Kirby points out, Latvian and Estonian nationalists 'were influenced far more than were the Finnish nationalists by events in Russia, where many of them studied or worked. This circumstance, and the deep hostility felt towards Germans, resulted in a more radical and uncompromising edge than was the case in Finland.'[8] The argument of how Slavophile views upon women and gender influenced the ideologists of the national awakening is a complex issue. However, the discussion of the Slavophiles' role in gender representations of the nation-building process falls outside the scope of this chapter.

Paternal Mapping of Differences/Filial Charting of Resistances

In 1636 Georg Mantzel published *Lettisch Vademecum* – a guideline to the rules of the proper Latvian language. In 1689 Ernst Gluck translated the Bible into Latvian. German educators also wrote about Latvians during European Enlightenment. Garlieb Merkel published the book *Letts, Particularly in Vidzeme, at the End of the Age of Philosophy* during the revolutionary changes in France. In this context, German cultural policies had been carving out a space for the development of local literary life, beginning with the foundation of the Latvian Literary Association in 1824. For the language of peasantry to be accepted as having a cultural value, and to 'be used as a vehicle of communication in public media'[9] meant a significant political change. At the same time, language became an ethnocultural boundary for literate Latvians. Those Latvians who had received education only in German had traditionally become Germanized. The fragile stratum of young educated Latvians in the middle of the nineteenth century were becoming increasingly aware of the problem of remaining in the periphery of the Baltic German elite and losing relations with Latvian-speaking members of the people. Later, a Latvian social democrat, Felikss Cielēns, saw these young literati as visionaries in a time when 'most people went on living in the mentality of past times.'[10]

As a leader of the national awakening Atis Kronvalds (1837–75) wrote, a *Lettisch Bauer* (a Latvian peasant) had been and remained nothing – not a man (*Unmenschen*). Thus, if a *Lettisch Bauer* (a Latvian peasant) had been nothing – not a man (*Unmenschen*) – then this ascriptive status had to be changed through the regeneration of a new Latvian nation.[11] A new collective identity was rhetorically constructed by Kronvalds and his compatriots as a progressive and emancipating movement out of the ascriptive status (*Unmenschen*) of an historical and dispersed *Lettisch Bauer* or 'zemnieks' (peasant) to a new notion of Latvian citizen.

The conceptual cradle for the 'awakeners' became the romantic 'organic body' of a German philosopher Johann Gottfried von Herder who lived in Riga for some time and, as an ethnographer, collected Latvian folk songs called '*daina*'. The concept of *Volk* created 'a 'Latvian' historiography in contrast to a historiography that dealt largely with the 'Baltic', and the elites thereof.'[12] Thus, as historian Rogers Brubaker points out, 'the *Volkssprache* was celebrated – most powerfully by Herder – as a matrix of creativity and individuality, and a conception of nation as founded on language and linguistically embedded culture took root among the flourishing German *Bildungsburgertum*. From this time on, the imagined community of the ethnocultural nation was available as a point of orientation, focus of value, source of identity, and locus of allegiance independent of – and potentially conflicting with – the state.'[13]

The hegemonic code of masculinity as Baltic Germans' paternal privilege for knowledge and God, dooming the doubly marginalized stratum of Latvian literati to the 'filial' passive role, needed new social and cultural forms. German was to be replaced by the vernacular as a purifying marker of the new nation and its different nationhood. The printing press became a linguistically unifying instrument for expunging Germanisms from the gradually developing literary language of Latvian. The young Latvian literati who sparked the national awakening movement of the 1850s propagated their ideas in two Latvian newspapers – *Pēterburgas Avīzes* and *Mājas Viesis*. The circulation of these two newspapers was important in those regions where primary education in parish schools was formally mandatory for rural people.

In this regional history, the nationalizing process is also the development of *Kultur*. It places a special stress on national differences and the particular identity of groups: 'Whereas the concept of civilization has the function of giving expression to the continuously expansionist tendency of colonizing groups, the concept of *Kultur* mirrors the self-consciousness of a nation which had constantly to seek out and constitute its boundaries anew, in a political as well as spiritual sense.'[14]

The constitution of boundaries could not operate with political identity, but it became possible to give cultural expression to 'spiritual roots' of the nationhood. The concept of *Kultiviert* collectivity needed then an historical dimension of national identity construction. Latvian literati had to employ or create narratives to incorporate into continuity of 'culture' to re-centre power relations in this region of the imperial periphery. They could not be found in works of art, books, religious or philosophical systems in which the individuality of a people expresses itself, as well as the related gendering of the representational systems. In the absence of a political medieval state of the type that existed in Lithuania, or political representation as existed in Finland, creating a moment of origin for textualizing 'the national awakening', a transition from marginality to 'a centre of their own', was an enormous task to perform. The national identity had to be constructed in socially mandated collective forms of possible and accessible narrative, visual and public spaces. The gendered affiliations, roles and statuses had to be translated into the concrete forms of the new collective identity.

Dainas: Imagining Ideal Womanhood

In building up transgenerational identity of communities and regions, folk songs known as *daina* were pronounced authentic sources to testify to the collectively shared antiquity and language. Tens of thousands of these folk songs from villages and farmsteads were collected by ethnographers, from the German philosopher Johann Gottfried von Herder to a passionate Latvian awakener Krišjānis Barons (1835–1923). For him and other awakeners, the folk songs collected and preserved by peasant women were unifying multiple evidences of the immanence of nationhood and the roots of *volk* spirit in the land. They became 'marker' texts for the representations of femininity, in particular, motherhood, in producing national and cultural difference.

Dainas were created on the principle of parallelism, when a character/ event/relationship/role/ status in the heavenly family has a reflecting parallel earthly/local plot in the same rhyme. The family of archaic gods and deities was organized around the sun–moon opposition.[15] In the Latvian language, the symbol of the sun, or *saule*, is marked grammatically in the feminine gender, whereas the moon is marked as masculine. *Saule* governs the *earthly world 'under the sun'* (*'pasaule'* in Latvian). *Dainas* were performed as mediating texts between singing performers and divine phenomena, revealing their endowing sacrality to performers during the act of singing.[16]

As the Latvian historian Dagmara Beitnere writes, 'they [*dainas*] had a didactic message aimed at creating an ideal person, harmonious and beautiful [daiļš]. Only the one who is ethical is also beautiful. A person is ethical when he/she is industrious and has many skills. In this way an ideal representation of a Latvian woman has been shaped. She was ethical [tikla] and, thus, industrious in terms of power in her household. Beauty was the last element in the hierarchy of womanhood. Morality implied beauty. When a young woman got married, it was the duty of her brothers to come to her new home and to observe whether she was being treated well in the family of her husband. If not, they had the right to take her back home. According to the *dainas*, brothers had a significant influence upon the status of a young wife in a husband's family.'[17] The brother-sister bonding was deeply rooted in pre-Christian agricultural cosmogony of Baltic tribes and reflected in *dainas*. Under *saule*, or *pasaulē* (the prepositional case of the noun), those people who sing *dainas* are earthly family members of *saule* – her brothers and sisters of a singing community among the deities revealing themselves in nature.

Herrnhuters: Brethren and their Sisters on the Margin of Modernity

The Herrnhuterian legacy was a seminal source of producing gendered representations of Latvian nationhood. It occupies a special place among other specific interpersonal and transgenerational interactions and practices in forming and representing gender and nationhood. Herrnhuterian ideas of pietism and *civitas Dei* structured gender representations of the nation long after the movement ceased to exist.

Latvian Herrnhuters' 'father', Count Nicholas Ludwig von Zinzendorf (1700-1760), a German Lutheran nobleman, founded a colony as *unitas fratrum* for emigrants from Moravia and called it The Brethren at Herrnhut. In 1736 Zinzendorf visited Livonia.[18] The Herrnhuterian idea of *civitas Dei* needed 'a promised land', and it found the land where thousands of folk songs *dainas* testified to preserved innocence and moral cleanliness of ancient peoples that 'had to be awakened from their lethargic sleep'.[19] It was the place where the deities revealed themselves in nature, and God would be revealed in Scriptures. Latvian Herrnhuters, or *brāļu draudzes* (the regions Vidzeme and Kurzeme), viewed themselves as models for materializing the project of *civitas Dei*. Wives, sisters and daughters of Latvian peasants and artisans were involved in Herrnhuterian activities. The relationship 'brother–sister', shaped in mythology, reflected in *dainas* and in customary laws, was consonant with the Herrnhuterian vision of brothers and sisters in faith with a rule of equality. Erdmute Dorotea, the wife of Zinzendorf, as well as wives of some other Baltic German Herrnhuters, helped her husband in disseminating pietism and Herrnhuterian ideas from the very beginning.

Herrnhuterian networking in Vidzeme and Kurzeme was significant both in transgenerational and translocal terms. They used to meet in *Gemeinhaus*, like their Baltic German brothers, to worship their *Herzens-religion*, or 'the religion of the heart' (Zinzendorf's phrase). His visions, as historian Detlef Henning has argued, 'influenced Latvian and Estonian peasant parish congregations. For the first time peasants who had worked as hired hands for German "brothers"and "sisters" were treated as equally valued members of a parish congregation. This change resulted in the development of the Latvian and Estonian languages.' [20]

Herrnhuterian congregations were divided in 'choirs' according to age, sex, marital status. Each choir was headed by an elder, either a man and or a woman. Women's choirs were marked by their dresses. Widows, unmarried young men, and young women were organized into separate choirs and supervised by the choirs' elders. Lovefeast was, for example, one of central fellowship gatherings. As the 'family meal' of a congregation, all members of a congregation attended it. They addressed each other as brothers and sisters, regardless of whether single, married, or widowed. The titles used in the congregations signified close spiritual affection and unity. Herrnhuterian brothers and sisters were organized into choirs, male and female groups including members in the same life situation. Typically, congregations were divided into the choirs of children, little boys, little girls, older boys, older girls, single brothers, single sisters, married people, widows, and widowers. Preachers and missionaries introduced ideas of equal access to education for both boys and girls as part of their religious enlightenment.

Latvian congregations of Herrnhuters were built on the principle of parafamily, or para-clan, entitlements. Individual identification with a local parish or Herrnhuters' congregation was no less significant than his/her farmstead identification. The spiritual entitlements were no less binding than familial bonds, because in these communities spiritual redemption was the desired destination of an individual fate. Congregations were not separated from peasant families. On the contrary, they penetrated household and clan relationships, across generations and across social and sexual differences. The bridging idea of equality despite social and ethnic differences drew up boundaries for belonging/not belonging to *civitas Dei*: 'people met brothers and sisters in Christ from other communities, particularly the lay preachers, called the preaching brothers, who often "crossed the borders" of their own communities with the message. Visits from one brotherhood to another were not rare, either, and in this way the Kingdom's work bound together men and women from near and far.'[21] A family was seen as a materialized bonding for bringing these spiritual principles into the sinful world.

This transgenerational model of a spiritually uniting 'family' was an adaptive experience of social interaction in peasants' responses to the consolidating calls of Latvian literati. Some historians of the Latvian Herrnhuters' movement point out that it is viewed as an all-peasant organization. Peasants, however, were already socially differentiated. A Baltic German Herrnhuter Karl Bruining wrote: 'frequently, the most prosperous and best farmers supported congregations.'[22] The posts of congregation leaders, or *tētiņi* (Daddies in Latvian) were typically occupied by well-off farmers and their sons. At the same time, lay teachers used the address 'Mother' when they referred to the Herrnhuterian faith as a whole.

The emancipation of peasantry in the early nineteenth century improved their economic and social positions and strengthened their aspirations. The agrarian bourgeoisie was only beginning to emerge, and had not yet split off from the majority of the peasantry. Thus, social divisions were not so deep that they could affect the growing longing for national consolidation. But in the 1830s–40s the movement still united thousands of peasants in Vidzeme and Kurzeme. It gradually changed into a network representing the interests of the growing rural bourgeoisie. The Herrnhuterian movement of religious consolidation as a form of ethnic identification was significant for all layers of the peasantry as it centred on the idea of 'equality across social and religious classes'. This idea was maintained by lay teachers so as to oppose the monopoly of the official Lutheran church in the ideological sphere. The long-term experience of Herrnhuterian consolidating strategies was very important for the ideologists of the national awakening in counterbalancing social and economic dissociations as well as the migratory tendencies among Latvians eastwards in a period of modernization and Imperial centralization. The awakeners appropriated Herrnhuterian rhetoric, adapting its unifying idiom of brothers and sisters in faith for the secular project of nationhood.

Gen(d)e(r)alogy of Singing Wars

Latvian song festivals became central to the historical process of nation-making. The first regional festivals of the 1860s and the first All-Latvian Song Festival in 1873 were derived from song festivals organized by Baltic Germans since the 1850s. In 1857, German singers from the Baltic provinces were invited to take part in the collective performance in Revel. In 1860 the joint concert of the 'Liederkrantz' and 'Liedertafel' choirs was organized in the Verman park in Riga. In 1861, the local singers' association took an initiative to organize the Baltic song festival: 670 singers participated in this event. Representatives of German choirs from the Baltic cities, Moscow, St Petersburg, Saratov, Tver gathered in Riga in 1863, with the only aim to organize the singing events according to the model of 'Deutscher Sängerbund'. The last and the biggest festival organized by German choir associations took place in 1880. A researcher of the Baltic German choir tradition F. Miller points to the exclusively male composition of 800 official participants. Moreover, as the researcher argues:

Figure 15.1 A kerchief for the memory of the Third Latvian Song Festival. (In: *The Guide Book of Song Festivals in Commemoration of the First Song Festival,* edited by I.E. Melngailis, Riga 1933.)

Latvian song festivals included more or less all layers of population whereas Baltic festivals of German songs were inclusive mainly for the representatives of the privileged strata. It is important to emphasize that Baltic German choirs included the singers from the elite of the society until the beginning of the 20th century. The social layer of so called ' petty Germans' (workers, petty traders, artisans) in general was small.[23]

This festival model was exclusive in social and gender terms. It was reinvented by local choirs and associations of Latvians into performances of political significance. A feminist philosopher Tuija Pulkkinen points to the importance of nationalizing processes in the imperial periphery and the focus on 'of the singularity of the communal subject, the singularity of the general will.'[24] The first festival laid groundwork to translate the future festival tradition into a hegemonic marker of national, cultural and linguistic difference for 'the singularity of the communal subject'. The national 'difference' translated itself into the derivative model of the festival by stepping out of the ascribed status of *unmenschen* and symbolically relocating Baltic Germans into otherness, beyond 'singing' boundaries of the singing nation.

The festival represented the unity of the nation of singers: 'Since times immemorial, the Latvian people have been known as the singing nation [or the singers' nation – *dziedataju tauta*]', wrote the poet Auseklis.[25] 'Each Latvian is a born singer,' wrote an ethnographer.[26] At the festival, the collective, congenial and harmonizing voice was projected from the local and regional into national performance of *dainas* as '*volk* property', the '*volk* dowry', 'the legacy of our dear grandfathers', and 'our ancient heritage.'[27] A Latvian ethnographer Dace Bula has pointed to the significance of the stereotype 'singers' people' for the foundational codes of collective Latvian identification.[28]

The festival tradition united peasants, artisans, mission-educated rural schoolteachers, preachers and urban literati and the maturing, national middle class. Festivals became symbolic and sacral connectors between local 'authenticity' on the one hand, and the 'new Latvians', on the other – to break through the common perception that an educated Latvian was a Germanized 'other' – alien to the *volk*. At the same time, the festival ritualized the 'one nation, one hero' scenario. The image of maternal home was instrumentalized for negotiating appropriated regional, social, religious legacies into performing/singing/enunciating the nation as a fraternal-sororal contract. The link *home-Rīga-Latvija* was later represented in an important poetic writing by Juris Alunāns (1832–64) in the symbolical parallelism of the title *Homestead. Nature. World* (*Sēta.*

Dāba. Pasaule – the feminine gender in Latvian).

What other public rituals were available to perform the ideals that were already formulated in Roman history and were now attuned to reclaimed national 'antiquity' – public agency, heroism, secularized values of self-control and self-sacrifice? It is no wonder that sometimes Latvia's folk song festivals have been known as 'singing wars', which started through the participation of choirs from communities and parishes, inspired by rural teachers in folk schools. Under conditions when dramatic 'inclusion' into modernity serves to destroy tradition, it is the tradition of nation-construction rituals to discriminate between 'insiders' and 'outsiders' that most explicitly seeks out performative forms of participation. The fact that Latvian song festivals as the major event of nationhood have been held regularly since 1873 has embodied Gilles Deleuze's paradox in *Repetition and Difference*: 'To repeat is to conduct oneself in terms of a singular or a particular, devoid of a similar or equally worthy. ... A festival has one obvious 'paradox' – to repeat 'the resumed'. Not to add the second or the third times to the first, but to allocate 'the' power to the first time; because of this power, the repetition is turned upside-down into interior-ization: as Pegui said, it is not a French holiday that honours or represents the overthrow of the Bastille, but the overthrow of the Bastille in advance celebrates and repeats all federations'.[29]

The first festival constituted a matrix of nationhood and its collective representation for the twentieth century. The central performers in the enormous song festival concerts were mixed choirs and male choirs, which collectively voiced the symbolic birth of the nation from different local places. Women as collectors and performers of folk songs and as partic-ipants in parish communities and Herrnhuterian congregations were included in the festivals. In this, women were called to demonstrate and to voice their individual and collective commitment to the stabilization of their roles of 'pillars of the nation'.

Many people from Herrnhuters' congregations took part in the festival. The organizers used Herrnhuterian images and idioms in their speeches. One of the 'founding brothers' and financiers of the first festival was a famous Latvian merchant called R. Tomsons (1834–92). Matis Kaudzite remembered his speech at the opening of the Festival:

> The honourable R. Tomsons, chairman of the festival committee, said in a speech that after many centuries, the time has come when people from Kurzeme and Vidzeme can come together for a people's festival, undivided by rivers or borders; that the sons and the daughters of the nation, as brothers and sisters of families, communities, parishes have come together from near and far, from

all social groups, to celebrate the festival and to disregard their differences, just as our ancient ancestors celebrated St. John's Day. But this festival also signifies the longing of the Latvian nation for enlightenment and education.[30]

As I have mentioned above, Herrnhuters called their church 'Mother'. The Rīga Latvian Association, which sponsored the event, took on the appropriating nickname of *Māmuļa*, or 'mommy', thus, confirming Rīga as the Latvian cultural capital and the centre (*Hertz*) of the nation. The headquarters of the Association are still called *Māmuļa*. A famous writer and a Herrnhuter elder, Matiss Kaudzīte, used the image of the morning sun as *balta māmuliņa*, or 'white mommy' that sanctified the participants of the event by addressing them as her sons.[31]

The Festival took place right after St John's Day, the archaic celebration of summer solstice. The script of choir performances reflected how Riga was symbolically and physically appropriated by the singing people and simultaneously marked as the mother of St John. A male choir performed a folksong typical for the St John's celebration that contained the lines 'Good evening, mother of St John, did you wait for us?' These lines were addressed to 'rich Rīga, St John's mother that did not expect Latvian singers and did nothing to accept them. Nothing was given for free, but the organizing committee gave much money and expected to benefit from the event.'[32]

The poems of Auseklis (the nom-de-plume of Miķelis Krogzems, 1850–79) introduced maternal imagery into the repertoire. The poetry of Auseklis accumulated maternal images common to Baltic and, specifically, Latvian mythologies. There were sixty *mothers* in Latvian mythological cosmology, for example – *Veļu māte* (the mother of the dead); the Sun's mother and daughter; *Ūdens māte* (the mother of the water); *Jūras māte* (the mother of the sea); *Vēja māte* (the mother of the wind); *Zemes māte* (the mother of the land) and so forth. The connection between the printed word of Auseklis' nationalistic poetry and the choral performance of his songs and *dainas* built up the performance script of the first song festival.

At the opening of the Festival Atis Kronvalds romantically spoke about the ancient maternal spirit embodied in the collective gathering of a nation redeemed from a paternalist legacy of oppression and revived in a spiritual harmony with nature and God. Other well-known speakers mentioned the cultural contribution of German schooling, Baltic German gentry, the legacy of Riga for the event. Kronvalds, on the other hand, stressed that the actual honour had to be granted to Latvian mothers, the Rīga Latvian Association and the collective spirit of Latvian people, that 'each child is fed from the maternal breast and hears the first sounds of the words from her lips – the language of the people.'[33]

In Kronvalds' public speech motherhood is represented as the uniting and inclusive symbol for all social groups of Latvians. The maternal symbolism in representing the nation as an 'organic unity' has to be considered in the context of Kronvalds' essays about new Latvian citizenship first published in the German language. In its Latvian translation, the image of a new Latvian citizen is grammatically marked in the masculine gender, both singular and plural. Kronvalds discusses differences between 'the Germanness' and 'the Latvianness' exclusively, by using nouns and adjectives in the masculine gender (for example, *vācietis* and *latvietis*, *vācisks* and *latvisks*) and knowledge. The passionate rhetoric of his essays is explicitly masculine in the argument with Germans about rights of a Latvian new *individual*, or *latvietis* (singular, masculine), and his access to education and knowledge. On the other hand, his speeches and the speeches of other festival organizers and witnesses are examples of inclusive rhetoric for consolidating people in the *collective* project of the nation.

Men and women are also equally important in Kaudzīte's memoirs as contributors to the creation of a '*volk*-song-body' – *dziedātāji un dziedātājas*, brothers and sisters in the singing nation. Their voices had to be synchronized and harmonized becoming equal in the creation of a unifying spirit of ethnic identity, in contrast to that their parents had remembered; becoming equal in creating a collective singing body in Rīga, putting aside and forgetting all divisions and differences; becoming equal in legitimizing the Latvian language in Rīga as the national and cultural territory; becoming equal sons and daughters in the *volk*-family; becoming equal in putting the 'grain' of the first festival into the 'soil' of *volk* consciousness for further cultivation; becoming equal in introducing the flag and the future hymn of the country. The flag was a collective present from nine young women, represented to the awakened nation as its *zeltenes* (golden flowers).

Folklore songs, ethnographic and religious legacies, literary texts and cultural events are as important as non-verbal materials, everyday objects, in the selection and use of 'given legacy' and its constructed images in creating a modern nation. Choirs, male and mixed, and guests played a role of uniting boundary-guardians in 'voice' (the festival repertoire) and in 'body' (local dress), integrating the festival into the permanence of local handicraft traditions presented at the festival. At the Third festival (1888) female participants were given kerchiefs as souvenirs that they could take home as a reminder of 'belonging' to and of 'passing' text/

textile memories to other women. The image on the kerchiefs, quint-essentially everyday objects, represented two young women dressed in national costumes, hand-in-hand, in the middle of a country farm. (It is interesting to note that 'two sisters' are a frequent image of womanhood in folk songs.)

The festivals were the first nationwide initiation rituals that invited rural young women to participate with self-esteem and in a public way, but only in the delegated roles of selected performers – 'sisters' in mixed choirs. The awareness of young women of belonging and of agency in the nation was legitimized en route from their parents, families, home-steads, communities, in mixed choirs, under the fraternal protection of the festival organizers. The politically instrumentalized cultural ritual of the festival was central to Latvian peasant women's individual and collective participation in the emancipatory vision of the national family, their consciousness of womanhood and motherhood confirming unity with nationhood.

An emerging masculine national subject was still marginalized from empowering positions in politics and economics and alienated from power positions in knowledge-production. He needed to solidify the spiritual, educational and harmonizing power of the nation by including a feminine 'subject' and by delegating to the national feminine the complementary qualities of strength, love, gallantry and morality. Strong women, mothers, daughters and sisters were then to tend the fire into the next day,[34] to act in a 'sisterly' way to secure an individual woman's inclusion into the nationhood.

Lāčplēsis: from Voice to Text/from Singing Mothers and Sisters to Filial Warriors and Ideal Maidens

Women's relations to the process of nation making underwent significant changes over the years of social and economic transformation of the 1870s and the 1880s. As A. Plakans argues, 'during the 1880s love of the Latvian *tauta[Volk]* began to dissociate itself from the desire for modernity, a union which the urban elite had brought into being and wishes to preserve.'[35] A national bourgeoisie emerged, a number of landless peasants were made proletarians, an active process of Russification in education was launched. The 1880s were a time when ethnic Latvian population of cities began to increase and the nuclearization of families occurred. Ideas about Latvian national citizenship and cultural autonomy reflected changes in the social stratification of the Latvian population and gradual development of the gendered dichotomy private/public. The private sphere of the nuclear family and the related ideology of the feminine were becoming more important for representations of gender order.

No woman's name, as an original historical or cultural figure, could have been drawn into scripting affection and the spirit of nationhood. Only mythological figures of female deities (Laima, Māra) could be drawn from tales. No woman's name emerged as an equally publicly acknowledged participant in the activities of the Latvian literati until the 1870s. In the 1870s and 1880s, only a few individual women tried to discuss women's issues. An example is Karoline Kronvalde, in her article 'Cienīgam Garram' ('For a noble spirit') in the newspaper *Baltijas Vēstnesis*.[36] In the article Kronvalde argued for equal rights and opportunities for both men and women in the public and cultural sectors by stressing the importance of equal education for both genders and by appealing to the imagined powers of ancient Latvian mothers.

Women's education and spiritual development was discussed as crucial to the nation's cultural life. An anonymous author wrote in a newspaper:

> A woman occupies a conspicuous position in the education of the people. She is the basic source of the people's education, thus, more significance should be given to the rise of women's education. Boys and girls are given equal gifts. Thus, it is wrong when the priority in education is given to one sex, and the second is neglected. The development of spiritual gifts is particularly necessary for girls because they maintain the people's virtues and the beauty of humanity grows out of them.[37]

In the 1880s, Maria Medinska tried to develop a public discourse on education and the importance of women in Latvian society:

> Also in the small nation the spiritually and seriously educated women-compatriots prove that the spirit of the people is alive and healthy. Serious men-compatriots also prove that their hands are the most powerful support and that they take care of female reason's spirit.[38]

Medinska proposed her views on new national woman derivatively, from the discourse of complementarity and equality under fraternal protection and care:

> Only through cooperation between men and women can we develop spirituality in our younger generations, and it is impossible for men to perform this task without women. Decent Latvian women are the most powerful basis in the hands of Latvian men. A women in her nation is the location where the nation's heart beats, and the nation's heart must be remembered.[39]

'The nation's heart' strongly evokes Herrnhuters' legacy, embedded as it was in educated women's emancipatory thinking. It also points to the choice of women's representations by the first Latvian writers. Matīss Kaudzīte, the chief elder of a Herrnhuterian Brotherhood and a writer, represented in his famous novel *The Times of Surveyors* the two Herrn-huterian women Ilze and Annuža, the Christ's 'pure in heart', idealized characters. His brother Reinis Kaudzīte (1839–1920) also tried to create a representation of an ideal Latvian woman for his Herrnhuterian vision of the nation.

Reinis Kaudzīte wrote the essay *Sieviškais cilveks* in the late 1880s, and the title of the essay is literally translated 'a feminine human being'. *Cilveks*, or 'a human being', a key word in his didactic writings, generally applies to both genders. For him a typical feminine person is 'everybody who is loveable, proud, everything that blossoms and sparkles, the whole smiling world [*pasaule*], because this human being is more a person of heart. To men belong the nature of autumn and winter.'[40] Women are so different and such special human beings that rights and obligations between genders should be rationally divided for each of the two genders to possibly fully accomplish his/her inborn, natural capabilities. A woman as 'a person of heart' is then the heart of a family that, in its turn, embodies the rational order of the universe in harmony with the social progress of the awakened nation. Thus, home economics is especially important for women's education because it is 'the first stone in the corner of the building of Latvian Enlightenment.'[41]

In 1888, Andrejs Pumpurs produced an epic narrative *Lāčplēsis* (*The Bear-Slayer*) – a tale of heroism:

> The poem threw caution to the winds as far as historical veracity was concerned and raised a minor legendary hero to the status of a symbol of all Latvian people ... the epic reminded its thousands of readers of the heroic battles their forefathers had once fought against another 'invader.'[42]

In describing Latvian life before the arrival of Germans in the twelfth and thirteenth centuries, the epic was meant to construct a past of the heroic battles of the Latvian nation's forefathers. Pumpurs used the models of *Kalevala*, German legends, and tales from the past as evidence of a happy and free ancient Latvian world that lived in harmony but ended up losing the battle against external enemies.

Lāčplēsis, a cultural hero of the epic narrative, opens an invented literary tradition of masculinity. His opposite is embodied in an internal enemy – Kangars, the traitor – who swears his faithfulness to the invaders who oppose his *volk*:

I swear to struggle with you against Perkons.
I swear that I will be a traitor of the motherland.
To destroy the defenders of the nation,
To deceive my own people for the benefit of other comers.
To bring the servants of alien faiths,
To kill everyone who resists,
And to put all Baltia into slavery's yoke. [43]

The names of cultural heroes – Lāčplēsis (the conqueror of the bear), Koknesis (keeper of the trees), and Burtnieks (the possessor of letters) – symbolize the trinity of epic heroes for an organic, masculine embrace of nature/culture in the mythology of the nation. When an enemy invades the land of Latvia, all are bound together despite any inner differences. All stages of this nation-cohering narrative are described in the foregrounding ascriptions and hierarchies of masculine roles from a single cultural hero to the brotherhood, and further to the binding presence of fathers and forefathers.

Femininity and motherhood are symbolically charted into several female characters. Staburadze, the crying mother of Baltic destiny, keeps the customs of her ancestors alive. In her image, the temporality of home is cyclically organized in regenerating this landscape into harmonious nation time. Staburadze, a reconciling symbol of the maternal, is simultaneously eternal and young. 'Light and eternal', she reproduces her maternal values in her daughter, and the mother-daughter continuity is ascribed symbolically into the plot of the renovation and the revival of the nation. She is the one who teaches young women and initiates them into marriage. The regenerated eternity of Staburadze and Staburags is drawn into a primordial model of family.

The author's desire to create a male hero, an extraordinarily strong warrior for his people's cause and its territory, determined the related representations of womanhood in the epic narrative. The central construction of the national feminine in the text is centred less around motherhood, but more around maidenhood and bridal virginity, reflecting the 'territorial' convolutions of sexuality, family, class and nation. The two female characters of Spidola and Laimdota are particularly significant in centring the representation of femininity on maidenhood. The oppositions day/night, white/black, good/evil, commitment/ betrayal, are all balanced between Spidola and Laimdota, a beautiful maiden with a pure and innocent heart. As Lāčplēsis says:

He gave himself a word:
To keep himself far from the first

And to deserve the respect of the second
With glorifying deeds. [44]

The beautiful witch Spidola spends her nights among dark and evil powers. With her access to uncontrolled dark forces, Spidola is associated with evil dominants in her symbolic alignment with Kangars, the traitor, thus magnifying the danger of potential 'complementary' betrayal of brother and sister through baneful deeds. The couple – the witch Spidola and the traitor Kangars – are constructed as a dormant and a perilous site of negativity against the collective designations of the *Volk* to its free memory of the independent progeny. It is not only Eve's sin when Spidola betrays her virginity. Falling into her charms and driven by curiosity, Lāčplēsis follows her witch flight to a feast of evil powers. He watches Spidola's dating with an *unknown* man, surrounded by other nefarious couples. Spidola's sexual appetites and uncontrolled evil powers are represented as an arcane, potential sin of belonging to aliens, to enemies. Later, Spidola is salvaged, purified and initiated into collectivity; she is accultured out of an invisible, dark, wild part of womanhood, free and unharnessed, into 'collective belonging' through the regenerating rite of bridehood.

Conclusion

The national awakening of a 'small national family' was occurring during the period of new divisions of power in Europe, the advent of mass consumption, and the nuclearization of the family. The visionary religious movement of Herrnhuters significantly framed the national emancipation process. Historian Eric J. Hobsbawm argues that 'religious and revolutionary movements often informed one another' as does Barbara Taylor who showed 'that the sexualized language of these visionary religious sects could be used to express profoundly radical critiques, and could lead women as well as men to participate in social action.'[45]

The leaders of the national awakening received their higher education in Russian and European universities, where they learned revolutionary and emancipating ideas about democracy. As political émigrés or residents outside of Latvia, they were able to overcome the provincialism of geography and history. They proposed nationalism as the emancipating ideology of equality and human rights that would in time change the status of the nation, as well as of women, in the struggle against oppression. In this political microhistory, the project of modernity entered its Baltic margins on controversial terms. Individual emancipation was viewed as being effected from collective cultural and, later, political emancipation. Emancipation as a social and national uplift in an agro-literate society under political and economic dominance was a complex process of negotiation with traditions. 'Tradition' and 'the traditional' were not constructed as a 'degenerate condition', but rather were part of the 'cultivation' of the nation and nationhood into modernity.

The new self-consciousness demanded an emancipated and 'enlightened' woman to embody the centring of the nation's roots in its antiquity. The past was not thrown off like a veil, but it was translated into the Maternal and protected in the Sororal and the Virginal. The image of the maternal home in consonance with traditional female roles in a pre-modern agrarian economy reconciled the overcoming of the local in the common past with the preserving of the local as the origin of language for the nation in the common present. Their duties were moral and spiritual to maintain the 'traditional' as ways of establishing markers of difference in the family and for the nation. Inclusion of the codes of femininity (mothers and sisters) was tuned into shared agency/responsibility for the boundary-construction and exclusion scripts of the nation-family. The feminine/maternal was articulated into glorifying the innate, emotional, continual, intimately organic and, more important, harmonizing bond of the national family as part of a 'new national womanhood'.

The ambivalent appropriation of the ideologies and discourses of difference and equality in the nationalizing process was also reflected in gendering national difference in the attributes of the feminine – cooperative, pacific, nurturing – as strongly positive faculties and harmonizing values in the model of nationhood. A new national order constructed and employed the idea of 'equality of sexes in their differences'. It was delegated into the vision of national citizenry that, following the traditional sex-role distribution in a nation-family, would need a male subject at its political helm. A woman, thus, remained on the moral pedestal. She was to maintain the boundaries of difference and exclusion.

Becoming aware of its own object-position, either within the autocratic regime or against Baltic German landowners, a masculine subject of the new Latvian nation, at the level of political symbolism, found a subversive escape from hierarchical repressions and exclusions in traditionally male spheres. The emerging masculine subject of the new nation contracted women into the realm of the collective symbolic. On the one hand, femininity was articulated as compensatory symbolical space for realigning power relations from the paternalism of Baltic German rule into the communal-fraternal contract of a modern nation. On the other hand, it symbolized 'a nonalienated, loving, cooperative social order'.[46]

Political history in the Baltic territories took a dramatic turn after the events of 1905–6 and 1914. Alternative solutions, with greater questioning of this ideology of difference in/of nation-construction vanished into the historical, conditional 'if . . .'

Notes

1. Scott J. (1988), *Gender and the Politics of History* (New York, Columbia University Press, 1988), 6.
2. Cf. Scott, *Gender*, 6.
3. Cf. Scott, *Gender*, 55.
4. It is also important to add: 'The differences between the German influence that was predominant in Central Latvia, and the Polish-Lithuanian influences which affected Eastern Latvia, were rather broad. As a result, for instance, the most of Latvia is Lutheran today, while Eastern Latvia (Latgale) is Catholic.' See: Høyer, S., Lauk, E., Vihalemm, P. (eds) (1993), *Towards a Civic Society: The Baltic Media's Long Road to Freedom. Perspectives on History, Ethnicity and Journalism* (Tartu), 14. Apart from these, Russian Orthodoxy was gaining influences in the span of the nineteenth century.
5. Haltzel, M.H. (1974), 'The Russification of the Baltic Germans: A Dysfunctional Aspect of Imperial Modernization' in A. Ziedonis, W. Winter, M. Valgem *Baltic History*, Columbus, 144.
6. Peasants received the right to participate in local (*pagasts*) and regional (*guberna*) self-government bodies (*zemstes*). The reform process spanned several decades until Latvians gained representation in the self-governmental bodies of communities, the right to purchase land from the German gentry, and a network of rural parish schools. Politically and economically privileged Baltic Germans were experiencing cursory and slow-paced marginalization of their entitlements, privileges, status and roles. All of this resulted from the redefined imperial visions of their positionalities in terms of loyalty policies toward Russia.
7. After 1905, the political representation of Latvians in the imperial parliament *Duma* resulted in a more complex understanding of the concept of citizenship in the nationalizing process. Even with this

factor, however, the economic question of land ownership (in 1914, 48 per cent of arable land in Latvia belonged to Baltic Germans) could not be divorced from the model of the Latvian family as a production unit. The family as a production unit with gender-role labour division, central to the nationalizing process, remained the focus of linguistic-cultural homogenization until 1940.

8. Kirby, D.G. (1995), *The Baltic World 1772–1993: Europe's Northern Periphery in an Age of Change* (New York: Longman Group Limited), 161.

9. Plakans, A., Haltzel, M.H., Lundin, C.L., Plakans, A., Raun, T.U., Thaden, E.C. (1981), 'The Latvians' in Thaden, E.C. (ed.) *Russification in the Baltic Provinces and Finland, 1885–1914*, coauthors (Princeton), 17.

10. Cielēns, F. (1998), *Laikmetu maina. Atmiņas un atziņas* (Rīga: Apgāds Memento), 39.

11. Kronvalds, A. (1994), *Tautiski centieni* (Rīga: Zvaigzne), 17.

12. Plakans, A. 'The Latvians', 211.

13. Brubaker, R. (1996), *Nationalism Reframed. Nationhood and the national question in the New Europe,* Cambridge: Cambridge University Press, 113–14.

14. Elias, N. (1995), *The Civilizing Process. The History of Manners and State Formation and Civilization.* translated by Edmund Jephcott, (Oxford UK and Cambridge US: Blackwell Publishers): 5.

15. I recommend the works of the late Haralds Biezais including his (1998) *Seņo Latviešu Debesu Dievu Ģimene* Rīga: Minerva.

16. Светлана Рыжакова (1997), 'Явление священного» в латышских Фольклорных текстах', *Latvijas Zinātņu Akademijas Vestis. A,* no. 1/2: 31–9

17. Дагмара Бейтнере, Ирина Новикова, 'Женщины Латвии и новое время' в *Феминистская теория и пракика: Восток-Запад. Материалы международной научно-практической конференции* ред. Ольга Липовская, (Санкт-Петербург, Репино, Центр гендерных исследований, 1996), 58.

18. Herrnhuterian groups were extremely important in constructing national identification as secularization of *civitas Dei*. Life according to strong discipline and equal work in the sustenance of the community were lenient features of Herrnhuterianism. Zinzendorf tried to found a 'fraternal community of Jesus that would represent everybody across ethnic and religious classes' See: Zutis, J. (1956) *Vidzemes un Kurzemes zemnieku brīvlaišana. XIX gadsimta 20. Gados,* Rīga: Latvijas Valsts Izdēvnieciba, 63. I would recommend

Constructing National Identity in Latvia

some available sources on Latvian Herrnhuters: Zutis, J. (1956), *Vidzemes un Kurzemes zemnieku brīvlaišana. XIX gadsimta 20. Gados,* Rīga: Latvijas Valsts Izdēvnieciba); Adamovičs, L. (1934), *Latviešu brāļu draudzes sākumi un pirmie ziedu laiki. 1738–1743,* Rīga, Latviju Kultura.

19. Švabe, A. (1990), *Latvijas vēsture,* Rīga: Avots, 23–4.

20. Henings, D. (1995), 'Nacionālā kustība un nacionālas balsts tapšana Latvijā', *Latvijas Vēstures Institūta žurnāls,* 1: 67.

21. Mezezers, V. (1975), *The Herrnhuterian Pietism in the Baltic. And its Outreach into America and Elsewhere in the World,* North Quincy, Massachusets, Christopher Publishing House, 75.

22. Zutis, J. (1956), *Vidzemes un Kurzemes zemnieku brīvlaišana. XIX gadsimta 20. Gados,* Rīga, Latvijas Valsts Izdēvnieciba, 192.

23. Millers, F. (1900), 'Baltvāču kordziedāšanas tradīciju pārmantošana', *Latvijas Zinātņu Akadēmijas Vēstis,* 6: 32.

24. Pulkkinen, T. (1996), *The Postmodern and Political Agency,* Hakapaino Oy, 160.

25. Auseklis (1879), 'Pa dziedāšanu pie latviešiem' *Latvijas Zemkopis,* no. 29–33.

26. Kohl, J.G. (1841),. *Die deutsch-russischen Ostseeprovinzen* (Dresden, Leipzig), 11.

27. Bula, D. (1997), 'Dziedataju tauta. Latviešu tautas dziesmu tradīcija un nacijas paštēls', *Latvijas Zinātņu Akadēmijas Vēstis. A,* 51 (1/2): 22–30.

28. Cf. Bula, *Dziedataju tauta,* 22–4.

29. Жак Делёз (1998), *Различие и повторение,* Санкт-Петербург: Петрополис, 13–14.

30. Kaudzīte, M. (1994), *Atmiņas no tautiskā laikmetā* (Rīga: Zvaigzne), 186.

31. Cf. Kaudzīte, *Atmiņas,* 193.

32. Cf. Kaudzīte, *Atmiņas,* 194.

33. Cf. Kaudzīte, *Atmiņas,* 189.

34. Cf. Kaudzīte, *Atmiņas,* 197.

35. Cf. Plakans, 'The Latvians', 130

36. Kronvalde, K. (1870), 'Ceenigam Garram', *Baltijas Vestnesis,* no. 46–8.

37. Brant, L. (1931), *Latviešu sieviete,* Rīga, Valters un Rapa): 62.

38. Cf. Brant, *Latviešu sieviete,* 22.

39. Cf. Brant, *Latviešu sieviete,* 171.

40. Kaudzīte, R. (1997), *Domu izteikumi,* Cesis: Sarma, 119.

41. Cf. R. Kaudzīte, *Domu izteikumi,* 149.

42. Cf. Plakans, 'The Latvians', 244.
43. Андрей Пумпурс (1975), *Лачплесис*, Москва, Художественная литература, 130.
44. Cf. Пумпурс, *Лачплесис*, 138.
45. Cf. Scott, *Gender*, 77.
46. Cf. Scott, *Gender*, 77.

Index

Note: Page numbers in bold refer to illustrations

Index

Index

Irish Parliamentary Party, 233, 244
Islam, in Egypt, 149, 151
Ismail, ruler of Egypt (1863-79), 139, 143

Jacobins, 86, 89
Jamaica, 112, 117–18, 120–1
  rebellion (1865), 109, 112
  slave rebellion (1831), 112, 118–20
Jamieson-Williams, M., feminist, 165
Japan, national symbolisms, 8, 9, 10
Jayawardena, Kumari, *Feminism and
  Nationalism in the Third World*, 5–6
Jewish women, 20
Jews
  and citizenship in England, 113–14
  and citizenship in Germany, 46, 49,
  198–9(n.12)
Jones, Edith, feminist, 165, 166, 172

Kaudzīte, Matiss, 322–3, 327
Kaudzīte, Reinis, *Sieviskais cilveks*, 327
Kettle, Andrew, Land League, 241
Khartoum, fall of, 143
Knibb, William, missionary (Jamaica),
  119
Kollár, Jan, *Daughter of Sláva*, 301
Kosmas chronicle (Czech), 298, 300
Krásnohorská, Eliska, 297
  Czech Woman Question, 306
Krok, father of Libuse, 298
Kronvalde, Karoline, 326
Kronvalds, Atis, Latvian writer, 314–15,
  323–4
kul slaves, in Egypt, 138–9, 141
Kurzeme (Latvia), 311, 318, 322

Ladies' Land League, 47, 56(n.23), 229
  America, 231
  Anna Parnell and, 236–7, **237**
  compared with Land League, 237–8
  development of individual feminism in,
  232–3
  disbanded, 241–2
  and imprisonment of Land League
  leaders, 239–41
Ladies' National Association, 231
Land League (Ireland), 233–4
  compared with Ladies' Land League,
  237–8

leaders imprisoned, 239–41
  status of women in, 233–4
Lange, Helene, 258–9, 261–2
  and ADF, 255, 257
  German BDF, 251, 255, 258–9
language
  Afrikaans, 207–8, 220
  German (in Bohemia), 295
  Latvian, 314, 324
  'mother tongue', 32, 57(n.28), 64
  women's role in teaching, 47–8
Latvia
  All-Latvian Folk Song Festival, 312,
  319
  cultural awakening, 314–15
  discourse on 'national' woman, 326–7
  ethnolinguistic nationalism, 47–8,
  321–5
  folk song festivals, 48, 319–25, **320**
  folk songs (*daina*), 312, 315, 316–17
  Herrnhuter religious movement, 311,
  317–19, 322–3
  maternal imagery, 323–4
  nationalist origins, 312–13
  peasants and land reform campaign,
  313–14, 331(n.6)
  and Russia, 312, 313, 314, 325,
  331–2(n.7)
  social stratification, 318–19, 325–6
Latvian language, 314, 324
Latvian Literary Association, 314
Lawson, Louisa
  Australian feminist and nationalist,
  159–60, 162
  The Dawn journal, 160–1
  poetry, 162–4
League of Nations, 46
liberal humanism, 275, 282
liberal political thought, 111
Liberal Unionist Association (Ireland),
  232
Libuse, Czech mythical princess, 48, 66,
  293, 294–5
  early images, 298–9
  as historical narrative, 300–1
  as popular heroine, 303–6
  as symbol of Czech statehood, 306
Libuše (Smetana's opera), 303–4, 305
literary tradition

Index

Czech, 299–300, 302–3
Latvian, 314–16
Lithuania, 316
Livonia (Baltic), 312, 317
Locke, John, role of women, 276
Lübeck Patriotic Women's Association,
259
Luise, Queen of Prussia, 66, 181, 192,
194
Luneville, J.J., portrait of Vieuzac, 95, **96**

Macaulay, Lord, 118, 121
Mahdi, the (Muhammad Ahmad), 143–4
Mahmud Pasha al-Barudi, 142
Mantel, Georg, *Lettisch Vademecum*
(1636), 314
marginalization, and international links,
19–20
margins
effect on political process, 36
and nation formation, 311
Marianne of Prussia, 'Appeal to the
Women of the Prussian State', 179, 181
marriage, Egyptian debate on, 149–50
marriage contract, analogous to political
representation, 281–2
masculinity, 67–9, 75(n.17)
as alterity, 82
and appropriation of feminine, 89
and defeat (Boers), 216–17
defined by military, 189–91
and epic heroes, 327–9
feminization of, 83, 84
and Latvian filial role, 315
linked with guns, 209–10
as middle class virtue, 124
and national identity, 17–18
O'Connell's, 114–15
and power, 271
and public rights, 10
and republican body politic, 275
sexualization of black, 94–5
see also men; military
Massachusetts, state constitution, 276–7
Maud, Queen of Norway, 13
Medinska, Maria, 326
Mehmet Ali Pasha (Muhammad 'Ali), as
Ottoman governor, 137, 138–9
Meiners, Christoph, *Geschichte des*

weiblichen Geschlects, 4
memory, collective, 64, 65–6
men
brothers in Latvian culture, 317–19
Bushman as Australian national type,
159
father figures in Japan, 9
and homo-social nation, 33, 159, 207
middle class (Prussia), 188
and national costume, 11, 13
as political citizens, 107
as protector of defenceless women,
189, 209–10
see also gender; masculinity
Merkel, Garlieb, *Letts* (Latvian history),
314
middle classes
Afrikaner, 209–10
and family virtues, 194–5
German, 255–6
Latvian, 319, 321
and masculine virtues, 124, 188, 190
and nationalism, 45
and Reform Act (1832), 121–2, 123,
124–5
significance of Western male dress, 14
women's domesticity, 289–90(n.15)
see also family; women, middle class
military
appeal to manliness, 45
and citizenship rights, 46, 65, 189, 196,
260
as community of brothers, 195
and image of soldier, 189–90
women's role in, 15
see also conscription; war
Mill, James, *Essay on Government*, 124
Mill, John Stuart, 233
Millar, John, *Observations Concerning
the Distinction of Ranks in Society*, 4
modernist theory, 34
money, as representative, 285–6, 291–
2(n.33)
Muhammad Ahmad (the Mahdi), 143–4
Muhammad 'Ali *see* Mehmet Ali Pasha
Muhammad Farid, al-Hizb al-Watani, 147
Muhammad Farid Wajdi, 149
Muhammad Sultan, 'King of Upper
Egypt', 139–40, 142

Index